Proxy Wars from a Global Perspective

Proxy Wars from a Global Perspective

Non-State Actors and Armed Conflicts

Edited by
Paweł Bernat, Cüneyt Gürer, Cyprian Aleksander Kozera

BLOOMSBURY ACADEMIC
LONDON • NEW YORK • OXFORD • NEW DELHI • SYDNEY

BLOOMSBURY ACADEMIC
Bloomsbury Publishing Plc
50 Bedford Square, London, WC1B 3DP, UK
1385 Broadway, New York, NY 10018, USA
29 Earlsfort Terrace, Dublin 2, Ireland

BLOOMSBURY, BLOOMSBURY ACADEMIC and the Diana logo are trademarks of
Bloomsbury Publishing Plc

First published in Great Britain 2024

Copyright © Paweł Bernat, Cüneyt Gürer and Cyprian Aleksander Kozera, 2024

Paweł Bernat, Cüneyt Gürer and Cyprian Aleksander Kozera have asserted
their rights under the Copyright, Designs and Patents Act, 1988, to be
identified as Editors of this work.

Series design by Adriana Brioso:
Cover image © Comstock/Getty Images

All rights reserved. No part of this publication may be reproduced or transmitted
in any form or by any means, electronic or mechanical, including photocopying,
recording, or any information storage or retrieval system, without prior permission
in writing from the publishers.

Bloomsbury Publishing Plc does not have any control over, or responsibility for, any
third-party websites referred to or in this book. All internet addresses given
in this book were correct at the time of going to press. The author and publisher
regret any inconvenience caused if addresses have changed or sites have
ceased to exist, but can accept no responsibility for any such changes.

A catalogue record for this book is available from the British Library.

A catalog record for this book is available from the Library of Congress.

ISBN:	HB:	978-1-3503-6928-3
	ePDF:	978-1-3503-6930-6
	eEook:	978-1-3503-6929-0

Typeset by FefineCatch Limited, Bungay, Suffolk

To find out more about our authors and books visit www.bloomsbury.com
and sign up for our newsletters.

Contents

List of Abbreviations	vii
List of Contributors	xiii

Introduction: The Necessity for a Global Perspective on Proxy
Warfare *Paweł Bernat, Cüneyt Gürer, Cyprian Aleksander Kozera* 1

Part One Theoretical and Historical Framework

1 Toward Conceptualization of Contemporary Proxy Warfare
Paweł Bernat and Cyprian Aleksander Kozera 11

2 US Proxy Warfare's New and Complex Paradigm
Richard D. Newton 23

3 States and Non-State Actors Interacting in Conflict: Explaining
State Use of Proxies *Cüneyt Gürer* 41

Part Two Proxy Forces in Various Theaters of Armed Conflicts:
Case Studies

4 Russian Proxy Use in the Hybrid War against Ukraine before the
2022 Invasion *Paweł Bernat, Viacheslav Semenenko, Pavlo
Openko and Daniel Michalski* 61

5 Ukraine's Legionnaires in the War against Russia *Tamir Sinai* 77

6 Insurgencies in Africa and the Middle East and the Future of
the Proxy Warfare in the Region *Jeffrey Kaplan* 95

7 Proxy Warfare in Mali: New Rendition of *Divide et Impera* and
Cautious French Saviorism *Cyprian Aleksander Kozera* 107

8 The Bifurcation of Violence: The Proxy Forces in the Central
African Republic *Błażej Popławski* 123

9 Libya: Fragmentation of the Country amid a Proxy War

vi   *Contents*

    Mehmet Alper Sozer and Emirhan Darcan   139

10 The Spheres of Influence: Multiple Proxy Wars in Syria
    Engin Yüksel   153

11 Iran's Hybrid Proxy Warfare through Palestinian Terrorism
    against Israel *Ori Wertman and Christian Kaunert*   167

12 The Conflict in Yemen through the Prism of Proxy
    War *James K. Wither*   183

13 When Proxies Win: The Impact of the Taliban's Changing
    Fortune on Pakistan's Leverage *Tova Norlen and Vinay Kaura*   201

Part Three Proxy Wars: The Emergence of a New Paradigm

14 Transnational Organized Crime Groups as State Proxies
    Ümit Namli and Cüneyt Gürer   225

15 The Salience of the New Proxy War Paradigm *Graeme P. Herd*   243

Afterword *Paweł Bernat, Cüneyt Gürer, Cyprian Aleksander Kozera*   257

Index   259

Abbreviations

3R	Return, Reclamation, Rehabilitation (CAR)
9/11	September 11, 2001 terrorist attacks on the USA
AIAI	*Al-Itihaad al-Islamiya*, Islamic Union (Somalia)
AKP	Justice and Development Party (Turkey)
AMISOM	African Union Mission in Somalia
APRD	People's Army for the Restoration of Democracy (CAR)
AQAP	Al-Qaeda in the Arabian Peninsula
AQIM	Al-Qaeda in the Islamic Maghreb
ARC	Autonomous Republic of Crimea (Ukraine)
ATO	Anti-Terrorist Operation (Ukraine)
A2R	Alliance for Revival and Rebuilding (CAR)
BBC	British Broadcasting Corporation
CAR	The Central African Republic
CIA	Central Intelligence Agency (USA)
CJTF	Civilian Joint Task Force (Nigeria)
COIN	Counterinsurgency
CPC	Coalition of Patriots for Change (CAR)
CPJP	Convention of Patriots for Justice and Peace (CAR)
CPSK	Patriotic Convention for Saving the Country (CAR)
CRS	Congressional Research Service (USA)
CT	Counterterrorism

viii   *Abbreviations*

CTC	Combating Terrorism Center (USA)
CTOC	Countering Transnational Organized Crime
DNR	Donetsk People's Republic (occupied territory of Ukraine)
DOP	Declaration of Principles
DPRK	Democratic People's Republic of Korea
DRC	Democratic Republic of the Congo
ECCAS	Economic Community of Central African States
ETIM	East Turkestan Islamic Movement (Syria)
EU	European Union
FACA	Central African Armed Forces
FDLR	Democratic Forces for the Liberation of Rwanda
FDPC	Democratic Front of the Central African People (CAR)
FMLN	Farabundo Martí National Liberation Front (El Salvador)
FOMUC	Central African Economic and Monetary Community
FPRC	Popular Front for the Rebirth of Central African Republic
FROCCA	Front for the Return of the Constitutional Order (CAR)
FSA	Free Syrian Army
FSB	Federal Security Service (Russia)
GATIA	Imghad Tuareg Self-Defence Group and Allies
GCC	Gulf Cooperation Council
GDP	Gross Domestic Product
GNA	Government of National Accord (Libya)
GNC	General National Congress (Libya)
GPS	Global Positioning System
GRU	Main Directorate of the General Staff of the Armed Forces of the Russian Federation

Abbreviations ix

Hamas	*Harakat al-Muqāwamah al-ʾIslāmiyyah,* Islamic Resistance Movement (Palestine)
HRW	Human Rights Watch
HTS	*Hayʾat Tahrir Ash-Sham,* a branch of Al-Qaeda (Syria)
ICU	Islamic Courts Union (Somalia)
IDF	Israel Defense Forces
IMU	Islamic Movement of Uzbekistan
IO	International organizations
IR	International relations
IRGC	Islamic Revolutionary Guard Corps (Iran)
IRGC-QF	Islamic Revolutionary Guards Corps-Quds Force (Iran)
IS, ISIL, ISIS	Islamic State, Islamic State of Iraq and the Levant, Islamic State of Iraq and ash-Sham (terrorist organization)
ISI	Inter-Services Intelligence (Pakistan)
ISIL-K	Islamic State of Iraq and the Levant—Khorasan Province (terrorist organization)
ITN	Iran's Threat Network
JeM	*Jaish-e-Mohammed,* a terrorist group (Pakistan)
KFF	Kashmiri Freedom Fighters
KGB	Komitet Gosudarstvennoy Bezopasnosti, Committee for State Security (Russia)
LAAF	Libyan Arab Armed Forces
LeT	Army of the Righteous or the Army of the Pure (Pakistan)
LH	Lebanese Hezbollah
LNA	Libyan National Army
LNR	Luhansk People's Republic (occupied territory of Ukraine)

LPDF	Libyan Political Dialogue Forum
LRA	Lord's Resistance Army (CAR)
M23	M-23 Movement (DRC)
MAA	Arab Movement of Azawad
MAD	Mutually-assured destruction
MANPADS	Man-portable air-defense systems
MIT	Turkish National Intelligence
MNLA	National Movement for the Liberation of Azawad
MNLC	National Movement for the Liberation of the Central African Republic
MOJWA	Movement for Oneness and Jihad in West Africa, also known as MUJAO
MPC	Central African Patriotic Movement (CAR)
MUJAO	Movement for Unity and Jihad in West Africa, also known as MOJWA
NATO	North Atlantic Treaty Organization
NDF	National Defense Forces (Syria)
NGO	Non-governmental organization
NPT	Non-Proliferation Treaty (Treaty on the Non-Proliferation of Nuclear Weapons)
NTC	National Transition Council (Libya)
OC	Organized Crime
OCCRP	Organized Crime and Corruption Reporting Project
OSCE	Organization for Security and Co-operation in Europe
PA	Palestinian Authority
PIJ	Palestinian Islamic Jihad
PKK	Kurdistan Workers' Party (Turkey)

PLO	Palestine Liberation Organization
PMC	Private Military Company
PYD	Democratic Union Party (Syria)
QF	Quds Force, one of five branches of IRGC (Iran)
RFI	Radio France Internationale
RUSI	Royal United Services Institute (United Kingdom)
SAA	Syrian Arabian Army
SADAT	International Defence Consultancy Construction Industry Inc. (Turkey)
SAM	Surface-to-air missile
SDF	Syrian Democratic Forces
SF	Army Special forces
SNA	Somali National Army
SOF	Special operations forces
SSC	Supreme Security Committee (Libya)
SSS	Sewa Security Services, a branch of the Wagner group (CAR)
STC	Southern Transitional Council (Yemen)
TFG	Transitional Federal Government (Somalia)
TOC	Transnational Organized Crime
TTP	*Tehrik-i-Taliban* Pakistan, the Pakistani Taliban
UAE	United Arab Emirates
UFDR	Union of Democratic Forces for Unity (CAR)
UK	United Kingdom of Great Britain and Northern Ireland
UN	United Nations
UNFPA	United Nations Population Fund
UNITAF	Unified Task Force (UN, Somalia)

UNSC	United Nations Security Council
UNSCR	United Nations Security Council Resolution
UNSMIL	United Nations Support Mission in Libya
UPC	Union for Peace in the Central African Republic
US, USA	United States of North America
US-SEALS	The United States Navy Sea, Air, and Land Teams
USSR	Union of Soviet Socialist Republics
UNOSOM	United Nations Operation in Somalia
VDV	Airborne Forces of the Russian Federation
WMD	Weapons of Mass Destruction
YPG	People's Defense Units also known as People's Protection Units (Syria)

Contributors

Paweł Bernat is a Senior Lecturer in Security Studies at the Polish Air Force University in Dęblin, Poland. His research interests focus on strategic and tactical aspects of outer space, with a special focus on the militarization and weaponization of Earth's orbit, the Russian Federation's space sector, space terrorism, and proxy and hybrid warfare, especially in Eastern Europe. He is a co-founder and Vice President of Andarta Education for Security Foundation, Deputy Editor-in-Chief of the *Safety & Defense* academic journal. He has published several dozens of academic articles on security and defense related issues.

Emirhan Darcan is a SAR scholar at the Institute for Penal Law and Criminology at the University of Bern, Switzerland. With a Ph.D. from Rutgers University, he has theoretical and hands-on experience in security, crime analysis, and international security cooperation. He has worked with security professionals, sociologists, politicians, and liaison officers to do fieldwork in various security-related topics, policy analyzes on legal aspects of governments' counterterrorism practices as well as political risk analysis.

Cüneyt Gürer is Professor of Transnational Security Studies at the George C. Marshall European Center for Security Studies in Garmisch-Partenkirchen, Germany. His research interests and areas of expertise comprise transnational security issues, regional security dynamics, democratic backsliding and security governance, and nonstate actors in contemporary conflicts. He lectures on the interaction of Turkey's domestic politics with its regional security policy process.

Graeme P. Herd is Professor of Transnational Security Studies in the Research and Policy Analysis Department of the George C. Marshall European Center for Security Studies in Garmisch-Partenkirchen, Germany. His latest publications include: Understanding Russia's Strategic Behavior: Imperial Strategic Culture and Putin's Operational Code (2022) and Russia's Global Reach: A Security and Statecraft Assessment (ed.) (2021).

Jeffrey Kaplan is Distinguished Senior Fellow at Danube Institute in Budapest, Hungary. He has published some twenty books and anthologies and over eighty articles and anthology chapters. His most recent books include Anti-Semitism in

Hungary (2 vols.) (2022), The 21st Century Cold War: A New World Order? (2020), Apocalypse, Revolution and Terrorism: From the Sicari to the American Revolt against the Modern World (2018), and the first volume in the Routledge distinguished author series, Radical Religion and Violence: Theory and Case Studies (2015). He has researched and taught in many countries, most recently China, Saudi Arabia, Pakistan, and Hungary.

Christian Kaunert is Professor of International Security at Dublin City University, Ireland. He is also Professor of Policing and Security, as well as Director of the International Centre for Policing and Security at the University of South Wales, UK. In addition, he is Jean Monnet Chair, Director of the Jean Monnet Centre of Excellence and Director of the Jean Monnet Network on EU Counter-Terrorism.

Vinay Kaura is Assistant Professor in the Department of International Affairs and Security Studies, Sardar Patel University of Police, Security and Criminal Justice, Rajasthan, India. He is also the Deputy Director of the University's Centre for Peace and Conflict Studies. His research interests include Afghanistan-Pakistan relations, counter-terrorism, conflict management and resolution, India's foreign policy, and the geopolitics of the Indo-Pacific. In addition to academic research, he has produced policy-relevant analyzes on a broad array of subjects, including institutional reforms, strategic communications, and public diplomacy.

Cyprian Aleksander Kozera is a military officer, researcher at the African Research Institute at the Obuda University in Budapest, Hungary, expert at the Interdisciplinary Research Centre of the University in Warsaw, Poland, member of the Polish Africanist Society and an alumnus of the George C. Marshall Center European Center for Security Studies. He researches and lectures on irregular warfare, terrorism, and proxy forces, focusing on Sub-Saharan Africa. He co-edited the *Security and Defence Quarterly* Special Issue on Proxy Forces and has contributed to i.a., *Safety and Defense, Security and Defence Quarterly*, and *Small Wars and Insurgencies*.

Daniel Michalski is a Polish military officer in the rank of major, lecturer, and the Head of the Security Studies Department at the Polish Air Force University, Dęblin, Poland. His research interests focus on air defense and air security. He has published several scientific articles on NATO's eastern flank air defense development.

Ümit Namli is a Financial Crime Investigator and Intelligence Analyst with fifteen years of investigation experience against financial crimes, money laundering, transnational organized crime groups, and their financial activities. Currently, he is working as the Analytics Analyst and Assistant Vice President of the AFC Threat Analytics Department at Deutsche Bank. Previously he worked as the Alexander von Humboldt Foundation Research Fellow at the Criminology Institute at Tübingen University, Germany, to conduct research on the structure of organized crime groups in Germany.

Richard D. Newton serves as the Chair of Strategic Futures and Research at the Center for Irregular Warfare Security Studies, Washington DC, US He is also an adjunct professor at Joint Special Operations University and the University of Alaska Fairbanks, US Newton served for twenty-two years as a USAF combat rescue and special operations helicopter pilot, combat aviation advisor, and strategic planner, before transitioning to international special operations and irregular warfare education. He holds a BSc from the USAF Academy, an MMAS from the US Army School of Advanced Military Studies, and a PhD from King's College London.

Tova C. Norlén is Professor of Counterterrorism and International Security at the George C. Marshall European Center for International Security in Garmisch-Partenkirchen, Germany. She previously served as a faculty member at the American University in Washington, DC, U.S, and as an Assistant Dean for Research at the George Washington University Elliott School of International Affairs in Washington, DC, US She publishes and researches in the areas of religious and territorial conflict, the motivations for terrorism, radicalization and extremism, irregular and hybrid threats, conflict mitigation and negotiation, NATO and emerging threats, and Middle East regional security.

Pavlo Openko serves as a colonel in the Ukrainian army, Senior Researcher, and the Deputy Head of the Department of Information Technology and Information Security of the National Defense University of Ukraine in Kyiv. His research interests focus on military policy and military strategy, logistic support, and weapon systems. He has published on military training, combat use, and logistical support of the security and defense sector of Ukraine. He is taking part in the Russian-Ukrainian war.

Błażej Popławski is a historian, sociologist, and museologist. He received his PhD in Humanities from the University of Warsaw, Poland. He is a member of the Polish Africanist Society. He conducted field research in East and West Africa, including Kenya, Tanzania, Uganda, Ethiopia, Nigeria, and the Ivory Coast. His research interests include the contemporary history of Africa, peacekeeping, constitutionalism, postcolonial theory, and development issues. He works as the Deputy Director of the Library of the Polish Parliament.

Viacheslav Semenenko serves as a colonel in the Ukrainian army, Associate Professor, and the Deputy Head of the Center for Military and Strategic Studies of the National Defense University of Ukraine in Kyiv. His major areas of research include hybrid war, military policy and military strategy, logistics, and armament. Currently, he is operating within the framework of the International Project SAS-161 (Military Aspects of Countering Hybrid Warfare: Experiences, Lessons, Best Practices). He is taking part in the Russian-Ukrainian war, which began in 2014 and continues to this day.

Tamir Sinai is a visiting instructor on European Security Issues at the Hebrew University, Jerusalem, Israel. His research interests focus on European security and unconventional warfare. His most recent publication is on the concept of "stay-behind" as a war-fighting tactic used by NATO in the Cold War.

Mehmet Alper Sozer is Assistant Professor at Roger Williams University in the School of Justice Studies, Bristol, RI, US His research interests focus on violent extremism and the prevention of radicalization. He has published numerous papers on radicalization and violent extremism besides his studies on crime and community policing. His most recent publication, titled NATO-Turkey: An Ambiguous Relationship in an Unpredictable Security Domain, appeared in Small Wars Journals.

Ori Wertman is a research fellow at the International Centre for Policing and Security, University of South Wales, UK, and a researcher at the Institute for National Security Studies (INSS), Tel Aviv University, Israel. He is an active member of the Jean Monnet Network on EU Counter-Terrorism at the University of South Wales. His areas of interest are National Security, the Israeli-Palestinian Conflict, Counter Terrorism, and Israeli Politics. Wertman has published his articles in academic literature and in the media in Israel and abroad. His recent book (co-authored with Christian Kaunert) is *Israel: National Security and Securitization* (2023).

James K. Wither is Professor of National Security at the George C. Marshall European Center for Security Studies, Garmisch-Partenkirchen, Germany. His main research interests are Irregular/Hybrid Warfare, Counterterrorism, and Total Defense. Recent publications include Hybrid Warfare Revisited (forthcoming 2023), Back to the Future: Nordic Total Defence Concepts (2021), and Outsourcing Warfare: Proxy Forces in Contemporary Armed Conflicts (2020).

Engin Yüksel is a PhD candidate at Leiden University Institute for History in the Netherlands. His current research focuses on the continuity and discontinuity of fundamental Russian military concepts, primarily over the twentieth century. He has over ten years of experience in Defense and Security organizations. Engin worked as an analyst at NATO's Operational Level Command in the Netherlands. He has also worked as a Research Associate at the Dutch Security Unit of the Clingendael Institute. His research has focused on strategy and international security with an emphasis on hybrid security organizations in the Middle East and proxy warfare.

Introduction: The Necessity for a Global Perspective on Proxy Warfare

Paweł Bernat, Cuneyt Gurer, Cyprian Aleksander Kozera

When we ask contemporary scholars what they think of proxy warfare, at least two issues come up: first, it is not exhaustively defined, and even in some cases, there are clear contradictions among those definitions, and second, proxies give the states the option of plausible deniability. If we pose the same question to an active military officer, we will probably get an answer related to the practice of outsourcing, which not only limits their footprint but reduces the risk to their lives. As for the broad public opinion, when confronted with this question we may hear of a rather peculiar confluence of Russian mercenaries and a German classical composer, Wagner. The perspectives differ, yet what they reveal is the curiosity about the phenomenon that may be deemed one of the oldest forms of outsourcing violence in civilized societies, its growing validity in the contemporary battlespace, and the practical interest of the practitioners.

This book, however ambitiously it may appear, is addressed to all audiences who might be interested in the contemporary proxy phenomenon: the broad public who wants to be informed about the phenomenon increasingly shaping modern conflict; military, law enforcement, and security practitioners who often are agents, employers, or patrons of proxy warfare; and, last but not least, academics, analysts, researchers, as well as students of International Relations and Security Studies.

For practical reasons, we kept the framework simple, followed a geographically defined structure, and used a language mostly free from technical jargon. Being active or former military and law enforcement professionals who have been actively involved in Academia, we understand the necessity to be brief and to the point and conceptualize theoretical discussions with case examples. We invited academics with similar "practical" backgrounds or approaches and asked them to deliver chapters that may be read by people akin to them or those who often do not have access to technical dictionaries and cannot afford a two-week-long library stay in order to fully and comprehensively grasp the meaning of intricate academic speech and dive into overlapping footnotes. On the other hand, we never wanted it to be "a field manual" but rather a legit but accessible academic book. For this reason, we kindly ask impatient readers for understanding when we sometimes dwell on definitions or try to over-validate a minor occurrence with too many references and sources.

The anthology gathers representative case studies of proxy wars from the "hottest" and volatile regions of the world and from various places of the vast and multi-dimensional specter of proxy warfare, which took place mainly in the second decade of the twenty-first century. Not to subscribe to a commonly known academic sentence, "when the reality does not fit your theory, change the reality"—we wanted the reality to shape the idea behind the book and not otherwise. We, therefore, did not start from the point of having a strict definition saying that, e.g., "proxy warfare is when a state uses a non-state actor to pursue its own interests," but we reached out to our colleagues specializing in different regions and domains and asked them: what does proxy warfare look like in your field? We allowed ourselves to be intellectually led by this constantly forming and reshaping thriving phenomenon controlled by no laws or too often contradicting them. Out of that and our practice-based nature came out a wide and comprehensive definition: proxy warfare is a way of outsourcing military tasks to a third party in an armed conflict environment. In a proxy war, there is a patron (principal) and a client (agent), but none of them has to be a state, and none of them has to be outside of the system (the conflict environment), as will be demonstrated on the further pages of this volume.

Such a definition may appear broad or even too broad, yet we would instead call it an inclusive one, and so is the phenomenon itself. It does not ask whether it fits into established academic definitions but defines and expands its semantic field through practice.

The book's rationale can be divided into two main goals, namely, to depict and discuss the current cases of proxy warfare and, based on those cases, to show the phenomenon's evolution and the need for its further conceptual development.

This book represents a global approach, looking at some dozen case studies of proxy wars from a decade-long perspective. Therefore, it cannot aim at being an academically exhausting encyclopedia of proxy wars, nor a historical study, nor it aims at creating new areas and perspectives within the field of study; it does not aim at working out a new definitional framework, semantic fields, or constantly shifting conceptual frameworks surrounding the phenomenon of proxy wars but describes how proxy warfare has been lately implemented around

Introduction 3

the globe. In this sense, this book partially defines proxy wars in an ostensive manner. It should be treated, however, as input data for further theoretical studies.

Putting the definitional considerations aside, there are a few indubitable facts we can be sure of after reading the chapters presenting case studies in the book. First, using proxies as a way of waging armed conflicts is still prevalent worldwide. Moreover, due to the geopolitical changes of the last three decades, it may have gained in popularity and significance. Secondly, as shown in many chapters of this volume, current iterations of proxy wars differ from their Cold War era predecessors. This evolution is fueled by geopolitical and technological changes. Thirdly, proxy wars are understudied, and the phenomenon requires more conceptual and theoretical analyzes. Lastly, as this book uniquely claims, current definitions of proxy use consider a limited version of what is happening on the ground. Therefore scholars and practitioners should refrain from limiting themselves to the definitions created in the previous era of proxy use but need to engage more with existing proxy structures and practices.

The anthology consists of three parts divided into fifteen chapters, preceded by an introduction and concluded with an afterword. The first part with its three chapters, respectively, serve as a theoretical-conceptual, historical, and social-scientific introduction to proxy warfare. The main body of the book—the recent cases of proxy wars from around the globe are described in chapters four to thirteen and enclosed in Part Two. The volume is concluded with Part Three that contains a chapter that deals with a *sui generis* case of proxy forces and the final chapter that brings all those cases together, indicating the differentiating characteristics of current proxy warfare.

In the first chapter, entitled "Toward Conceptualization of Contemporary Proxy Warfare," Paweł Bernat and Cyprian Aleksander Kozera explain why the notion of proxy war has become too ambiguous to serve as a successful explanatory tool and where these ambiguities come from. They argue that proxy wars substantially change over time, twenty-first-century proxy wars qualitatively differ from proxy wars of the Cold War era, and many conceptual and explanatory frameworks still used today were created in the previous era or are based on past realities and experiences. In consequence, there is a lot of conceptual vagueness and confusion, which directly contributes to the degrading explanatory power of the notion of proxy warfare. In order to close the gap between the reality of current proxy warfare and its comprehension patterns, the authors postulate establishing new explanatory tools, which should be based on and being able to explain current proxy wars.

The second chapter was written by Richard D. Newton, and it is devoted to the US approach to proxy warfare and its evolving nature throughout the days of the Cold War and the three following decades. The US, presently one of the biggest patrons of proxies worldwide, holds a strong Cold War expertise of this type of warfare from its struggle against the Soviet camp. The experiences from the Philippines, El Salvador, and Afghanistan are briefly discussed in Newton's chapter, while its main attention is focused on the case study offered by the protracted Somali conflict. When discussing changes, the US approach to proxy warfare undergoes, Newton concludes that to wage wars "through, with, or by" will remain the leading US attitude to warfare. Even—or especially—in the times of the global power muscle flexing, as the prime competitors (namely the US, China, and Russia) will seek to stay below the threshold of direct armed confrontation. Similarly, within the counter-terrorism and counter-insurgency contexts, outsourcing warfare against jihadist groups will probably remain the best course of action, as well.

Cüneyt Gürer, in his chapter "States and Non-State Actors Interacting in Conflict: Explaining State Use of Proxies," argues that proxy use has been considered as an alternative way of the state's indirect involvement in the conflict and that there is a need to look at proxy use from different perspectives. He provides insights using international relations (IR) theories to explain why states prefer proxies in contemporary conflict. Using the three major theories of the IR discipline, Gürer encourages scholars to apply their interpretation to explain proxy use from different disciplinary perspectives. His chapter gives an alternative approach to proxy use and takes the proxy discussion to the IR field.

Chapter Four, "Russian Proxy Use in the Hybrid War against Ukraine before the 2022 Invasion," co-authored by four scholars, Paweł Bernat, Viacheslav Semenenko, Pavlo Openko and Daniel Michalski, is the first discussion of a proxy use case study. It describes and analyzes the use of proxy forces by the Russian Federation in its hybrid war against Ukraine, from the 2014 attack on Crimea to the beginning of the full-scale invasion on February 24, 2022. The authors argue that in that aggression, Russian proxy forces were used in a very different manner. During the first stage of the operation, in Crimea, Russians attacked under the guise of local actors but also used local actors to seize (with little or no violence) the peninsula. Russian incursion into the regions of Donetsk and Luhansk that occurred later that year involved the engagement of regular proxy forces, which in the form of Russian-supported militias fought against the Ukrainian army along with Russian special forces. The chapter describes the

Introduction

events that took place during the conflict and analyzes them via the prism of hybrid war and proxy warfare.

Tamir Sinai, in Chapter Five, entitled "Ukraine's Legionnaires in the War against Russia," focuses on proxy use on the other side of the Russian-Ukrainian conflict. Sinai shows how noncitizens uniformed members of Ukraine's military, or "legionnaires", have taken prominent roles since February 2022 when Ukraine launched an all-out mobilization and commenced mass recruitment of legionnaires to defend against the Russian invaders. Using Grasmeder's model of state enlistment of legionnaires, the chapter analyzes the employment of noncitizens in different stages of the war with Russia between 2014 and 2023. It provides a study of Ukraine's "legionnaires" in terms of their functions, formations, integration into the armed forces, and the dynamics and motivation behind their recruitment. The chapter is concluded with the suggestion of adding the category of "foreign volunteers—legionnaires" to the typology used in the discourse on contemporary warfare and the role of proxy forces.

The next chapter, "Insurgencies in Africa and the Middle East and the Future of the Proxy Warfare in the Region," written by Jeffrey Kaplan, examines insurgent conflicts in Africa and the Middle East from two perspectives: the bipolar model of the Cold War and the current situation in the post-Cold War world as it involves state and sub-state involvement. Based on this discussion, it concludes with some consideration of the future of proxy warfare in these regions.

In the following chapter, "Proxy Warfare in Mali: New Rendition of *Divide et Impera* and Cautious French Saviorism," Cyprian Aleksander Kozera presents the Malian theater of proxy warfare, where two allied governments, the Malian and the French, supported, in a very different manner, opposing proxies with contrasting goals. The chapter explains the Malian and the French approach to proxy warfare on the Sahelian stage. Kozera argues that the former employed it for strategic gains, lack of other possibilities, or a will to find them, while for the latter, it was just a way of gaining a tactical edge over jihadi groups and limiting one's own risks in hostile terrain. Consequently, the results were very much different, and some of the far-reaching aftereffects resonate in today's yet more divided, impoverished, and war-torn Sahel.

Błażej Popławski, in Chapter Eight, "The Bifurcation of Violence: The Proxy Forces in the Central African Republic," discusses the multifaceted proxy warfare in the Central African Republic. He starts with laying the historical and social foundation of proxy warfare in Sub-Saharan Africa, arguing that the continent has been heavily affected by this type of violence in the Cold War. Overlapping the phenomenon of "repeat civil wars," proxy wars on the African continent fall into, as Popławski calls it, "postcolonial cycles of violence" that contribute to state failure and further perpetuation of civil violence. Popławski's case study focuses on various proxy actors that have been operating in the country and profiting from various patronage since the outbreak of the last civil war in 2013. Last but not least, the author argues that this central African country is a stage of a postcolonial proxy war between France and Russia.

Chapter Nine, written by Mehmet Alper Sozer and Emirhan Darcan, is dedicated to the analysis of the Libyan conflict as a proxy battlespace with its multitude of actors and the enormous complexity of their relationships with internal and external patrons. The chapter entitled "Libya: Fragmentation of the Country amid a Proxy War" begins with a brief description of the pre-existing conditions for proxy warfare in Libya, namely Gaddafi's rule and the subsequent Arab Spring, which is followed by an examination of armed non-state proxy groups in the country. The authors argue that the Libyan war has turned into a proxy war of nation-states fighting each other for the influence and control of energy resources, and provide an in-depth analysis of the proxy warfare from a historical, political, and thematic perspective. The chapter is concluded with a risk assessment for the potential escalation of this conflict toward a multiparty conventional war and a damage report of this devastating proxy war.

The following chapter, entitled "The Spheres of Influence: Multiple Proxy Wars in Syria," moves the analysis of proxy warfare from Africa to the Middle East. In the chapter, its author, Engin Yüksel, investigates different ways in which Turkey, Iran, and the US have performed various proxy war strategies in Syria. The chapter analyzes how regional actors, namely Turkey and Iran, have capitalized on existing shared identity networks while building proxy relationships, whereas the US has pragmatically established linkages to promote democracy and eliminate extremism threats. One of the more significant findings of the study was that, unlike Turkey and the US, Iran has employed peculiar relational and processual methods of waging proxy war, such as utilizing non-Syrian Shia groups as intermediaries or building an auxiliary relationship with the Syrian Arabian Army.

Ori Wertman and Christian Kaunert, in their chapter "Iran's Hybrid Proxy Warfare through Palestinian Terrorism against Israel," delve deeper into Iran's ways of utilizing proxies. The study reviews how Hamas and Palestinian Islamic Jihad (PIJ), serving as Iranian proxies, have conducted a hybrid terror campaign against Israel, and how the latter confronted this security threat. The authors argue that not only Palestinian terrorist organizations who have been conducting hybrid terror campaigns against the state of Israel acted as Iranian proxies, but also the Lebanese Shiite terror organization Hezbollah should be accounted as such, for it has received significant financial and logistical support from Iran over the years. Consequently, as it is argued further, Hamas and PIJ are integral to the Iranian strategy of indirect war through its proxies against Israel, the West, and other regimes in the Middle East.

In Chapter Twelve, "The Conflict in Yemen through the Prism of Proxy War," James Wither argues that the armed conflict in Yemen should not be simplified as a proxy war between the Saudi and Iranian contenders for dominance in the Middle East. Neither, it should be reduced to just a local struggle between the Houthis and the government. Such a binary and reductionist approach obscures the complex, local origins of the conflict and differing military and political objectives of domestic combatants. In consequence, it leads to overlooking the multi-cause and multiparty struggle that occurs in Yemen—the struggle that is, however, full of various proxy actors.

Chapter Thirteen focuses on Central Asia. Tova Norlen and Vinay Kaura, in their study "When Proxies Win: The Impact of the Taliban's Changing Fortune on Pakistan's Leverage," approach the issue of proxy use from changing power dynamics, with the emphasis on the hierarchical nature of the relationship between principal and agent. They argue that the policy objectives of both sides define the nature of the relationship. The authors further point out how the ability of the principal to control the agent also plays an important role in explaining the relationship between the Taliban and Pakistan as a recent example of power relations between the patron and the agent. The chapter explores the historical context and the dynamics of the relationship after the Taliban becomes an actor holding the state power of Afghanistan from August 2021. It is concluded with the claim that Taliban's new position as a "state actor" and the increasingly divergent goals between Pakistan and the Afghan Taliban have greatly diminished Pakistan's ability to exert control over their proxy, arguably giving rise to an inverted proxy-patron relationship, in which the proxy partially dictates its patron's policies.

Chapter Fourteen, "Transnational Organized Crime Groups as State Proxies," written by Ümit Namli and Cüneyt Gürer proposes a non-traditional take on the utilization of proxies. The chapter approaches proxy use from a different perspective and argues that not only armed groups that are considered part of an ongoing conflict but also transnational organized crime (TOC) groups could also be used as state proxies. The authors, claiming that proxies can be used as a part of the strategic power competition among the global actors, examine how TOC groups are used as state proxies in the contemporary security environment.

Their analysis demonstrates that authoritarian regimes are more likely to use TOC groups as proxies to reach their objectives in international competition with other states.

The last chapter of the volume, "The Salience of the New Proxy War Paradigm," written by Graeme Herd, is a systematic summary of the case studies presented in the book. Based upon four distinct defining features of the structure of proxy use in the contemporary era, namely, the multiplicity of sponsors, the fluidity and complexity of proxy sponsor motivations, sponsor delegation or orchestration relations with proxies are governed by increasingly complex costs/ benefits trade-offs, proxy-sponsor relations trend towards convergence, the author examines the case studies presented in the book. Building on those and other examples of proxy warfare, Herd argues for the existence of a new, post-Cold War proxy warfare paradigm.

All these chapters construct our geographically-oriented narration about the last decade's proxy warfare. They are by no means exhaustive—as they do not cover every case in the world, not even every continent—yet hopefully, they are updative, instructive, and informative, as they pertain to significant and diverse cases from around the world. Last but not least, we do hope that, as scholars, we added value with this volume to the academic discourse on proxy warfare.

Dear Reader, we hope that after reading this anthology, you will feel better informed about this phenomenon—more and more visible on the contemporary battleground.

We wish you an inspiring lecture.

The Authors
Paweł Bernat, Cüneyt Gürer, Cyprian Aleksander Kozera

Disclaimers

The views expressed in this book are those of the authors. They do not reflect the policy and should not be seen as an official position of any institution or government the authors otherwise may represent or may be affiliated with.

The opinions expressed in this volume are those of the author(s) and do not necessarily reflect the official policy or position of the George C. Marshall Center, the government of the United States of America or the Federal Republic of Germany.

Part One

Theoretical and Historical Framework

1

Toward Conceptualization of Contemporary Proxy Warfare

Paweł Bernat and Cyprian Aleksander Kozera

Introduction

For some time now, there has been a consensus among scholars working in the field of proxy warfare that there is not enough conceptual work being done on proxy wars. They are "chronically under-analysed" (Mumford 2013b: 1), "under-theorized" (Rondeaux and Sterman 2019: 11), "under-researched" (Ivanov 2020: 39), and "understudied" (Rauta 2020: 10).

Apart from the obvious fact that there are not enough studies carried out and researchers involved in the analysis of the phenomenon, the reason for such a state of affairs is rather complex. Generally speaking, as demonstrated in this chapter, the term has become too ambiguous and, in consequence, has lost much of its explanatory power.

The goal of this chapter is to explain why where this ambiguity of the proxy war notion comes from. The main argument, simply put, is based on three premises: (1) proxy wars substantially change in time, (2) current, twenty-first-century proxy wars qualitatively differ from proxy wars of the Cold War era, and (3) many conceptual and explanatory frameworks still used today were created in the previous era. The conclusion is straightforward—these frameworks are unable to encompass the complexities of the current much more convoluted proxy wars; the definitions stemming from these frameworks are inadequate to the actual reality of proxy warfare today. Consequently, there is a lot of conceptual vagueness and confusion, which directly contributes to the degrading explanatory power of the notion of proxy warfare. The calls to analyze, research, and study it are the response to that situation and a plea to reinstate the conceptual order.

It is worthwhile to mention that proper depiction and understanding of proxy wars are not only needed by academia but also by policymakers. There is an important practical aspect to it from a national and international security perspective.

In recent years, a few valuable conceptual frameworks were created (they are described in more detail at the end of the chapter). However, if such frameworks are to be successful explanatory tools, they have to be based on a thorough understanding of the current proxy wars reality. The ultimate goal of this book is to provide such knowledge by presenting and discussing the newest occurrences of proxy wars from around the globe.

The structure of the chapter responds to the structure of its main argument. It is divided into three sections. The first one is dedicated to presenting a brief history and development of proxy wars up to the end of the Cold War era. In the second section, the authors examine the evolution of proxy warfare in the twenty-first century. The argument presented here shows that currently fought proxy wars have evolved to be qualitatively different from their predecessors. The third section, entitled "The Conceptual Struggle and Possible Ways Out," meticulously analyzes the incompatibility of the traditional explanatory frameworks to current conflicts and several "new" definitions and models that take into account at least some of the complexities of the "new" proxy wars.

Brief History of Proxy Warfare

Yaacov Bar-Siman-Tov, in his article "The Strategy of War by Proxy," proposes two general understandings of proxy warfare. According to the first one, a proxy war takes place when in a regional armed conflict, at least one of the parties involved has the support of a superpower, which provides indirect military assistance. The major reason behind such involvement of a superpower is the superpower's will to use a local conflict to "advance its global and regional strategic or political interests without the need to intervene by its own forces" (1984: 263). The second type of proxy warfare, as Bar-Siman-Tov further argues, occurs when despite the external power's indirect intervention, the supported state is losing the war, and the superpower takes the decision to intervene directly (1984: 263–4). This straightforward definitional ambiguity—to engage one's troops or not, which may even be perceived as a contradiction, should not come as a surprise when discussing proxy warfare. The fact is that the phenomenon of using proxies is probably as old as the war itself and has been evolving throughout the whole of warfare history. Apart from providing introductory information on proxy warfare, the very purpose of this chapter (and the whole book) is to demonstrate the evolution of the phenomenon and conceptual struggle that it brings forth. Bar-Siman-Tov is not wrong in his attempt to theoretically grasp the gist of proxy warfare. However, one must remember that these definitions were proposed in the 1980s. i.e., during the Cold War—in times of two global powers that used their power and influence over weaker states to gain more domination on the globe and, ultimately, to defeat their adversary.

One of the first well-documented use of proxies was the assistance given by Rome to the Mamertines in their fight against Carthage during the First Punic War (264–41 BCE). In spite of initial reluctance stemming from moral reasons, the Senate eventually decided to provide the assistance to Messene it asked for. In the end, Rome's will to broaden its influence over Sicily and simultaneously erase, at little expense, the Carthaginian threat by the hands of Mamertines tipped the scales (Pfaff 2017: 305).

Several centuries later, the Byzantine–Sasanian War of 572–91 provided a discussion-worthy example of the use of proxy warfare, where two superpowers of that time, the Eastern Roman Empire, ruled by emperor Justinian, and the Sasanian Empire of Persia led by Khosrow I, also known as Anushirvan, used Arab tribes as intermediaries at the beginning of the war. Banu Lakhm was an Arab kingdom that encompassed the territory of Southern Iraq and Eastern Arabia and was a stable ally of the Sassanians in the sixth century. The Lakhmids posed a serious threat to Byzantine. In 529, Justinian supported Al-Ḥārith ibn Jabalah (Arethas) in becoming the king of the Ghassanids—a pre-Islamic Christian Arab tribe that occupied the lands to the west of Banu Lakhm, current Jordan, Southern Syria, Northern Iraq, and Saudi Arabia. The two rulers built a close relationship. Justinian's intentions were, as Dignas and Winter put it, obvious—the creation of a force loyal and strong enough to become a counterpart to the Lakhmids. The plan worked because, throughout the sixth century, the two kingdoms were in permanent military confrontation (Dignas and Winter 2007: 169–71).

In Middle Ages Europe, the proxyization of warfare was something rather natural. O'Brien argues that rulers of that time actually preferred hiring mercenaries, preferably groups of trusted foreigners, to fight their wars. Such a solution helped avoid substantial losses of their own troops. In time, many independent free companies of knights were formed, who sold their services to various military and political leaders across the continent and beyond (O'Brien 2011: 111). Outsourcing of warfare reached such a pathological level that contemporary political writers such as Niccolò Machiavelli strongly argued against hiring mercenaries (2014: 53–6).

In the nineteenth and early twentieth century, the colonial powers often participated in regional armed conflicts in an attempt to save or strengthen their global influence, and quite frequently, they found themselves on opposite sides of the battle. United Kingdom, Austria, Russia, and Prussia stood against France and Spain in the 1839–41 Egyptian–Ottoman War. In the first phase of the Samoan Civil War, 1887–9, the US and British Royal Navy stood against German warships. Ultimately, the Matafans supported by Germany were defeated, just as plans of the latter to expand their empire. In the 1918 Finnish Civil War, Germany clashed with Soviet Russia. In the Spanish Civil War of 1936–9, Spanish Nationalists had the support of Italy, Nazi Germany, and Portugal, while the Republicans were backed by the Soviet Union and Mexico. In all of those cases, the superpowers of that time fought against one another, more or less directly, on territories of different states. These were proxy wars in the classic sense of the term.

The geopolitical aftermath of the Second World War and the invention of nuclear weapons accelerated the development and significantly increased the scale of the use of proxies. The world became bipolar, and the two powers, i.e., the United States and the Soviet Union, did not want to take the risk of waging a full-scale war against their adversary that would inevitably result in MAD (mutually-assured destruction). Another key element in this puzzle was the threat of using atomic bombs. More frequent use of proxies after 1945 seems to be a natural consequence of that state of affairs. As Andrew Mumford rightly noted, this threat "ensured more acute selectivity in conflict engagement" (2013a: 40). In this new global security environment, the majority of proxy wars structurally looked very similar to the Byzantine–Sasanian War described above. The attempts to theoretically grasp the essence of the phenomenon mirrored the bipolar reality. In his 1964 article entitled "External Involvement in Internal War," Karl Deutsch defines proxy war as "an international conflict between two foreign powers, fought out on the soil of a third country; disguised as a conflict over an internal issue of that country; and using some of that country's manpower, resources and territory as a means for achieving preponderantly foreign goals and foreign strategies" (1964: 102). The major wars that occurred after the Second World War and before the collapse of the Soviet Union in 1991 perfectly fit this definition.

Many proxy wars were fought during the Cold War period. The largest and most important ones, i.e., the ones in which the United States and the Soviet Union participated on opposite sides, were the 1950–53 Korean War, the 1952–75 Vietnam War, the wars in Afghanistan, the 1979–89 Soviet-Afghan War, and the 1989–92 Afghan Civil War. All of those armed conflicts are well-researched,

Toward Conceptualization of Contemporary Proxy Warfare

analyzed, described, and understood also from the proxy warfare perspective—the Korean War (Bar-Siman-Tov 1984; Macdonald 2019; Lee 2001; Millett 2001), the war in Vietnam (Lind 2002; Brown 2016; Miller and Vu 2009; Daum, Gardner and Mausbach 2003), and Afghanistan (Marshall 2006; Loveman 2002; Rondeaux and Sterman 2019; Shahrani 2002). In general, a large majority of books on proxy warfare, regardless of whether trying to construct an explanatory model of proxy wars or just providing descriptions of case studies, focused on conflicts that occurred during the Cold War, and the wars themselves followed the pattern of Deutsch's definition.

The conclusion stemming from this brief historical review is that there have been various types of proxy wars, and their evolution depends on and is fueled by the current geopolitical situation and military capabilities. If the character of proxy wars mirrors the global political order, then it was a natural course of action that after the collapse of the Soviet Union and the bipolar world, the proxy wars changed as well. The intention behind this book is to show this evolution with the use of the chosen case studies of the recent proxy wars.

The Evolution of Proxy Warfare in the Twenty-First Century

Rondeaux and Sterman, in their 2019 study, write that "Cold War norms, however, no longer apply in a highly networked, multipolar world" (2019: 3). Among the arguments they provide to support this thesis, they mention "erosion of state power," "rise of transnational social movements," and "proliferation of advanced military and communications technology" (Rondeaux and Sterman 2019: 3). The conclusion seems straightforward—Washington and Moscow no longer set the rules in the environment where a growing number of various entities, states and non-states, sponsor proxy interventions. Nowadays, as Rondeaux and Sterman argue further, "a complex mesh of partnerships among states, corporations, mercenaries, and militias is changing the way wars are fought and won" (2019: 3).

Similar conclusions are drawn by Ivanov, who analyzed the reasons behind recent changes in proxy warfare. He rightfully argues that proxy warfare "is a product of mutual relationships between actors, as well as the surrounding conditions, and has an influence within any given geostrategic environment" (Ivanov 2020: 38). He is also right in claiming that both those elements have significantly changed in the recent years and that their change influenced the development of the proxy warfare. Let us have a closer look at the new geopolitical, military, and technological environment, which constitutes the background of proxy warfare; the background which, it has to be added, determines the character of the proxy groups and how they participate in the proxy wars.

Analyzing proxy warfare during the times of the Cold War, from today's perspective, seems a much easier task than trying to today conceptually grasp it, describe and analyze it, and solve the policy challenges stemming from it. Current proxy conflicts are simply much more complex and interlinked than before. The fall of the Cold War order brought forth a collapse of the bipolar world, which was superseded by multipolarity. Globalization of the twenty-first century has significantly strengthened the role of the internet and soft power. Geopolitics has changed substantially due to global alliances being broken off, expanded, or created. International sanctions on "rogue" states have become a progressively more important tool for diminishing economies, isolation, and punishment. It has also changed, as Rondeaux and Sterman argue, the role of proxies and their sponsors by "elevating transnational social movements, an array of armed actors enabled by interconnected supply chains, and conflict entrepreneurs" (2019: 4). From the perspective of the states, this new environment—multipolar and based on almost not limited markets and integrated transportation, information, and economic systems, "is providing states with great opportunities to covertly sponsor organized crime, terrorism, and insurgencies" (Ivanov 2020: 43). It is especially relevant in times of growing cost of human life of one's own troops and still persistent lack of will of open involvement in armed conflict, when the geopolitical goals of the state may be achieved with the use of proxies. In consequence, various proxy groups, including militias, paramilitary organizations, and private military security forces, play a considerable role in the strategies of main global actors (Rondeaux and Sterman 2019: 4), including the Russian Federation, the United States, Turkey, Iran, Iran, Saudi Arabia, and France. The case studies chapters of this book analyze the proxy involvement of these states in various armed conflicts.

Technology has always been entwined with warfare, and very often, the latter was a driving force for technological development creating new weapons and, in consequence, new tactics for the battlefield. The way the current proxy wars are fought, their evolution, is also determined by the technologies that are used. We observe a progressive democratization of communication and weapon systems. It basically means that traditionally weak agents, like proxy groups, have now access, via their proxy sponsors, to very advanced and sophisticated weapon systems, which are able to change the outcome of the conflict. Attack drones,

MANPADS, GPS-based weapons, 3D printers, and signal-jamming devices are just a few examples. Moreover, new communication technologies allow proxy groups to have global reach and, sometimes, to operate independently. As Ivanov accurately sums it up, technological innovations, apart from altering the global security environment, "are substantially influencing the character of the proxy force" (Ivanov 2020: 46).

The Conceptual Struggle and Possible Ways Out

The fact that proxy wars have changed, due to the reasons described above, has not stayed unnoticed by the analysts of the issue, as well as policymakers. The inadequacy of the established explanatory tools based on and pertinent to the Cold War era and the actual way proxy warfare is currently conducted has created a theoretical gap. Many researchers, recognizing the growing need for the conceptualization of the phenomenon, wanted to bridge this gap by creating new, suitable to the new reality descriptions and definitions. It is not an easy task, especially if we take into account the fact that proxy warfare is still evolving and not much time has passed since the collapse of the former bipolar world order and the occurrence of new characteristics of proxies and how they are used.

Therefore, we are today in a situation of terminological confusion, especially among non-specialists, because some "old" definitions are still in circulation together with the "new" ones. In this sense, this book is an attempt to shed some light on the current proxy warfare and show through the case studies of recent proxy wars, including non-traditional ones, how they are conducted. This contribution, we believe, should provide new information on the evolution of the phenomenon of proxy warfare, which can be helpful in constructing a new explanatory framework.

Let us now briefly analyze the history and development of the two definitional frameworks of proxy wars. The first one, from the Cold War era, had its main focus on how two superpowers of that time waged conflicts against each other without open participation to avoid escalation, which in consequence, may have brought about nuclear war and total destruction of the planet. It was, of course, recognized, e.g., by Philip Towle (1981: 21), that proxy wars had happened before, but also that the current world determined much more frequent calling for this kind of conducting wars. Towle's historical analysis demonstrates the quantitative evolution of proxy warfare from the times before the Second World War to the Cold War period. In that picture, the only difference is in the current superpowers and their technological and military capabilities, and the engagement of proxies is examined in three aspects, i.e., arms transfers, volunteers, military bases and alliances (Towle 1981: 21–4). Such an approach is naturally a reflection of the times it was created in, and it cannot be successfully used to adequately describe and understand the use of hybrid warfare as it takes place, e.g., in the Russian-Ukrainian war (see Chapter Four) or Israeli-Iranian conflict (see Chapter Eight).

Other "old" definitions, already discussed in this chapter, define proxy war as an armed conflict where "at least one of the parties involved has the support of a superpower" (Bar-Siman-Tov 1984: 263) and as "an international conflict between two foreign powers, fought out on the soil of a third country" (Deutsch 1964: 102). Such an understanding also does not fit the current, much more complex, and complicated reality of today's proxy warfare, as it is clearly visible in all the case studies of proxy wars published in this book. There are no doubts, among the specialists, that there is a qualitative difference between the "old" Cold War era proxy wars and the ones that came after.

"New" conceptual frameworks, in order to catch up with the changing reality, tend to be very broad and general. Rondeaux and Sterman argue that today "proxy warfare is best defined as sponsorship of conventional or irregular forces that lie outside the constitutional order of states" (2019: 4). According to Mumford, current proxy wars are "the indirect engagement in a conflict by third parties wishing to influence its strategic outcome," and are "the logical replacement for states seeking to further their own strategic goals yet at the same time avoid engaging in direct, costly and bloody warfare" (2013b: 11). Kozera et al. define it as "a phenomenon that entails employment of an intermediary in pursuing aims of and by an external state actor in armed conflict" (2020: 79). These are just exemplary definitions, but they are consistent with the trend of the comprehension of proxy wars within the framework consisting of four constitutive elements, namely (1) sponsorship or engagement, (2) intermediaries, (3) goals of the engagement, and finally (4) the engaged sponsor.

Each of these four categories is not straightforward and sometimes should be perceived as a scale and not in terms of the one-zero logic. In practice, it means that classifying an armed conflict as a proxy war requires arbitrary decisions, which, as argued before, may contribute to theoretical disorder and pose a serious challenge to policymakers. For example, in the first case, the following questions arise: When is the patron state's sponsorship significant enough for the state to be accounted as a proxy sponsor? Is providing reconnaissance data enough? Financial assistance? Or maybe just training the troops of the sponsored country? In the second category, the intermediaries: What do irregular forces consist in? Do they necessarily have to be armed troops, or maybe well-trained hackers are even more suited for some forms of more and more occurring hybrid warfare? The category of goals, although easier to delineate or diagnose, is not univocal. Is "feeding the chaos," proposed by Tyrone Groh as one of the aims of proxy engagement as indirect intervention (2019: 8), a good enough reason to assess an engagement, of course, without any serious military or financial involvement, as a proxy war? And finally, the engaged sponsor has been almost always identified as a state, a superpower in the Cold War era. It seems, however, that in times of large international corporations, private military companies, and transnational crime, it does not have to be.

The above nexus of questions and possible answers to them is responsible for the lack of a comprehensive and detailed definition of today's proxy warfare. At this point, it is difficult to say whether such a definition is even possible. Of course, the phenomenon of proxy warfare is understudied, but there is also a possibility that since it broke off the shackles of twentieth-century limitations, it has become too broad and internally differentiated to be closed in one unconditional and unambiguous definition. In other words, the term might have been misused, and in time it lost its core meaning. Or maybe we just need more time to gain a fuller perspective and more data to methodologically sort it out?

Fortunately, there are good models already being constructed. Let us briefly discuss two of them, namely Groh's aims-oriented classification and Vladimir Rauta's definitional structure of the "proxy war" notion. Groh's model, presented in his 2019 book entitled *Proxy War: The Least Bad Option*, is based on the understanding of proxy war as a type of indirect intervention which can be undertaken by the sponsor state due to various reasons (Groh 2019: 26–40). A different policy objective is a key differentiating issue among four proposed types of proxy wars, namely, (1) in it to win it, (2) holding action, (3) meddling, and (4) feed the chaos. Each type, Groh explains, "has a specific purpose based on a state's perception of what is at stake and its commitment to the outcome" (2019: 35). This framework allows him to classify the open-source confirmed proxy wars that took place in 1945–2001, and he believes that it will be a successful explanatory tool for the proxy wars of the future because it provides an insight into "how and why an intervening state would choose [proxy war] as a policy option" (Groh 2019: 40).

The second model, proposed by Rauta, takes a different approach. This complex proxy warfare conceptualization model has been consistently developed over the last several years (Rauta 2019; Rauta 2021). It is an attempt to construct an all-encompassing definitional matrix for proxy wars, which is organized around three elements, namely, (1) a material-constitutive feature, (2) a processual feature, and (3) a relational feature (Rauta 2021: 1). The material-constitutive feature of the notion comes down to the fact that external support is materially required for an armed conflict to be called proxy war, and its constitutive element. The support may, of course, vary depending on the case, and should be understood as a spectrum between, but not limited to "provision of finance, training, to help with intelligence, safe havens, and permission for transit" (Rauta 2021: 13). The support itself may be direct or indirect, "where 'direct' refers to the country's own troops and indirect speaks of the above-mentioned categories: supplies of weapons, financial assistance, or sanctioned use of a neighbouring state's territory" (Rauta 2021: 13). A processual feature explains the "modalities through which the material-constitutive component is provided" (Rauta 2021: 14). Rauta here distinguishes two possible options. The first one takes place when the government and all of its involved institutions "form complex chains of responsibility over the intervention and allow its aims to be met through a third party," while the second option presupposes that the assistance can be given via an entirely external intermediary (2021: 14). The final feature—a relational one stems from the need to acknowledge that various entities, not necessarily states, can be actors engaged in proxy warfare, also on the sponsor side. In this respect, focusing on the relational component has an advantage over actor-centric definitions, which are not always adequate and too limiting (Rauta 2021: 15). Rauta's model for conceptually addressing the complexities of the contemporary proxy war phenomenon, we believe, is the most comprehensive. It is best suited to systematically classify and explain the rich variety of this type of conducting warfare today.

Conclusion

In summary, the chapter presents the commonly acknowledged fact that current proxy wars, and especially their theoretical framework, are understudied. There is a gap between a quickly developing phenomenon and its conceptual grasp. The terminological and definitional confusion that exists today can negatively influence policymaking (Rondeaux and Sterman 2019: 11), which, in consequence, may bring forth a threat to national and international security. The goal of the chapter was to show the need for the development of more reality-based explanatory frameworks that would be able to accurately grasp the complexities of the twenty-first-century proxy wars. This book, in its attempt to scrupulously describe the cases of recent and current proxy wars, is an answer to this call.

Bibliography

Bar-Siman-Tov, Y. (1984), "The Strategy of War by Proxy", *Cooperation and Conflict*, 19 (4): 263–73. http://www.jstor.org/stable/45083584.

Brown, S. (2016), "Purposes and Pitfalls of War by Proxy: A Systemic Analysis", *Small Wars & Insurgencies*, 27 (2): 243–257. https://doi.org/10.1080/09592318.2015.1 134047.

Daum, W., L. C. Gardner, and W. Mausbach, eds (2003), *America, the Vietnam War, and the World*, Cambridge: Cambridge University Press.

Deutsch, K. W. (1964), "External Involvement in Internal War, in H. Eckstein (ed.), *Internal War, Problems and Approaches*, 100–110, New York: Free Press of Glencoe.

Dignas, B. and E. Winter (2007), *Rome and Persia in Late Antiquity: Neighbours and Rivals*, Cambridge: Cambridge University Press.

Groh, T. L. (2019), *Proxy War: The Least Bad Option*, Stanford: Stanford University Press.

Ivanov, Z. (2020). "Changing the Character of Proxy Warfare and Its Consequences for Geopolitical Relationships", *Security and Defence Quarterly*, 31 (4): 37–51. https://doi.org/10.35467/sdq/130902.

Kozera, C. A., P. Bernat, C. Gürer, B. Popławski and M. A. Sözer (2020), "Game of Proxies— Towards a New Model of Warfare: Experiences from the CAR, Libya, Mali, Syria, and Ukraine", *Security & Defence Quarterly*, 31 (4): 77–97. https://doi.org/10.35467/sdq/131787.

Lee, S. H. (2001), *The Korean War*, London: Routledge. https://doi.org/10.4324/9781315840222

Lind, M. (2002), *Vietnam: The Necessary War*, New York: Touchstone.

Loveman, C. (2002) "Assessing the Phenomenon of Proxy Intervention", *Conflict, Security & Development*, 2 (3): 29–48. https://doi.org/10.1080/14678800200590618.

Macdonald, J. M. (2019), "South Korea, 1950–53: Exogenous Realignment of Preferences" in E. Berman and D. A. Lake (eds), *Proxy Wars: Suppressing Violence through Local Agents*, 28–52, Ithaka: Cornell University Press.

Machiavelli, N. (2014), *The Prince*, Penguin Classics UK.

Marshall, A. (2006), "From Civil War to Proxy War: Past History and Current Dilemmas", *Small Wars & Insurgencies*, 27 (2): 183–195. https://doi.org/10.1080/0959 2318.2015.1129172.

Miller E. and T. Vu, (2009), "The Vietnam War as a Vietnamese War: Agency and Society in the Study of the Second Indochina War", *Journal of Vietnamese Studies*, 4 (3): 1–16.

Millett, A. R. (2001), "Introduction to the Korean War", *The Journal of Military History*, 65 (4): 921–935.

Mumford, A. (2013a), "Proxy warfare and the future conflict, *The RUSI Journal*, 158 (2): 40–46. https://doi.org/10.1080/03071847.2013.787733.

Mumford, A. (2013b), *Proxy Wars*, Cambridge: Polity.

O'Brien, K. (2011), "Surrogate Agents: Private Military and Security Operators in an Unstable World", in M. Innes (ed.), *Making Sense of Proxy Wars: States, Surrogates & the Use of Force*, 109–36, Lincoln: University of Nebraska Press.

Pfaff, C. A. (2017), "Proxy War Ethics", *Journal of National Security Law & Policy*, 9 (2): 305–353.

Rauta, V. (2019), "Conceptualising the Regular-irregular Engagement: The Strategic Value of Proxies and Auxiliaries in Wars amongst the People", in D. Brown, et al., (ed.), *War amongst the People*, 101–24, Havant: Howgate Publishing Limited.

Rauta, V. (2020), "Framers, Founders, and Reformers: Three Generations of Proxy War Research", *Contemporary Security Policy*. https://doi.org/10.1080/13523260.2020.1800240.

Rauta, V. (2021), (2021) "Proxy War'—A Reconceptualisation', *Civil Wars*, 23 (1): 1–24. https://doi.org/10.1080/13698249.2021.1860578.

Rondeaux, C. and D. Sterman (2019), *Twenty-First Century Proxy Warfare: Confronting Strategic Innovation in a Multipolar World Since the 2011 NATO Intervention*, New America.

Shahrani, N. M. (2002), "War, Factionalism, and the State in Afghanistan", *American Anthropologist*, 104 (3): 715–722. https://doi.org/10.1525/aa.2002.104.3.715.

Towle, P. (1981), "The Strategy of War by Proxy", *The RUSI Journal*, 126 (1): 21–6. https://doi.org/10.1080/03071848108523403.

2

US Proxy Warfare's New and Complex Paradigm

Richard D. Newton

Introduction

In July of 1969, President Richard Nixon articulated a new approach to US national security objectives. As a newly elected president who had inherited the very unpopular war in Vietnam, President Nixon's vision was to pursue American national security goals through partnership with friends and allies, essentially a manifesto for outsourcing American small wars to others. That announcement, known as the Nixon Doctrine, affirmed to the world that the U.S would keep its treaty commitments and in the case of aggression short of nuclear confrontation, the US would furnish military and economic assistance, but would expect the nations being attacked to assume the primary responsibility for furnishing the manpower to defend themselves (Nixon 1969). The Nixon Doctrine, allowing advice, training, and monetary and material assistance, but eschewing direct military involvement, has been reaffirmed by every US President since. More importantly, Nixon's 50-year-old pronouncement continues to provide the policy basis for modern proxy warfare by the US

Throughout the Cold War, both the United States and the Soviet Union used a collection of military surrogates to further their political agendas. The world was a very different place then and the global economy was barely interdependent. While the US sought trading partners and stable markets for American goods and services, the Soviet Union could hardly sustain its own population and had little of value to export beyond military hardware. Its goal for confrontation with the West was to expand its sphere of influence and gain political clout within international institutions such as the United Nations. Since 2019, though, Russia has become a leading exporter of petroleum and gas, coal, iron, nickel, and wheat. Although Moscow is a net exporter and maintains a favorable trade surplus, Russia must still import manufactured goods such as vehicles, packaged medicines, and telecommunications equipment (OEC 5.0 2021). Modern Russia now has the ability to wield an economic cudgel it did not have during the Cold War, especially among those nations needing Moscow's oil, gas, and critical minerals, or wanting access to Russian markets.

The Cold War was also an era of mutual nuclear deterrence—neither the US nor the Soviet Union were willing to risk a war that might escalate into an exchange of thermonuclear weapons. Therefore, military confrontations were intentionally limited, often irregular, conflicts fought by proxies away from the central plains of Europe. Over 50 years of "small wars," or indirect confrontations between the two superpowers manifested in scores of limited conflicts in Africa, the Middle East, Southeast Asia, South Asia, Central America, and South America as the two superpowers sought to bring "Third World" nations into their competing "camps." The Soviets and the US fought for influence and access on the peripheries. The unexpected result of five decades of indirect superpower confrontation was that US Special Operations Forces (SOF), primarily Army Special Forces (SF), developed the skills, attitudes, doctrines, and ethos they later employed in the successful unconventional warfare campaigns waged in Afghanistan (2001) and northern Iraq (2003).

The SFs' core ideology of conducting operations "through, with, or by" indigenous populations or host nation security forces has its origins in the beginning of the Republic (Boyatt 1998: 36). Both the British and the French enlisted and armed native American surrogates in their frontier battles of the seventeenth and eighteenth centuries. During America's westward expansion before and after the Civil War, the US Army recruited native Americans to fight against other natives who opposed the settlers moving west. In 1901, after the Spanish-American War, the Army organized friendly Filipinos into the Philippine Constabulary to fight and pacify indigenous groups opposed to the American occupation. Throughout the Second World War, the Army's Office of Special Services, the forerunner to today's Army Special Forces and the Central Intelligence Agency (CIA), equipped, trained, and led proxy forces in Southeast Asia to fight against the Japanese and in Europe to fight against the Axis powers. It was only natural, then, for the US to continue using local and regional surrogates during the Cold War to contain Soviet aspirations.

After the Allied victory in 1945, many former European colonies in Asia and Africa saw an opportunity to assert themselves and gain independence from the colonial powers. The Soviet Union and to a much lesser extent, China, used these independence movements or "wars of national liberation," as opportunities to export the communist form of socialism and to gain international supporters as a counter to the US and its primarily European allies. The US, flush with victory, but exhausted and nearly bankrupt after years of a global war, sought a low cost means of supporting its treaty commitments, assisting its allies, and countering the spread of communism. Training indigenous forces and advising friendly foreign governments and their security forces became the Special Forces' *raison d'être* (Cleveland and Egel 2020: 19–24).

The US Army and the US Air Force, though, kept their organizational, training, procurement, and planning efforts almost exclusively focused on conventional warfare.[1] Both services left the uncomfortable and "messy" environment of limited warfare, guerrilla warfare, counterinsurgency, counter-terrorism, and irregular warfare to their respective SOF, "Basically, the task of Air Force COIN forces is to provide advice, training, and assistance to indigenous forces" (Tactical Air Operations—Special Air Warfare 1967: 1).

This division of labor was not necessarily a bad thing. While the conventional services focused on what the nation perceived to be the most dangerous threat to the US national survival—deterring direct confrontation with the Soviet Union, SOF conducted irregular warfare activities on the peripheries. For over five decades, Army SF and to a much lesser extent, Air Commandos from the Air Force, quietly practiced and perfected the regional, cultural, diplomatic, and trainer skills so necessary for success in proxy warfare. Their quiet efforts in the far-flung regions of the world bred a cadre of special operators comfortable with this unique form of warfare, one more inclusive of political, social, cultural, economic, and civil aspects than conventional military forces should be.

Although "low intensity conflict"[2] was the most prevalent form of conflict the US engaged in during the 1960s, 1970s, and 1980s, they were intentionally economy-of-force efforts. Small SOF teams would deploy for months at a time to remote locations to train, assist, and advise indigenous forces and governments. In addition to the small-unit tactical skills they employed and taught their hosts, the training included a healthy dose of regional familiarization, local languages, cultural immersion, and instructor development. An SF soldier had to become part anthropologist, part diplomat, part social worker, and part cultural attaché, as well as being an excellent soldier and trainer. Operating embedded with their native hosts around the world, Army SF became this nation's principal tool to recruit, organize, train, and lead proxy forces sympathetic to US national interests, while at the same time serving as a force for change and gaining legitimacy with host nation governments (Cleveland and Egel 2020: 4).

The Special Forces' irregular warfare methodology—embedding with their counterparts, speaking the hosts' languages, and using the hosts' equipment—proved to be relatively inexpensive for the United States to sustain, kept the American presence to a minimum in areas that may have had political or cultural aversion to foreign involvement, and improved the ability of the host forces to provide for their nations' defenses. In return, the SF gained tactical skills related to the native environment (e.g., jungle warfare or desert warfare) that they then brought home and passed on to their US counterparts. The lessons learned in scores of anti-communist campaigns around the world between 1947 and 1989 were applied with great success during the early unconventional warfare campaigns in Afghanistan and in northern Iraq. The seeds of those two proxy wars were sown during the four decades of anti-Soviet containment.

Cold War Legacy

In order to establish a context for the current, twenty-first-century incarnation of proxy warfare, it is helpful to quickly review a few case studies from the Cold War.

Between 1946 and 1954, the US assisted the government of the Philippines to overcome a communist-sponsored insurgency that very nearly put the Philippines into the Soviet sphere of influence. After a series of heavy-handed missteps that alienated the population and aggravated the peasants' grievances, the Filipino government finally began a series of needed financial and land reforms. In addition, the president appointed a new secretary for national defense, Ramon Magsaysay, who set out to eliminate corrupt and inept leaders from the army and the national police, demanded accountability for human rights abuses, and promoted officers who understood the need to win back the peoples' support as a means to ensure the legitimacy of the civilian government.

The US was unwilling to recall its citizens back into uniform to fight another Asian war, so it provided money, equipment, training, and advisors to assist Magsaysay's efforts. American advisors, from the battalion level to Minister of Defense, taught counter-guerrilla tactics and advised their counterparts to find local, Filipino solutions to the problems they were facing. The advisors also imparted Magsaysay's passion for improving the treatment of civilians, helped reorganize the battalions into lighter and more mobile combat teams, and assisted the Filipinos to create a responsive logistics system. Lt Col Edward Lansdale, Magsaysay's advisor, said after the war, "the Filipinos best knew the problems, best knew how to solve them, and they did it—with US aid and advice, but without US domination of their effort" (Greenberg 1987: 98).

On the other side of the Pacific Ocean, in El Salvador, communists returned to their country in 1971 after years of training and indoctrination in Cuba and North Vietnam. By 1979, there were at least five major communist insurgent groups vying for control of the country.

The five insurgent groups gathered in Havana to organize into a single, coordinated effort, and the result was the Farabundo Martí National Liberation Front (FMLN in Spanish). The El Salvadoran rebels were funded, armed, and trained by the Soviets. In the US, the threat from communist expansion into the Americas caused Presidents Carter and Reagan to commit political, economic, financial, and military assistance to help El Salvador fight back. Traumatic memories of the Vietnam experience were still raw and so the size of the US military contingent was limited to 55 trainers and advisors in the country at any one time. Two to three advisors were embedded with each of the six El Salvadoran brigades, their mission being to reinforce the lessons taught at US schools and US-sponsored training camps, provide real-time assessments of the units' combat effectiveness, and change the El Salvadoran army's historically terrible human rights record.

The small American presence in the country, while initially a "no more Vietnams" response by the American leadership, ended up being a blessing and affirmed the value of small teams assisting host nation forces out of any spotlights. The SF advisors ensured the El Salvadorans took the lead in this fight and the institutional reforms needed to correct the human rights abuses and restore the legitimacy of the El Salvadoran army were implemented (Cleveland and Egel 2020: 57–8).

The Soviet Union began supporting Afghan rebels in 1919, on the heels of the Russian Revolution. At the time, Afghans were fighting the British and the Bolsheviks were supplying money, arms, and training. That support continued through the 1970s, ensuring the USSR occupied a strategic position between the two US allies in the region, Pakistan and Iran. In 1977, though, the president of Afghanistan, Mohammed Daoud Khan, asked for US help to move away from the Soviets. Saudi Arabia, Egypt, and Iran, with US concurrence, began sending aid and assistance to Afghanistan. Unfortunately, Daoud was assassinated by Soviet-trained officers and a pro-Soviet Marxist was installed as president. The new government proved so unpopular with the Afghan people that open rebellion broke out and the Soviet Union had to send an airborne battalion to protect their puppet government.

28   *Proxy Wars from a Global Perspective*

In the spring of 1980, the situation had deteriorated to the point where Soviet ground troops were needed to stabilize the country and an airborne division was deployed to Bagram AB. Rather than calming things down, though, the Soviets' presence united the disparate tribes. For the next five years, the Russians fought a counter-guerrilla campaign, with Soviet troops and their Afghan clients occupying the cities while the mujahideen controlled the countryside. By 1985, there were over 100,000 Soviet troops in Afghanistan.

Both Presidents Carter and Reagan found ways to assist the Afghans fighting the Russians. The US provided intelligence and aid packages, and encouraged allies and partners to provide money, arms, and training. The US contracted for surrogates from Saudi Arabia, the United Arab Emirates, Egypt, and Iran to join the anti-Soviet fight. Special Forces advisors in Pakistan helped the Afghans expand upon their traditional fighting methods–ambushes and raids, to exploit the vulnerabilities inherent in the Soviets' conventional, mechanized style of warfare. The US and its partners supplied heavier, modern weapons such as machine guns, anti-armor missiles, and rocket-propelled grenades to enhance the Afghans' guerrilla fighting methods. When the Russians countered with air mobile formations and aerial fire support, the US negated the Russian advantage by supplying Stinger surface-to-air missiles (SAM) to the guerrillas. In 1988, Prime Minister Mikhail Gorbachev began withdrawing Soviet forces from Afghanistan (Encyclopedia Britannica 2022).

These, and other, similar, irregular warfare campaigns, demonstrated that the US could effectively and inexpensively confront Soviet-sponsored aggression by outsourcing the fighting to proxies. The US was fortunate to have empathetic partners willing to provide funds, economic assistance, training, humanitarian aid, agricultural assistance, and equipment, in addition to military support. What the Americans' successful experiences during the Cold War showed was (1) a small US presence was usually the most successful course of action, (2) that the host nation had to "own" the causes of the conflict and commit to addressing the grievances and problem areas that spawned the rebellion, (3) security assistance efforts needed a whole of government approach with civic, judicial, social, informational, and political aspects, in addition to internal security efforts, and (4) successful US training, advice, and assistance avoided creating host nation security forces in the US Army model. Local security forces needed to reflect their nations' cultures, traditions, and ethos if they were to succeed after US assistance ended. Unfortunately these lessons were only embraced by a small segment of the military leaders who would command US and partner forces during the guerrilla conflicts of the twenty-first century. By the time any mistakes were recognized and accepted, it was too late and the US and her allies were pulling out, exhausted after decades of frustrating conflicts that had no definable stopping points and defied conventional Western military paradigms.

To illustrate the complex challenges of modern proxy warfare, we will use Somalia as a case study. While many may question the choice, especially those still wedded to the Cold War definition of "war instigated by a major power which does not itself become involved." A definition more appropriate for the current era is offered by Cambridge University Press, "a war fought between groups or smaller countries that each represent the interests of other larger powers and may have help and support from these" (Cambridge English Dictionary 2021). This definition better captures how diluted and widespread the sponsors of proxy warfare have become and the diversity of their motives for becoming involved. Unlike during the Cold War, today's sponsors and supporters may include global jihadi movements, regionally powerful nations, international governmental organizations, or transnational criminal cartels, in addition to the three major powers: US, Russia, and China. From this perspective, the wicked problem that is Somalia is very appropriate to consider.

Background

In 1969, General Mohammed Siad Barré, with support from the Soviet Union, led a coup and took control of Somalia's fledgling democratic government. Barré, who had trained and exercised with the Soviets advising Somalia's army, took advantage of Cold War politics and in 1974 signed a Treaty of Friendship and Cooperation to formalize the Soviets' security assistance programs that had been ongoing since 1963. (Ingiriis 2016) The USSR and Cuba provided aid, arms, aircraft, advisors, and training to the Somali army and air force to balance US aid and military assistance to Ethiopia. In July 1977, against the will of the Soviets, Barré invaded the Ogaden region of eastern Ethiopia to unify all ethnically Somali areas in the Horn of Africa. When the Soviet Union publicly disapproved, Barré kicked the communists out. The Cubans and Soviets promptly switched to the Ethiopian side. The USSR then supported Ethiopia by airlifting over $1 billion in supplies, tanks, armored vehicles, artillery, MiGs, and helicopters to Addis Ababa. Cuba and South Yemen sent 12,000 soldiers to assist Ethiopia and the USSR provided 1,500 advisors (Urribarres 2021; Ingiriis 2016). By March 1978, the combined Ethiopian and Cuban ground and air force had recaptured all major cities and most of the territory in the Ogaden region. Barré ordered the army to disengage and return to Somalia. All Somali combat units were out of Ethiopia by March 15, 1978, the official end of the conflict.

The Ogaden War caused a massive turnaround in popular support for Barré. His military was devastated and in 1979, disgruntled army officers formed the first opposition party. In an attempt to restore his prestige and power in the region, Barré actively courted the US and its allies for support, offering the US the former Soviet base at Berbera as a counter to Soviet influence in the region. That effort had mixed results, especially given Barré's terrible human rights record and increasingly dictatorial government policies. With the 1989 fall of the Soviet Union, Somalia's importance to the West's containment strategy disappeared and the US never followed through on developing the facilities at Berbera (Mitchell, 1985). Civil war broke out among rival Somali clans and militias and in January 1991, Barré was forced into exile. He died in 1995, in Nigeria.

Since 1991, the country has existed in a perpetual state of chaos and crisis. Without an effective central government, it has been difficult to call it a nation. No one group was able to control the country nor provide any sort of lasting security and stability. The United Nations has been trying since mid-1992 to ensure the safety and security of its humanitarian aid programs, beginning with the UN Operation in Somalia (UNOSOM I). The weak mandate of UNOSOM I peacekeeping forces, though, rendered them impotent and warring Somali clans disregarded the UN's authority, held UN aid packages hostage. and used stolen food aid as a means of securing power and loyalty. The Somali people endured massive poverty, ethnic cleansing, continuous fighting, and a series of famines. Hundreds of thousands died and millions fled the country (UN Background Paper, Somalia: UNOSOM II 2021; Wise 2011; Office of the Historian, Foreign Service Institute 2021).

In November 1992, the UN accepted the US's offer to organize a military coalition, Unified Task Force (UNITAF), and to lead Operation RESTORE HOPE to stem the humanitarian disaster, provide stability, and ensure the delivery of aid. UNITAF was replaced by a new UN mission, UNOSOM II in May 1993, also led by the Americans. The US subsequently expanded UNOSOM II's mission to include removing the main warlord in southern Somalia, General Mohammed Fareh Aideed, and added restoring Somalia's failed government institutions to the mandate (Clark and Herbst 1996; Woods 1997). UNOSOM II was soon fully embroiled in Somalia's civil war. In 1994, President Clinton withdrew US forces from Somalia after the October 1993 Battle for Mogadishu ("Blackhawk Down"). The UN withdrew in March 1995, leaving the country in disarray, without a central government, and still facing widespread famine, corruption, and violence.

Ten years later, in 2002, the factions finally agreed to accept a new coalition government. The Transitional Federal Government (TFG) parliament was formed in 2004 and in 2006 it had its first-ever meeting inside Somalia. Unfortunately, the Islamic Courts Union (ICU) challenged the TFG's authority. Predominantly Christian Ethiopia, fearing the implications of a fundamentalist Islamic state on its eastern border, intervened and sent 10,000 troops to protect the TFG.

Politicized Islam in Somalia began in the 1970s as an underground movement during the Barré years. Al-Itihaad-al-Islamiya (AIAI) began in the 1960s as a Wahabi terrorist group. During the 1980s, the group received funding from various Islamic charities, including Osama bin Laden. Its armed wing was made up primarily of Somali fighters who had returned from fighting the Soviets in Afghanistan. After Barré's exile, AIAI officially announced its existence and its intent to create a regional Islamic state. The group began mounting attacks into Ethiopia and in August 1996, Ethiopian forces entered Somalia and attacked the group's encampments, effectively destroying AIAI's militant capabilities. Many of the AIAI fighters would go on to join with the Islamic Courts Union and form a new youth militia (Stanford University Center for International Security and Cooperation 2019a).

The Islamic Courts Union was formed in 2000 to provide a semblance of security, manage crime, and offer a rule of law in the absence of an effective Somali government. The courts were effective because they used local militias to enforce their authorities. When the courts united, they also united their militias and created the first armed organization not loyal to a single clan or warlord. The ICU began extending its control outside of Mogadishu, providing security and government services, and also managing schools and medical clinics. Many of the AIAI's more fundamentalist and militant fighters joined the ICU and formed a youth militia, al-Shabaab ("The Youth") (Wise 2011; Stanford University Center for International Security and Cooperation 2019b).

By 1995, the CIA assessed that Somalia, an ungoverned space the size of Texas, was becoming a safe haven for radical Islamic terrorist groups. The CIA funded warlord groups in and near Mogadishu, and used those militias as US proxies to find and apprehend suspected terrorists linked to al-Qaeda. US support to unpopular warlords and the specter of greater foreign intervention caused resentment among the Somalis and galvanized popular support for the ICU. In June 2006, the ICU took full control of Mogadishu and its fighting wing, al-Shabaab, had driven the warlords out of the city. (Stanford University Center

32   *Proxy Wars from a Global Perspective*

for International Security and Cooperation, 2019b) The success of the ICU caused concern because of their stated goal to expand into Ethiopia and Kenya to create an Islamic state based on strict interpretation of sharia law. In 2006 the UN Security Council passed a resolution authorizing a military intervention under the African Union. With US political and military support, Ethiopia again invaded southern Somalia, destroyed the ICU, and took control of Mogadishu. Al-Shabaab, though, was not destroyed and became an independent group that evolved into a more radical and better organized violent extremist organization (Klobucista, Masters and Aly Sergie 2021).

Al-Qaeda purportedly began training Somali AIAI militants in response to the UN and US humanitarian aid and peacekeeping missions. Even though hundreds of thousands were starving, Somalia was unable to address the symptoms nor the causes of the famine, and rich Muslim nations did not mobilize to assist. Radical Islamic elements inside and outside of Somalia successfully characterized the humanitarian missions as foreign interventions.

The 1998 bombings of the US embassies in Nairobi and Dar es Salaam were planned by al-Qaeda's top commander in East Africa, Fazul Abdullah Mohammed, a Kenyan, working out of a camp at Ras Kiamboni, Somalia (United States Senate 2010). After Al-Shabaab separated from ICU it informally aligned itself with al-Qaeda and since 2008 has benefited from that organization's training, funding, and ideological guidance. In February 2010, al-Shabaab publicly declared allegiance to al-Qaeda (Wise 2011). In February 2012, Ayman al-Zawahiri announced the two groups' formal affiliation.

Al-Shabaab's anti-foreigner rhetoric plays well with traditional Somali dislike of outsiders. The organization's justification for its attacks outside Somalia and against African peacekeepers operating in Somalia echo al-Qaeda rhetoric— retaliations for foreign military operations in Somalia and for Western persecution of Muslims worldwide (Blanchard 2020a). Since 2010, the terrorist group has carried out terrorist attacks in Uganda and Kenya with the intent of notifying "every country who is willing to send troops to Somalia that they will face attacks on their territory" (Klobucista, Masters and Aly Sergie 2021).

Outsourcing Modern War, or the New "Faces" of Proxy Warfare

In about 2007, both the US and the UK dropped the Bush-era terms, "war on terror" and "global war on terror" as being unhelpful and misleading because nations go to war against nations or organizations, but not against a tactic—terrorism. While the decision was correct, there have been no replacements that capture the globalization and interconnectedness of the threats to liberal and secular democracies posed by jihadi terrorist groups. Modern warfare, at least in its current incarnation has been hybrid—a mix of conventional, irregular, cyber, economic, informational, etc.; and is often motivated by religious, cultural, or ethnic extremism. The US, the Soviet Union, and their respective allies generally played by an agreed upon set of rules and when small wars threatened to escalate beyond acceptable limits, the superpowers were able to push the situation back inside the lines. Those rules have been pretty much discarded in this new version of modern warfare.

Where Barré's Somalia was a willing pawn during the final decades of the Cold War, intentionally playing the US and the Soviet Union against each other, the landscape drastically changed in the early 1990s, creating a new paradigm that made the current situation unlike the Cold War (Moolla 2018). The fall of the USSR opened a path for regional powers to flex their "muscles" unconstrained by the earlier controls imposed from Moscow or Washington. Second, the politicization and radicalization of Islam affected vulnerable Muslim communities, and the religious wars that began in 1979 against the Soviets in Afghanistan, have produced cadres of trained and battle-hardened fighters, leaders, and technicians able and anxious to go where needed to fight for their causes. The third and very troubling characteristic of the new post-Cold War landscape is the proliferation of modern weapons and the ease and speed weapons, money, people, and information are able to travel across traditional borders. As General David Petraeus noted, the current incarnation of great power competition is very different from the Cold War; the world's economies have become interdependent and it is nearly impossible to contain and isolate modern conflict and violence away from innocent and uninvolved populations (Petraeus 2021). Thus, as the world has become more complex and more dangerous, proxy warfare has followed suit. Instead of superpowers competing for influence, global and regional powers are outsourcing their wars to smaller, usually poor, nations who offer their militaries for hire, to civilian contractors, to local militias and paramilitaries, and to the host nations' security forces. Little of this is new. The scale of the outsourcing is surprising, but understandable when one accepts that great powers often need to separate themselves from messy wars in distant locales, where operational necessity often requires partnering with ethically, legally, or morally questionable entities, or if the nature of the conflict defies the doctrine, tactics, training, and organizational structures of conventional military forces. Which brings us back to Somalia . . . .

The threat from al-Shabaab, one of the most well organized and well-funded terrorist groups on the continent, has caused a number of nations to focus on Somalia to neutralize the joint threat from al-Shabaab and al-Qaeda (Savage and Schmitt 2022). Since 2007, Western powers have been paying for African troops to fight in Somalia (Blanchard 2020b). Under the auspices of the Africa Union, about 20,000 soldiers from Kenya, Ethiopia, Burundi, Djibouti, and Uganda have been in Somalia helping to stabilize the central government, provide security, and fight al-Shabaab. It speaks volumes about the security challenges in Somalia that China, India, and Russia have refused to help fund the African Union Mission in Somalia (AMISOM) (Al-Shabab in Somalia 2021; Williams 2017). The African forces in Somalia, under the mantel of "African forces protecting Africans," are essentially surrogates contracted by Western nations that fear the threats posed by jihadi terrorists.

This African veneer on the West's peace and security mission does little to allay traditional Somali xenophobia. To Somalis, other Africans in their country are just as unwelcome and considered equally foreign as Westerners. AMISOM peacekeepers have often been the targets for terrorist attacks. Making matters worse is that with al-Qaeda's help the terrorists have become more sophisticated in their attacks and have been able to move beyond their borders (Wise, 2011). In 2010, dozens of innocent spectators were killed by an al-Shabaab bomb while watching a World Cup match at a bar in Uganda. In 2011, al-Shabaab conducted over 150 attacks in Kenya. And in 2013, 2015, and 2019 they pulled off three spectacular bombings in Kenya, at the Westgate Mall in Nairobi, Garissa University, and the DusitD2 hotel.

Since April 2010, the European Union has maintained a training mission for Somalia, in addition to funding, training, transporting, and equipping AMISOM battalions. The EU has been sending approximately 200 trainers and mentors from seven to nine contributing nations to train, advise, and equip the Somali National Army (SNA), to create a professional security force that is able to successfully stand against al-Shabaab and provide stability and security to the people of Somalia. It is classic indirect approach, using money, equipment, and training to grow and improve host nation security forces so that they can defend their nation . . . a relatively inexpensive and politically acceptable version of outsourcing conflict.

In 2009, the CIA, with the government of Somalia's concurrence, established a secure base in Mogadishu and joined the fight against al-Shabaab and al-Qaeda. The US quietly bankrolled counter-terrorism (CT) training and supplied arms, equipment, uniforms, and money. The US also provided technical intelligence from its aerial surveillance systems. The actual number of Americans on the ground was small and unobtrusive so as to avoid scrutiny and public pressure. By outsourcing CT operations to the Somalis, American casualties were avoided and collateral damages became the Somalis' responsibility. In 2011, Somali CT forces found and killed Fazul Mohammed, the al-Qaeda operative who had masterminded the 1998 embassy bombings. In 2013, after al-Qaeda confirmed the linkage between itself and al-Shabaab, the US confirmed it was training Somali CT units (Walsh, Schmitt and Barnes 2021).

One of the US's more overt outsourcing methods for the last twenty years has been to employ private military contractors for both surrogate force training and equipping and aerial intelligence collection. Beginning in about 2011, the US began using contractors to provide civilian trainers to assist and advise Somali and AMISOM forces (Bancroft Global Development 2021). The contractors use SF methodology to empower, enable, and support local security forces. The contractors also fully immerse themselves with the units they are training, showing their counterparts they have confidence in their hosts' abilities to defend and protect them (Naylor 2015).

The other aspect of outsourcing the conflict has to do with airborne intelligence collection. It is no secret that the US does not have enough military aircraft to meet all its global requirements. Thus, the US has turned to specialized contractors to provide airborne intelligence and surveillance capabilities optimized to suit the characteristics of different operating areas—short, unimproved runways; limited support services; and dedicated, on-call support to a very small number of tactical units. This is completely anathematic to the Air Force's ethos of large, multirole aircraft designed to support entire theaters of operations. In small wars, though, outsourcing airborne reconnaissance and surveillance capabilities to contractors makes fiscal sense and allows the military to quickly discard contractor-provided aircraft and capabilities when US national priorities and Service budget requirements change.

Beginning in 2014, US SOF quietly joined the effort in Somalia, working with an army commando unit, the Danab Brigade (Lightning in Somali). Contractors provided basic military training while SOF delivered advanced skills training, helped share operational intelligence, and sometimes accompanied Danab units during operations. In November 2020, the Department of Defense declared the Danab as "the most capable ground assault force in the SNA" (Ersozoglu 2021).

Conclusion

The war against al-Shabaab does not rank among the United States' or Europe's top priorities. President Biden's decision to follow through on President Trump's promise to end the "endless" wars in Iraq and Afghanistan has given the US a rare moment of peace. There is little appetite in Washington or Europe to send large numbers of troops to Africa to hunt down al-Shabaab and al-Qaeda. Still, the threat posed by al-Shabaab and al-Qaeda to the US and Europe must be addressed lest we and our allies face another spectacular attack. After twenty years of conflicts in Afghanistan and the Middle East, outsourcing the fight against al-Shabaab and other jihadi extremist groups is probably the best course of action.

In Somalia, the war to constrain and degrade al-Shabaab and al-Qaeda was intentionally outsourced to willing proxies: friendly African nations, Somali military units, and contractors in order to constrain the American and European presence and also avert risks to Western troops. The proxy warfare model used in Somalia followed the precedence established decades earlier, as summarized in the Philippines, El Salvador, and Afghanistan case studies. In each of those instances, the US trained, equipped, funded, and often controlled, surrogate forces to achieve US national objectives. It is no different in Somalia. The West is paying the bill so as to control the threat al Shabaab poses to Europe and the US In May 2022, President Biden sent US SOF back to Somalia, but capped the number of US military personnel in Somalia at 450, (Savage and Schmitt 2022) fully in keeping with President Nixon's 1969 vision of training, advising, and assisting others, but not sending US battalions to fight Somalia's war.

The US is also facing a new era of great power competition, though, and must deter the threats posed by China and Russia. The US and European armed forces need to restore and replenish their formations and equipment depleted and exhausted by the past twenty years of war. The Special Forces model, then, small units teaching indigenous communities to defend themselves with the equipment they have, must be embraced by the national security community. The lesson that should have been learned from the wars in Afghanistan and Iraq is that large conventional formations of US and European militaries do not fare well in remote guerrilla conflicts. What Cold War era proxy wars showed was that great power competition on the fringes limited the cost of confrontation without threatening great power survival. Going forward, then, the US and its partners should strengthen their abilities to organize, train, and equip proxies and

US Proxy Warfare's New and Complex Paradigm

surrogates who will most likely be the ones contracted to do the fighting in future modern wars.

Notes

1 In 1970, a general told an interviewer from the RAND Corporation, "I'll be damned if I permit the United States Army, its institutions, it doctrine, and its traditions to be destroyed just to win this lousy war [Vietnam War]" (Beckett 2001: 24).

2 Low intensity conflict was a pseudonym used in the 1970s and 1980s to refer to the conflicts usually fought by guerrillas, most often revolutionaries and insurgents seeking to change the political status quo.

Bibliography

"Al-Shabab in Somalia" (2021), *Global Conflict Tracker*. Available online: https://www.cfr.org/global-conflict-tracker/conflict/al-shabab-somalia (accessed 12 November 2022).

Bancroft Global Development (2021). *Project Profile: Somalia*, Available online: https://www.bancroftglobal.org/project-profile-somalia/ (accessed 2 November 2021).

Beckett, I. F. W. (2001), *Modern Insurgencies and Counter-Insurgencies*, London: Routledge.

Blanchard, L. P. (2020a), *Al Shabaab*. Washington, DC: Congressional Research Service.

Blanchard, L. P. (2020b), *Somalia*. Washington, DC: Congressional Research Service.

Boyatt, M. (1998), "Special Forces: Who Are We and What Are We?", *Special Warfare*, Summer 1998: 36–7.

Cambridge English Dictionary (2021), "Proxy War". Available online: https://dictionary.cambridge.org/us/dictionary/english/proxy-war (accessed 1 November 2021).

Clark, W., and Herbst, J. (1996), "Somalia and the Future of Humanitarian Intervention", *Foreign Affairs*, March-April 1996: 70–85.

Cleveland, C. T., and Egel, D. (2020), *The American Way of Irregular War: An Analytical Memoir*, Santa Monica: RAND Corporation.

Encyclopedia Britannica (2021), "Soviet Invasion of Afghanistan". Available online: https://www.britannica.com/event/Soviet-invasion-of-Afghanistan (accessed 1 November 2021).

Ersozoglu, E. (2021). "Danab: Somalia's Lightning Commandos", *Grey Dynamics*. Available online: https://www.greydynamics.com/danab-somalias-lightning-commandos/ (accessed 10 November 2021).

Greenberg, L. M. (1987), *The Hukbalahap Insurrection: A Case Study of a Successful Anti-Insurgency Operation in the Philippines, 1946–1955*, Washington, DC: US Army Center for Military History.

Ingiriis, M. H. (2016), *The Suicidal State in Somalia: The Rise and Fall of the Siad Barré Regime, 1969–1991*, Lanham, MD: University Press of America.

Klobucista, C., Masters, J., and Aly Sergie, M. (2021), "Al-Shabab", *Council on Foreign Relations*. Available online: https://www.cfr.org/backgrounder/al-shabab (accessed 19 May 2021).

Mitchell, C. (1985), "US Losing Interest in Military Bases in Somalia: Port, Airstrip no Longer are Key Part of Plans for Gulf of Aden Emergency", *Los Angeles Times*, March 17. Available online: https://www.latimes.com/archives/la-xpm-1985-03-17-mn-35349-story.html (accessed 10 November 2021).

Moolla, F. F. (2018), "Figuring the Dictator in the Horn of Africa: Nuruddin Farah's Dictatorship Trilogy and Ahmed Omar Askar's Short Stories", in C. Baker and H. Grayson (eds), *Fictions of African Dictatorship: Postcolonial Power Across Genres*, 199–214, Oxford, UK: Peter Lang.

Naylor, S. D. (2015), "Profit and Loss in Somalia", *Foreign Policy*, January 22. Available online: https://foreignpolicy.com/2015/01/22/delta-force-somalia-terror-blackwater-bancroft/ (accessed 10 November 2021).

Nixon, R. M. (1969), *Address to the Nation on the War in Vietnam*, November 3. Available online: www.presidency.ucsb.edu/ws/index.php?pid=2303 (accessed: 10 November 2021).

OEC 5.0. (2021), *Observatory of Economic Complexity*. Available online: https://oec.world/en/profile/country/rus#:~:text= Exports%20The%20top%20exports%20of,and%20Italy%20(%2416.7B) (accessed 4 November 2021).

Office of the Historian, Foreign Service Institute. (2021), *Somalia: 1992–1993*. Available online: https://history.state.gov/milestones/1993-2000/Somalia (accessed 6 November 2021).

Petraeus, D. (2021), "The Future of Geopolitics Post-Pandemic", interview, October 28, *RUSI*. Available online: https://rusi.org/events/members-events/general-david-petraeus-future-geopolitics-post-pandemic (accessed 10 November 2021).

Savage, C. and E. Schmitt (2022), "Biden Approves Plan to Redeploy Several Hundred Ground Forces Into Somalia", *New York Times*, May 16. Available online: https://www.nytimes.com/2022/05/16/us/politics/biden-military-somalia.html (accessed 16 November 2021).

Sperber, A. (2020), "The Danab Brigade: Somalia's Elite, US-Sponsored Special Ops Force", *Pulitzer Center*, August 11. Available online: https://pulitzercenter.org/stories/danab-brigade-somalias-elite-us-sponsored-special-ops-force (accessed 10 November 2021).

Stanford University Center for International Security and Cooperation. (2019a), *Mapping Militant Organizations: Al Ittihad Al Islamiya*. Available online: https://

cisac.fsi.stanford.edu/mappingmilitants/profiles/al-ittihad-al-islamiya (accessed 10 November 2021).

Stanford University Center for International Security and Cooperation. (2019b), *Mapping Militant Organizations: Islamic Courts Union*. Available online: https://cisac.fsi.stanford.edu/mappingmilitants/profiles/islamic-courts-union (accessed November 10, 2021).

Tactical Air Operations—Special Air Warfare (1967), *Air Force Manual 2-5*. Washington, DC: HQ US Air Force.

Timberg, C. (2006), "Guns Finally Silent in Somalia's Capital", *Washington Post*, June 17.

"United Nations Background Paper, Somalia: UNOSOM II" (2021), *United Nations*. Available online: https://peacekeeping.un.org/sites/default/files/past/unosom2backgr2.html (accessed 7 November 2021).

United States Senate (2010), *Al Qaeda in Yemen and Somalia: A Ticking Time Bomb. A Report to the Committee on Foreign Relations*, January 21, Available online: https://www.govinfo.gov/content/pkg/CPRT-111SPRT54494/html/CPRT-111SPRT54494.htm (accessed 10 November 2021).

Urribarres, R. (2021), *The Cuban Air Force in the Ethiopian War (Ethiopia)*. Available online: http://www.urrib2000.narod.ru/Etiopia.html (accessed 7 November 2021).

Walsh, D., E. Schmitt, and J. E. Barnes, (2021), "A Faltering Shadow War Against Somali Militants", *New York Times*, October 25.

Williams, P. D. (2017), "Paying for AMISOM: Are Politics and Bureaucracy Undermining the AU's Largest Peace Operations?", *International Peace Institute Global Observatory*, January 11. Available online: https://theglobalobservatory.org/2017/01/amisom-african-union-peacekeeping-financing/ (accessed 10 November 2021).

Wise, R. (2011), "Al Shabaab", *Center for Strategic & International Studies*, July 15. Available online: https://csis-website-prod.s3.amazonaws.com/s3fs-public/legacy_files/files/publication/110715_Wise_AlShabaab_AQAM%20Futures%20Case%20Study_WEB.pdf (accessed 7 November 2021).

Woods, E. (1997). "Somalia", *Institute for Policy Studies*, January 1. Available online: https://ips-dc.org/somalia/ (accessed 10 November 2021).

3

States and Non-State Actors Interacting in Conflict: Explaining State Use of Proxies

Cüneyt Gürer

Introduction

Why do States use proxies? How can we best explain a State's policy choice of using proxies rather than directly involving in a conflict? Why does proxy use matter for States and what are the main arguments to justify their involvement in a conflict outside their borders? What can the international relations literature offer to explain States' policy choice of using proxies? These are some of the questions this chapter will address to provide an alternative explanation to State proxy use, a phenomenon that has become a critical issue in contemporary conflicts (Gürer and Kozera 2020: 11–5). Previous studies provided wide range of explanations why States use local groups as proxies in different conflict scenarios, and how proxy-State interaction occurs (Ahram 2011: 7–24; Groh 2019: 83–124; Berman and Lake 2019: 1–27; Salehyan 2020: 493–515). Studies examining the proxy use consider the dynamics of a given conflict as the central element that leads to the decision of proxy use (Hauter 2019; Fox 2019b; Brown, 2016), therefore the decision to use proxy forces is made as a response to the conflict/war context. However, this chapter argues that States' decision of proxy use and the choice of proxies could be also related to other factors and shaped by both domestic and international policy priorities of the State (or a combination of them.)

This chapter therefore, goes beyond the conflict and war context and in addition to that, explains proxy phenomenon with the theories of international relations. In a way, this study follows the suggestions of Farasoo (2021: 6–12) pointing that current studies on proxy war should go beyond the principle-agent conceptualization in explaining the reasons and mechanisms of the State use of proxies or what he calls proxy war as a "multi-layered mechanism rather than a 'single-faced' phenomenon" (Farasoo 2021: 15). This chapter argues that proxy use is a policy decision, similar to any other State decision, which has direct consequences on a State's foreign policy behavior. Taking the discussion out of the conflict context and considering an alternative approach to traditional principle-agent model gives an opportunity to consider various elements of a State's choice of using proxies. International relations theories provide significant amount of explanatory power to understand what causes State decision of proxy use and choice of their proxies. Therefore, this chapter expands the understanding of proxies as a subject of security studies which is provided in the first chapter of the book and argues that using international relations (IR) theories, we can provide alternative insights and increase the predictability of the State behavior using proxies in conflict.

Proxy use is a product of a State's policy process and decision outcome which is not different than any other policies of a State at the international level. Nevertheless, IR scholars and foreign policy analysts have not paid much attention to State behavior in this specific policy field and most analysis has therefore relied on case studies that lack a comprehensive theoretical framework. Studies connect the State-proxy interaction to the discussion of alliance making in international relations connect the concept to the IR literature (San-Akca 2017: 1–42), and attempt to bridge scholarly discussions from various disciplines and develop a theoretical framework to understand proxy war (Rauta and Mumford 2017: 100). Some of these attempts limit their understanding of proxy war within the military doctrine discussions (Fox 2019a: 11–3; Fox 2019b: 44–71; Fox 2020: 50–8). All these discussions bring important insights to understand the contemporary proxy war and background conditions of States use of proxies in the modern warfare. According to this chapter; there are at least two types of interaction explaining the process of proxy use; the first one is related to strategy and policy making processes based on the "why" question that results with the use of proxies as a strategy and policy choice. The second type of interaction is at the tactical phase includes the process of using proxies also related to the "how" question of proxy use. Explaining "how" States engage with proxies requires understanding the process of interaction between States and their designated proxies. This interaction has been addressed by number of studies, looking mostly at the support mechanisms and institutional level engagement of supporting States (Carment and Belo 2020: 21–41; Fox 2019b: 44–71). This chapter, however, focuses on the first phase of interaction to explain the "why" question by focusing on States' motivations to use proxies.

States and Non-State Actors Interacting in Conflict

Explaining State behavior at the international level is a challenging task. As the main unit of analysis in international relations, States act for a variety of reasons and foreign policy outcomes are often shaped by domestic, regional, and systemic interactions. How States define and execute certain policy preferences has been a matter of international relations for decades, and theories of international relations provide a significant amount of insights to explain State behavior at the international level. By emphasizing various aspect of international and State structures, actors, identities and social interactions, theories help scholars understand, categorize, and predict State behavior, as well as analyze the working mechanisms of international State behavior. IR literature explains State-proxy behavior as an outcome of the policy processes of States. It can therefore provide significant insight to understand States' policy preferences and at the same time predict potential State-proxy behavior in future conflicts. Different theories emphasize different actors, institutions, structures and interactions, and therefore provide us alternative dimensions to understand a State's motivations and calculations of proxy use. As an example; from a Realist international relations perspective, States use proxies to pursue their national interests and State power is the most important determinant of proxy use. Powerful States can use proxies because they have the means to support the proxy and at the same time can coerce proxy groups to pursue supporting States' interests. Realist interpretation would argue that proxy groups have limited choice but to cooperate with the supporting States and their objectives are irrelevant because the most important issues are the interests of the supporting States.

From the perspective of Liberalism, however, States' interactions with proxy groups are another form of cooperation which benefits both sides. A Proxy group and supporting State can both reach a common objective and an analyst using liberalist international relations would argue that supporting proxies is about supporting their rights against a more powerful adversary, rather than pursuing the interests of the supporting State. Constructivism would argue and proxy interaction is only possible when the identities of both the supporting State and proxy group matches. This chapter will use these three major theories of IR (Realism, Liberalism, and Constructivism) to explain proxy use by States more in detail.

By explaining State use of proxies using IR theories, this chapter contributes to the IR literature by providing an alternative look at the use of proxies from an international relations perspective. This chapter also sets the stage for the following chapters in the book by discussing the main determinants of policy choices to help explain the case studies. The overall approach to the chapter is straightforward: applying the main arguments and assumptions of the three major IR theories to explain why States use proxies. Alternative explanations of State behavior using IR theories and applying those theories to different policy issues will give scholars and practitioners insights into the decision-making process, which could help them predict State behavior under similar conditions. Applying IR perspective to the proxy literature will allow readers to put the discussions in this book in a theoretical context and explore alternative ways of approaching States' calculations of proxy use.

State Motivations to Use Proxies

State-proxy interaction starts with the State's decision to intervene in a conflict. However, due to various considerations, States may prefer to not commit their militaries or other forces, to the conflict, but instead decide to support a group that is not directly connected to its own institutions. Rauta (2019: 11) defines proxy forces as "armed groups that are not part of the regular forces, but that fight for and on behalf of States." Therefore, the first condition for proxy use is the State's expected strategic outcome. The following action, then, for the States, is to engage with a non-State actor to delegate their intervention into the conflict. (Salehyan 2010 in Rauta 2019: 11). In defining the structure of interaction and examining why States use proxies, this chapter follows the distinction made by Groh (2019: 26–40) between *donated assistance* and *proxy war.* Proxy use in a conflict or proxy war is different than the donated assistance which refers to the act of "aiding an indigenous actor engaged in a civil conflict without strings attached—without the intent or need to control proxy's actions" (Groh 2019: 28). Proxy war, however, requires a State establish a principle-agent relationship and a hierarchy with a local actor (Yüksel 2020: 139). Berman and Lake (2019: 1–27) develops a principle-agent framework to explain indirect involvement of States to conflicts in other countries through proxies. Principle refers to a relatively powerful actor that aims to increase its influence or reduce the likely effect of the conflict; an agent is the proxy group that the principle uses to achieve its objectives.

The main motivation in the principle-agent interaction is the desire to pursue a strategic interest in the conflict. Therefore, we can argue that the main motivation for the State to use a proxy is connected to the desired strategic outcome of the conflict. As an example, Turkey changed the policy of donated assistance to Syrian armed opposition groups at the beginning of the Syrian conflict to using these groups as proxies, and assuming the outcome of conflict would increase the Turkey's influence in the region (Yuksel 2020: 137–52). Similarly, Iran has used proxy forces in the Middle East to balance and pursue its own interests for decades (Kaunert and Wertman 2020: 99–114), while the US supported Kurdish armed groups during the Syrian conflict without committing US military forces, but still expecting ISIS would be defeated (Wither 2020: 17–34). Proxy use could also be related not only to strategic goals, but also to political, statutory, or domestic limitations on direct involvement and the use of force. Domestic political constraints on a supporting State can result in a proxy strategy which reduces the domestic pressure and lowers the risks for the ruling government, but allows the government to pursue national interests at the same time (Mumford 2013: 40–6; Byman 2018).

According to Groh's elaborations (2019: 4) States' abilities to use proxies as a policy option occurs under one or more of the following conditions: (1) the interest of the State is connected to its identity outside its borders, (2) the State's well-being is connected to developments in the other State, or (3) when the State has the capacity to engage in international affairs.

Groh (2019: 32) also makes a distinction between a State's vital and desirable interests that will require direct intervention, non-intervention, or intervention through proxies. He proposes four types of proxy wars: *in it to win it, holding action, meddling, and feed the chaos.* Each category identifies different types of actions by the supporting State and the expected outcome from the interaction. The first category (*in it to win it*) requires more support and decisive actions for The proxy to win and achieve the desired outcome. *Holding action* and *meddling* give the supporting State more room to act and identify the appropriate level of support since the State can adapt and the outcomes are not vital to core interests. *Feeding the chaos* requires actions to prolong the conflict to prevent the opposing State from winning. In addition to these explanations of States' motivations to engage in proxy war, geopolitical considerations should be also added to the discussion.

In a recent article Ivanov (2020: 38) argues that State-proxy interaction should go beyond the engagement mechanisms during the conflict and take a holistic approach that considers the geostrategic environment. Therefore, understanding proxy war in a global context requires paying more attention to the international and related structural explanations when States decide to use proxies instead of becoming directly involved in a conflict. In other words, there is a need to apply the literature of international relations to understand the motivations and decision-making processes of proxy war. The rest of the chapter will apply IR theories to the concept of States use of proxies in conflict.

Using IR Theories to Explain Proxy Use

In order to explain States' choices of using proxies, this chapter uses three major theories of international relations: Realism, Liberalism and Constructivism. There are other theories making significant contributions to the understanding of State behavior at the international level, however these three theories shape the main understanding of the world affairs (Walt 1998: 29–46; Snyder 2004: 52–62). These theories also have internal variations emphasizing different aspects of the assumptions of the theory and adapting their focus based on the new developments in the world politics. As an example, realism emphasizes the power of States in international relations, but neo-realism accepts the value of power but changes the focus from power itself to the structure of the international system that allows or limits using the power that States hold. This chapter will now describe how the three IR theories explain States' use of proxies.

Realism: Realist interpretation of world politics considers the State as the main actor in the international relations. Realism has a distinct State-centric approach to proxy use and connects the State use of proxies with its power and capacity. According to the realist understanding, the international system is anarchical and the system has no overarching authority over the States to change their behavior. What really matters is the power States hold and how other States balance the power structure at the international level (Morgenthau 1948; Morgenthau 2006; Gellman 1988: 247–66). States either compete or balance each other based on the amount of power they hold and the structure that allows using that power (Waltz 1979). The overall approach of realism to non-State actors in international politics is related to how States consider them as the part of their national interests and how useful they are to pursue the States' interests. States' use of non-State actors and proxies to increase their advantages and to pursue their interests is a natural outcome of their national interest calculations in the power politics. In order to create a power against other States and increase their relative gain, powerful States will use proxies. According to realism, international relations are conflictual and international conflicts are resolved by force, and relative gain is an important outcome of the power competition which refers to, in simple terms, getting more than the rival state. In an anarchical international structure, proxy use is an option for States to solve conflicts. State survival is the main driving force of international politics when viewed through the lens of a realist approach. States therefore have the right, if they have the power to do so, to use proxies for their survival, increase their security, and protect their interests. Realism considers rational calculations and strategic thinking as a part of the foreign policy-making process and argues States can deal with the threats and dangers with rational calculations and strategic thinking (Schellig 1980: 18–9). Thinking about different options helps States to find the best solution for their national interests. Leaders should approach threats strategically if they want to be successful (Jackson et al. 2019: 83). Strategic thinking considers less about what is good or bad but mostly focuses on what is required for a policy to be successful (Schellig 1980: 3–53). Therefore, from a strategic realism perspective, proxy use is part of strategic calculations and options for States and is not connected to any value judgments because the possible use of proxies is part of a State's survival strategy.

Due to the anarchic nature of the international system, no overarching authority exists to regulate State behavior, therefore, powerful States can use proxies without any restrictions originating from the international system. Different from classical realism, neo-realism argues that proxy use is a policy outcome after considering structural limitations of the international system. Therefore, according to neo-realism, States take the structural limitations of the international system into consideration to use their power and proxy use becomes an alternative way of applying force at the international level. Putting the State at the center of its analysis, realism does not consider non-State groups used as proxies as unitary actors. Realism partially accepts the principle agent framework by looking at the relationship between the supporting State and the proxy as a hierarchical one, i.e. the State as the principle and the proxy as the agent. However, realism does not accept the fact that the agent would have a separate objective in this interaction. The proxies role is to pursue the interest of the supporting State.

Realism has limitations in explaining how to control proxies when they pursue an agenda that is different than the supporting States' objectives and the methods acceptable for them. Since realism doesn't apply the morality for individuals to morality of States (Morghentau 2006: 34–8; Art and Jervis 2014: 167), realism's assumption that the proxy follows the principle's agenda fails when the proxy pursues its own interests and acts against the interests of the supporting States.

Liberalism: Liberal understanding of world politics builds its arguments on the rule of law, individual rights, and existence of international law. From this perspective, proxy use and cooperation with non-State actors should be based on international law and basic principles of liberalism and should not violate those principles. According to liberal understanding of world politics, States have certain interests to pursue, and cooperation is an important aspect of getting what they want. From a liberal perspective, proxy use is a part of this cooperation. Liberalism considers States' interactions with non-State actors different than how realists see these interactions. Although liberalism still accepts the States as the main actors of the international system, they argue that international relations include other actors that hold separate interests than States. In other words, international relations occur not only between States, but also among States and non-State actors such as private companies, individuals, non-governmental organizations, and international organizations. Liberalism considers non-State actors as legitimate and active actors in the system, not as entities whose values and interests are dependent on the supporting States. Liberals argue non-State actors and proxies would have their own agendas and their cooperation and working for States is based on their own interests.

Liberal interpretation of proxy use considers proxy groups as local groups with their own agenda independently constructed from the States that they cooperate with. Therefore, each party has their own agenda and defends their interests based on common objectives. The liberal approach would argue that the reason for supporting local groups as proxies is not only to pursue national interests, but also to help the proxy groups defend their rights to exist against the oppressing States. Defending liberal values and self-determination principles is an important element of proxy support. From the liberal IR perspective, proxy use is connected to both cooperation and liberal value promotion. Therefore, liberalism would argue that States will cooperate with proxy groups because they believe cooperation brings both sides what they want. The main focus of the supporting State is the cooperative behavior and support of the group to pursue its interests in the conflict.

A social base interpretation of liberalism, sociological liberalism, sees the relations among people and social groups as an important supplement of the State-State relations at the international level (Rosenau 1980 in Jackson and Sorensen 2016: 111). The idea behind sociological liberals defending the social connection between different countries is that they are more prone to produce peace. Liberal international relations theory, therefore, would interpret the use of proxies from a perspective which allows more social interaction as an alternative to government-to-government interaction. For that reason, proxy use requires supporting States' acceptance of the demands of the proxy groups, their cultural features, and providing assistance for the group to make social connections.

States and Non-State Actors Interacting in Conflict

Liberals see proxy use from a larger perspective, as a way of establishing liberal values in illiberal States. Liberals can explain the role of diaspora communities when States select certain groups as their proxies in conflict. Sociological liberalism can help one to understand when members of certain groups in one country are more likely to support the members of a similar group in another country. However, when the social groups in the supporting State join the armed conflict on proxy side, this condition violates the main assumption of the liberal understanding that social interaction should promote peace. In the liberal tradition, a better explanation for proxy use by States comes from Robert Keohane and Joseph Nye (1977:25) in what they called "complex interdependency." According to their approach, international politics is becoming more integrated as different issues require a variety of coalitions across governments (Keohane and Nye 1977 in Jackson and Sorensen 2016: 115). Complex interdependency considers military force irrelevant in most conflicts, therefore States will pursue different goals and different State institutions will be independently interacting with various actors including non-State actors. According to this approach, the cooperation between State and non-State groups is a natural outcome of complex interdependency.

Constructivism: Both realism and liberalism focus on the material structure of the international system and explain State behavior based on the power they hold, their institutions, structural positions in the international systems, and mechanisms of international behavior. Constructivism approaches State behavior from a different perspective and considers non-material issues as the most important issues that define State policies and actions at the international level. The first step of the constructivist approach at the international level is putting more emphasis on human awareness, consciousness, and the creation and interpretation of reality (Jackson et al. 2019: 236).

Behind the mechanism of human awareness, ideas, beliefs, and identities play an important role in informing the actors about the structures and how the structures function. Constructivists do not reject the material aspect of international relations and accept the fact that States will pursue their national interests. What constructivists add to material base conception of the international behavior of States is the meaning that States give to their national interests and the role of identities shaping those interests (Hurd 2009: 298–305). As famously put and widely cited by the IR scholars, Alexander Wendt (1992: 391–425) argues that anarchy, a core realist concept, does not exist independently and States themselves determine the nature of the anarchy, therefore it is constructed and interpreted by the States. According to constructivist accounts, international relations are based on the social construction that the States and leaders shape to establish a reality. The important aspect of policies is not how much reality exists in their structure but how we perceive them. In other words, the meaning we give to the events are much more important than their actual existence. Interests and identities are central elements of a constructivist approach to world politics; therefore, State interests and identities are the main determinants of the policy behavior which is under constant construction by many actors. Identities define how State and non-State actors define themselves against each other, which also shapes the interests of the actors.

A constructivist's interpretation of State foreign policy behavior is as an outcome of constant reality construction and connected interests based on shared identities. Constructivists do not ignore the existence of institutional structures and their values, nevertheless, they argue that structures are only meaningful with a set of norms that are connected to the identities and constructed realities. Therefore, in order to have successful policy outcomes, it is more important to know the situational factors related to the identities of actors, and their discourses, rather than distribution of material power. Hopf (1998: 175) argues that "one will need to know about the culture, norms, institutions, procedures, rules, and social practices that constitute the actors and the structures alike." Constructivists would, therefore, argue that States not only choose proxies based on their identities, but also construct the norms of their engagement with these groups based on cultural and social explanations. Constructivism explains the policy changes of States to support groups that share common identities and values, therefore it provides more flexibility in explaining policy changes over time.

Connecting Theories with Cases and Analysis

There is no single theory that explains every aspect of a State's proxy choice and one single case does not fit into the main assumptions of every theoretical approach presented in this chapter.

As discussed earlier, Groh (2019: 4) emphasized three main conditions for States to use proxies; identity, interests, and State's capacity. All these conditions refer to a decision-making mechanism prioritizing different aspects of national interests. The first condition of proxy use, identity, is considered as a subject of constructivist approach to IR. Second and third conditions, State interest and capacities, could be related to both realist and liberal understanding of international relations. Proxy use is an international behavior of States and is used as a foreign policy tool, therefore, applying IR theories to understand, explain, and predict State behavior is essential to bringing additional insights to proxy discussions both at the academic and practical levels. This section will apply theories to selected contemporary cases to explain the use of proxies by States in the contemporary security environment.

Realist emphasis on power better explains when powerful States force local groups to act as their proxies. In this regard, realism doesn't give much choice to proxies to decide whether they want to cooperate with the intervening State or not. Therefore, realism does not adequately explain why proxy groups pursue their pursue their own interests rather than the interest of the supporting State. Realism explains the relationship between great powers and local groups, focusing on the coercive power of States when proxy groups act as agents of States. Realism has obvious limitations to explain the States' constraints on using its own security forces in conflict and other domestic constraints forcing them to use proxies.

Liberalism provides more powerful explanations to the interaction of States and proxies, as the theory puts more emphasis on cooperation mechanisms and domestic level variables of the decision-making process. According to liberals, States use proxies not because of the power they hold but but because of domestic considerations. However, domestic constraints are not limited to the economic pressures, but also the changing priorities of domestic politics that limit the use of military forces and them to think of using proxies instead. The US took a liberalist approach and did not become directly involved in the Syrian conflict, due to the domestic political pressures of overseas military intervention forced the US to use proxies. As the US changed its priorities during the conflict from overthrowing Assad to fighting ISIS, proxy use remained the same, but the name of proxies changed over time (Hussain 2018; Kozera et al. 2020: 77–97).

Democracies are more sensitive to domestic constraints, therefore, we can assume that democratic States would prefer to use proxies more often than non-democracies based on their domestic calculations. Arnold (2018) introduces the concept of "liberal-democratic proxy war" and argues that liberal democracies have the additional responsibility to protect individual liberties while at the same time pursuing national interests. Therefore, according to his argument, democracies are expected to support those proxies that would not act against liberal democratic ideals during and after the conflict. Therefore, as liberal IR theory would argue, democracies have the responsibility of considering internal dynamics of proxy use while constructivists would claim, values are still important for States to consider when thinking of using proxies. Taking US proxy use at the center of his research, Arnold hypothesizes that "the US is likely to support armed rebellious groups only when a president assesses that doing so both can serve the nation's strategic interests and can be defended in terms of liberal-democratic ideals." His argument puts a limitation to the realist approach and considers value judgments as the significant part of the policy outcome. In the case of US support for Mujahidin, Arnold argues that the support was based on the ideal self-determination, regardless of the fact that the Mujahidin were not liberal democrats (Arnold 2018: 16). In the cases of US support for rebel movements in Libya and Syria, both were consistent with the US interests and liberal-democratic ideals "because the rebel movements in question were fighting authoritarian regimes responsible for large-scale human rights abuses against civilians."

In another case, Bamidele (2020: 172) argues that, to counter Boko Haram violence in Borno State, Nigeria, the local population in Borno communities created a Civilian Joint Task Force (CJTF) which later created a collaboration mechanism with the military forces of the country. In the later stages, after being recognized by the government and receiving support, the CJTF received support from international organizations such as the International Community of the Red Cross and the UN Development Program.

Although there has been distrust between government forces and local groups, they have been included in the counterinsurgency operations of the government and because of their effectiveness they are considered a crucial part of efforts to counter Boko Haram violence. This example demonstrates a cooperation mechanism between State and local groups based on a mutual benefit of successful operations against a violent actor. Liberal argument explains this specific case better as the cooperation between a local group and government forces structured around a shared interest. Constructivism offers an identity-based explanation of this interaction and argues that what really brought local task forces and the State together is their shared identity. However, it was more of a shared threat and the need to act against Boko Haram terrorists rather than the identity forcing the joint action. As Bamidele's research indicates (2020: 171–88) CJTF used religion as a way of generating momentum and recruiting new members, arguing that Boko Haram was not representing the real face of their religion. Religious arguments were instrumental to stabilize the structure of the organization, but their real power came from the State recognition. It is possible to argue that both liberalism and constructivism explain this case, where liberalism posits the cooperation with the government and constructivism expansion of the organization. The only criticism for this example could be that the State and the proxy interaction happened internally and not at the international level. However, international operations of the threat and the involvement of international organizations qualifies this example to demonstrate the use of liberalism and constructivism to explain Nigeria's use of a local group as a proxy to counter Boko Haram.

Bruchmann (2020: 53–75) examines the power brokers in weak States and explains their role in socio-political life in Afghanistan, Lebanon and Mali. He defines power brokers as "rational and unitary actors within a weak or failed State … a social pyramid of patriarchic, pre-modern, kinship-based societal structures that build self-defense militias and band together during conflict with the center or foreign powers." According to his analysis, power brokers grow in self-ruling communities and they play an important role between community interests and external involvement. They hold a place between tradition and global pressures and are expected to defend the local interests. His analysis of Afghanistan between 1995 and 1997 concluded that the Taliban's victory was made possible by alliances of power brokers based on their rational calculations rather than ethnic base actions. The liberal approach can explain this assuming that the local actors based on their own rational actors can have an impact on how States use proxies. Even when there is an initial construction of the group based on ethnicity or local connections, the level of support from the external actor can strengthen local proxy structures.

As a different example upon which to apply IR theories, Turkey's use of proxies during the Syrian conflict can be better explained by constructivism. Putting the religious and nationalist identities at the center of the support, Turkey's use of Syrian opposition as a proxy had a lot of identity related discourses (Yuksel 2019; Yuksel 2020). Turkey also used national identity to counter Kurdish influence in the region and opposed US support for Kurdish YPG groups against ISIS. Because Turkey defined Kurdish identity as a threat to the Turkish State and social structure, US support for these groups, even against a common threat (ISIS) did not change the opposition of Turkey to US support for the Kurds. As it would be predicted by the constructive approach, non-material power, religious and national identities, cultural arguments, and defining an enemy based on the identity created significant power for Turkey to mobilize support for its actions in Syria.

Conclusion

How States have used proxy forces in different conflicts has been studied extensively from a security sciences perspective and this chapter argued that IR theories can also provide valuable insights into States' choices of and relationships with proxies. By using three major theories of IR: realism, liberalism, and constructivism, this chapter demonstrated that all three theories have a great deal of explanatory power. Realism provided a powerful explanation as to why strong States use proxies when the proxy did not have much choice but to become an agent of the supporting State. However, realism could not provide much insight into how the State-proxy interaction would work and why a proxy might act on its own agenda in this principle-agent relationship. Realism therefore, is a theory whereby we can gather more information at the international and structural level, but when we need more information on the domestic dynamics of the proxy use, liberalism tends to provide better insights.

Liberalism provides many insights into the structure of interaction between the supporting State and the proxy group, as well as the limitations preventing the State from using their own security forces. A liberalist argument would also close the gap that realists leave in understanding the problems of controlling proxies and addressing the violations and abuses committed by the proxies. Liberalism would argue both the decision to use proxies and process of employing them should serve liberal principles, Therefore, proxies should follow the same rules that apply to States when engaged in conflict. Liberalism supports the idea of common good and strengthening international norms regulating proxy use. The liberalist argument emphasizes that groups and States sharing common goals and objectives and operating under the same institutional structures, will act together when conflict occurs.

As the third theory this chapter examined, begins from where the liberals end and argues that in these types of commonality shared identities play a bigger role. Putting religious, national, and cultural identity structures at the center, constructivists argue that States prefer proxy groups with shared identities. Norms and discourses are also necessary to understand a State's choice of a proxy group and constructivists would argue that identity is more important than the material structures and institutions of the international system. Constructivism helps us to better understand the State-proxy connections when the State and proxy group justify their relationship based on their shared identity, culture, or discourses they use to justify their actions.

Applying IR theories to how States choose and use proxies is not a common practice and more discussion is necessary to explain States' choices and the practice of State-proxy interactions. This chapter discussed three IR theories that help to understand why States choose to work with proxies rather than using their own forces during conflict. The different theories and their variations will also help readers to reach alternative explanations and better predict State and proxy behavior. The chapter did not investigate the issues of how States establish the connection with proxies and once established, how this connection works. Future studies should examine how different motivations could affect the State-proxy relationship.

Bibliography

Ahram, A. (2011), *Proxy Warriors: The Rise and Fall of State-Sponsored Militias*, Stanford: Stanford University Press.

Andrew M. (2013), "Proxy Warfare and the Future of Conflict", *The RUSI Journal*, 158 (2): 40–46. https://doi.org/10.1080/03071847.2013.787733.

Arnold, J. (2022), "Supporting Rebellion: Liberal Democracy and the American Way of Proxy War", PhD thesis, Princeton University, Princeton. Available online: https://dataspace.princeton.edu/handle/88435/dsp01j098zd87g?mode=simple (accessed 11 September 2022).

Bamidele, S. (2020), "Sweat is invisible in the rain": Civilian Joint Task Force and counter-insurgency in Borno State, Nigeria', *Security and Defence Quarterly*, 31 (4): 171–88. https://doi.org/10.35467/sdq/130867.

Berman, E. and D. A. Lake, eds (2019), *Proxy Wars: Suppressing Violence Through Local Agents*, Ithaca: Cornell University Press.

Brown, S. (2016), "Purposes and Pitfalls of war by Proxy: A Systemic Analysis", *Small Wars & Insurgencies*, 27 (2): 243–257. https://doi.org/10.1080/09592318.2015.113404 7.

Bruchmann, S. (2020), "Towards a Structural Understanding of Powerbrokers in Weak States: From Militias to Alliances", *Security and Defence Quarterly*, 31 (4): 53–75. https://doi.org/10.35467/sdq/130935.

Byman, D. L. (2018), "Why Engage in Proxy War? A State's Perspective", *Brookings Institute*. Available online: https://www.brookings.edu/blog/order-from-chaos/2018/05/21/why-engage-in-proxy-war-a-states-perspective/ (accessed 13 October 2021).

Carment D. and D. Belo (2020), "Gray-Zone Conflict Management: Theory, Evidence, and Challenges", *European, Middle Eastern and African Affairs*, Summer: 21–41.

Farasoo, A. (2021), "Rethinking Proxy War Theory in IR: A Critical Analysis of Principal–Agent Theory", *International Studies Review*, 23 (4): 1835–1858. https://doi.org/10.1093/isr/viab050.

Fox, A. C. (2019a), "In Pursuit of a General Theory of Proxy Warfare", *Land Warfare Paper*, 123. Available online: https://www.ausa.org/publications/pursuit-general-theory-proxy-warfare (accessed 17 September 2021).

Fox, A. C. (2019b), "Conflict and the Need for a Theory of Proxy Warfare", *Journal of Strategic Security*, 12 (1): 44–71. https://doi.org/10.5038/1944-0472.12.1.1701.

Fox, A. C. (2020), "Five Models of Strategic Relationship in Proxy War", *Georgetown Security Studies Review*, 8 (2) 50–58. https://doi.org/10.13140/RG.2.2.28382.25925.

Gellman, P. (1988), "Hans J. Morgenthau and the Legacy of Political Realism", *Review of International Studies*, 14 (4): 247–266. https://doi.org/10.1017/S0260210500113130.

Groh, T. L. (2019), *Proxy War: the Least Bad Option*, Stanford: Stanford University Press.

Hauter, J. (2019), "Delegated Interstate War: Introducing an Addition to Armed Conflict Typologies", *Journal of Strategic Security*, 12 (4): 90–103. https://doi.org/10.5038/1944-0472.12.4.1756.

Hopf, T. (1998), "The Promise of Constructivism in International Relations Theory" *International Security*, 23 (1): 171–200.

Hurd, I. (2009), "Constructivism", in *The Oxford Handbook of International Relations*, Oxford: Oxford University Press.

Hussein H. (2018), "What is Behind the US' Support of the YPG?" *Middle East Monitor*, 30 January. Available online: https://www.middleeastmonitor.com/20180130-what-is-behind-the-us-support-of-the-ypg/ (accessed 18 May 2022).

Ivanov, Z. (2020), "Changing the Character of Proxy Warfare and its Consequences for Geopolitical Relationships", *Security and Defence Quarterly*, 31 (4): 37–51. https://doi.org/10.35467/sdq/130902.

Jackson R. H. and G. Sørensen (2016), *Introduction to International Relations: Theories and Approaches*, 6th edn, Oxford: Oxford University Press.

Jackson, R., G. Sørensen and J. Møller (2019), *Introduction to International Relations: Theories and Approaches*, Oxford: Oxford University Press.

Jervis, R. and R. J. Art (2014), *International Politics: Enduring Concepts and Contemporary Issues*, London: Pearson Education.

Kaunert, C. and O. Wertman (2020), "The Securitisation of Hybrid Warfare through Practices within the Iran-Israel Conflict: Israel's Practices to Securitize Hezbollah's Proxy War" *Security and Defence Quarterly*, 31 (4): 99–114. https://doi.org/10.35467/sdq/130866.

Keohane R. O. and J. S. Nye (1977), *Power and Interdependence: World Politics in Transition*, Boston: Little Brown.

Kozera, C. A., P. Bernat, C. Gürer, B. Popławski and M. A. Sözer (2020), "Game of Proxies—Towards a New Model of Warfare: Experiences From the CAR, Libya, Mali, Syria, and Ukraine", *Security and Defence Quarterly*, 31 (4): 77–97. https://doi.org/10.35467/sdq/131787.

Kozera, C. A. and C. Gürer (2020), "Introduction to the Special Issue 'Proxy Forces in Modern Warfare', *Security and Defence Quarterly*, 31 (4): 11–15. https://doi.org/10.35467/sdq/132287.

Morgenthau, H. (1948), *Politics Among Nations: The Struggle for Power and Peace*, New York, Alfred Kopf.

Morgenthau H. J. (2006), *Politics Among Nations: The Struggle for Power and Peace*, 7th rev. edn, K. W. Thompson and D. Clinton (eds), Boston: McGraw-Hill Higher Education.

Powell, R. (1991), "Absolute and Relative Gains in International Relations Theory", *American Political Science Review*, 85 (4): 1303–20.

Rauta, V. and A. Mumford (2017), "Proxy Wars and the Contemporary Security Environment", in R. Dover, H. Dylan and M. S. Goodman (eds), *The Palgrave Handbook of Security, Risk and Intelligence*, 99–115, London: Palgrave Macmillan.

Rauta, V. (2019), "Towards a Typology of Non-State Actors in 'Hybrid Warfare': Proxy, Auxiliary, Surrogate and Affiliated Forces", *Cambridge Review of International Affairs*, 33 (6): 868–87. https://doi.org/10.1080/09557571.2019.1656600.

Salehyan, I. (2010), "The Delegation of War to Rebel Organizations", *Journal of Conflict Resolution*, 54 (3): 493–515. https://doi.org/10.1177/0022002709357890.

San-Akca, B. (2017), "States and Nonstate Armed Groups (NAGs) in International Relations Theory", in W. R. Thompson (ed), *Oxford Research Encyclopedia of Politics*. Available online: https://oxfordre.com/politics/display/10.1093/acrefore/9780190228637.001.0001/acrefore-9780190228637-e-303?rskey=m3kI0W&result=1 (accessed 20 October 2021).

Schelling, T. C. (1980), *The Strategy of Conflict*, Cambridge: Harvard University Press.

Snyder, J. (2004), "One World, Rival Theories", *Foreign Policy*, (145): 52–62. https://doi.org/10.2307/4152944.

Walt, S. M. (1998), "International Relations: One World, Many Theories", *Foreign Policy*, Spring: 29–46. https://doi.org/10.2307/1149275.

Waltz, K. N. (1979), *Theory of International Politics*, Long Grove, IL: Waveland Press, Inc.

Wendt, A. (1992), "Anarchy is What States Make of it: the Social Construction of Power Politics", *International Organization*, 46 (2): 391–425. https://doi.org/10.1017/S0020818300027764.

Wither, J. K. (2020), "Outsourcing warfare: Proxy Forces in Contemporary Armed Conflicts", *Security and Defence Quarterly*, 31 (4): 17–34. https://doi.org/10.35467/sdq/127928.

Yüksel, E. (2019), "Strategies of Turkish Proxy Warfare in Northern Syria", *Clingendael*. Available online: https://www.clingendael.org/pub/2019/strategies-of-turkish-proxy-warfare-in-northern-syria/ (accessed 10 October 2021).

Yüksel, E. (2020), "Turkey's Approach to Proxy War in the Middle East and North Africa", *Security and Defence Quarterly*, 31 (4): 137–152. https://doi.org/10.35467/sdq/130916.

Part Two

Proxy Forces in Various Theaters of Armed Conflicts: Case Studies

4

Russian Proxy Use in the Hybrid War against Ukraine before the 2022 Invasion

Paweł Bernat, Viacheslav Semenenko, Pavlo Openko
and Daniel Michalski

Introduction

The events described in this chapter, i.e., the Russian aggression on Ukraine that started in 2014 and the occupation of Crimea and large parts of eastern Ukraine, have eventually led to the initiation of the full-scale Russian-Ukrainian war in 2022. Russia's attack on its neighbor could be perceived as a demarcation line between an old, post-Cold War geopolitical order and a new one that is currently, that is at the end of 2022, being written by Ukrainian and Russian armed forces and authorities in the fields and cities of Ukraine. The outcome of the war is not yet known, but what is certain is that we are witnessing a beginning of a geopolitical change and a forming of a new global security environment.

The reasons why the Russian Federation decided to invade Ukraine are described in detail in the second section of the chapter. In a nutshell, it felt it started losing its influence in Ukraine, which democratically decided to orient itself toward the West. At that time, the Ukrainian economy was weak, the society seemed divided, and prospects for the future were not very optimistic. Russian authorities found it to be a great opportunity to strengthen its global posture and gain more territory and therefore decided to attack Ukraine and "annex" some of its lands.

In order to pursue its strategic goals, the Russian Federation had to be careful not to induce a broader international conflict. It has to be remembered that in 1994 the Budapest Memorandum was signed, in which three nuclear powers, i.e., the Russian Federation, the United States, and the United Kingdom, gave assurances to Ukraine that its independence and sovereignty in the existing borders were secured in exchange for getting rid of its nuclear capabilities and signing the Treaty on the Non-Proliferation of Nuclear Weapons (UN 1994: 169). Therefore, Russian authorities decided to use hybrid and proxy warfare as tools for the creation of the "fog of war." The obscurity they created was enough to generate uncertainty among the western powers, which then translated into their weak reaction to the Russian aggression on Ukraine. The third part of the chapter is dedicated to a brief discussion of the definitions of hybrid war and proxy warfare and the constitutive elements of the phenomena. A clear understanding of these ways of conducting an armed conflict is necessary to properly examine to what extent and how Russia used them against Ukraine since 2014 and up to the beginning of the full-scale invasion of February 24, 2022. In the fourth section of the chapter, we provide a concise, factual description and the timeline of the events leading to the occupation of Crimea (2014) and the "static war" that was taking place in the eastern part of Ukraine (2014–22). The international response is covered in section five. It is a significant piece in the puzzle because, as we believe and argue, the weak response of the international community to Russia's aggression was one of the reasons leading to the largest war in Europe since the Second World War. The only consequences the Russian Federation suffered were economic and technological sanctions, which, as we demonstrate, did not impede the Russian economy. The business continued as usual, especially the import of Russian fossil fuels. In this respect, as we further argue, the Russian authorities' choice to realize their goals by conducting a hybrid war and employing proxy forces was, from their perspective, a proper one. The chapter is closed with bringing together the main arguments and answering the questions regarding the employment of hybrid warfare and proxy forces by the Russian Federation against Ukraine in the 2014–22 armed conflict and before the full-scale invasion of February 2022.

The Political Background of Russia and Ukraine before the Beginning of the Conflict

At the beginning of the twenty-first century, the imperial ambitions of the Russian Federation were reborn, and the actions to realize these ambitions intensified. They have deep historical roots—they originated in the early days of the formation of "Muscovy" and then developed further during the Russian Empire and the Soviet Union. The Kremlin's leaders managed to build imperialism in post-Soviet Russia in a relatively short period of time. It was, generally speaking, modeled on the communist ideology, namely, the unlimited power of capital, the ruthless exploitation of the working class, the militarization of the economy, the arms race, and world domination (Frolov and Semenenko 2021: 8).

The main long-term interest of the Russian Federation, up to 2013, presupposed a favorable political and economic attitude toward Ukraine. At that time, Russia was able to keep Ukraine on a non-allied military-political course, which would guarantee the absence of military bases of unfriendly, from the Russian perspective, states on Ukrainian territory. Integration with Ukraine was much more desirable, as it provided better guarantees for Ukraine to stay on this favorable for Russia course. In order to execute this strategy, the Russian Federation worked to weaken Ukraine's central government, ensure the country's neutral status, and institute significant economic and political independence of its regions (NATO 2020; Syrotenko 2020; Pacek, Pievtsov, and Syrotenko 2021).

At the same time, Ukraine's internal conditions, mainly the problematic economic situation, partly contributed to the conflict. Overcoming these difficulties depended on the country's choice of how to steer its military-political course and shape the orientation of its economy. In world trade, there is an almost unequivocal rule: if you want to supply goods to a particular country, your military-political course must go in line and facilitate it by adopting friendly relations and cooperation with this country. After the Orange Revolution of 2004–5 and the election of Viktor Yushchenko for president, Ukraine intensified its pro-Western policy in the political and military dimensions. Russia, the leading importer of Ukrainian goods (especially high-value-added goods), began, at that time, to gradually replace Ukrainian supplies with domestically produced goods and thus reduced access to its market for Ukrainian products. The economic situation became more dire in Ukraine, whose main trading partner was Russia. The connection between the military-political course, foreign trade, and the pace of development of the export-oriented economy was clearly visible in this case. In 2005, despite the growth of the global economy, a sharp slowdown in Ukraine's GDP growth was observed. According to the World Bank (2022), the annual economic growth shrank from 11.8 in 2004 to 3.1 percent in 2005.

The strengthening of the cooperation between Ukraine and the West continued even even though Viktor Yanukovych, a pro-Russian politician, was elected president in 2010. The elections, it is worthwhile to mention, were assessed by the Council of Europe as meeting "most OSCE and Council of Europe commitments" (Council of Europe 2010: 13). The situation drastically changed on November 21, 2013, when Yanukovych's administration, due to

64   *Proxy Wars from a Global Perspective*

enormous pressure put by Russia (Göler 2015: 300), suspended preparations for the EU trade agreement (BBC 2013). The refusal to abandon the treaty on closer trade ties with the EU triggered a chain of actions resulting in the emergence of nationwide protests and a social movement, later named Euromaidan. In late November 2013, approximately 100,000 people attended a demonstration in the Ukrainian capital city—Kyiv. A few weeks later, the numbers grew, and in early December, 800,000 Ukrainians occupied Kyiv city hall and Independence Square (BBC 2014). On December 17, Presidents Yanukovych and Putin signed the Ukrainian-Russian action plan. Presumably, it was Putin's attempt to quiet down the political situation in Ukraine and keep it in the Russian sphere of influence by strengthening Yanukovych's regime. The action plan included a major discount in energy prices and pledged $15 billion in aid (Tsygankov 2015: 284). The protests, however, continued and spread to other parts of the country. In late February 2014, violent clashes erupted, and the Kyiv Independence Square turned into a regular battlefield. On February 18–21, 88 protesters were killed. Later on, the number of deaths increased to 113, including the ones who died from injuries sustained during the fight (Shveda and Park 2016: 88). On February 22, Yanukovych fled the country, and the parliament speaker–Olexander Turchynov was named as interim president. The new President—Petro Poroshenko, a West-oriented supporter of Euromaidan, was elected on May 25, 2014 (BBC 2014). In other words, Ukraine started to slip away from Russian influence, and President Putin called the change of power in Ukraine a coup that was executed by Nationalists, neo-Nazis, Russophobes, and anti-Semites (Putin 2014)—a neat segue and setting the stage for the actions to come.

Theoretical Background: Hybrid Wars and Proxy Forces

Armed aggression is usually a continuation of a foreign policy goal that is not achieved through the use of soft power. Russian aggressive policy and finally its invasion of Ukraine can be conceived in such terms, i.e., as a consequence of the conviction that Ukraine was invertedly moving away from the Russian sphere of ideological, political, and economic influence.

This chapter aims to answer whether this armed conflict before the full-fledged war started by Russia on February 24, 2022, can be accounted as a hybrid and proxy warfare. Both terms of hybrid and proxy warfare are broad, ambiguous, dynamic, dependent on geopolitical and technological changes, and therefore defined variously. For the purpose of this analysis, we shall rely on the definition of hybrid threats proposed by the United States Joint Forces Command, which defines it as "Any adversary that simultaneously and adaptively employs a tailored mix of conventional, irregular, terrorism and criminal means or activities in the operational battle space. Rather than a single entity, a hybrid threat or challenger may be a combination of state and nonstate actors" (Glenn 2009: 2). This understanding of hybrid warfare is especially applicable to the analyzed case because it includes the use of non-state agents that potentially could meet the criteria for proxy agents.

The concept of proxy warfare, similarly, is vague and has been an object of conceptual, methodological, and definitional battles (Rauta 2021:1). The classical definition coined by Karl Deutsch (1964: 102) in the midst of the Cold War describes the phenomenon as "an international conflict between two foreign powers, fought out on the soil of a third country; disguised as a conflict over an internal issue of that country; and using some of that country's manpower, resources and territory as a means for achieving preponderantly foreign goals and foreign strategies." More current elucidations of the phenomenon usually abandon the state-centricity present in that definition and put more emphasis on the role of the proxy actors. A very general definition proposed by Rondeaux and Sterman sees proxy warfare "as sponsorship of conventional or irregular forces that lie outside the constitutional order of states" (2019: 18). Mumford, on the other hand, provides a more detailed definition where proxy wars are understood as "effects-based operations," which are undertaken to limit potential consequences of "conflict escalation with a rival superpower," and carried out without the engagement of the state's military forces (Mumford, 2013: 45). What stems from these definitions is the fact that the use of proxies does not always translate into conducting a proxy war.

It will be argued in this chapter that in 2014 the Russian Federation started a hybrid war against Ukraine and used various proxies in the process to reduce risk and minimalize plausible consequences of initiating an armed conflict. This strategy, as it turned out and will be demonstrated in this chapter, was on the whole successful.

Russian 2014 Military Aggression Against Ukraine

Planning, organization, support, management, and carrying out of Russia's military aggression against Ukraine can be described as taking place at four levels (Frolov and Semenenko 2021: 10–11). (1) The strategic idea of military aggression was developed by the Russian Federation's political authorities under President Vladimir Putin's direct leadership as the Supreme Commander-in-Chief of the Russian Federation's Armed Forces. Direct planning, organization, and comprehensive support were carried out by the Federal Security Service (FSB), the Ministry of Defense, the General Staff of the Armed Forces, the Armed Forces, the Airborne Forces of the Russian Federation (VAT), and the Southern Military District Headquarters. (2) The political platform of the Russian hybrid aggression in Ukraine consisted of the Party of Regions, the Communist Party of Ukraine and the Autonomous Republic of Crimea (ARC), pro-Russian parties, and Crimean movements (Zhegulev 2017). Among the main executors of the decisions of the separatist political forces were: the pro-Russian part of the population of the eastern regions and the ARC, pensioners of Soviet orientation, representatives of the criminal business who were threatened with criminal liability for illegally acquired business, management of local governments, law enforcement agencies, and the Armed Forces, which have sided with the aggressor. Separatist political parties and movements formed the occupying authorities, organized the administration of the occupied territories, harshly persecuted and destroyed Ukrainian patriotic organizations and their leaders under the guise of restoring the occupation "order," and organized rallies to support the Russian aggression. (3) The direct management of military aggression against Ukraine was carried out by operational groups of the Ministry of Defense, the General Staff, and the FSB of the Russian Federation from the joint command posts of the Southern Military District and the Black Sea Fleet in Sevastopol. Apart from regular Russian military formations, illegal military formations created in the occupied territories and staffed by the pro-Russian, anti-state population of Ukraine, and the "patriots" of the "Russian world" took an active part in the military actions. (4) Finally, the last group contributing to the hybrid war against Ukraine consisted of various criminal individuals who undertook spontaneous actions in the occupied territory and other regions of Ukraine. Their primary purpose was to seize archival documents and criminal cases in the bodies (archives) of the Ministry of Internal Affairs, the Security Service of Ukraine, and the courts. Some materials were destroyed on the spot or sold (Frolov and Semenenko 2021: 10–11).

Russian Hybrid Actions and Occupation of the Crimea

The first target of the Russian hybrid aggression against Ukraine was the Autonomous Republic of Crimea. Long before the occupation, Russia created a robust network of agents on the peninsula, ready to destabilize the socio-political situation at any moment. Russia's armed aggression against Ukraine was just another step in a long-planned and organized anti-Ukrainian hybrid war (NATO 2020; Syrotenko 2020).

The operation to seize the Crimean peninsula began on February 20, 2014, when the Russian armed forces, contrary to international legal obligations, crossed the state border of Ukraine through the Kerch Strait (Verkhovna Rada 2015a).

On February 23, a rally of 20,000 people took place in Sevastopol, during which a Russian citizen, Oleksiy Chaly, was proclaimed mayor (Ukrainian Institute of National Memory 2019). On the night of February 27, 2014, the Russian Federation's special purpose units and airborne troops seized the buildings of the Council of Ministers and the Verkhovna Rada of the Autonomous Republic of Crimea, over which the flag of the Russian Federation was raised. In the morning, deputies of the Verkhovna Rada of Crimea gathered in the session hall, where they decided to hold a so-called referendum on the status of the peninsula. On the same day, Russian troops seized media and communication facilities, Simferopol airport, Belbek airport in Sevastopol, and a ferry to Kerch. Soon the Russian Black Sea Fleet blocked the naval bases where the ships of the Naval Forces of the Armed Forces of Ukraine were located (Verkhovna Rada 2015b).

In March, regular Russian troops and paramilitary forces continued to use force to block Ukrainian military camps in Crimea, seize administrative premises, and control highways and other strategically important facilities. No military targets were captured at once. Meanwhile, contrary to the Decree of the Acting President of Ukraine Turchynov on the suspension of the decision of the Crimean Parliament and the decision of the Constitutional Court of Ukraine, which recognized the announcement of the referendum inconsistent with the Constitution of Ukraine, despite the disapproving position of the UN Security Council, despite the boycott of the referendum by the Mejlis of the Crimean Tatar people, the so-called referendum on the status of Crimea took place on March 16. In the presence of a large number of armed Russian servicemen, the referendum in the Autonomous Republic of Crimea and the city of Sevastopol allegedly collected more than 1.7 million filled ballots (corresponding to 82.7% of the total number of voters), of which almost 97% voted "for the reunification of Crimea with Russia as a subject of the Russian Federation (Zolotukhin 2018: 200).

On March 18, in Moscow, the so-called "Agreement on the Accession of the Republic of Crimea to the Russian Federation" was signed by President Putin

68 — Proxy Wars from a Global Perspective

and Russian-appointed Crimea government representatives. On March 20, it was ratified by the State Duma of the Russian Federation, and on March 21, by the Federation Council (National Institute for Strategic Studies 2016: 11–2).

Russian Hybrid War and the Use of Proxies in the East of Ukraine

The armed conflict in east Ukraine can be divided into three periods, namely, (1) the attack of Russian special forces and mobilized proxy groups (early April—September 5, 2014), (2) containing and localization of the conflict in some districts of Donetsk and Luhansk regions, (September 5, 2014—February 23, 2022), and finally (3) full-scale invasion of Ukraine by the Russian Federation and open war (since February 24, 2022). Since the war continues (the last updates of the chapter were made in April 2023), we shall focus only on the two first periods due to two reasons—the first two stages of the conflict fit the carried out analysis, which mainly focus on proxy and hybrid warfare, and secondly, the "special military operation," as Russian authorities call it, is still underway. In 2017, Ukraine's Ministry of Defense published "The White Book Of The Anti-Terrorist Operation in the East of Ukraine 2014–2016," where the timeline of the first two years of the conflict is described in detail (the report proposes the first part of the above division, i.e., the first period from April to September 5, 2014, and the second—after September 5, 2014). (Ministry of Defense 2017: 19–39).

At the beginning of the armed conflict in eastern Ukraine, the Russian special services focused on destabilizing the situation in the Eastern region, which included creating illegal armed groups, using weapons and terrorist methods, and teaching the ways to oppose legitimate authorities. Russia sent truly mixed forces to eastern Ukraine that consisted of troops who were "on leave" or "not active duty," Russian nationalists, the so-called "soldiers of fortune" (i.e., non-commissioned soldiers willing to serve whoever would hire them), veterans of the Caucasus and Balkan wars, soldiers from other "hot spots," and simple criminals who would fight alongside the recruited locals (Ministry of Defense 2017: 20).

The Russians coordinated the sabotage groups, which on April 6, 2014, almost simultaneously seized the buildings of regional state administrations in Donetsk and Kharkiv, and in Luhansk—the premises of the Security Service of Ukraine. As early as April 7, 2014, Russian intelligence-led collaborators proclaimed the creation of the Donetsk People's Republic and the Kharkiv People's Republic, and in Luhansk, they established the Southeast Resistance Headquarters and demanded that the eastern regions secede from Ukraine (the creation of the

Luhansk People's Republic was proclaimed on April 27) (Ministry of Defense 2017: 20–1).

The actions of special units of the Ministry of Internal Affairs of Ukraine in Kharkiv were effective, and by April 8, they managed to liberate administrative premises and detain offenders. However, the situation in the Donetsk and Luhansk oblasts turned out to be more difficult for the Ukrainian forces. In Luhansk, on April 11, 2014, Russian terrorist groups laid siege to the regional council and issued an ultimatum to proclaim the Luhansk People's Republic independent from Ukraine's government. The coordinated actions of Russian saboteurs were evidenced by the simultaneous capture on April 12 of the city council in Artemivsk, the police department, and the city council in Kramatorsk, and a failed attempt to seize the city council in Horlivka. On the same day, Igor Girkin's sabotage group (up to 60 people), which had arrived from Crimea, captured Slovyansk. Volodymyr Sysenko's group (up to 70 people), formed in the Russian Federation, arrived in Donetsk. Igor Bezler's group operated in Horlivka. All the leaders of these groups were Russian officers (Marko 2016: 46).

In July 2014, the total number of troops of the Russian-created forces in eastern Ukraine exceeded 15,000. Up to 50 militant training camps were set up, both in Russia and in the occupied territories of Ukraine (Ministry of Defense 2017: 27).

In August 2014, after realizing the impending collapse of the Novorossiya project, the Russian military and political leadership decided to move regular troops into eastern Ukraine. On the night of August 24–25, 2014, the situation in the area changed dramatically. After a powerful artillery strike from the territory of Russia, which involved about 200 units of artillery, Russian units secretly invaded the territory of Ukraine. Russian servicemen, as during the Crimean events, did not have documents and identification marks on uniforms and military equipment (Muzhenko 2015: 10–1). This period ended with the repulse of Russian aggression and the withdrawal of Ukrainian Anti-Terrorist Operation (ATO) forces to positions and frontiers, which were later enshrined in the Minsk agreements as a line of demarcation between the parties.

Since the beginning of September 2014, due to the invasion of Russian troops, anti-terrorist operation forces have been forced to take defensive action. A characteristic feature of this stage was the beginning of large-scale construction of the defense lines in eastern Ukraine. Two defensive lines were created: the first—on the line of contact with the Russian hybrid occupation troops, the second—approximately 15–20 km away from the first. The basis of the frontiers was a system of bases with checkpoints, trenches, shelters, passages, firing positions of armored combat vehicles, and other fire means. The winter of 2015 was equally intense as the summer of 2014. In January, the Russian Federation began to implement a plan to expand the controlled territories, which led to offensive operations simultaneously in Luhansk, Donetsk, Debaltseve, and Mariupol areas. One of the "hottest" places in the anti-terrorist operation was the Donetsk airport, the defense of which lasted 242 days (Shtohrin 2016: 352).

After the repulse of the second offensive of the Russian occupation forces in January and February 2015, the construction of lines of defense in eastern Ukraine became the business of the entire Ukrainian people. Since September 2016, the Russian-Ukrainian confrontation in eastern Ukraine has undergone significant changes, mainly due to the signing by the Trilateral Contact Group (consisting of the representatives of Ukraine, Russia, and OSCE) of the agreement on disengagement in Donbas on September 21, 2016. The document provided for the diversion of the parties from the occupied positions in both directions to form sections 2 km wide and 2 km deep (Ministry of Defense 2017: 38).

Up to February 24, 2022, when Russia began a full-scale war against Ukraine, the Russian proxies, with the support of the regular troops of the Russian Armed Forces, continued activities aimed at destabilizing the internal socio-political situation in the occupied regions of Donetsk and Luhansk (Shovkoplias 2022). On September 23–27, 2022, the so-called "referenda" were held in Donetsk and Luhansk regions for joining the Russian Federation (Tass 2022a). They did not meet any transparency criteria and violated Ukrainian and international law (UN 2022a), and were condemned by 143 countries (UN 2022b). On September 30, 2022, President Putin announced the annexation of Donetsk, Luhansk, Kherson, and Zaporizhzhia regions (Tass 2022b), although the latter two were not under Russia's entire control.

International Response to the Russian Federation's Aggression

The majority of the world condemned the actions of the Russian Federation from the beginning. On March 27, 2014, i.e., six days after the Russian Federal Council ratified the "annexation" of Crimea, the UN General Assembly adopted a resolution in support of the territorial integrity of Ukraine (UN 2014). On July 2, 2014, the OSCE Parliamentary Assembly recognized Russia's actions as "military aggression" (OSCE 2014: 18).

The first attempt to resolve the crisis was a meeting of the heads of diplomacy of the European Union, the United States, Ukraine, and Russia in Geneva on

April 17, 2014, which adopted a joint statement on the crisis in Ukraine. The document stated that "all parties" shall refrain from any form of violence, intimidation, or provocation, all illegally armed groups must be disarmed, all illegally occupied buildings, squares, and streets in Ukrainian cities must be released, all "protesters" and those who voluntarily lay down their arms will be granted amnesty, apart from those who were found guilty of committing serious crimes. The parties also agreed that the OSCE Special Monitoring Mission should play a leading role in providing assistance to the Ukrainian authorities and local communities in the immediate implementation of the de-escalation measures. The US, the EU, and Russia pledged to support the OSCE Mission, including by sending observers (Geneva Statement, 2014). Although this document contained a list of steps that would lead to a de-escalation of the crisis, it was very general and left each side a wide field for interpretation, including the key phrase "all parties" to the conflict, which would not necessarily cover the Russian proxies used in the invasion.

Due to the escalation of the conflict, on September 5, 2014, the first Minsk Protocol (Minsk I) was signed. The representatives of Ukraine, Russia, the OSCE, and separatists signed a protocol on a ceasefire in eastern Ukraine. Two weeks later, due to ceasefire violations, a memorandum was signed, which clarified the implementation of the Protocol. Despite the negotiated agreements, the situation in the east of Ukraine has not been stabilized. On February 12, 2015, the "Package of Measures for the Implementation of the Minsk Agreements," the so-called Minsk II, was agreed upon (Duncan 2020: 10–6).

It is worth emphasizing that both agreements are considered to be more beneficial for Russia rather than Ukraine (Åtland, 2020). For example, Pełczyńska-Nałęcz and Buras argue that "the full implementation of Minsk II would bring Russia closer to fully achieving its political goals: to make Ukraine unstable or even to transform it into a vassal state" (2017: 2). Regardless of the imparity, eight years after Minsk II it should be noted that none of the 13 measures of Minsk II were fully implemented. Despite the agreements, the static war, which had formed, was a cause of a significant number of casualties before the full-scale Russian invasion in 2022 (UN 2022c). Among the main reasons for such a state of affairs was the difference in the interpretation of the agreements (Kobzar, 2016; Stępniewski, 2016).

As a result of the violation of the agreements and escalation of the Ukrainian conflict, western countries imposed sanctions on the Russian Federation. The list of sanctions was long and, at that time, consisted of over one hundred positions. The list was renewed every six months based on an assessment of the Minsk agreements implementation. However, many studies showed that the actual impact on the Russian economy was limited (Dreger et al. 2016: 5–8; Kholodilin and Netšunajev 2018: 41–8).

Taking into account the immediate and middle-term consequences for the Russian Federation, it has to be said that the western countries' reaction was insufficient—the sanctions had no significant impact on the Russian economy, and military aid for Ukraine, on the other hand, was inadequate. Both failed to become a deterrent to further Russian military actions against Ukraine.

Conclusions

The chapter's main goals were to provide information about the Russian Federation's aggression against Ukraine from the beginning of the conflict in 2014 to the outbreak of the full-scale war on February 24, 2022, and to analyze the hybrid nature of the attack and the use of proxy forces.

Hybrid war, as discussed in section three above, presupposes the use of "conventional, irregular, terrorism and criminal means" by "state and nonstate actors" (Glenn 2009: 2). The actions of Russian and Russian-inspired forces, described in section four of the chapter that led to the occupation of Crimea and the seizure of parts of the Donetsk and Luhansk regions definitely meet these criteria. Russia adopted the whole spectrum of means and groups of people, from disguised regular troops to convicted criminals.

The question of whether proxy warfare took place during the war is methodologically more challenging to answer. Undoubtedly, it does not fit into the traditional, Cold War-created understanding of the phenomenon. As it was argued, the constitutional features of proxy warfare evolve along the geopolitical and technological changes. The actions undertaken by the Russian Federation can be perceived as proxy warfare according to new attempts to elucidate the concept, including the works of Mumford (2013) and Rondeaux and Sterman (2019). As demonstrated, the separatist movement in Donetsk and Luhansk was primarily set off and then supported by the Russian Federation, which later sent its regular troops and openly admitted it.

It is worth adding that the way hybrid warfare was conducted and the proxy forces used during the conflict in Ukraine are information that should be used for further current conceptual studies of both phenomena.

It was argued that one of the main reasons for the use of proxies by Russia was the fear of provoking large-scale international reactions, and the employment of proxy forces "allow low-level armed conflict to be induced and sustained without suffering repercussions" (Kozera et al. 2020: 83). The decision to use proxy forces at the beginning of the war turned out to be the right one for Russia. The Minsk Agreements, as it was demonstrated, addressed more Russian than Ukrainian interests. It should be added that the direct result of Russia's invasion was illegal. It refers to the actual incorporation of the Crimea Peninsula and significant parts of eastern Ukraine into the Russian Federation in 2014 and 2022. The sanctions imposed by the West were limited and, as many argue, failed, especially regarding their deterrence aims. From this perspective, it was a military and political victory for Russia. On the other hand, the easiness of reaching these goals led President Putin to make what seems a very irrational decision to invade the whole of Ukraine; the war, as many believe in April 2023, cannot be strategically won by the Russian Federation.

Bibliography

Åtland, K. (2020), "Destined for Deadlock? Russia, Ukraine, and the Unfulfilled Minsk Agreements, *Post-Soviet Affairs*, 36 (2): 122–39. https://doi.org/10.1080/106058 6X.2020.1720443.

BBC (2013), "Ukraine suspends preparations for EU trade agreement", *BBC*, 21 November. Available online: https://www.bbc.com/news/world-europe-25032275 (accessed 10 November 2022).

BBC (2014), "Ukraine crisis: Timeline", *BBC*, 13 November. Available online: https:// www.bbc.com/news/world-middle-east-26248275 (accessed 10 November 2022).

Council of Europe (2010), "Observation of the Presidential Election in Ukraine (17 January 2010)". Available online: https://www.ecoi.net/en/file/ local/1068999/1226_1264701636_edoc12132.pdf (accessed 12 November 2022).

Deutsch, K. W. (1964), "External Involvement in Internal War, in Harry Eckstein ed., *Internal War, Problems and Approaches*, 100–110, New York: Free Press of Glencoe.

Dreger, C. et al. (2016), "Between the Hammer and the Anvil: The Impact of Economic Sanctions and Oil Prices on Russia's Ruble, *Journal of Comparative Economics*, 44 (2): 295–308. https://doi.org/10.1016/j.jce.2015.12.010.

Duncan, A. (2020), "The Minsk Conundrum: Western Policy and Russia's War in Eastern Ukraine", Ukraine Forum, May 2020. Available online: https://www.chathamhouse. org/sites/default/files/2020-05-22-minsk-conundrum-allan.pdf (accessed 10 November 2022).

Frolov, V and V. Semenenko (2021), "Formuvannya perspektyvnoyi modeli orhanizaciyi oborony Ukrayiny", *Nauka i oborona*, 3 (2019): 3–9. https://doi.org/10.33099/2618- 1614-2019-8-3-3-9.

Frolov, V and V. Semenenko (2021), "Orhanizaciya terytorial'noyi oborony Ukrayiny v umovax hibrydnoyi vijny z Rosiyeyu", *Nauka i oborona*, 2 (2021): 8–16. https://doi. org/10.33099/2618-1614-2021-15-2-8-16.

Geneva Statement (2014), "Mission of Ukraine to the North Atlantic Treaty Organization", 17 April. Available online: https://nato.mfa.gov.ua/en/news/1067-zhenevsyka-zajava-vid-17-kvitnya-2014-rokuukrros (accessed 12 November 2022).

Glenn, R. W. (2009), "Thoughts on Hybrid Conflict", *Small Wars Journal*, 2 March. Available online: http://smallwarsjournal.com/blog/2009/03/thoughts-on-hybrid-conflict/ (accessed 10 November 2022).

Göler, D. (2015), "Wenn normative Macht zur geostrategischen Herausforderung wird: Überlegungen zur aktuellen Ukraine-Krise", *ZfP*, 62 (3):289–305.

Kholodilin K. A. and A. Netšunajev (2018), "Crimea and Punishment: The Impact of Sanctions on Russian Economy and Economies of the Euro Area", *Baltic Journal of Economics*, 19 (1): 39–51. https://doi.org/10.1080/1406099x.2018.1547566.

Kobzar, S. (2016): "Mind the Gap: Interpreting the Minsk II Agreement", *Policy Brief*, 2016 (3). Available online: http://aei.pitt.edu/82524/1/Policy_Brief_2016_3.pdf (accessed 9 November 2022).

Kozera, C. A., P. Bernat, C. Gürer, B. Popławski and M. A. Sözer (2020), "Game of Proxies—Towards a New Model of Warfare: Experiences from the CAR, Libya, Mali, Syria, and Ukraine", *Security & Defence Quarterly*, 31 (4): 77–97. https://doi. org/10.35467/sdq/131787.

Marko, S. (2016), *Khronika hibrydnoyi vijny / Hibrydna vijna v Ukrayini XXI storichchya*, Kyyiv: Al'terpres.

Mumford, A. (2013), "Proxy Warfare and the Future Conflict", *The RUSI Journal*, 158 (2): 40–6. https://doi.org/10.1080/03071847.2013.787733.

Muzhenko, V. (2015), "Dvanadcyat' dniv, shho zminyly khid ATO", *Narodna armiya*, 21 August.

National Institute for Strategic Studies (2016), "Proceedings to the Second Anniversary of the Russian Aggression against Ukraine", 20 February. Available online: https://niss.gov.ua/sites/default/files/2016-02/Eng_ru.pdf (accessed 9 November 2022).

NATO, Science and Technology Organization (2020), *Military Aspects of Countering Hybrid Aggression: Ukrainian Experience (STO-TR-SAS-161)*.

OSCE (2014), *Baku Declaration And Resolutions Adopted By The OSCE Parliamentary Assembly at the Twenty-Third Annual Session*, Baku, 28 June to 2 July 2014. Available online: https://www.oscepa.org/en/documents/annual-sessions/2014-baku/declaration-2/2540-2014-baku-declaration-eng/file (accessed 11 November 2022).

Pacek, B, H. Pievtsov and A. Syrotenko (2021), *Current Issues of Military Specialists Training in the Security and Defence Sector under Conditions of Hybrid Threats*, Warsaw: Wydawnictwo Instytutu Bezpieczeństwa i Rozwoju Międzynarodowego.

Pełczyńska-Nałęcz, K. and P. Buras (2017), *The Minsk (Dis)Agreement and Europe's Security Order*, Warsaw: Stefan Batory Foundation. Available online: https://www. batory.org.pl/upload/files/pdf/rap_otw_eu/The%20Minsk%20(dis)agreement%20 and%20Europe%E2%80%99s%20security%20order.pdf (accessed 10 November 2022).

Putin, V. (2014), "Address by President of the Russian Federation", 18 March. Available online: http://en.kremlin.ru/events/president/news/20603 (accessed 10 November 2022).

Rauta, V. (2021), (2021) "Proxy War'—A Reconceptualisation', *Civil Wars*, 23 (1): 1–24. https://doi.org/10.1080/13698249.2021.1860578.

Rondeaux, C. and D. Sterman (2019), *Twenty-First Century Proxy Warfare: Confronting Strategic Innovation in a Multipolar World Since the 2011 NATO Intervention*, New America. Available online: https://d1y8sb8igg2f8e.cloudfront.net/documents/ Twenty-First_Century_Proxy_Warfare_Final.pdf (accessed 10 November 2022).

Shovkoplias, I. (2022), "The Invisible War: 8 Years of Battles in Donbas", BRAND UKRAINE NGO, 14 July. Available online: https://war.ukraine.ua/articles/8-years-of-war-in-donbas/ (accessed 10 November 2022).

Shtohrin, I. (2016), 352) *Ad 242. Istoriya muzhnosti, braterstva ta samopozhert-vy*, Kharkiv: Knyzhkovyj Klub "Klub Simejnoho dozvillya".

Shveda, Y. and J. H. Park (2016), "Ukraine's Revolution of Dignity: The Dynamics of Euromaidan", *Journal of Eurasian Studies*, 7 (1): 85–91. https://doi.org/10.1016/j. euras.2015.10.007.

Stępniewski, T. (2016), "Konflikt zbrojny Rosji z Ukrainą i negocjacje pokojowe w Mińsku", *Studia Europejskie*, 3 (79): 43–59.

Syrotenko, A., ed. (2020), *Voyenni aspekty protydiyi hibrydnij ahresiyi: dosvid Ukrayiny*, Kyyiv: Nacional'nyj Universytet Oborony Ukrayiny Imeni Ivana Chernyaxovs'koho. Available online: https://nuou.org.ua/assets/monography/mono_gibr_viin.pdf (accessed 12 November 2022).

Tass (2022a), "Referendum to mark a new stage in Donbass development—DPR premier", 21 September. Available online: https://tass.com/politics/1511039 (accessed 10 November 2022).

Tass (2022b), "Putin signs decrees to recognize independence of Zaporozhye, Kherson regions", 29 September. Available online: https://tass.com/politics/1515559 (accessed 13 November 2022).

Tsygankov, A. (2015), "Vladimir Putin's Last Stand: The Sources of Russia's Ukraine policy", *Post-Soviet Affairs*, 31 (4): 279–303. https://doi.org/10.1080/106058 6X.2015.1005903.

Ukrainian Institute of National Memory (2019), "Do 5-richchya vid pochatku zbrojnoyi ahresiyi Rosijs'koyi Federaciyi proty Ukrayiny", 27 February. Available online: https:// uinp.gov.ua/informaciyni-materialy/viyskovym/do-5-richchya-vid-pochatku-zbroynoyi-agresiyi-rosiyskoyi-federaciyi-proty-ukrayiny (accessed 11 November 2022).

UN (2014), "General Assembly Adopts Resolution Calling upon States Not to Recognize Changes in Status of Crimea Region", 27 March. Available online: https://press.un. org/en/2014/ga11493.doc.htm (accessed 10 November 2022).

UN (2022a), "So-called Referenda in Russian-controlled Ukraine 'Cannot be Regarded as Legal': UN Political Affairs Chief", 27 September. Available online: https://news.un.org/en/story/2022/09/1128161 (accessed 11 November 2022).

UN (2022b), "Ukraine: UN General Assembly demands Russia reverse course on 'attempted illegal annexation", 12 October. Available online: https://news.un.org/en/story/2022/10/1129492 (accessed 13 November 2022).

UN (2022c), "Conflict-related civilian casualties in Ukraine", 27 January. Available online: https://ukraine.un.org/sites/default/files/2022-02/Conflict-related%20civilian%20casualties%20as%20of%2031%20December%202021%20%28rev%2027%20January%202022%29%20corr%20EN_0.pdf (accessed 11 November 2022).

UN [United Nations] (1994), "Memorandum on Security Assurances in Connection with Ukraine's Accession to the Treaty on the Non-Proliferation of Nuclear Weapons", Budapest, 5 December 1994. Available online: https://treaties.un.org/doc/Publication/UNTS/Volume%203007/Part/volume-3007-I-52241.pdf (accessed 12 November 2022).

Verkhovna Rada (2015a), "Information of the Verkhovna Rada (VVR), 2015, No. 46, Article 417". Available online: https://zakon.rada.gov.ua/laws/show/685-19#Text (accessed 11 November 2022).

Verkhovna Rada (2015b), "Pro Zayavu Verxovnoyi Rady Ukrayiny 'Pro vidsich zbrojnij ahresiyi Rosijs'koyi Federaciyi ta podolannya yiyi naslidkiv': Postanova Verxovnoyi Rady Ukrayiny vid", 21 April. Available online: https://zakon.rada.gov.ua/laws/show/337-19#Text (accessed 11 November 2022).

World Bank (2022), "GDP growth (annual %): Ukraine", The World Bank. Available online: https://data.worldbank.org/indicator/NY.GDP.MKTP.KD.ZG?locations=UA (accessed 12 November 2022).

Zhegulev, I. (2017), "Esli by nas ne podderzhal Patrushev, v Krymu stojal by amerikanskij flot' Interv'ju krymskogo politika Leonida Gracha o tom, kak FSB pomogala Krymu s 2005 goda', *Meduza*, 21 March. Available online: https://meduza.io/feature/2017/03/21/esli-by-nas-ne-podderzhal-patrushev-v-krymu-stoyal-by-amerikanskiy-flot (accessed 10 November 2022).

Zolotukhin, D., ed. (2018), *Bila knyha special'nyx informacijnyx operacij proty Ukrayiny 2014–2018*, Kyyiv: Meha-pres hrup. Available online: https://mkip.gov.ua/news/3793.html (accessed 11 November 2022).

5

Ukraine's Legionnaires in the War against Russia

Tamir Sinai

Introduction

In her article "Leaning on Legionnaires: Why Modern States Recruit Foreign Soldiers," Elizabeth Grasmeder looks at why modern nation-states still recruit foreigners against the conventional wisdom that since the French revolution, the most important part of state power—military fighting might—should be based on citizens as recruits (Grasmeder 2021). She rightly points out that the myth of the citizen-soldier, even though being the norm cannot cover the fact that legionnaire recruitment continued widely. She brings forward "supply" and "demand" explanations—"supply" being the numerical or political limits of potential recruits from amongst the population and "demand", the perceived external threat to the sovereignty and territorial integrity of the state to explain when states are likely to recruit legionnaires in order to satisfy their demand for more manpower. The case study Grasmeder provides is about the changing recruitment patterns of the German Wehrmacht in the Second World War. She then concludes that the state's military power, directly under its control, can be extended beyond the confines of the capabilities and capacities of its citizenry, allowing the state to mobilize skilled and combat-tested recruits and to pursue strategies beyond its nominal demographical means.

The following case study will focus on Ukraine's recruitment of foreign volunteers between 2014 and February 2022, when Russia attacked Ukraine and invaded the country on four fronts. It was then that Ukrainian President Volodymyr Zelenskyy called on foreign volunteers willing to fight to join the Ukrainian Armed Forces and help resist this unprovoked attack. Since then, many have joined the war effort and occupied a not insignificant position in the discourse about the war.

But where do they fit into the "proxies" debate? Here one could argue that definitions of "foreign fighters" which do not allow an analysis of "legionnaires" (noncitizens who are uniformed personnel of the state's armed forces) must be incomplete, given their prominence and noncitizen status. As we explore in this volume how the state interacts with combatants fighting on its behalf, there is a case to be made that legionnaire recruitment, and their use is becoming an integral aspect of contemporary warfare. Even if legionnaires are arguably on the fringe of proxy use, they need to be included if we want to gain a more complete understanding of the contemporary battle-space.

This chapter will first look at definitions and some of the literature, followed by an identification of the different stages in which Ukraine enlisted foreign citizens between 2014–2022 using Grasmeder's "supply" and "demand" dynamic influencing the changes in government policy at each stage. Concluding, we will evaluate the case and its implications for our understanding of a state's military pillar of power and how a state's behavior and choices are influenced by the possibility of legionnaire recruitment, but also what the limits of this theory are as seen in this case.

Legionnaires in Nation States' Armies

Grasmeder defines legionnaires as "foreigners who are neither citizens nor subjects of the state whose military they serve" and, "[u]nlike mercenaries or contractors, who fight outside a state's military hierarchy, legionnaires are members of its armed forces" (Grasmeder 2021: 147).

In a discussion on states' use of proxies, i.e., in the widest sense, combatants who are not the nation states' citizen-soldiers, legionnaires have so far been somewhat overlooked. They do not quite fit the varied but often incomplete typologies of "non-state actors" in warfare offered so far. This is to be expected, considering the heterogeneity of combatants found in modern conflicts from Syria, to Libya, the Central African Republic, and, indeed Ukraine. They can also display quite different characteristics when compared to citizen soldiers, as we will see in this case study of Ukraine. In fact, they are on the continuum of regular, citizen soldier to proxy, to militiaman or mercenary—on the fringes between proxies and citizen soldier.

In one recent typology, four categories of non-state actors in "hybrid warfare," which can serve as a starting point for our examination of legionnaires in Ukraine between 2014 and 2022, are described (Rauta 2019: 868–87). Rauta's category of "surrogates"—indirectly embedded combatants, supplementary to the armed forces, and fighting internally—in fact corresponds to fighters we see in the first phase of foreign recruitment covered in this study, namely the volunteer militias raised after Russia's invasion of Ukraine in 2014 and the occupation of Crimea (Rauta 2019: 880). While this is not a factor addressed in Rauta's study, these formations did include foreign volunteers. The units were in due course integrated into the Ukrainian regular armed and territorial forces, turning these "volunteers" into "legionnaires."

The term proxy usually refers to non-state actors fighting on behalf of/ alongside a state, often externally. In this case, the actors are noncitizens fighting for the state and as members of the regular armed forces. Yet, they are not your usual citizen soldiers, and this is of importance, not only because of the centrality of "citizenship" in the discussion of nation-states' armies, but also as it fundamentally changes the relationship between the state and that soldier fighting on its behalf. The legionnaire-state relationship is in a way reminiscent of the relationship between the state and a "classical" proxy. It is thus the lack of a category that describes on the one hand "noncitizens" but on the other "state actors" that becomes evident here.

The added quality of "noncitizen," not addressed in current definitions, is relevant when trying to understand the relationship between the state and these noncitizen combatants. We will thus focus on the units which primarily draw their manpower from foreign recruits, the *Georgian* and *Chechen* units fighting for Ukraine, as well as the *International Legion* (to include units like the *Belarussian* as well as *Russian* formations that were created in 2022). This is not to say that noncitizens did not serve in other units of the Ukrainian military all along. While the *Legion* has taken center stage in the discussion of legionnaire recruitment in Ukraine in 2022, the other formations (Georgian and Chechen) merit a closer look within the dynamic of state-legionnaire relations as they have gone through all the stages described—from their formation around 2014, integration in the consolidation phase 2016–2021 and their surge/revival in the all-out war that was unleashed by Russia in 2022.

In the effort to better grasp the dynamics of noncitizen soldiers serving the state, we will look at the motivation for Ukraine to recruit or allow for the recruitment of foreign volunteers in the fight against Russia using the "supply" and "demand" dynamics offered by Grasmeder. As mentioned, the model explains states' recruitment of noncitizens into its armed forces as a function of internal "constraints" combined with its "perception of external territorial threats" and the recruitment of noncitizens being in apparent contradiction to the intuitive understanding that modern nation-states view their own citizens as the most loyal, best suited, and motivated "to fight effectively and reliably" in defense of their state (Grasmeder 2021: 148–51). Please note that the motivation of volunteers to join the Ukrainian military are manifold. This side of the equation is not subject of this analysis though.

Ukraine's Armed Forces: Post-Soviet Baseline

With independence in 1991, Ukraine inherited the armed forces stationed in the territory of the erstwhile Soviet Socialist Republic of Ukraine, including the strategic nuclear weapons. Consequently, Ukraine had the second largest army in Europe and indeed could have become a de-facto nuclear power. While the Soviet Union withdrew its tactical nukes from non-Russian republics to Russia proper by March 1992, and command and launch control over the strategic nuclear missiles remained under Moscow's control, Ukraine did have negative operational control, i.e., it could block a potential launch from its territory. The nuclear warheads all the while remained under strict Russian control (Budjeryn 1996: 9–20). By 1994, Ukraine had finally given up any aspirations for an independent nuclear arsenal after signing the Budapest Memorandum on Security Assurances, obtaining security assurances from the Non-Proliferation Treaty (NPT) depository states, the Russian Federation, the United Kingdom, and the United States.

At this stage, the Ukrainian Armed Forces, as were all former Soviet armies, were manned exclusively by citizens of Ukraine without any provision for the inclusion of noncitizens. During this period of early statehood, however, Ukraine's armed forces were adversely affected by corrupt leadership and low spending and in devastating decline. In 1996 the first attempt was made at defense reform, away from a Soviet fighting force geared to do battle with NATO and towards a force for the protection of Ukraine, first and foremost against a perceived growing threat from Russia. In the period of interest to us here, Ukraine went through distinct phases of noncitizen recruitment between 2014–2022, and we witnessed the emergence of a variety of foreign volunteer uses in different units. Three stages, that illustrate Grasmeder's dynamics can be identified in those years—from the baseline of all-citizen armed forces, as we have seen, through a stage of integration and consolidation, and all the way to the mass recruitment and creation of the *International Legion*. Each stage is characterized by changing internal contexts ("supply") on the one hand, and external threat levels ("demand") on the other, causing the acceptance of foreign volunteers or their active recruitment by the state. Over those eight years, Ukraine offers a case study that covers a state characterized by "high" then "reduced" and finally "existential" demand or threat factors. On the "supply" side, corruption and loyalty questions fluctuated but continued and reinforced the "demand" issues. In the following section, we will look in more detail at these developments.

Early Stage of Foreign Recruitment 2014–2015

When Russia invaded Ukraine, annexed Crimea, and fomented the war in the Donbas (in the period between February 2014 and February 2016), the country found itself in a situation of "high-level external threat" and stifling "domestic constraints" that explain the acceptance by the state of limited recruitment of foreign volunteers. Its dysfunctional armed forces could not or would not face up to either the Russian invaders or the Russian-backed separatists in the Donbas. Local, grassroots, most often privately-financed volunteer units took up the fight and recruited foreign volunteers with the approval of the central authorities in Kyiv.

In early 2014, following the Euromaidan protests and the "Revolution of Dignity," pro-Russian unrest stirred in southern and eastern Ukraine, providing Russia with cover for the take-over of Crimea by Russian troops and the annexation of the territory as well as a destabilizing and rapidly escalating armed separatist conflict in the Donbas. Ukraine at that time was not in good shape militarily. Morale was low and thousands of servicemen defected to the separatists' side in the face of over 40,000 Russian troops massed across the border (Kofman et al. 2017: 41–2). When Russia invaded and annexed Crimea and started the war in the Donbas, Ukraine's military had been weakened by years of neglect, underfunding, and corruption. The ground forces had an estimated mere 6,000 combat-ready troops (Bowen 2022). Defections to the Russian side and the Russian-sponsored insurgency in the Donbas further drained Ukrainian manpower resources. The state was quite unable to fight off the invading Russians and their local proxies. The Minister of Internal Affairs Arsen Avakov noted, "the internal military troops and police were demoralized. There were only a couple of units actually capable of resisting the separatists. Something innovative and efficient had to be done" (Käihkö 2022). Kyiv arguably had no choice but to allow the formation of grassroots-devised and created, privately funded, while at the same time highly-motivated battalions of volunteers willing to fight and defend the territorial integrity of Ukraine, which coincidentally were also accepting international recruits. Between 2014 and 2019, an estimated 900 foreign volunteers from around the world and about 3000 Russians joined these various units (Soufan Center 2019). Next to the newly established National Guard, the volunteer units and their foreign recruits helped Kyiv meet its manpower needs.

When the tide was turning in Ukraine's favor by the summer of 2014, not least through the stellar efforts of the volunteer units, Russia quickly escalated and overtly introduced its own armed forces directly into the conflict for the first time, halting the Ukrainian advance and establishing a line of separation the separatists could hold. Not forcing the issue further, Russia seemed happy to leave the conflict at a stalemate with rising and lowering intensity and bloodletting.

The Ukrainian volunteer battalions mentioned were at first formed as militias (i.e., not as territorial defense formations) and not as part of the state's regular armed forces. They were able to hold a certain degree of autonomy in 2014-2015, autonomy rooted in their military strength and successes (notably the Azov and Donbas Battalions) compared to regular state forces, their mainly corresponding goals and agendas, and indeed their popular/grassroots character. The phenomenon was gradually sanctioned by the central authorities by nominally integrating or co-opting them into state structures of the National Guard under either the Ministry of Internal Affairs (as *Special Tasks Patrol Police*) or the Ministry of Defense (as Territorial Defense Battalions) (UCMC 2015). Still, for quite some time, these units received insufficient funding from the state and continued to be crowdfunded or sponsored by local oligarchs. This led some of these units to be infamously politicized (i.e., Azov Battalion or the Right Sector's *Ukrainian Volunteer Corps*) or turned, in the eyes of some, into quasi "private armies" with foreign volunteers.

All these units are discussed at length elsewhere (Käihkö 2018: 147–66). The focus here is on the primarily foreign-staffed units like the Georgian National Legion (ethnic Georgian and/or English-speaking) as well as the Dzhokhar Dudayev Battalion and Sheikh Mansur Battalion (ethnic Chechen and Muslim) that were created in the early stages of the war in the East and, with some ups and downs, still exist today.

The Georgian National Legion was formed in April 2014 by six Georgian veterans of wars with Russia who believed that the fate of their country, Georgia, would be decided on the battlefields of Ukraine as, should the Kremlin succeed in subjugating Ukraine, it would then refocus on the Caucasus and threaten Georgian sovereignty and independence. The legion was fully independent from the Ukrainian armed forces and its soldiers true "foreign fighters" in the conventional sense. It was self- and crowd-funded and supplied itself by raiding weapons depots in the Donbas. It was also tiny, numbering twenty to forty soldiers by the end of 2014, platoon strength. In 2016 it counted about one hundred fighters, including non-Georgians from Germany, the US, the UK, Australia, Greece, Azerbaijan, Moldova, Armenia, and Israel (UNIAN 2018).

The transition to the next phase was gradual. By 2015, with the Ukrainian central government and armed forces "finding their feet," the various foreign volunteer units were ordered to withdraw from the frontline in the Donbas and were subsequently integrated into the now-reforming, state armed forces. A codification of this new situation, recruitment of foreign volunteers, happened in 2015 when the Ukrainian parliament formally legalized foreigners serving in the Ukrainian armed forces and regulated their status and eventually established a path towards citizenship. The process, however, was turbulent, as we will see below.

Consolidation Stage 2016–2021

After that initial shock and the loss of large swathes of its sovereign territory, the Ukrainian state entered a phase of consolidation and much-needed reconstruction of its armed forces. When the frontline in the East stabilized and regular army units took over the positions previously held by volunteer units, Kyiv forced their integration into the Ukrainian armed forces. This showcases the natural tendency of a sovereign nation-state to monopolize the means of violence under its control. It could do so, as the earlier domestic constraints (i.e., corruption, dubious loyalty issues, mismanagement), were slowly addressed (if not fully resolved), and Western-sponsored reorganization and training missions supported Ukrainian efforts to reshape its armed forces. External pressure also reduced as Russia evidently did not want to force a Ukrainian defeat in the Donbas but seemed, for the time being, satisfied with a frozen conflict along a tense line-of-contact.

As mentioned, the inherent erosion of the sovereign state monopoly on violence caused by "non-embedded" armed formations demanded that as soon as the central authorities were able to, they felt they must rein in, integrate, or disband the volunteer battalions. The Ukrainian state did this in various ways, by co-opting, incorporating, and coercing these units (Käihkö 2018: 148).

The Minsk II agreement of February 2015 signaled a change in the legal status of foreign volunteers as it stipulated the disbandment of all non-state armed formations, including volunteer and mercenary units, in Ukraine. After its sluggish implementation, due to continuous fighting in the Donbas, a law allowing foreigners to join the Ukrainian armed forces under contract was signed in November 2015 (VVR 2015). Thus, the Georgian National Legion became part of the Armed Forces of Ukraine in 2016 when it was integrated into the *25th Independent Motorized Battalion "Kyivan Rus."* This was the first time in Ukraine's history that foreigners were officially accepted into the Armed Forces of Ukraine (Musaeva and Buderatskyi 2022) and fully integrated into its command structures (Blatchford 2022). The unit also grew steadily in size as new members, no longer necessarily Georgians but Westerners and even many Ukrainians were admitted. Allegations of incompetence against its parent unit *"Kyivan Rus"* led to the legion being reassigned to a different parent unit (UAWIRE 2018). The fact that a small unit has a say in its place in the order of battle is rather unusual for modern armies and a sign in itself of special status.

Other units, like the Sheikh Mansur Battalion, were integrated into the *Ukrainian Volunteer Corps*, a military formation of the "Right Sector" movement that remained independent from the Ukrainian Armed Forces Until Russia invaded in 2022. Made up of primarily Chechen fighters, the unit had fought from 2014 in the Donbas with staunch pro-Ukrainian fervor and continued to do so as part of the *Volunteer Corps*. These Muslim units were subject to scrutiny and even perceived persecution by the Ukrainian state.

In a traumatic case in 2018, a member of the unit, Timur Tumgoev, was extradited to Russia by Ukrainian authorities based on allegations of him having fought for an ISIS affiliate in Syria. Tumgoev was subsequently tortured and sentenced to eighteen years in prison by Russia. Several other cases were pending when the war broke out in 2022 (Belov 2022). The Ukrainian President's Office stated in April 2022 that extraditions and sanctions against fighters had been the work of pro-Russian elements within the Ukrainian government to include the former Minister of the Interior. These elements continue to be identified and removed from positions of power. Unjustly sanctioned individuals have been returned to their units and are once again on the front line.

During this "consolidation phase," the Ukrainian state more or less integrated the largely foreign-staffed units, but both the Georgian Legion as well as the Chechen units continued to enjoy varying degrees of independence—see the example of the Georgians, mentioned above. In all this, the units received and followed orders from the Ukrainian command of operations in the East, the

Anti-Terrorist Center. They never challenged state authority, unlike, at some stage, the *Right Sector,* which threatened to march on Kyiv if pro-Russian officials were not purged (Global Security Website 2022).

The build-up of Russian invasion forces in 2021 found these units performing routine tasks, if not manning positions on the line-of-separation in the Donbas. The Georgian Legion was apparently involved in training Ukrainian civilian volunteers in the newly stood-up Home Defense Battalions (Hauer 2022). This process of incorporation of legionnaire units arguably continued right up until the massive Russian build-up on Ukraine's border in 2021, when intelligence confirmed an imminent invasion of the country by what was widely perceived as a vastly superior enemy. In February 2022, the situation turned undeniably into one of an "existential" external threat that warranted the mass mobilization of Ukrainian citizens and stimulated the mass recruitment of foreign volunteers.

All-out War and Mass Recruitment 2022

With the brutal assault on Ukraine on February 24, 2022, the situation changed dramatically. When Russian President Vladimir Putin began the large-scale invasion of Ukraine from Belarus, Russia, the Donbas, and occupied Crimea, his declared war aim was a complete regime change, and the occupation of Ukraine vaguely disguised as a "Special Military Operation" to "de-nazify" and "demilitarize" the country. Everyone, not least Putin himself, believed that the complete subjugation of Ukraine was a matter of weeks, if not days. In this situation, the "supply," as well as the "demand" dynamics, went to their highest possible values, as martial law was declared and a general mobilization conducted. The "demand" part of the equation seemed blindingly clear: "Russia has sufficient conventional military power to reinforce each of its current axes of advance and overpower the conventional Ukrainian forces defending them" and "Russia will likely defeat Ukrainian regular military forces and secure their territorial objectives at some point in the coming days or weeks" (Clark et al. 2022).

On the "supply" side, the mood was that every man was needed—tens of thousands of Ukrainians were hurriedly drafted into *Territorial Defense Units,* and all male Ukrainian citizens between eighteen and sixty were barred from leaving the country in view of the dire need for every potential fighting man (President of Ukraine 2022). Ukrainians living abroad returned in droves—over 20,000 in the first week of the war—as women and children fled in their millions across the borders to safety in the West.

On February 27, 2022, President Volodymyr Zelenskyy called for the *International Legion of Territorial Defense of Ukraine* to be created and manned by volunteers willing to fight in the defense of Ukraine (Shoaib 2022). Alongside universal statements on social media, he also addressed specific communities, in particular in countries with a sizable Ukrainian diaspora, a case in point being Canada. Soon the general call for "everyone willing to defend Ukraine," became more focused by specifying combat or other specialized experience like medical, cyber, etc., as a prerequisite for acceptance. The enthusiastic crowd of volunteers that had poured into the country and included so-called "war tourists" and an assortment of inexperienced fantasists proved at times counterproductive. Headlines of disillusioned "wannabes" who experienced a rude awakening with their first contact with modern urban warfare threatened to discredit the propaganda value of the legion. Thus, formally, the three conditions for joining, as stated on the Legion's website, were given as (1) being a noncitizen, (2) having a willingness to actively fight for European freedom and democracy, (3) having combat experience and passing, reportedly stringent, background checks and psychological exams (FightForUA 2022).

It is notoriously hard to get accurate data on the units formed as, for legal and other reasons, much of their activities are covert. Evidence is often anecdotal, and media reports often biased. A Legion spokesperson stated previously that more than fifty nationalities from every continent were represented in the legion and that former soldiers from the US and UK were the most common—a claim disputed by some. Realistic estimates put the number at a maximum of "a few thousand," much lower than the official pronouncements of over 20,000 (Murauskaite 2022). The Georgian National Legion numbered an estimated 250 soldiers, Georgian as well as from a number of different countries when Ukraine was invaded. (Shamsian 2022). It grew significantly in size as more volunteers found their way to Ukraine to join that unit. Ukrainian presidential adviser Oleksiy Arestovych said in June 2022 that a *Freedom of Russia Legion*, made up of Russian volunteers and deserters, had a "few hundred" members, with the unit itself claiming it consisted of two "fully manned battalions," which could potentially mean more than 1,000 fighters (The Moscow Times 2022). Another formation, the Belarussian-manned Kastus Kalinouski Battalion, adds to the colorful variety of legionnaire units.

In a net assessment and in order to weigh the eventual impact of these legionnaire units, one needs to look at the actual numbers. If Ukraine managed to recruit and retain a few thousand volunteers, this number does not significantly relieve numerical "supply" issues in a country with millions of potential recruits but offered an opportunity to enlist specialist and combat-experienced recruits. But other factors also play a role: combat unit integration has proven difficult even for experienced soldiers due to the lack of arms, organizational support, and coordination, as well as the obvious language barrier. Furthermore, many combat veterans from the West are much more accustomed to efficient supply and rotation routines. While evidence of such issues remains for the time being anecdotal, it remains to be seen how the selection of volunteers developed during the war, what *modi operandi* were found, and how Ukraine overcame such difficulties. Whilst it is undeniable that legionnaires have taken part in significant battles like the retaking of Irpin, and the fight for Hostomol, Severodonetsk, Lysychansk, Bakhmut, and indeed the breathtaking counter-offensive of fall 2022, the actual fighting power gained through legionnaire recruitment might be small or at least hard to measure at this stage.

Considering how savvy Kyiv was in its use of strategic messaging and how skillfully Kyiv dominated the information space, one can come to a different conclusion on what the primary aim of legionnaire recruitment was. It is safe to assume that the call for volunteers was an effort to shape the narrative that the freedom of the West was being defended on Ukrainian battlefields—thereby internationalizing the war (Arielli et al. 2022). While NATO nations categorically rejected any call for direct involvement in the fighting—by refusing to provide and enforce a no-fly zone over Ukraine—the image of Western volunteers engaging in firefights with Russian invaders strongly supported this narrative. If states could not participate actively, they could still allow their citizens to contribute to the fight. One volunteer expressed: "NATO isn't doing anything about it, so the only thing we can do is take up arms and do it ourselves" (Zitser, 2022; Miller 2022).

Measuring such intangibles is notoriously hard. Some critics have voiced doubt about the Legion's public relations value based on the number of searches for keywords like "Foreign Legion Ukraine" on Google, which was not long-lived (it peaked for a week following the call for volunteers) (Google Trends 2022), as was pointed out in a recent study (Habtom 2022). Yet, to base one's evaluation on this might be premature. It is a fact that some volunteers like the author and analyst Malcolm Nance (1.1m followers on Twitter) and several Georgian, Finnish, and Latvian politicians have gained a remarkable following on social media and are regular contributors to news networks, helping to shape public opinion in their countries and around the world. This contributes to, as mentioned before, the effort to gain and now sustain Western support solidified in the weeks after the initial assault on Ukraine. When the realization took hold in the West that Ukraine did indeed have a fighting chance, the messaging by the

Ukrainian government garnered a wide and supportive coalition, that could focus on concrete material/martial support.

Conclusions: Legionnaires on the Twenty-First-Century Battlefield

Legionnaires are a common phenomenon in modern states' militaries. The notion that the defense of the realm is an exclusive task for citizen-soldiers does not quite hold true. As Grasmeder suggested and the case of Ukraine shows to some extent, legionnaire recruitment can be reasonably linked to "supply" and "demand" dynamics. Coincidentally, it probably has much in common with states' use of proxies, be they private military companies, militias, or any other form of proxy forces discussed in this book (just refer to the Russian use of the above in the same war depicted in Chapter four). The main and most important difference remains that legionnaires are members of the states' armed forces and not of non-state formations. Exclusively looking at these non-state actors in our analysis of proxy forces has for a long time narrowed our focus. As Grasmeder formulated: "scholarship should prioritize examining how states expand the military manpower that they *control directly*, and that its focus on states' use of private military and security companies may be, if not misguided, incomplete" (emphasis added) (Grasmeder 2021: 192–193).

As seen in the Ukraine case study, legionnaire recruitment fulfills functions beyond the numerical or qualitative needs of a state in situations of perceived vulnerability to defeat in war. The public relations benefits of legionnaire enlistment by Ukraine in 2022 certainly equaled or outweighed the numerical relief of its manpower resources—and this can be linked to the Ukrainian center of gravity: continued international support.

This is a valid goal in the face of an existential external threat. Having identified its center of gravity, the government quite logically used every line of effort to tie Western governments and the public to their struggle. The recruitment of thousands of volunteers created a concrete image of that connection and helped shape the perception of an international struggle against evil. In this regard, the experience is not unlike the Finnish use of legionnaires in the Winter War. The recruitment of legionnaires by Finland, too, had a dual role of fielding (quality) manpower (pilots, etc.) but also allowing the expression of solidarity by European states. In times of social media, this effect is amplified manyfold and was used skillfully by Ukraine. All this is not to lessen the possibly significant impact foreign volunteers have had and still have in actual war-fighting and training, nor does it diminish the significance of the sacrifices many have made and are making in solidarity with Ukraine—something that does not go unnoticed with the Ukrainian population.

The case has thus shown that there are causal links between the "supply" and "demand" dynamics and the state's recruitment policy. It also shows that beyond the combat *manpower* calculus indicators suggested by Grasmeder, just as powerful but far more intangible factors need to be included in our analysis of legionnaire recruitment. The case suggests that, in Ukraine, the recruitment of foreign volunteers in 2022 was a strategic messaging tool to shape the narrative and internationalize the war, thereby ensuring unprecedented material support. The benefits of gaining combat-experienced recruits are an added value still difficult to assess given the tight information control practiced by Kyiv as the fighting continues.

In general, one should draw the line between what we witness in the case of Ukraine, a state at war since 2014, and other state-recruited legionnaires like noncitizen members of the US, UK, or various European armed forces. The dynamics there can be much more complex beyond the "supply" and "demand" of and for military manpower logic. This would incidentally answer some of Grasmeder's "puzzles" mentioned in her dissertation (Grasmeder 2020: 506).

Some cases like Luxembourg, Belgium, and Norway may be better explained by intangible factors like concepts of European/Nordic Integration/Citizenship. Other cases show the influence of history and tradition (*Pontifical Swiss Guard, Brigade of Gurkhas*) or considerations that might change over time. Grasmeder's model seems to explain recruitment best in extreme cases, like the case of the Wehrmacht, and not necessarily in peacetime armies. But there is a continuum between the recruitment of legionnaires into for example, the army of Luxembourg, and armies in an all-out war like Ukraine. Further up on that continuum, we can certainly find examples where states conduct a very proactive foreign policy and often prefer to use legionnaires for their expeditionary operations (French Foreign Legion). In the case of Ukraine in 2022, we have seen that Grasmeder's manpower-centric model needs to be modified to include intangible power generators like international support and the resulting very tangible supply of lethal weaponry. These can be as crucial to stand up to an existential threat as manpower; indeed, legionnaire recruitment can be a means to help generate international support and promote the provision of necessary platforms and munitions.

In conclusion, a definition of "legionnaire" as a type of combatant on the contemporary battlefield and in the context of proxy warfare is needed. Legionnaire units fight with and are integrated in the command hierarchy of the state's armed forces. What makes them distinct from other units is the fact that they are staffed by noncitizens and not draftees or citizen soldiers. They can sometimes also, as seen in this case study display a special in not autonomous status. Furthermore, legionnaires, as noncitizens, are subject to special regulations – in Ukraine they are prevented from attaining officer rank. A case in point would be Mamuka Mamulashvili whose rank is given as "Commander"—not a Ukrainian armed forces' rank.

Concerning their subjugation under the military system of justice, under which they fall according to Ukrainian law, it is doubtful if Ukraine will prosecute noncitizens for absence without leave or similar offenses. They certainly did not spend any time or effort on this following the desertion of volunteers in the early stage of the war but apparently took it as a mechanism of selection. Another distinction these noncitizen soldiers need to consider is the fact that the enemy might, rightly or wrongly, not recognize them as legal combatants under International Law. The threat of execution or incarceration as mercenaries, if captured by a ruthless enemy, looms over the volunteers. All this although Vladimir Putin himself signed a decree allowing foreigners to serve in the Russian army, including in wartime, "in accordance with admitted principles and norms of international law" (Grasmeder 2020: 4).

All these peculiarities create a distinct relationship between the state and these combatants, even though they are uniformed members of the regular armed forces, and justify the inclusion of "legionnaire" as a separate category in our typology of proxies as actors in the grey zone and indeed the conventional battlefield of the twenty-first century.

Bibliography

Arielli, N. and K. Karvinen (2022), "Fighting for Ukraine: The Role Foreign Volunteers can Play in Wartime", *The Concersation*, 8. March. Available online: https://theconversation.com/fighting-for-ukraine-the-role-foreign-volunteers-can-play-in-wartime-178685 (accessed 11 October 2022).

Belov, E. (2022), "Chechency—jeto ljudi, kotorye za nas'. Predstavitel' prezidenta Ukrainy—o dobrovol'cah i jekstradicijah', *Kavkazr*, 20 April. Available online: https://www.kavkazr.com/a/chechentsy-eto-lyudi-kotorye-za-nas-predstavitelj-prezidenta-ukrainy-o-dobrovoljtsah-i-ekstraditsiyah-/31812827.html (accessed 10.10.2022).

Blatchford, A. (2022), "Band of Others: Ukraine's Legions of Foreign Soldiers are on the Fontline", *Politico*, 24 March. Available online: https://www.politico.com/news/2022/03/24/ukraine-legion-foreign-soldiers-00020233 (accessed 12 September 2022).

Bowen, A. S. (2022), *Ukrainian Armed Forces*, Washington: Congressional Research Service.

Budjeryn, M. (1996), "Was Ukraine's Nuclear Disarmament a Blunder?", *World Affairs*, 179 (2): 9–20. https://doi.org/10.1177/0043820016673777.

Clark M., G. Barros and K. Stepanenko (2022), "Russia-Ukraine Warning Update: Initial Russian Offensive Campaign Assessment", *Institute for the Study of War*, 24 February. Available online: https://www.understandingwar.org/backgrounder/russia-ukraine-warning-update-initial-russian-offensive-campaign-assessment (accessed 10 October 2022).

FightForUA (2022), "FAQ," Fight for Ukraine. Available online: https://fightforua.org/ (accessed 10 October 2022).

Global Security Website (2022), "Volunteers", *Global Security Website*. Available online: https://www.globalsecurity.org/military/world/ukraine/volunteers.htm (accessed 10 October 2022).

Google Trends (2022), "Foreign Legion Ukraine". Available online: https://trends.google.com/trends/explore?q=foreign%20legion%20ukraine (accessed 11 October 2022).

Grasmeder, E. (2020), "Brothers in Arms: Foreign Legions, National Armies, and Reexamining Citizenship and Military Service", PhD diss., George Washington University, Washington DC.

Grasmeder, E. M. (2021), "Leaning on Legionnaires: Why Modern States Recruit Foreign Soldiers", *International Security*, 46 (1): 147–195. https://doi.org/10.1162/isec_a_00411.

Habtom, N. K.-T. (2022), "The Composition and Challenges of Foreign Fighters in Ukraine", *Scandinavian Journal of Military Studies*, 5 (1): 79–90. http://doi.org/10.31374/sjms.151.

Hauer, N. (2022). "The Georgian Fighters Stiffening Ukraine's Defences against Possible Russian Attack", *National Post*, 16 February. Available online: https://nationalpost.com/news/world/the-georgian-fighters-stiffening-ukraines-defences-against-russia (accessed 10 October 2022).

Käihkö, I, (2018), "A Nation-in-the-Making, in Arms: Control of Force, Strategy and the Ukrainian Volunteer Battalions", *Defence Studies*, 18 (2): 147–166. https://doi.org/10.1080/14702436.2018.1461013.

Käihkö, I. (2022), "The War between People in Ukraine", *War on the Rocks Website*, 21 March. Available online: https://warontherocks.com/2018/03/the-war-between-people-in-ukraine/ (accessed 11 October 2022).

Kofman, K, K. Migacheva, B. Nichiporuk, A. Radin, O. Tkacheva, and J. Oberholtzer (2017), *Lessons from Russia's Operations in Crimea and Eastern Ukraine*, Santa Monica: RAND Cooperation.

Miller, C. (2022), "NATO Won't Put Troops in Ukraine, but Western Foreigners are Volunteering to Join the Fight against Russia". Available online: https://www.buzzfeednews.com/article/christopherm51/russia-invade-ukraine-western-fighters-nato (accessed 26 April 2022).

Murauskaite, E. (2022), "Foreign Fighters in Ukraine: What Concerns Should Really Be on the Agenda?", *Russiamatters.org,* 18 August. Available online: https://www.russiamatters.org/analysis/foreign-fighters-ukraine-what-concerns-should-really-be-agenda (accessed 11 October 2022).

Musaeva, S. and Y. Buderatskyi (2020), "Mamuka Mamulashvili, Commander of the Georgian Legion: Ukraine is the Only Country to Take on the Challenge of the Barbaric Terrorist State that is Russia", *Ukrainska Pravda,* 10 July. Available online: https://www.pravda.com.ua/eng/articles/2022/07/10/7357256/ (accessed 12 September 2022).

President of Ukraine (2022), *Decree of the President of Ukraine of 24.02.2022 No 64/2022 On the imposition of martial law in Ukraine.* Available online: https://www.president.gov.ua/documents/642022-41397 (accessed 10 October 2022).

Rauta, V. (2019), "Towards a Typology of Non-state Actors in 'Hybrid Warfare': Proxy, Auxiliary, Surrogate and Affiliated Forces", *Cambridge Review of International Affairs,* 33 (6): 868–887. https://doi.org/10.1080/09557571.2019.1656600.

Shamsian, J. (2022), "A Georgian Commander Fighting Russian Forces in Ukraine Says More International Support Will Help Defeat Putin", *Business Insider Website,* 7 March. Available online: https://www.businessinsider.com/georgian-legion-commander-ukraine-army-russia-war-mamuka-mamulashvili-2022-3 (accessed 26 April 2022).

Shoaib, A. (2022), "President Zelensky Appeals for Foreign Volunteers to Come to Ukraine and Enlist in a Newly-formed 'International Legion' to Fight the Russian Invasion", *Business Insider,* 27 February. Available online: https://www.businessinsider.com/ukraine-international-legion-foreigners-join-fight-2022-2 (accessed 10 October 2022).

Soufan Center (2019), *White Supremacy Extremism: The Transnational Rise of the Violent White Supremacist Movement,* The Soufan Center.

The Moscow Times (2022), "Switching Sides: The Elusive 'Russian Legion' Fighting With Ukraine", 8. August, Available online: https://www.themoscowtimes.com/2022/08/08/switching-sides-the-elusive-russian-legion-fighting-with-ukraine-a78459 (accessed 11 October 2022).

UAWIRE (2022), "'Georgian Legion' Leaves Ukrainian Armed Forces", *UAWIRE,* 6 January. Available online: https://uawire.org/georgian-legion-left-the-ukrainian-armed-forces (accessed 9 September 2022).

UCMC (2015), "Volunteer battalions in the East of Ukraine: who are they?", *Ukraine Crisis Media Center,* 16 March. Available online: https://uacrisis.org/en/20026-volunteer-battalions-eastern-ukraine (accessed 12 October 2022).

UNIAN (2018), "British Conflict Medic Joins Ukrainian Forces in Donbas", UNIAN Information Agency, 10 April. Available online: https://www.unian.info/

war/10099904-british-conflict-medic-joins-ukrainian-forces-in-donbas.html (accessed 10 September 2022).

VVR (2015), "About the Legal Status of Foreigners and Stateless Persons", Art.4, p. 20, Information of the Verkhovna Rada of Ukraine. Available online: https://zakon.rada.gov.ua/laws/show/3773-17 (accessed 12 September 2022).

Zitser, J. (2022), "A Nightclub Worker, a Boxer, and a Pizza-Maker are among the Stream of Volunteers Arriving at Ukraine's Embassy in London to Sign up for Zelensky's International Legion", 4 March. Available online: https://www.businessinsider.com/ukraine-the-uk-volunteers-joining-zelenskys-international-legion-2022-3 (accessed 26 April 2022).

6

Insurgencies in Africa and the Middle East and the Future of the Proxy Warfare in the Region

Jeffrey Kaplan

Mercenaries are useless, disunited, unfaithful
They have nothing more to keep them in a battle
Other than a meager wage
Which is just about enough to make them wanna kill for you
But not enough to make them wanna die for ya

John Cale, "Mercenaries (Ready for War)"

Introduction

Proxy warfare is as old as the history of warfare itself. Roman legions depended on proxy forces to control their vast empire. The Ummayad and Abbasid empires, through a constant pattern of shifting alliances, leveraged tribal forces to conquer and control vast empires with quite small and limited standing armies. The British Raj utilized proxies in India and East Africa. More recently, corporate entities like the American Blackwater and the Russian Wagner Group offer mercenary fighters for rent. Gone are the days when wannabe mercenaries could peruse the ads in publications like *Soldier of Fortune* magazine to sign on to conflicts in such remote regions as Angola, Mozambique, or Rhodesia (Lamy 1992).

As the articles in this volume demonstrate, the historical patterns of proxy warfare still exist but much too has changed. The twenty-first century is a far more complex stage, and the role of multiple audiences, mass media, social media, and increasingly multipolarity with the decline of the post-Cold War West and the humiliation of Russian forces in theaters from Afghanistan in the 1990s to Ukraine today diminishes the threat of Russian global or even regional power projection. China, for its part, prefers economic to military imperialism, flexing its security muscle only in its immediate proximity.

This paper will, therefore, briefly examine current uses of proxy forces in Africa and the Middle East as a clue to what the future of proxy warfare portends.

Insurgency

Following Daniel L. Byman (2018) and James K. Wither (Chapter twelve in this volume), insurgency comes in two basic forms; alliances made openly between allies and proxy relationships where a state overtly or covertly aids an insurgent group. For our purposes, both forms of insurgency fall into our discussion. Whether through overt alliance relationships or by covert support, proxy groups engage in warfare that states deem to be in their interest.

The literature on insurgency is voluminous (Rich and Duyvesteyn 2012) and has been since the 1960s and the appearance of Ted Gurr's classic text *Why Men Rebel* (1970). In the Cold War, insurgency was the dominant form of proxy warfare. Perceived nuclear parity mandated that western and Soviet forces avoided direct engagement at all costs. As a result, both the US and the Soviet Union waged war through local proxies, largely small militias which operated in the rural areas and were beyond the capacity of weak states to effectively counter or control.

Proxy warfare in the Cold War was primarily ideologically driven. Local grievances were therefore interpreted through the lens of great power competition and used socialist or democratic rhetoric to both attract the support of a foreign sponsor and to position themselves as an alternative to the governing regime. Soviet supported insurgencies in Latin America and the Caribbean challenged and engaged American forces throughout the 1960s and 1970s and, with the triumph of Fidel Castro in 1959, provided a beachhead that effectively projected Soviet influence in the region (Rosenberg et al. 2010; Brands 2012). In the case of Cuba, the failure of the 1961 Bay of Pigs invasion to inspire a counterinsurgency to overthrow the Castro regime paved the way for the 1962 Cuban Missile Crisis that for a moment appeared to be the trigger for a nuclear exchange (Kornbluh 1998; Kennedy 2011). In the process, a generation of counterculture heroes, from Che Guevera to the Sandinistas, emerged to inspire leftists throughout the world.

The United States countered by supporting insurgencies at the peripheries of Soviet influence, particularly in Africa. These however did not trouble the Soviets greatly. It was not until the Soviet invasion of Afghanistan that American support of local insurgencies was telling. These, however, were tribal and religious in nature, despite the illusion in Washington that the Northern Alliance led by Ahmad Shah Massoud were rough hewn proto democrats.

There remained a few outliers such as the Maoist insurgency in Nepal or, until its most timely demise, Sendero Luminoso (the Shining Path) in Peru. But ironically, Maoist insurgencies in the post-Mao era have largely lost their proxy status. State sponsors are hard to come by for such archaic ideologies, so their struggles were both local and localistic.

Today, ideologically inspired insurgencies are largely a thing of the past. Ideology, communist, democratic or anarchist, no longer lights a fire in the hearts of men. They will surely not play a significant role in proxy warfare in the foreseeable future.

Yet, as many of the chapters in this volume attest, insurgency supported through proxy warfare is far from extinct. Where Cold War insurgencies fought by proxy the ideological struggles of East and West, insurgencies today are more complex and far more intractable. Insurgencies based on ethnicity and tribe predominate in Africa and the Middle East, as do insurgencies based on religious faith or sectarian identification. For these, state sponsors are to be found. But unlike the Cold War era, these sponsors tend to be regional and the interests they espouse are of confessional and largely regional import.

Several of the articles in this volume deal well with African insurgency in Mali and the Central African Republic. Even in the Cold War, these insurgencies were primarily tribal in nature. They could be trained and equipped by the superpowers directly or, more often, indirectly through regional surrogates. Libya became the conduit for Soviet weapons and influence in the Cold War years, impacting conflicts throughout Sub-Saharan Africa. Although this aid was seldom decisive, it did have an impact. Over time, Libyan aid also became more sophisticated as assistance could be withheld from one rebel faction in favor of another should a proxy force become recalcitrant in its support of Libyan or Soviet wishes (Tamm 2006).

The fall of Gadhafi in 2011 put paid to most of this remote assistance, which had lost much of its Russian patronage in the post-Cold War era in any case. However, in a crowning irony, new forms of proxy warfare found a fertile testing ground in the Libyan Civil War that followed. In what has aptly been dubbed "coalition proxy warfare", a number of states have backed factions in the conflict, most notably Russia which supports the Libyan National Army (LNA) while Turkey backs the Government of National Accord (GNA). The United Arab

Emirates and Saudi Arabia have also taken a hand with the introduction of Syrian and Sudanese mercenaries (Wither 2020: 17).

On the western side, while the United States in the Cold War era often took a direct hand in training and supplying proxy forces, Israeli military and intelligence operators were often thick on the ground. This sometimes did not go well, as in the Israeli support of the coup that brought Idi Amin to power in 1971 (Schmidt 2013: 32). One of the most visible Israeli actions was in the Horn of Africa with the first outbreak of the Eritrean wars of secession from Ethiopia. Acting together with American troops, Israelis acted in a counterinsurgency role against the Eritrean Liberation Movement (Schwab 1978: 17). Ethiopian support for the Anya Naya rebellion among the Nilotic tribes, most notably the Dinka, in southern Sudan led to extensive Israeli support for the rebels in the Sudanese conflict that went on for almost two decades (Aalen 2014).

However, as Wither and others point out, African insurgency has become more complex (Mumford 2013; Krieg and Rickli 2018). What was once a game for two, the United States and the Soviet Union and their respective allies has become complex, and much more deadly. Tribalism has become more pronounced and in many cases such as Rwanda, Darfur and Uganda, frankly genocidal (Kaplan 2010). The intensity of the violence however has not deterred regional and local sponsors from establishing proxy relationships, although these are far more short-lived then their Cold War predecessors.

The Middle East follows some of the African patterns. Certainly, tribalism is present and in some conflicts important. But here, ethnicity and religious identification is the dominant factor. Iran has emerged as a primary sponsor of proxy warfare, including insurgency. In this, Iran has become something of a global actor whose activity has expanded from the Middle East to Africa and South Asia (Jahanbani 2020). The Iranian case is fascinating and will be a central focus of this brief review.

Iran is the only Shi'ite state in the world, although in the so-called "Shi'ite Triangle" (Iran, southern Iraq, and southern Lebanon), there is a clear Shi'ite majority in Iraq and very likely a Shi'ite plurality, if not an outright majority, in Lebanon as well (Louër 2021). In the Cold War, Iran was a staunch US ally. Until the Iranian Revolution in 1979, the United States relied on a security alliance between Iran and Saudi Arabia as the basis of Gulf security (Chubin 1992: 63–4). That ended in 1979 and for a brief moment, Iran became in the words of Claire Sterling "terror central" as both Sunni and Shi'a Islamists flocked to Tehran and came away with promises of support and training (Sterling 1981). It didn't last long, and soon Iran reverted to its sectarian Shi'ite roots, and support for Sunni groups slowly faded away (although in the twenty-first century, Iranian support has become less sectarian and more pragmatic). Indeed, Saudi Arabia soon became an implacable foe as, with Iranian support, a Shi'ite uprising in Eastern Province, centered in Qatif, was put down with great violence (Matthiesen 2014; Hegghammer 2010; Keynoush 2016). Today, Iranian support for the Houthi uprising in Yemen has inflicted considerable damage on the Saudis.

Today, Iran is involved in one form or another in numerous insurgencies in the Middle East, Africa, and South Asia. As these proxy relationships developed, Shi'ism was the linking factor, but soon sectarian relationships gave way to a wider array of state interests as Sunni groups too benefitted from Iran's largess. One lesser-known example is the Iranian involvement in the Iranian support of the predominantly Sunni Baluchi insurgency in Pakistan (Taheri 2012; Rehman 2014), though Iranian involvement is far wider than this. Best known is Iranian involvement in the Houthi conflict in Yemen and in the multiparty scrum in Syria. Yemen and Syria will therefore be the focus of this discussion.

In the area of insurgency, Iran is an interesting model in that it is a state that acts directly, often through the Revolutionary Guards (Iranian Islamic Revolutionary Guards Corps or IRGC), but rarely alone. The Lebanese Hezbollah, often seen as an Iranian proxy, has developed a military force that probably eclipses that of the Lebanese state, is a regular presence fighting in coordination with the ICRG. This chapter would argue, however, that Hezbollah is much more of an Iranian ally than a proxy, and acts most effectively as a force multiplier rather than as either support or stand in. Moreover, this is no recent development but can be traced to the quality of the leadership of the group when it first emerged in the wake of the Israeli incursion into Lebanon in 1982.

At the time, the Lebanese Shi'a were centered in southern Lebanon, which made them contiguous with the border with Israel and in south Beirut. Shi'a saw themselves, with considerable justification, as "the deprived"; the underdogs versus the Sunni and Maronite Christian overdogs to borrow an oft-used term in Islamist discourse. At the time, it was only natural that the Lebanese Shi'a would identify with the other underdog of the Arab world, the Palestinians, and thus was formed the "natural alliance" between the two. This allowed PLO fighters to take positions near the Israeli border, fire Katyusha rockets into northern Israel, and in an equally oft-told description, "run like hell", leaving the Shi'ite villages in the South to bear the incredibly destructive brunt of Israeli air raids launched in reprisal (Norton 2007b; Gabriel 1984).

The Shi'a of southern Lebanon in the 1960s and 1970s were primarily governed by traditional tribal elites who kept them in a position of virtual serfdom on the land. By the 1960s, poverty and the increasing violence along the Israeli border forced a massive urban migration where Shi'ite rural migrants flooded into the southern suburbs of Beirut, bringing their poverty with them and finding few jobs or means of feeding their families. The role was filled again by wealthy Shi'a who created dependencies not unlike the migrants had known in the south.

It was at that point that Imam Musa al-Sadr, himself a scion of the powerful clerical family with roots in Iraq and Iran, entered the country in 1959 and over the course of the next half decade slowly built a new, independent movement that uncannily resembled the kind of civil rights movement emerging in the United States which he dubbed Amal (Hope). Amal was remarkably successful, for the first time not only offering Lebanese Shi'ites an alternative to their traditional leaders, but actually challenging those elites for dominance in the Shi'ite community. Unfortunately, the escalating violence between Palestinians and Israel in southern Lebanon left little space for a civil rights movement, and with Operation Litani, a full-scale Israeli military incursion into southern Lebanon in 1978, Amal took the step of creating its own militia, becoming one of the many militias that by 1982, again in the wake of an Israeli invasion, would fall on each other in the Lebanese Civil War (Siklawi 2012). Imam Musa, however would not live to see the Civil War. He and two of his companions disappeared from the baggage area of the Tripoli airport in 1978, never to be seen again. Posthumously many saw Imam Musa, the vanished Imam, in the eschatological terms of Twelver Shi'ism, refusing to believe he was dead but instead waiting in occultation for the Last Days (Ajami 1986).

The loss of Imam Musa left a vacuum in Lebanese Shi'ite politics which had to be filled. The success of the Iranian Revolution and the radicalization within the Shi'ite community which, under the tutelage of the PLO had taken root in the 1960s, combined to offer fertile ground for the Iranian Revolutionary Guards and for the teachings of Imams such as Sheikh, later to become Grand Ayatollah Muhammad Hussein Fadlallah, whose book *Islam and the Logic of Force* would inspire a generation of young Lebanese Shi'ites (Miller 1994; Browers 2012).

Hezbollah emerged publicly in the wake of the Israeli invasion of 1982, although its roots are better traced to the influence of Iran and the Islamic Revolution in 1979 (Norton 2007a). Although its foundational document stated that its primary aim was the liberation of al-Quds (Jerusalem), it was clearly aligned with Iran and the Shi'a ulema (scholars of religion) who followed Imam Khomeini and the Revolution. Its history is fascinating and, with the Egyptian Ikkwan (Muslim Brotherhood) provides a model for emulation for

Islamic groups around the world, although few if any have the capacity to follow the path.

For our purposes, however, we need only note two factors that even in its early days kept it from being entirely an Iranian proxy. First, it was careful not to become dependent solely on Iranian funding, training or weapons. Rather, it balanced Iranian support with that of Hafez al-Assad in Syria. By skillfully playing Iran against Syria, it was able to carve out a position of relative independence (Ali 2019).

Second and in the long run more important, Hezbollah was not conceived as merely a terrorist group. Initially, it had to overcome the challenge for dominance among Lebanese Shi'ites with Amal, making it first and foremost a political faction. Borrowing the model of the Ikkwan, it tempered its revolutionary rhetoric with a social outreach that provided medical clinics, schools, and support in rebuilding homes leveled by the Israeli invasion. Hezbollah's bombing of the US Embassy in Beirut and the death of almost 200 marines branded it a terrorist group forever in the eyes of the West, while American intelligence, which had been provided by the group with a video of its torture and murder of CIA Station Chief William Francis Buckley in 1985 brought a series of reprisal killings by the agency (Hastedt 1988; Levitt 2015).

For the West Hezbollah was a terrorist group and nothing more. It was a terrorist group, but it was also much more. In the next decade, it developed into a powerful political party that carefully played by democratic rules. It became a media empire and a social welfare agency that successfully filled the gaps that the massive failures of the Lebanese state could not. And it developed conventional armed forces that not only dwarfed that of the Lebanese state but was credited by the Israeli military itself with having defeated Israel in its 2006 invasion of southern Lebanon (Kalb and Saivetz 2007). Hezbollah is now truly a state within a state in Lebanon, and an ally rather than a proxy in Iran's insurgent conflicts throughout the region (Javed 2022).

The extent of Iran's involvement in Syria with Hezbollah at its side is well illustrated by the research of Nakissa Jahanbani (2020: 42):

Turning to Syria, Iran's proxy network extended into the country prior to the civil war. Just before the conflict's outbreak, Tehran launched a multi-pronged foreign policy to assist the Assad regime, such as sending in IRGC and Iranian army forces in an advisory capacity to train the Syrian military and transport supplies from Tehran. Another pillar included raising new and bolstering existing militias and other non-state violent organizations in the country. Toward the latter, Ariane Tabatabai wrote in this publication that the Fatemiyoun

Brigade, for example, was established under the guidance of the IRGC-QF in 2012 and was intended to serve as an affordable means of Iranian support to the Assad regime: "fighters would be paid a few hundred dollars per month and promised residency rights to essentially serve as cannon fodder for Iran's efforts in Syria."

In Syria, in addition to raising militias, Iran also directed Lebanese Hezbollah's (LH) and proxies' fighters from Lebanon and Iraq, respectively. In 2012, both LH and Iraqi proxies began moving forces into Syria. Those from Iraq included Iranian-backed militias within the Hashd al-Shaabi, such as Asa'ib Ahl al-Haq and Harakat al-Nujaba. In addition to forming militias, Iran also worked with existing militias in Syria, such as Al-Ghaliboun, among several others. LH was also pivotal in training pro-regime militias and establishing several Iranian-supported militias in Syria, for example Quwat al-Ridha, one of the groups that is now part of the Syrian Hezbollah groups. The salary incentives and recruitment strategies used for the Fatemiyoun Brigade were also employed for other proxies operating in Syria, such as the Zeinabiyoun Brigade o and Kata'ib Aimmah al-Baqiyah (a Syrian Shi'a Iranian-backed militia). The IRGC-QF also incentivized recruitment for other Syrian proxies, paying directly from its coffers or through Iraqi proxy intermediaries.

And beyond Syria, Iran and Hezbollah are involved in insurgencies in Africa and South Asia but have been most effective in their support of Ansar Allah and the Houthi insurgency in Yemen. The Houthis, with Iranian arms and the support of the IRGC Hezbollah's fighters, have not only staved off the ill-considered Saudi incursion but with Iranian missiles have been able to threaten Riyadh and other Saudi cities. They have made occasional attacks on Abu Dhabi as well in this fashion.

In writing of the Houthi uprising, Michael Knights notes that, like its other forays into foreign insurgencies, Iran and Hezbollah, in stark contrast to many Cold War models, play support roles and do not seek to direct or control the factions they support (2018: 22):

Iran does not appear to control the Houthi leadership, but it did ramp up its support to the Houthis at precisely the moment that their ambitions broadened not only to control northern Yemen but also to build defensive bulwarks far outside the traditional Zaydi heartland. The Houthis could arguably have taken northern Yemen without Iran's help, and there are indications Tehran warned against this step. But Iran has provided critical aid in allowing the Houthis to slow down the Gulf-backed Yemeni government recapture of terrain. The relationship between Iran and the Houthis could remain transactional or it could deepen. Iran, Lebanese Hezbollah, and Ansar Allah share a strikingly similar worldview opposing the United States, Israel, and Saudi Arabia, as underlined by the Houthi slogan: "Death to America, Death to Israel, Curse upon the Jews, Victory to Islam." Hardliner military commanders within the Houthi movement such as Abdullah Eida al-Razzami and Abdullah al-Hakim (Abu Ali) may be more susceptible to IRGC influence than other parts of the Houthi hierarchy, and this wing of the movement could be strengthened over time, particularly if the current war continues. As one expert on Yemen told the author, "some Houthi leaders think the Saudis want to exterminate them down to the last man, woman and child, and they want to continue the war to Makkah" (in Saudi Arabia). Though it clearly lacks the capacity to take such 0ffensive action, Ansar Allah is more than capable of becoming a "southern Hezbollah" on the Red Sea, flanking Saudi Arabia and Israel from the south, a factor that continues to drive the Gulf coalition's efforts to deprive the Houthis of a coast through which to draw on Iranian and Hezbollah assistance in the future.

Conclusions

The Cold War world was a simpler place, and insurgencies were supported by one or both sides on the peripheries of the global chess board. Today as we have seen, life and proxy support for insurgencies are far more complex.

Looking to the future, this complexity has only deepened, and forces that once served as great power proxies have taken on a more central role. Certainly, the greatest changes are on the Russian side. The Russian defeat in Afghanistan did much to tip the Soviet Union, already teetering on the brink economically and politically, over into the abyss. Never one not to double down on failure or to learn the lessons of their mistakes, Russia, ill-prepared, poorly led, and following a set of preconceived perceptions that beggar the imagination, embarked on a campaign of conquest in Ukraine that dwarfs in scale the disaster in Afghanistan.

As a result, Russian supplies of arms and influence can only diminish. Worse, as of this writing, Russian forces are forced into retreat from areas of the Ukraine that they had only months before claimed, with great fanfare to annex, Russia is forced to import weapons and equipment from such former proxies as Iran (Iran International 2022; Hernández 2022). While it would be chimeric to believe that this will dry up the supplies of arms and materiel to insurgent groups in Africa and the Middle East, it can be expected to greatly increase the influence of states once seen as great power proxies in those theaters.

In the zero-sum calculations of the Cold War, this loss for Russia would be seen as a net gain for the United States and the West, but this, too is illusory. The COVID pandemic absorbed considerable resources in western states, making support for foreign conflicts less saleable. However, this will pale in comparison to another effect of the Ukraine war. Western support for Ukraine and European dependence on Russian energy is a contradiction that leaves Europe facing a winter of steeply rising energy prices that will force governments to offer energy support to their own citizens. The massive economic impact of the closing off of Russian oil and natural gas will leave far less room for the support of distant insurgent conflicts. Rather, the west has so far held fast to its military and political support for Ukraine. How long this will last in the face of winter cold is debatable, but as of this writing, the consensus holds.

With the decline of great power support, it is conceivable, but unlikely, that the many insurgent conflicts around the world will decline. But just as the end of the Cold War did not quell local and regional conflicts, in all likelihood, they will continue, but with the greater dependence on regional powers such as Iran, Saudi Arabia, and increasingly the UAE.

Bibliography

Aalen, L. (2014), "Ethiopian State Support to Insurgency in Southern Sudan from 1962 to 1983: Local, Regional and Global Connections," *Journal of Eastern African Studies*, 8 (4): 626–41.

Ajami, F. (1986). *The Vanished Imam: Musa Al Sadr and the Shia of Lebanon*. Ithaca, NY: Cornell University Press.

Ali, M. H. (2019), "Power Points Defining the Syria-Hezbollah Relationship", *Carnegie Endowment for International Peace*, 2019.

Brands, H. (212), *Latin America's Cold War*. Cambridge: Harvard University Press.

Browers, M. (2012), "Fadlallah and the Passing of Lebanon's Last Najafi Generation", *Journal of Shi'a Islamic Studies*, 5 (1): 25–46. https://doi.org/10.1353/isl.2012.0022.

Byman, D. L. (2018), "Why Engage in Proxy War? A State's Perspective", *Brookings*, 21 May. Available online: https://www.brookings.edu/blog/order-from-chaos/2018/05/21/why-engage-in-proxy-war-a-states-perspective/ (accessed 22 December 2022).

Chubin, S. (1992), "Iran and Regional Security in the Persian Gulf", *Survival*, 34 (3): 62–80.

Gabriel, R. A. (1984), *Operation Peace for Galilee: The Israeli-Plo War in Lebanon*, New York: Hill and Wang.

Gurr, T. R. (1970), *Why Men Rebel*. Princeton, N.J.: Princeton University Press.

Hastedt, G. (1988), "Intelligence Failure and Terrorism: The Attack on the Marines in Beirut", *Journal of Conflict Studies*, 8 (2): 7–22.

Hegghammer, T. (2010), *Jihad in Saudi Arabia: Violence and Pan-Islamism since 1979*, Cambridge: Cambridge University Press.

Hernández, G. R. (2022), "Iran Supplies Arms to Russia", *Arms Control Association*, November. Available online: https://www.armscontrol.org/act/2022-11/news/iran-supplies-arms-russia (accessed 22 December 2022).

Iran International (2022), "Iran Supplying Russia With More Weapons For Ukraine War", 2 November. Available online: https://www.iranintl.com/en/202211025274 (accessed 22 December 2022).

Jahanbani, N. (2020), "Reviewing Iran's Proxies by Region: A Look toward the Middle East, South Asia, and Africa", *CTC Sentinel*, 13 (5): 39–48.

Javed, M. (2022), "Hezbollah a State within a State: An Overview", *International Journal of Research Publication and Reviews*, 2582: 169–77.

Kalb, M. and C. Saivetz (2007), "The Israeli—Hezbollah War of 2006: The Media as a Weapon in Asymmetrical Conflict", *Harvard International Journal of Press/Politics*, 12 (3): 43–66.

Kaplan, J. (2010), *Terrorist Groups and the New Tribalism: Terrorism's Fifth Wave*, London: Routledge.

Kennedy, R. F. (2011), *Thirteen Days: A Memoir of the Cuban Missile Crisis*, New York: WW Norton & Company.

Keynoush, B. (2016), *Saudi Arabia and Iran: Friends or Foes?*, New York: Palgrave Macmillan.

Knights, M. (2018), "The Houthi War Machine: From Guerrilla War to State Capture", *CTC Sentinel*, 11 (8): 15–23.

Kornbluh, P. (1998), *Bay of Pigs Declassified: The Secret Cia Report*, New York: New Press.

Krieg, A. and J.-M. Rickli (2018), "Surrogate Warfare: The Art of War in the 21st Century?, *Defence Studies*, 18 (2): 113–30. https://doi.org/10.1080/14702436.2018.14 29218

Lamy, P. (1992), "Millennialism in the Mass Media: The Case of 'Soldier of Fortune' Magazine", *Journal for the Scientific Study of Religion*, 31 (4): 408–24.

Levitt, M. (2015), "Why the Cia Killed Imad Mughniyeh", *Politico Magazine*, 9 February. Available online: https://www.politico.com/magazine/story/2015/02/mughniyeh-assassination-cia-115049/ (accessed 22 December 2022).

Louër, L. (2021), *Shiism and Politics in the Middle East*, Oxford: Oxford University Press.

Matthiesen, T. (2014), *The Other Saudis: Shiism, Dissent and Sectarianism*, Cambridge: Cambridge University Press.

Miller, J. (1994), "Faces of Fundamentalism: Hassan Al-Turabi and Muhammed Fadlallah", *Foreign Affairs*, 73: 123–42.

Mumford, A. (2013), "Proxy Warfare and the Future of Conflict", *The RUSI Journal*, 158 (2): 40–6. https://doi.org/10.1080/03071847.2013.787733.

Norton, A. R. (2007a), *Hezbollah: A Short History*, Princeton: Princeton University Press.

Norton, A. R. (2007b), "The Role of Hezbollah in Lebanese Domestic Politics", *The International Spectator*, 42 (4): 475–91.

Rehman, Z. U. (2014), "The Baluch Insurgency: Linking Iran to Pakistan", *NOREF Report*, May.

Rich, P. B. and I. Duyvesteyn (2012), *The Routledge Handbook of Insurgency and Counterinsurgency*, London: Routledge.

Rosenberg, E. S., F. Katz and J. Olcott (2010), *A Century of Revolution: Insurgent and Counterinsurgent Violence During Latin America's Long Cold War*, Durham, NC: Duke University Press.

Schmidt, E. (2013), *Foreign Intervention in Africa: From the Cold War to the War on Terror*, Cambridge: Cambridge University Press.

Schwab, P. (1978), "Cold War on the Horn of Africa", *African Affairs*, 77 (306): 6–20.

Siklawi, R. (2012), "The Dynamics of the Amal Movement in Lebanon 1975–90", *Arab Studies Quarterly*, 34 (1): 4–26.

Sterling, C. (1981), *The Terror Network: The Secret War of International Terrorism*, New York: Holt, Rinehart, and Winston.

Taheri, A. (2012), "Baloch Insurgency and Challenges to the Islamic Republic of Iran", *Society for the Study of Peace and Conflict*.

Tamm, H. (2016), "Rebel Leaders, Internal Rivals, and External Resources: How State Sponsors Affect Insurgent Cohesion", *International Studies Quarterly*, 60 (4): 599–610.

Wither, J. K. (2020), "Outsourcing Warfare: Proxy Forces in Contemporary Armed Conflicts", *Security and Defence Quarterly*, 31 (4): 17–34. https://doi.org/10.35467/sdq/127928.

7

Proxy Warfare in Mali: New Rendition of *Divide et Impera* and Cautious French Saviorism

Cyprian Aleksander Kozera

Proxy Actors' Definitional Conundrum

Proxy warfare related terms are oftentimes used differently by various actors and that may cause some confusion. For this reason and for the need of our narration, let us split proxy actors of the agent side of principal-agent (or patron-client) equation into four categories based upon such a previous attempt by Vladimir Rauta (2019). Let us follow his categorization in slightly simplified terms and thus as actors of proxy warfare, besides principal (patron) distinguish: auxiliaries, affiliated agents, surrogate agents, and proxies per se. These actors can be characterized as originally external or internal to the conflict environment. The external proxy agents being auxiliaries and proxies per se, while the internal are affiliates and surrogates. Secondly, these agents differ in their principal's (patron's) involvement. If the patron is not embedded in the conflict zone—they are either proxy agents per se or surrogate agents. If the patron is embedded in the conflict environment (through its very geographical location or deployment of armed forces): these are auxiliaries or affiliated agents.

Consequently, a proxy agent per se is an agent originally external to the conflict environment introduced to the conflict environment by a patron that remains external and is involved only indirectly—by such a proxy.

The auxiliary agent is also originally external to the conflict environment yet is incorporated there alongside its patron, who is involved directly as well. The affiliated agent is originally internal to the conflict and works for the patron, who is likewise directly involved.

The surrogate agent, while being internal to the conflict, acts on behalf of the external patron, who thus remains not involved directly. This classification of proxy actors will be further use in this chapter.

The Socio-Ethnic Context and Different Approaches to the Employment of Proxy Forces in the Malian Theater

Understanding the proxy use by state patrons in Mali requires us to devote a few words to the ethnic and historical context of conflicts, that arguably spans for centuries, between various ethnic groups inhabiting the territory of the present day Mali, the colonial indirect administration system, and the post-colonial governance model preferred by the Bamako elites.

It is widely believed that the Niger river belt divides the "white" (the Arab and Tuareg) north from the "black" south of Mali. This simplification, however, overlooks intraregional, inter- and intra-ethnic diversity and dynamics. Namely, northern regions are inhabited not only by the Tuareg and Arabs (both pastoralist and nomadic communities) but primarily by the black and sedentary Songhai people (45 percent of the northern population) and other Sub-Saharan peoples (e.g., the Fulani, also called Fula, Fulbe or Peul). Northern communities are highly internally diversified (where "white" or "black" do not necessarily refer to the skin color but to status), segmented (into traditionally noble, free, and servile status), and in state of constant competition over power (e.g., the Imghad Tuareg vs the Ifogha Tuareg) and resources (access to grazing lands that sedentary communities use as farming fields, what causes tensions, especially in times of droughts; Harmon 2014: 4–9). Occasionally, some Tuareg groups revolt against the central government due to lack of economic development (north of Mali being among the poorest and least developed regions in Africa), institutional negligence, and their perceived marginalization (Pezard and Shurkin 2013: 6). At the same time, however, race-based clichés have been used by various narrations and propaganda aiming at creating animosity between the peoples from the south and the north. President Moussa Traoré's propaganda unleashed against the Tuareg specifically, in the 1990s, tagged them as "white-dominated feudal society" responsible for centuries of enslavement of the black people from the south (Wing 2008: 160). Yet outside of governmental propaganda, reality remains far more nuanced. This complexity has been efficiently exploited by Bamako elites in times when the Malian state lacked the physical and institutional capacity to impose its superiority over the north.

The complexity of the traditional socio-political structures is well exemplified by the Tuareg society, a basic understanding of which is vital to the arguments presented. The Tuareg are divided into confederations of clans. Such a confederation consists of traditionally noble and commoner clans (i.e., formerly vassal). For instance, the people of the Kel Adagh confederation are divided into numerous clans of various traditional social status inside the structure. There are more significant noble clans like Kel Afella (the politically dominant one, from which the chief of Kel Adagh, *amenokal*, comes), Iriyaken, Imezzekarren, etc., collectively known as Ifoghas (sing.: Afaghis), other less important noble clans like e.g. Idnan, and commoner clans such as Imghad (Boilley 1999: 10, 47–48; Pezard and Shurkin 2013: 4). Their place in this socio-political ladder is by no means eternal, and at various occasions, some clans intend to rise their status at the expense of others (cf. Boilley 1999: 59). This intra-ethnic dynamic has been an important tool at hands of the Malian government often acting as a patron towards certain "socially" rebellious groups.

The type and character of proxy forces in the battlespace differ, and so does the approach to their employment by various patrons. Consequently, it leads to multitudinous combinations of patron-client (principal-agent) relationships. In a specific conflict theater, we can observe different and competitive approaches that are rarely repeated in other places or by different actors. The case study of the Malian conflict of 2012–2013 provides us with two distinct and different approaches to the proxy forces management. The first case is that of the Malian government, which predates the conflict, yet continues alongside and evolves with the insurgency. The second one—that of the intervening French forces which rather cautiously, limitedly, and risk-aversely employed local partners to minimize their own exposure to danger and to gain access to local physical and human terrain knowledge.

Despite their common geographical and temporal denomination regarding the use of proxies, these two patrons strongly differed in their relationship with locally "outsourced" actors. For this reason, it is entirely appropriate to consider both cases separately and compare these case studies in the conclusive part of this chapter.

The Malian Government's Use of Proxy Forces: To Rule by Creating Divisions

The year 1960, known as "the year of Africa", brought independence to many African states but few nations. Perhaps the biggest "nation" on the continent left without a sovereign entity was the Tuareg. With the inheritance of colonial administrative divisions and borders by newly independent African states (so-called *uti possidetis* rule), many of the Tuareg were assigned to the newly emerged Mali Federation. Pierre Boilley even called this transformation of power "a substitution of the European colonization by the African colonization" (Boilley 1999: 12). Ancient divisions resurfaced quickly.

The first Tuareg and Arab revolt against the central government in Mali occurred already in 1963 and was brutally, or even arguably genocidally, put down by the Malian armed forces. In the post-independence environment, Bamako possessed (Soviet-provided) technological superiority over under-armed rebels fighting in the traditional way on camels. This superiority, however, worn down over time with—on the one hand—post-independence erosion of Malian army and state institutions due to corruption and mismanagement, and—on the other hand—self-arming of the Tuareg, who also profited from training in the ranks of the Libyan military in 1980s (Stewart 2013: 3–4).

The second rebellion of the 1990s was thus managed differently by the central government with increasing use and the rising role of the governmental proxies. Lacking sufficient resources to effectively combat the insurgents, Bamako convinced a rebelled Ifoghas Tuareg leader, Iyad ag Ghali, to change allegiance and then helped him defeat his rival Tuareg militias, thus weakening the uprising but cementing locally strong position of the Ifoghas Tuareg. Additionally, the Malian army supported Ganda Koy, an ethnic (Songhai-dominated) militia, to target the "white" civilian populations of the Arab and the Tuareg. The conflict scaled down with a coup d'état in Bamako and an Algerian-brokered peace, called Tamanrasset Accord, in 1992, yet in some places continued well into 1996. (Lecocq 2010: 249–307; Pezard and Shurkin 2013: 4, 8–9; Stewart 2013: 34–5).

Interestingly, Iyad ag Ghali is a man of swinging loyalties and of his own particular considerations—in 2006 he joined another Ifoghas-led rebellion. This time, to deal with the new northern insurgency, the government of president Amadou Toumani Touré sent Arab and Tuareg army commanders to the north to transform the revolt against the state into fragmented ethnic and clans-based clashes. A Malian army officer and a Tuareg dispatched for this purpose, Haji ag Gamou, was also a sworn Ifoghas' enemy with a history of inter-clan fighting against the Ifoghas in the previous uprising. The Arab and his clan fighters fought off the Ifoghas, and another peace deal (the Algiers Accords) was signed in 2006. A double ex-rebel and ex-governmental agent, Iyad ag Ghali, was reintegrated into the Malian political class (Pezard and Shurkin 2013: 9; Stewart 2013: 36). Yet to undermine Ifoghas' positions in the region and to ensure that the loyal clans are in the dominant position in the north, in the late 2000s, the Malian leadership handed the control of Kidal smuggling routes over to the traditionally vassal tribe of Imghad (that of ag Gamou) and some pro-government Ifoghas (Lacher 2011: 3). Thus, Bamako exploited its links to organized crime groups and allowed its allies to engage in and profit from illegal activity. By doing so, however, the Malian leadership increased the competition between the armed groups on the ground and "[i]t eventually lost control over the conflicts this generated, while the rule of law and the legitimacy of state institutions were eroded through complicity with organized crime" (Lacher 2012: 11).

The fall of Qaddafi regime in Libya (2011) had a devastating effect on the region and served as a catalyst for another insurgency in northern Mali. Trained, armed and battle-hardened Tuareg who served in the Libyan military came back to northern Mali on the revolutionary wave to face no economic prospects there except for extortion, smuggling, and kidnapping for ransom. A broad coalition of the Tuareg, Arab and other factions revolted against Bamako again in January 2012. The nationalist Tuareg were gathered in the National Movement for the Liberation of Azawad (*Mouvement National de Libération de l'Azawad*, MNLA), a group dominated by a "noble" Idnan clan, supported by some Ifoghas, and led by col. Mohamed ag Najim, an Idnan and former Qaddafi officer. Despite their secular and nationalist agenda, MNLA fought alongside radical and terrorist groups such al-Qaeda in the Islamic Maghreb (Algerian Arab dominated), Ansar Din (a radical Tuareg group, led by Iyad ag Ghali) and more heterogeneous Berrabiche Arab-led Movement for Oneness and Jihad in West Africa (*Mouvement pour l'unicité et le jihad en Afrique de l'Ouest*, MUJAO). By the end of June 2012, the role of MNLA was marginalized in the insurrection by the aforementioned radical elements, and the group was ousted of the main northern cities. This time the corrupt regime of Touré was too weak to respond and the incapacitated Malian army was incapable of any military action except for undertaking another coup d'état in March 2012. Facing the risk of spill-over and the jihadists attacking the capital, the transition government asked France to intervene, what followed in January 2013 with Operation Serval (Assemblée Nationale 2013: 19–21, 31; Comolli 2015: 101–2; Pezard and Shurkin 2013: 6; Sénat 2013: 34, 38–9, 43, 70; McGregor 2017: 10–2).

The French victory over jihadists resulted in the restoration of the precarious order in the north that characterized status quo ante rebellion. Thus the unsolved Tuareg question returned on the Bamako agenda. Under the leadership of Ibrahim Boubacar Keïta, Mali resorted to its traditional strategy of ruling the north—*divide et impera*, to rule by dividing northern alliances into fragmented and feuding elements.

The Imghad, the Tuareg of a lower status within the traditional hierarchy, formed the Imghad Tuareg Self-Defence Group and Allies (Groupe autodéfense touareg Imghad et alliés, GATIA). By being loyal to Bamako, the Imghad Tuareg aimed at improving their position in northern politics at the expense of other Tuareg clans. The group was unofficially led by a Malian army general and an Imghad Tuareg, Haji ag Gamou, known from his previous exploits against northern rebellions led by other Tuareg clans. GATIA was later incorporated into so called the Platform, a movement assembling various ethnic militias loyal to Bamako (including Ganda Koy, its sister group, Ganda Izo, and Arab loyalist militias) (RFI 2014; RFI 2016; McGregor 2017: 10).

Interestingly, during the fourth Anefis battle (September 14–17, 2015) which was the first violent infringement of the peace accords, GATIA "was equipped with brand new vehicles (surprisingly the same Korean vehicles that Malian forces [had] recently received)". It is also alleged that in the fourth Anefis and the Menaka battle (April 27, 2015) GATIA was logistically supported by the Malian army (Interview 1 2015). It may suggest that some groups might have been closely associated, or rather virtually incorporated into the Malian military. GATIA, however, claimed being independent, especially when it was convenient for the group, e.g., when they were reluctant to honor agreements made by the government with enemy factions (cf. Jeune Afrique 2015). We cannot, therefore, dismiss GATIA's claims to limited independency from the government and, especially, particular interests of the Imghad or that of ag Hamou that were not necessarily in line with the Keïta government approach (cf. Maiga 2016: 6). The support of the Malian leadership towards pro-government militias was also confirmed by the author's source within the Malian military, yet without giving concrete evidence (Interview 2, 2015). Later, the very same findings were confirmed by the UN Panel of experts in its 2020 report (UN 2020).

Its leadership structure and logistical support it obtained strongly suggests that GATIA might have been a surrogate or affiliated proxy force of Bamako— yet certainly a proxy force very closely tied to the government. We can classify GATIA as a surrogate rather than an affiliated agent due to the Malian government otherwise being de facto external to the conflict environment. This, however, can be debated as much as Bamako's presence in the north: it can be considered on *de iure* terms (then it was present as a legitimate and sovereign actor) or de facto—then rather politically and militarily absent at that period.

Similarly, when the insecurity spread over the central areas of Mali (i.e., the Mopti region), and the government sovereignty was undermined by extremists from the Macina Liberation Front (also known as the Katiba Macina, dominated by the Fulani), Bamako resorted to local ethnic militia of the Bambara and the Dogon, the traditional hunters called Dozo, and particularly the Dogon hunters' brotherhood's group named Dan Na Ambassagou (since 2016). When Dogon villages were attacked, Dozos responded with violence against Fulani villages, contributing to further escalation of the conflict, and increasing civilian casualties (Lebovich 2017; BBC 2018; Lebovich 2019; L'Obs 2019). In a leaked UN report virtually all armed groups operating in the north were accused of war crimes in the years 2012–2018, yet Dan Na Ambassagou, alongside terrorists groups, was accused of even more severe crimes against humanity (RFI 2020; UN 2020: 1–2).

There have been many premises pointing out that the government, through the security services and the army, arms and trains the Dozos, and particularly Dan Na Ambassagou. It is specifically visible in change of their equipment (military assault weapons) and military tactics (HRW 2018; Lebovich 2018). Furthermore, the Malian army has committed abuses itself, including massacres on the Fulani civilian population (BBC 2018; Lebovich 2018; RFI 2020). Such a solution of employing the Dozo militias was also suggested to the author by his source in the Malian military (Interview 3, 2016). Thus, once more being unable to provide security for its population, the government again resorted to proxy warfare and chose one ethnicity as an affiliate (the Bambara and the Dogon, traditionally agriculturalists—worth noting that the Bambara have been Malian political and military elites for centuries; Pezard and Shurkin 2013: 3) to counter another (the Fulani, traditionally a pastoral community). In consequence, constructing a vicious circle of violence between these communities. Although Bamako officially dismantled the group in 2018, it continues to receive support from local officials (UN 2020: 7).

The discussed Bamako's proxy-based approach to counterinsurgency is nothing new, however, and indirectly stems from the previous, colonial experiences of the French who decades earlier had faced similar circumstances in their scramble for the African interior and the Sahel.

The French Use of Proxy Forces: With a Little Help from the Old Friends

When the French colonial forces were conquering the areas of today's northern Mali in the late nineteenth century, they faced violent opposition from the local Tuareg and Arab tribes (also known as the Moors). Quick and surprising raids, called *rezzou*, haunted French forces, that had taken over Timbuktu in February

1894. Lacking skills and resources to deal with such a typical irregular insurgency, the French resorted to proxy warfare. The strategy of use of affiliated forces in this geographical context was first outlined in a letter of the governor of the French Sudan, Lieutenant-Colonel Audéoud, who already in 1898 proposed to use indigenous militias armed with older weaponry and briefly trained at local military posts (Audéoud, 1898; Boilley 1999: 61; Grémont 2010: 4–5). In 1900 the French armed some Kunta Arabs with relatively modern rifles, which Kunta's foes lacked. The then dominant Tuareg tribe in the north—the Iwellemmedan, who led the resistance—were pacified in 1903. However, some time later, the Kunta made a pact with the Iwellemmedan and they launched another revolt in 1916. Then, the French employed the Shaamba Arabs, the Kel Ahaggar and Kel Adagh (i.e., the Ifoghas) Tuareg to counter another Iwellemmedan-led irredentism (Grémont 2010: 4–5). In 1928, Kel Adagh, acting again on behalf of the French, put an end to the *rezzous* of Moroccan Arabs, thus introducing some kind of peace and stability to the region (Pezard and Shurkin 2013: 6).

Parties to these "proxy deals" had their own considerations—the French were putting down the insurgency as they lacked men to do it on their own—in 1913, a group of approximately sixty four officers and non-commissioned officers were commanding more than a thousand of Malian soldiers in northern Mali (Boilley 1999: 116), and in the whole Timbuktu region in 1920 there were only around thirty French (Grémont 2010: 8). The local political, economic and personal interests played their part for the Kuntas, Kel Adagh, and others. In the first revolt at the turn of the twentieth century, the Kuntas had personal dealings with the Iwellemmedan that had not gone well, and fighting for the French allowed them to acquire technological superiority and "settle the scores." In the latter rebellion the French affiliates raided Iwellemmedans' camps to steal camels and cattle. For Kel Adagh, situated lower in the local political hierarchy of those days, it was not only about spoils of war, yet also a chance of rising their status at the expense of the dominant neighbors (Grémont 2010: 8).

Realizing that the French dominance in the region is not tenable without local support, the French resorted to so-called indirect administration, where they recognize and incorporate local tribal structures and employ local forces to realize policing and auxiliary tasks. Thus the Arab and Tuareg served as reconnaissance units and affiliated forces in combating hostile raids that plagued the French Sudan, as the land was then called. On the other hand, serving the colonial power provided local groups with a unique opportunity to get better armament, receive regular funding, settle scores with competing groups, rob foe's cattle, and raise their own status in the social hierarchy. Namely, in due course, Kel Adagh (led by the Ifogha clans) rose to prominence at the expense of the Iwellemmedans, who—interestingly—were also broadly employed by the colonial administration (Grémont 2010: 7–10). The colonial administration was constantly wary of their northern proxies revolting against them (cf. Grémont 2010: 10), it did not hamper, however, the emergence of a romanticized legend of the "noble warriors" and "the blue people of the desert" who helped the French secure their foothold in western Sahel. The legend that keeps on resounding in Europe yet a hundred years later.

The French were back to Mali after half of a century since their departure—this time to save the country, not to subjugate it. French forces came at the invitation of the Malian interim government troubled with the Islamist insurrection in the north. The rebels moving south constituted the greatest threat to the Malian state sovereignty since independence. Thus, with the Operation Serval, the French were to renew their conquest of western Sahel—yet this time from the hands of terrorists groups. Similarly, like a century earlier, the French intended to resort to the well-remembered strategy of employing local affiliates, and even from the same tribes.

With a force of almost 5,200 soldiers top, supported by a Chadian contingent of up to 2,000 men and a Malian army in disarray, Paris had to subjugate large swaths of mostly semi-desert land, equal to the size of France. The air superiority allowed the French to instantly stop the incursion of armed terrorist groups into central territories that had been moving towards Bamako in early January 2013. It was instantly followed by an organized push of allied troops northwards that evicted armed groups from the main cities and towns. The mountainous massive of Adrar des Ifoghas on the border with Algeria remained, however, a stronghold of the extremist militias (Kozera 2018). The name of the area is by no means accidental—it has been traditionally inhabited by the Kel Adagh (Ifoghas), yet after the marginalization of the MNLA, the extremist groups took over the region. At least for several decades, it has served as a safe haven for the Tuareg (Kel Adagh) irredentists, Algerian terrorists, trans-regional traffickers, and troublemakers of all sorts (Assemblée Nationale 2013: 20–1, 52–4, 63, 100; Kozera 2018: 53).

The French forces were already overstretched trying to secure the vast lands of Mali's northern provinces with its troops numbers not adequate to effectively control the area. They were, however, to conduct the final blow to the terrorists in their stronghold in a treacherous and inaccessible terrain, not without a reason compared to the Afghanistan's Tora-Bora mountains. Although using local Tuareg "guides" provided the French with access to exclusive local physical and human terrain knowledge, and thus reduced their operational risk.

The employment of the Tuareg "guides" and militias by the French is obscured by the latter's initial denial of any such dealings. However well-founded are military premises to use local affiliates, the problem lied in their political recognition of any sort. The region where the French needed most of the local expertise and support was, as it has been discussed, the fiefdom of Kel Adagh, and particularly their noble clans, Ifoghas. Not coincidentally, the Kidal region is the stronghold of the MNLA, which derives much of its support from Kel Adagh (Idnan and Ifoghas). The same group that co-initiated the latest insurgency and declared an independent state of Azawad in northern Mali in April 2012. Balancing between the operational necessities, risks of unnecessary deaths, and the accusations of legitimizing groups that undermine Mali's integrity, Paris was careful in revealing the operational cooperation between its expeditionary forces and local Tuareg "facilitators", undoubtedly of the MNLA pedigree. Initially, denying any form of cooperation with incriminated groups (Sénat 2013: 42; Powelton 2014), later the French admitted working with some "Tuareg militias" (Goya 2013), and more openly when MNLA dropped any independence claims and entered the peace process (Sénat 2013: 57, 70).

There was, however, one incident that not only confirmed French cooperation with the MNLA at an early stage of Operation Serval yet also revealed its nature and the depth of the French trust that MNLA enjoyed. MNLA returned to its traditional fiefdom of the Adrar des Ifoghas area at the end of February 2013. The return of anti-Islamist combatants seemed to be a strategy coordinated with the French to encircle the jihadists taking refuge in Adras des Ifoghas and control the trafficking routes towards Algeria. MNLA thus re-installed itself in Il-Khalil (aka El-Khalil or al-Khalil), a border post previously occupied by the Arab-dominated AQIM (Al-Qaeda in the Islamic Maghreb).

Alleged exactions against local Arab population, of which MNLA was accused, drew attention of the Arab Movement of Azawad (MAA), a secular ethnic self-defense militia. The group clashed with MNLA on February 23, 2013. In consequence of the attack, a French air strike hit the positions of MAA near Infara, destroying their vehicles and wounding four combatants. MNLA claimed that they were attacked by the MUJAO supported by members of MAA and Ansar al-Sharia (a MUJAO's splinter group)—passing this version on to the French allowed to convince MNLA's patron to launch the airstrike against "the terrorists". Although MNLA claimed taking MUJAO's prisoners, the presence of the group on the Il-Khalil battleground cannot be verified (Le Point 2013; RFI 2013a; RFI 2013b; McGregor 2013).

The battle of Il-Khalil not only confirms French cooperation with MNLA yet also reveals its military nature par excellence, that run much deeper than just "guiding" and intelligence gathering: the Tuareg militia was trusted with cutting off the jihadists and even identifying targets for lethal airstrikes. More importantly though, France's local partner might have abused its relationship with the patron for its own purposes—to weaken its rival in competition over the control of (legal and illegal) trade routes—as all points to the fact that the February 23 clashes between MNLA and MAA, and the airstrike that followed were irrelevant to the anti-terrorist mission and constituted an example of typical clashes between competing armed groups. It is thus highly likely that, as a side effect of cooperation with MNLA, the French were drawn into inter-ethnic rivalry under the guise of a counter-terrorism mission.

In later years, as the French mission expanded from one-country-based ("Operation Serval") into much broader and encompassing five Sahel countries ("Operation Barkhane," since 2014), the French also enlarged their cooperation with local armed groups. Their new allies encompassed that of the Movement for the Salvation of Azawad, the Imghad Tuareg of GATIA (hostile towards MNLA), and the Islamic Movement of Azawad, that consisted of ex-Ansar Din fighters who were expected to deliver their former companions to the French authorities (McGregor 2013; Guibert 2018). These relations, however, were not as deep as with MNLA.

The supposedly privileged relationship between MNLA and the French was business-like, and the results of both groups' alignment of common interests rather than any political choice of Paris, that after all supported the integrity of Mali, saving Bamako from the jihadist peril. The French profited from their allies' intimate knowledge, presence, and legitimacy in the northern territories, and their secular ideology was certainly not a reason for discomfort. The Tuareg of MNLA, on the other hand, profited from unofficial patronage that translated into the group's legitimacy and status on the political arena. Possibly they also exploited their position to weaken their political competition and opponents (cf. Il-Khalil incident).

Conclusions: Proxy Governance *à la Malienne* vs Limited French Outsourcing

From the perspective of Bamako, use of proxy forces seemed an easy alternative for lack of institutional capacity of the state to effectively project its power outside of the capital, and specifically in the northern provinces of Gao,

Timbuktu, and Kidal. In times of weakening state institutions, increasing insecurity and rebellion, the state monopoly on violence was partially delegated to non-state armed groups loyal to the Malian elites. In exchange, Bamako's proxy forces (affiliates and in some cases also arguably surrogates) profited from special status and protection of the officials and military to rise their status over competition and enrich themselves from regional trafficking (provided that they shared with their patrons, cf. UN 2020: 2), or raids.

The French approach to the use of proxies differed as did the French aims and needs in the Malian theater. The employment of the northern groups in the counter-terrorism operation resulted from the operational, or even tactical, necessities and not strategic considerations. While Bamako, seemed not be capable of holding the country without its "divide and rule by proxy" strategy, the French needed local guides and allies to diminish their operational costs of counter-insurgency warfare in inaccessible terrain. Paris did not embrace nor support the Tuareg irredentism, yet rather exploited the business-type offer of the Tuareg, who, through this cooperation, intended to legitimize themselves as a constructive and meaningful actor on the political stage of Mali.

While Bamako seems not to consider the consequences of use and support towards non-state armed groups (both of ethnic or criminal character), what resulted in some of them gaining considerate independency (e.g., GATIA or Dan Na Ambassagou), the French were cautious not to over-play their local affiliates. Paris understood that giving too much credit and providing too much support for a specific group could raise its status over others and even over the government, create a "monopolist power-broker" in the north and thus perpetuate the armed struggle at the expense of a political solution. As the Il-Khalil incident exemplifies, however, it may not have been that smooth and entirely successful. Thus, the French, with their arguably post-colonial resounding saviorism towards the Malian state, wanted to profit from local facilitators' capacities sustainably and outsourced to affiliated proxies with moderation, as not to create long-term disadvantage for the peace process.

Bamako, however, lacking resources and the will to resolve local conflicts constructively and peacefully, had been employing the proxy-based *divide et impera* strategy in order to fragmentarize and weaken local political alliances, counter irredentist movements, or basically provide some sort of aberratively understood order. By playing one against another and sowing discord among the heterogeneous populations of Mali, the government aimed at exercising control over the territory through a precarious balance, the elites seemingly favored over positive peace. In consequence, however, what Bamako obtained was further

Proxy Warfare in Mali 119

escalation of violence, erosion of state institutions, fragmentarization of conflict, and perpetuation of its underlying causes.

Afterword

The end of 2021 brought a new and possibly perilous opening in the Malian employment of proxies. Drifting away from their traditional European allies and democratic values, the military junta in Bamako tilted towards cooperation with the undemocratic regime of Vladimir Putin. Citing historical ties with the Soviet Union and accusing France of Neo-colonialism, the Malian military leaders were in fact tempted by promises of efficiency of the Russian hard-power approach and quasi-special-forces operations by the infamous paramilitary Wagner Group. Arrival of the Russian "instructors" and "military advisors" (in late December 2021, which was preceded by the appearance of Russian geologists seeking possibilities of natural resources extractions to pay for the contract), caused a rupture with European allies operating within the counter-terrorism Barkhane mission and the "Takuba Task Force," and consequently expulsion of the French-led endeavor out of Mali in 2022.

In 2022 Russian-advised and assisted Malian army continued to struggle with non-state violence in various parts of the country. Their tactics of stark disregard towards local populations well-being bring new accusations of summary murders and other human rights abuses, so reminiscent of the Soviet atrocities and the Russian military actions in Eastern Europe. They are also further isolating the military regime in Bamako and deepening the crack between the government and increasingly insecure local populations.

Albeit, from the Russian perspective, this proxy installation in Mali, altogether with other political and relatively inexpensive and unsophisticated efforts of Moscow, proved very efficient in marginalizing influence of the traditional and post-colonial power of France. Thus, at a little expense, Russia achieved a strategic gain. The proxy warfare—however unsuitable for democratic regimes— is strategically efficient for those disregarding the norms.

Bibliography

Assemblée Nationale (2013), *Rapport d'information déposé en application de l'article 145 du Règlement par la Commission de la Défense Nationale et des Forces Armées en*

120   *Proxy Wars from a Global Perspective*

conclusion des travaux d'une mission d'information sur l'opération Serval au Mali, 18 July.

Audéoud, R. (1898), "Lettre du lt-cl. Audéoud lt. Gouverneur, au lt-cl. Commandant la Région Nord de Tombouctou" [A letter from LTC Audéoud, Governon of the French Sudan to the Commandant of the Region North-Timbuktu], 13 September 1898, Kayes, Service historique de l'armée de terre (SHAT), carton Soudan 6; as quoted by: Cormier-Salem et al. (eds.) (2005), *Patrimoines naturels au Sud: Territoires, identités et stratégies locales*. Paris: Institut de recherche pour le développement: 254.

BBC. (2018), "Mali Fula villagers were killed 'in cold blood'", *BBC,* 24 June 2018. Available online: https://www.bbc.com/news/world-africa-44594595 (accessed 12 May 2022).

Boilley, P. (1999), *Les Touaregs Kel Adagh; Dépendances et révoltes: du Soudan français au Mali contemporain*, Paris: Karthala.

Comolli, V. (2015), *Boko Haram. Nigeria's Islamist Insurgency.* London: Hurst & Company.

Grémont, C. (2010), *Le Maghreb dans son environnement régional et international: Touaregs et Arabes dans les forces armées coloniales et maliennes. Une histoire en trompe-l'oeil.* Note de l'Ifri, Institut Français des Relations Internationales. Paris: IFRI. Available online: https://www.ifri.org/sites/default/files/atoms/files/gremont_touaregs_et_arabes.pdf (accessed 22 August 2020).

Goya, M. (2013), "Mali :'Le risque, c'est que l'on s'engage dans un combat extrêmement long", interviewed by Christine Muratet, *Radio France Internationale*, 20 February. Available online: https://www.rfi.fr/fr/afrique/20130220-mali-le-risque-est-on-s-engage-combat-extremement-long (accessed 22 August 2020).

Guibert, B. (2018), "Au Sahel, 'je n'ai pas besoin de canons supplémentaires, mais il nous faut gagner en mobilité", *Libération*, 9 July. Available online: https://www.liberation. fr/planete/2018/07/09/au-sahel-je-n-ai-pas-besoin-de-canons-supplementaires-mais-il-nous-faut-gagner-en-mobilite_1665186 (accessed 22 August 2020)

Harmon, S. A. (2014), *Terror and Insurgency in the Sahara-Sahel Region. Corruption, Contraband, Jihad and the Mali War of 2012–2013*, Farnham: Ashgate.

HRW (2018), "We Used to Be Brothers': Self-Defense Group Abuses in Central Mali", *Human Rights Watch.* 07 December. Available online: https://www.hrw.org/report/2018/12/07/we-used-be-brothers/self-defense-group-abuses-central-mali (accessed 22 August 2020).

Interview 1. (2015), Interview with an official of the MINUSMA intelligence division conducted by the author. Anonymized.

Interview 2. (2015), Interview with a member of the FAMA conducted by the author. Anonymized.

Interview 3. (2016), Interview with a member of the FAMA conducted by the author. Anonymized.

Jeune Afrique (2015), "Mali: que se passe-t-il à Anéfis?", *Jeune Afrique*, 28 August. Available online: https://www.jeuneafrique.com/260397/politique/se-passe-t-a-anefis/ (accessed 12 May 2022).

Kozera, C. A. (2018), "Black Holes of Insecurity: The North of Mali", in J. Besenyő and V. Marsai (eds), *The Dynamics of Conflicts in Africa in the Early 21st Century*, 43–61, Budapest: Dialog Campus.

Lacher, W. (2011), *Organized Crime and Terrorism in the Sahel. Drivers, Actors, Options*. SWP Comments, Berlin: Stiftung Wissenschaft und Politik—German Institute for International Affairs.

Lacher, W. (2012), *Organized Crime and Conflict in the Sahel-Saharan Region*. Carnegie Endowment for International Peace, 13 September. Available online: https://carnegieendowment.org/2012/09/13/organized-crime-and-conflict-in-sahel-sahara-region-pub-49360 (accessed 22 August 2020).

Lebovich, A. (2017), "Stabilising Mali—Why Europe Must Look Beyond Technicalities", *European Council on Foreign Relations*, 24 May. Available online: https://ecfr.eu/article/commentary_stabilising_mali_why_europe_must_look_beyond_7293/ (accessed 12 May 2022).

Lebovich, A. (2018), "Mali's impunity problem and growing security crisis", *European Council on Foreign Relations*, 28 June. Available online: https://ecfr.eu/article/commentary_malis_impunity_problem_security_crisis/ (accessed 12 May 2022).

Lebovich, A. (2019), "Mapping armed groups in Mali and the Sahel", *European Council on Foreign Relations*, May. Available online: https://ecfr.eu/special/sahel_mapping (accessed 12 May 2022).

Lecocq, B. (2010), *Disputed Desert. Decolonization, Competing Nationalisms and Tuareg Rebellions in Mali*, Afrika-Studiecentrum Series, Brill.

Le Point (2013), "Mali: bombardements français sur une base d'un groupe armé, quatre blessés". *Le Point*, 25 February. Available online: https://www.lepoint.fr/monde/mali-bombardements-francais-sur-une-base-d-un-groupe-arme-quatre-blesses-25-02-2013-1632127_24.php (accessed 12 May 2022).

L'Obs. (2019), "Mali: des chasseurs traditionnels 'dozos' tuent 37 habitants d'un village peul". *L'Obs [Nouvel Observateur]*, 2 January. Available online: https://www.nouvelobs.com/monde/afrique/20190102.OBS7844/mali-des-chasseurs-traditionnels-dozos-tuent-37-habitants-d-un-village-peul.html (accessed 12 May 2022).

Maiga I. (2016), "Armed Groups in Mali: Beyond the Labels", *West Africa Report*. Institute for Security Studies, 17. Available online: https://media.africaportal.org/documents/WestAfricaReport17.pdf (accessed 12 May 2022).

McGregor, A. (2013), "French Cooperation with Tuareg Rebels Risks Arab Rising in Northern Mali", *Terrorism Monitor*, 11 (5), 8 March, Jamestown Foundation, Available online: https://www.refworld.org/docid/513d9e922.html (accessed 22 August 2020).

McGregor, A. (2017), "Anarchy in Azawad: A Guide to Non-State Armed Groups in Northern Mali", *Terrorism Monitor*, 15 (2), 27 January. Available online: https://jamestown.org/program/anarchy-azawad-guide-non-state-armed-groups-northern-mali/ (accessed 12 May 2022).

Pezard, S. and M. Shurkin (2013), *Toward a Secure and Stable Northern Mali. Approaches to Engaging Local Actors*, RAND Corporation. Available online: https://www.rand.org/content/dam/rand/pubs/research_reports/ RR200/RR296/RAND_RR296.pdf (accessed 22 August 2020).

Powelton, F. (2014), "Mali : Discrétion de l'armée française sur sa collaboration avec les Touaregs", *Sahel Intelligence*, 1 October. Available online: https://sahel-intelligence.com/5349-mali-discretion-de-larmee-francaise-sur-sacollaboration-avec-les-touaregs.html (accessed 22 August 2020).

Rauta, V. (2019), "Towards a Typology of Non-state Actors in 'Hybrid Warfare': Proxy, Auxiliary, Surrogate and Affiliated Forces", *Cambridge Review of International Affairs*, 33 (6): 868–87.

RFI (2013a), "Mali: ce que l'on sait des affrontements entre Touaregs et groupes armés à Il Khalil", *RFI*, 23 February. Available online: https://www.rfi.fr/fr/afrique/20130223-mali-incertitudes-affrontements-touaregs-groupes-armes-il-khalil-mnla-maa-mujao-tchad-hollande (accessed 12 May 2022).

RFI (2013b), "Mali: les affrontements entre MNLA et MAA inquiètent". *RFI*, 25 February. Available online: https://www.rfi.fr/fr/afrique/20130225-mali-affrontements-entre-mnla-maa-inquietent-tinzaoutene-in-farah-in-khalil (accessed 12 May 2022).

RFI (2014), "Nord du Mali: naissance d'un groupe armé opposé à l'autodétermination", *RFI*, 15 August. Available online: https://www.rfi.fr/fr/afrique/20140815-nord-mali-naissance-groupe-arme-oppose-autodetermination-maa-gatia-mnla-gamou-almahmoud (accessed 12 May 2022).

RFI (2016), "Mali: le général El Hadj Ag Gamou affirme appartenir au Gatia", *RFI*, 23 September. Available online: https://www.rfi.fr/fr/afrique/20160923-mali-general-el-hadj-ag-gamou-affirme-appartenir-gatia-touareg (accessed 12 May 2022).

RFI (2020), "Mali: l'armée épinglée dans un rapport de l'ONU pour crimes de guerre", *RFI*, 23 September. Available online: https://www.rfi.fr/fr/afrique/20201223-mali-l-arm%C3%A9e-%C3%A9pingl%C3%A9e-dans-un-rapport-pour-des-crimes-contre-l-humanit%C3%A9 (accessed 12 May 2022).

Sénat (2013), *Rapport d´information fait au nom de la commission des affaires étrangères, de la défense et des forces armées (1) par le groupe de travail « Sahel », en vue du débat et du vote sur l'autorisation de prolongation de l'intervention des forces armées au Mali*, 16 April.

Stewart, D. J. (2013), *What is next for Mali? The Roots of conflict and challenges to instability*, Strategic Studies Institute, Carlisle: US Army War College.

UN (2020), *Final report of the Panel of Experts established pursuant to Security Council resolution 2374 (2017) on Mali and renewed pursuant to resolution 2484 (2019)*. United Nation Security Council, 13 August.

Wing, S. D. (2008), *Constructing Democracy in Africa: Mali in Transition*, New York: Palgrave Macmillan.

8

The Bifurcation of Violence: The Proxy Forces in the Central African Republic

Błażej Popławski

The Tradition of Proxy Wars in Africa

Proxy wars are the perennial element of modern, hybrid warfare. They can be defined as "the indirect engagement in a conflict by third parties wishing to influence its strategic outcome. They are constitutive of a relationship between a benefactor, who is a state or non-state actor external to the dynamic of an existing conflict, and their chosen proxies who are the conduit for weapons, training, and funding from the benefactor" (Mumford 2013: 11). Proxy war occurs when state or non-state (non-governmental organization or international organization) actor, based on a perception of interest, ideology, and risk accepts that direct intervention in a conflict would be either unjustifiable or too costly (in political as well as financial sense) (Loveman 2002: 29–48; Bar-Siman-Tov 1984: 263–4). The main components of a proxy war include the provision of manpower (mercenaries, non-combatant military "advisers"); the delivery of materials (arms, ammunition, and other military technology); financial assistance (Groh 2019: 35–7).

The frequency of proxy wars increased in the countries of the Third World during the Cold War (Ahram 2011: 2–5). The avoidance of nuclear war has been a prime reason for the enhancement of these kinds of conflict. Africa, especially the Sub-Saharan part of the continent, became the polygon of the struggle between the United States and the Soviet Union during the period of decolonization (Kalyvas, Balcells 2010: 415). Not only superpower states were exploiting African states or non-state actors as agents of global conflict after the Second World War—a similar strategy was adopted by former colonial powers (e.g., France, Belgium). There are many Sub-Saharan examples of proxy wars on the continent during the Cold War: the Congo Crisis (1960–1965); the Rhodesian Bush War (1964–1979); the South African Border War / Namibian War of

124 *Proxy Wars from a Global Perspective*

Independence (1966–1990); the Nigerian Civil War (1967–1970); the first phase of the Angolan Civil War (1975–2002) (Porter 1984; Schmidt 2013).

Postcolonial Cycles of Violence

The rise of "failed states" caused in part by post-Cold War power vacuums increased the number of proxy wars in postcolonial Africa—mostly, but not only, in the Sub-Saharan part of the continent (e.g., the Second Libyan Civil War 2014–2020). After the fall of the Soviet Union, "proxy wars were primarily used by smaller, regional powers rather than those with global reach and interests" (Groh 2019: 10). At the turn of the twentieth and the twenty-first centuries superpower-induced proxy wars have largely been replaced by multilateral proxy wars driven by regional (often: non-state) powers via the cross-border percolation of indigenous militia groups, warlord factions, clans, tribes, opportunistic criminal gangs, terrorists, jihadists and professional Private Military Companies (PMCs) (Hills 1997: 35–51; Lock 1998: 1393–426). "Those who are armed can easily switch from a passive/defensive to an active/offensive role and can commit human rights violations and even destabilize governments. They cannot be considered soldiers either, since they are not part of the army or in the chain of command, and often belong to a large number of different nationalities (Gomez del Prado 2009: 436). It is important to notice that 90 percent of recent state-based armed conflicts are "repeat civil wars" (Walter 2015: 1242–3)—old wars restarted by the same proxy after a period of time.

There are many examples of these armed conflicts when regionally influential Sub-Saharan African states use proxy war to indirectly intervene in another state: the second phase of the Angolan Civil War (1975–2002); the First and the Second Liberian Civil Wars (1989–1997; 1999–2003); the Sierra Leone Civil War (1991–2002); the First and the Second Congo Wars (1996–1997, 1998–2003); the First and Second Ivorian Civil Wars (2002–2007, 2010–2011) the Chadian Civil War (2005–2010) (Singer 2001–2002; Williams 2016). An interesting example of the use of proxy forces in Africa and the devolution of state control over violence to non-state actors is the newest history of the Central African Republic (CAR).

The Collapse of the Central African Republic

The CAR is diamond-, uranium- and gold-rich but crippled by poverty and civil war. Nowadays the country is one of the least developed countries in the world

(Binoua 2005; Pascal 2015). Decades of conflict, corruption, and poor governance have made military coups (e.g., 1966, 1979, 1981, 1996, 2001, 2003—supported by proxy forces from France, Libya, Democratic Republic of Congo (DRC), Chad, Sudan a de facto political manner in which political power is transferred (Faes, Smith 2000: 284–91).

The main axis of the conflict in CAR in the twenty-first century is the religious and ethnic identification of the inhabitants. The nation is divided into over eighty ethnic groups. The country's population of 5.45 million is about eighty-nine percent Christian. Muslims constitute about nine percent of the population and are mostly concentrated in the far northeast of the country, close to the borders with Chad and Sudan. The most numerous tribes are: Gbaya (28.8%); Banda (22.9%), Mandjia (9.9%), Sara (7.9%), M'Baka-Bantu (7.9%), Arab-Fulani (Peuhl) (6%), Mbum (6%), Ngbanki (5.5%), Zande-Nzakara (3%). Another face of the proxy war, strictly connected with the religious-ethnic situation, is the tension between pastoralists (predominantly Muslim) and farming (mostly Christian) communities, the economic competition for natural resources (land and water) (Roitman 2005), and postcolonial relationship between the center and the peripheries of the country (the predominantly Muslim north of the country—prefectures of Vakaga and Bamingui-Bangoran—has been largely excluded from political power, held by a majority Christian political elite in Bangui) (Brown, Zahar 2015: 15–6).

According to various human rights organizations, the central government of CAR is de facto unable to provide basic security (Doui Wawaye 2017). "The absence of the state in the rural areas of CAR is so striking that the position in certain respects has almost reached the level of caricature" (Bierschenk, de Sardan 1997: 441). Local politicians in CAR are increasingly relying on proxy forces—including armed groups, special operations units, and private military and security companies. On the other hand, with a closed political system governed by a corrupted elite and no other means of accessing political power, creating armed groups or hiring foreign mercenaries may become a way for politico-military entrepreneurs to get a position within the government and access to profits garnered by exploitation of the country's resources (Reno 2011: 242–56).

The Séléka Coalition and the Role of Chad and Sudan

During the rule of President François Bozizé (2003–2013), one third of the country (mainly northern part) was not effectively controlled by the government in Bangui, and the control of this area was exercised by three major armed rebel groups: Union of Democratic Forces for Unity (*Union des forces démocratiques pour le rassemblement*; UFDR); People's Army for the Restoration of Democracy (*Armée Populaire pour la restauration de la république et la démocratie*; APRD); Convention of Patriots for Justice and Peace (*Convention des patriotes pour la justice et la paix*; CPJP). This part of CAR was also troubled by raids conducted by the Janjaweed from Sudan, which crossed the border with CAR to chase fleeing residents of Darfur (Kisangani 2015: 49–50).

Though rebellions were present for almost a decade, a qualitative change occurred at the end of 2012 with the emergence of the Séléka rebel alliance, comprised of a collection of armed men hailing from north-eastern CAR, Chad, and Sudan. The CPJP and CPSK signed the first agreement on August 20, 2012. This organization quickly became a wide, heterogeneous coalition of several militia groups: CPJP presided over by Noureddine Adam, Charles Massi; CPSK led by Mohamed-Moussa Dhaffane; Democratic Front of the Central African People (*Front démocratique du peuple centrafricain*; FDPC) led by Abdoulaye Miskine; UFDR headed by Michel Am Nondroko Djotodia; Patriotic Convention for Saving the Country (*Convention Patriotique pour le Salut du Kodro*; Alliance for Revival and Rebuilding (*Alliance pour la Renaissance et la Refondation*; A2R) coordinated by Salvador Edjezekanne (Maynero 2014: 179–93).

The emergence of the Séléka in north-eastern CAR resulted from the government's abandonment of the region and the growing influence of Chad and Sudan. There are strong historical ethnic and trade linkages between populations in northern CAR, Chad and Sudan. In terms of culture, north-eastern CAR is oriented towards Abéché in eastern Chad and Nyala in South Darfur as opposed to Bangui or any other part of CAR. It should be noticed that Chad and Sudan supported the Séléka because they needed to secure their borders and prevent a situation where armed opposition groups fighting against the governments in Ndjamena and Khartoum would use CAR as a staging post to launch attacks. Furthermore, Chadian and Sudanese business networks are known to enjoy lucrative relationships with rebel groups (especially composed of Arab-Fulani) in control of the oil fields located in southern Chad and northern of CAR (Tubiana 2008: 20–1).

The government in Ndjamena supported Séléka rebels and even trained some of them. A lot of Séléka's soldiers come from Chad and Sudan (Berg 2008: 2), mostly from Zaghawa tribe (Marchal and Bawtree 2006: 471) (it is worth to add that Chadian President Idriss Déby, killed in April 2021, was a member of a clan within the Zaghawa tribe). They mostly use Arabic and in the vast majority of cases do not know French or Sango (however, the word Séléka means "Coalition" in Sango) (Klosowicz 2016: 40).

The main goals of the Séléka were to seek comprehensive political reform after one decade of the regime led by Bozizé (it should be stressed that the president maintains power by appealing to foreign sponsors, especially France, and by monopolizing power in the hands of family members and members of his ethnic group, the Gbaya). Djotodia, a Soviet-trained civil servant who turned into a rebel commander, called for the national fight against corruption and tribal clientelism. His political program was—de iure—concentrated on the reconstruction and improvement of the government (Käihkö and Utas 2014: 73).

In 2012 5,000 fighters of Séléka, supported by 700 Chadian combatants under the rebel Baba Laddé, began a military campaign against Bozizé (Klosowicz 2016: 40). In 2013, rebels took control of Bangui, the capital city. Having lost Chad as a close ally, and unsuccessfully appealed to France to intervene, Bozizé was overthrown. Civilians were reportedly frequently subjected to attacks by fighters of the Séléka, involving mass looting, destruction of property, killings, and sexual violence (Agger 2014: 5).

Djotodia suspended the constitution and installed himself as interim president (the first Muslim president in CAR's history). On September 13, 2013, he formally dissolved the Séléka, which he had lost effective control of shortly after taking power. Only a part of the militias were integrated into the Central African Armed Forces (Forces armées centrafricaines; FACA). The process of integration was not successful because of the tribalism (recruitment for national armed forces in CAR was always conducted in line with the ethnicity) (Welz 2014: 603).

In January 2014, Djotodia was invited to attend a summit of the Economic Community of Central African States (ECCAS) in Ndjamena. He then resigned following the pressure put on him by Deby. Next political changes (on 20 January 2014, Catherine Samba-Panza, the mayor of Bangui, was elected as the interim president) had little effect in stopping abuses by the militia soldiers who now began being referred to as ex-Séléka (Welz 2014: 603). Their opponents used to name themselves "Anti-Balaka".

Anti-Balaka Militias: A Warlord Army or a Village Protection Force?

The Anti-Balaka were formed by non-state actors (tribal leaders, village strongmen, local Notables) as village self-defense forces in response to the acts of violence committed by the units of the Séléka (Lombard and Batianga-Kinzi

2015: 54). The name "Anti-Balaka" means "anti-machete" in Sango. The group dates back to the mid-2000s and was created with the unification of local Christian militias and former armed security forces that remain loyal to ousted Bozizé (the president had a close relationship with many of the leaders of the Anti-Balaka, i.a., Maxime Mokom and Patrice-Edouard Ngaissona). It needs to be highlighted that this kind of self-defense force fits in a long tradition of "culture of resistance" by the several ethnic groups (Gbaya, Banda, Mandjia, and Mbum), which supported each other during anti-colonial insurrections (Ndéma 2015).

Initially composed of mixed membership drawn from Christians, Muslims, and animists, the group became dominated by Christian militias by 2013. The Anti-Balaka framed their grievances using the idioms of religion and foreignness (many citizens of the country became xenophobic towards inhabitants of alleged Arabic origin—whom they call "Chadians"). The Christian-dominated anti-Balaka had the initial goal of counterinsurgency, and self-defense against the onslaught of the Séléka rebels. The majority of them come from the tribes situated in the central and southern parts of CAR (Lombard and Batianga-Kinzi 2015: 54).

The Anti-Balaka began to engage the Séléka forces militarily in June 2013. The Anti-balaka attacked nomadic cattle camps of the ethnic Peuhl Muslim community. By the end of 2014, the country was de facto partitioned, with the Anti-Balaka controlling the south and west, from which most Muslims had evacuated, and ex-Séléka groups controlling the north and east (Pettersson and Wallensteen 2015: 543).

They became more organized in 2014, apparently with the integration of numerous former members of FACA. Their core goals shifted to one that was clearly political: to bring former President Bozizé back from exile to resume his role in national politics; to minimize the influence of Chadians in CAR; to abolish the domination of members or sponsors of the Séléka in commercial and business sectors of the economy of CAR (Ntuda Ebodé 2014: 9–10).

The Anti-Balaka was able to grow their numbers to 50,000-75,000 through the recruitment of young men who had been victims of the Séléka. By the end of 2013, they had gained enough resources and personnel to stage a major attack in Bangui, allegedly financed by the Front for the Return of the Constitutional Order (FROCCA), which was established by Bozizé in August 2013. These groups contain some heavily armed former soldiers, including elements of Bozizé's Presidential Guard (Garde Républicaine), commonly known as the Red

Berets (it is worth to add that the Guard consisted almost exclusively of those who had supported Bozizé's rebellion in 2001, as well as the Chadians) (Klosowicz 2020: 180–1).

Rather than operate with a centralized command structure, the Anti-Balaka militia is a loose coalition; one in which leadership is decentralized with respective local commandants having specific areas under their control. Since the 2016 general elections, several more brutal factions of the Anti-Balaka militia have emerged in the eastern and central parts of the country, mostly targeting Muslim civilians—not only connected with the Séléka.

The Bifurcation of Proxy Forces: Ex-Séléka Militias

Although officially the Séléka had been dismantled in September 2013, the group persisted. By 2014, disagreements over resource control and strategy disputes among the Séléka leadership led to the group splitting into several factions, predominantly along ethnic lines, who fight each other for control of resource-rich areas and seasonal migratory movements. The different factions continued to perpetuate violent acts (Flichy de La Neuville, et al. 2013).

The ex-Séléka recruited new members from Chad and Sudan by promising combatants financial gains in the form of looting. In 2015 the number of armed fighters of the ex-Séléka was 12,000, with 2,000 stationed in camps in Bangui. They also control large areas across the country, including strategic roads in the north and the east parts of CAR. The separatists have their own police, gendarmes, prisons, and military bases. They also collect taxes and fees. They profit from gold and diamond mines in areas they control. French and Chadian support these guerrillas and help to gain control over two-thirds of the country (Dukhan 2017: 4).

Popular Front for the Rebirth of Central African Republic (*Front populaire pour la renaissance de la Centrafrique*; FPRC) was formed in July 2014 in Birao. Union for Peace in the Central African Republic (*Unité pour la paix en Centrafrique*; UPC) was created in September 2014 by Ali Darassa. Return, Reclamation, Rehabilitation (*Retour, Réclamation et Réhabilitation*; 3R) was formed in December 2015 by Sidiki Abbas. Central African Patriotic Movement (*Mouvement patriotique pour la Centrafrique*; MPC) was established July 2015 by a Chadian—Mahamat Al-Khatim. National Movement for the Liberation of the Central African Republic (*Mouvement national pour la libération de la Centrafrique*; MNLC) was formed in 2017 (Dukhan 2017: 26–8).

The most important changes on the political scene in CAR (Faustin-Archange Touadéra won the presidency in 2016 and in 2021) did not intervene in the activity of the ex-Séléka militias. The factions are still competing against each other. Some of these groups have a political agenda (some of the Séléka fighters even began calling for the north to secede from the CAR), but many seem to be motivated primarily by tribal xenophobia and, what should be noticed, economic opportunities. In the Southeast of the country, three ex-Séléka splinters (FPRC, UPC, and MPC) fight each other, with the FPRC targeting Fulani, who are seen as supporters of UPC and the latter targeting Goula and Runga, who constitute the FPRC's support base (Lombard 2016).

The ex-Séléka groups build short-term alliances. For example, UPC and FPRC split after Adam, leader of the latter, demanded independence for CAR's predominantly Muslim north, a move opposed by UPC leader Darassa. FPRC fighters and allies from MPC, have joined with a faction of the anti-Balaka (which itself has split into two factions) to fight the UPC. Another example: in December 2020 different armed groups (Anti-Balaka militias, UPC, FPRC, 3R, MPC) who accused Touadéra of trying to fix the elections, formed Coalition of Patriots for Change (*Coalition des patriotes pour le changement*; CPC). However, this coalition is not very stable—on April 6, 2021, UPC left CPC.

Lord's Resistance Army: Searching for the Asylum

The east of CAR had seen an increase in incidents attributed to the Lord's Resistance Army (LRA). LRA was formed by Joseph Kony in northern Uganda in 1987 as a religiously-inspired militia group. Since its founding, the group has been responsible for widespread and systematic abuses of human rights across central Africa, including in Uganda, DRC, CAR, and South Sudan (Prunier 2004: 366–7). The government of Uganda claimed that at the beginning of the twenty-first century, the LRA had only 500 or 1,000 soldiers in total (Titeca and Costeur 2015: 100). The LRA uses the eastern region of CAR, especially the Haut-Mbomou district, as a safe haven to evade Ugandan troops. The rise of the activity of LRA in the country comes also as a result of a reduced presence of Ugandan military operating in CAR under the auspices of the African Union Regional Task Force (in early 2017, the Ugandan government stated its intention to withdraw troops from the counter-LRA operations in CAR, citing a lack of international support) (Dukhan 2017: 26–8).

The presence of LRA in CAR should be also put in the context of the relationship between Kampala and Khartoum. Throughout the 1990s, the two countries were fighting a proxy war. Uganda was arming and training the dissident Sudan People's Liberation Army (SPLA), fighting for autonomy for the Nilotic peoples of the south, while Sudan was supporting the LRA, providing bases, supplies, and training. After the proclamation of the new country—South Sudan, the cooperation between governments in Khartoum and Ndjamena has created an opportunity for LRA in CAR. There are also reports that the guerrilla has trafficked gold, diamonds, and ivory through CAR in cooperation with some ex-Séléka militias (Faber 2017: 17–8).

In response to the security vacuum in the Southern Sudan-DRC-CAR border area, various local self-defense groups—sometimes affiliated to the Anti-Balaka factions—have emerged to protect their communities against the LRA, generally to greater effect than the armies and peacekeeping missions in the region (Faber 2017: 17–8). However, the existence of these groups in CAR poses a dilemma to the acting governments, who struggle to monopolize the legitimate use of force and therefore have tended to be hesitant to endorse, let alone encourage their formation.

A New Chapter in the Crisis: the Wagner Group

The CAR has been a particular focus for the Russian government because of the mining investments. For trading weapons and providing advisors under a fragile civil war setting, Russia gains access to one of the most coveted natural resources in Africa: oil, diamonds, gold, iron, uranium, diamonds, timber, cotton, and coffee (Carter 2020). From the perspective of the Kremlin, the geographical situation of the CAR—thanks to the decreased presence of France in this country (Yanis 2016)—is crucial. The country is positioned along a vital crossroad between the western and eastern parts of the continent, it borders the Sahel as well as Sudan, traditionally influenced by Russia (Maslanka 2020: 1–2).

Russian support for CAR President Touadéra's administration, which has struggled to wrest back control over parts of the country from local warlords since 2016 has included military assistance, and information operations. In these fields, Russia cooperates with Rwanda (Lobez 2019: 13). Russia's surge in the CAR had its genesis in a 2017 exemption to the UN arms embargo that allowed the African country to acquire a modest quantity of light arms (Goodison 2019: 38–40). Russia began its purposive actions in CAR by donating a large cache of

AK-47s to Bangui and sending 170 "civilian instructors" from the Wagner Group. The Wagner Group is a Russian organization that has served as a private military contractor in several African countries. Although presumed to be founded by Dmitri Utkin, former Lieutenant colonel in the 2nd Spetsnaz Brigade based in the Russian city of Pskov, and owned by billionaire restaurateur Yevgeny Prigozhin, there are varying beliefs about control of the organization; some believe that it is a semi-state force connected to Russia's Main Intelligence Directorate (GRU) (Østensen and Bukkvoll 2018: 19–20).

Wagner's physical presence in Africa has been widely reported on, particularly in unstable and dysfunctional countries and conflict zones: CAR, Sudan, Mozambique, Mali, Libya, and Madagascar. Estimates of Wagner Group PMCs in Africa vary between 1,350 and 2,000 (while hard data is difficult to come by, it can be assumed that there are 3,500–5,000 fighters in the Group) (Grossman et al. 2019: 2).

The camp of PMCs from the Wagner Group was set up about sixty kilometers from the capital Bangui at the Berengo. Sewa Sécurité Services (SSS), a private company registered in CAR in 2017, became the legal framework through which 178 Russian trainers were officially authorized to deploy and train CAR soldiers on how to handle the weapons delivered by Russia. The PMCs also provide security for senior officials of the government. Valery Zakharov, a former member of the Russian security services and an associate of Prigozhin, was named the Special Security Advisor to President Touadéra. The Group has provided there the military training to CAR special forces (Bugayova and Regio 2019: 6).

The issue of the Wagner's presence in CAR became even more fraught in July 2018, when three Russian investigative journalists, Orkhan Dzhemal, Aleksandr Rostorguev, and Kirill Radchenko, were shot dead while trying to make a documentary on the PMCs in CAR and the size of the corruption among African politicians associated with the Kremlin. These journalists were killed by unidentified assailants, while they were on their way to a town located in the area of deposits of gold, diamonds, and uranium, which is being currently under the protection of Prigozhin's people. Dzhemal, Rostorguev, and Radchenko worked under the auspices of the Investigations Management Center, an organization run by Mikhail Khodorkovsky, a political opponent of Putin (Kuczynski 2019: 19).

The murder of three Russian journalists was never independently investigated. For the majority of the analysts, this case became a clear signal that the Kremlin will not quit its business in CAR. Moreover, in 2019, with Moscow's

The Bifurcation of Violence

encouragement, the government of CAR signed the African Union-sponsored Khartoum agreement with fourteen armed groups controlling most of the provinces of the country, a deal that still serves as the country's roadmap to peace today. "Through this agreement, Wagner had several objectives: to position Russia as a dealmaker in a conflict that Western powers have failed to meaningfully resolve, to consolidate Russian investments and contracts in CAR by ensuring Touadéra's reelection in 2020, to obtain the support of leaders of armed groups so that the population living in areas under their control would vote for Touadéra, and to agree on terms that would allow Wagner's companies— and, sometimes, Chinese entrepreneurs—to access and exploit natural resources in rebel-controlled areas" (Dukhan 2020: 3). Russia probably will continue its current strategy—using para-military personnel (a hybrid combination of legal military advisors and members of PMCs) to reap economic profits in the country.

Summary

Proxy warfare will shape twenty-first century conflicts in postcolonial regions for the foreseeable future. The erosion of state power, rise of transnational social movements, and proliferation of advanced military and communications technology are shifting this process (Rondeaux, Sterman 2019: 3). The recent history of CAR, one of the weakest countries all over the world, is an example of the phenomena of proxy wars. During the last decade CAR became "the ghost country". Over one million Central Africans have been displaced. About half a million have been driven into neighboring countries, while over 700,000 are displaced within CAR. The government in Bangui lost "monopoly on violence" (Berman 2006). Currently, the most important politicians build support on the basis of a short-term alliance with local or foreign proxies.

In CAR well-trained Muslim- and Christian-affiliated militias, guerrillas, and professional mercenaries from abroad, mostly from Chad and Sudan, are operating in all of the regions of the country since the outbreak of the civil war in 2013. Armed groups can be divided into fluent categories: the Séléka, the Anti-Balaka. The fact that the Séléka and the Anti-Balaka each have a single name masks the fact that they are not groups in the sense of having a united structure. Both groups should be understood as diffuse mobilizations of a range of actors, rather than structured organizations with clear chains of command. These all forces (particularly ex-Séléka militias) can be affiliated with the political

134 *Proxy Wars from a Global Perspective*

actors—from CAR and foreign powers—who compete against each other and try to control natural resources (gold, diamonds, uranium).

The loyalties of the proxy forces during the civil war in CAR are very fluid. The engagement of Chadians in the conflict is an example of this phenomenon. Firstly, Chadian soldiers participate in the Multinational Force of the Central African Economic and Monetary Community (Force multinationale en Centrafrique, FOMUC). Secondly, since Bozizé's takeover, Chadian soldiers have secured his stay in power. Thirdly, Chadian rebel forces have used northeast CAR as a rear base. Fourthly, Chadian regular forces have conducted raids in CAR to fight with another Chadian armed groups and assist Central African armed forces. Finally, Chadian combatants have joined the UFDR (Debos 2008: 227–8). It should be also considered, that a lot of decisions made by the government in N'Djamena had been consulted previously in Paris.

The competition between the proxy forces is also strongly supported by Russia and a former colonial power—France. Nowadays, it is clear that Franco-Russian postcolonial proxy war and the political struggle between different ethnic actors in CAR are major source of instability in the region.

Bibliography

Agger, K. (2014), *Behind the Headlines: Drivers of Violence in the Central African Republic*, Washington DC: Enough Project.

Ahram, A.I. (2011), *Proxy Warriors: The Rise and Fall of State-Sponsored Militias*, Stanford, CA: Stanford University Press.

Bar-Siman-Tov, Y. (1984), "The Strategy of War by Proxy", *Cooperation and Conflict*, 19: 263–73.

Berg, P. (2008), *The Dynamics of Conflict in the Tri-Border Region of Sudan, Chad and the Central African Republic*, Berlin: Friedrich Ebert Stiftung.

Berman, E.G. (2006), *La République Centrafricaine: une étude de cas sur les armes légères et les conflits*, Geneva: Small Arms Survey.

Bierschenk, T. and J.-P. de Sardan, (1997), "Local Powers and a Distant State in Rural Central African Republic", *Journal of Modern African Studies*, 35 (3): 441–68.

Binoua, J. (2005), *Centrafrique. L'instabilité Permanente*, Paris: Harmattan.

Brown, M.J. and M.J. Zahar, (2015), "Social Cohesion as Peacebuilding in The Central African Republic and Beyond", *Journal of Peacebuilding & Development*, 10 (1): 10–24.

Bugayova, N., and D. Regio, (2019), *The Kremlin's Campaign in Africa: Assessment Update*, Washington: Institute for the Study of War.

Carter, P.M. (2020), *Understanding Russia's Interest in Conflict Zones*, Washington: United States Institute of Peace.

Debos, M. (2008), "Fluid Loyalties in a Regional Crisis: Chadian 'Ex-Liberators' in the Central African Republic", *African Affairs*, 107 (427): 225–41.

Dukhan, N. (2017), *Splintered Warfare: Alliances, Affiliations, and Agendas of Armed Factions and Politico-Military Groups in the Central African Republic*, Washington: Enough Project.

Dukhnan, N. (2020), *Central African Republic: Ground Zero for Russian Influence in Central Africa*, Washington: Atlantic Council.

Faber, P. (2017), *Sources of Resilience in the Lord's Resistance Army*, Washington: Center for Naval Analyses.

Faes, G. and S. Smith, (2000), "République Centrafricaine: La Solitude et le Chaos", *Politique Internationale*, 88: 284–91.

Flichy de La Neuville, T. and V. Mézin-Bourgninaud and G. Mathias, (2013), *Centrafrique, Pourquoi la guerre?*, Limoges: Lavauzelle.

Gomez del Prado, J.L., (2009), "Private Military and Security Companies and the UN Working Group on the Use of Mercenaries", *Journal of Conflict and Security Law*, 13 (3): 429–50.

Goodison, K. (2019), "Russia in the Central African Republic: Exploitation Under the Guise of Intervention", *Philologia*, 1 (11): 34–42.

Groh, T.L. (2019), *Proxy War. The Least Bad Option*, Stanford: Stanford University Press.

Grossman, S. and D. Bush, and R. DiResta, (2019), *Evidence of Russia-Linked Influence Operations in Africa*, Stanford: Stanford Internet Observatory.

Hills, A. (1997), "Warlords, Militia and Conflict in Contemporary Africa: A Re-Examination of Terms", *Small Wars & Insurgencies*, 8 (1): 35–51.

Käihkö, I. and M. Utas, (2014), "The Crisis in CAR: Navigating Myths and Interests", *Africa Spectrum*, 49 (1): 69–77.

Kalyvas, S.N. and L. Balcells, (2010), "International System and Technologies of Rebellion: How the End of the Cold War Shaped Internal Conflict", *The American Political Science Review*, 104 (3): 415–29.

Kisangani, E.F. (2015), "Social Cleavages and Politics of Exclusion: Instability in The Central African Republic", *International Journal on World Peace*, 32 (1): 33–59.

Klosowicz, R. (2016), "Central African Republic: Portrait of a Collapsed State After The Last Rebellion", *Politeja*, 42: 33–52.

Klosowicz, R. (2020), "Identity, Ethnic Conflict and Communal Conflict in Sub-Saharan Africa", *Politeja*, 68: 171–90.

Kuczynski, G. (2019), *Russia in Africa: Weapons, Mercenaries, Spin Doctors*, Warsaw: Warsaw Instutute.

Lobez, C. (2019), "Activisme croissant de la Russie en RCA", *Diplomatie*, 97: 12–17.

Lock, P. (1998), "Military Downsizing and Growth in the Security Industry in Sub-Saharan Africa", *Strategic Analysis*, 22 (9): 1393–426.

Lombard, L. (2016), *State of Rebellion: Violence and Intervention in The Central African Republic*, London: Zed Books.

Lombard, L. and S. Batianga-Kinzi, (2015), "Violence, Popular Punishment, and War in The Central African Republic", *African Affairs*, 114 (454): 52–71.

Loveman, C. (2002), "Assessing the Phenomenon of Proxy Intervention", *Conflict, Security and Development*, 2 (3): 29–48.

Marchal, R. and V. Bawtree, (2006), "Chad/Darfur: How Two Crises Merge", *Review of African Political Economy*, 33 (109): 467–82.

Maslanka, L. (2020), "France and the Russian Presence in Africa", *Bulletin of the Polish National Institute of the International Relations*, 47 (1477): 1–2.

Maynero, A.C. (2014), "La Centrafrique, de la rebellion Seleka aux groups anti-Balaka (2012–2014): Usages de la violence, scheme persécutif et traitement médiatique du conflit", *Politique africaine*, 134: 179–93.

Mumford A. (2013), *Proxy Warfare*, Cambridge: Polity Press.

Ndéma, J. (2015), *Le Dialogue isiamo-chrétien en Centrafrique*, Paris: Harmattan.

Ntuda Ebodé, J. V. (2014), "La Centrafrique à la croisée des chemins", *Diplomatie*, 68: 8–12.

Østensen, Å.G. and T. Bukkvoll (2018), *Russian Use of Private Military and Security Companies—The Implications for European and Norwegian Security*, Kjeller: Norwegian Defence Research Establishment.

Pascal, L. (2015), *République Centrafricaine. Douanes et corruption, causes de la déliquescence du pays?*, Paris: Harmattan.

Pettersson, T. and P. Wallensteen, (2015), "Armed conflicts, 1946–2014", *Journal of Peace Research*, 52 (4): 536–50.

Porter, B.D. (1984), *The USSR in Third World Conflicts: Soviet Arms and Diplomacy in Local Wars, 1945–80*, Cambridge: Cambridge University Press.

Prunier, G. (2004), "Rebel Movements and Proxy Warfare: Uganda, Sudan and the Congo (1986–1999)", *African Affairs*, 103 (412): 359–83.

Reno, W. (2011), *Warfare in Independent Africa*, Cambridge: Cambridge University Press.

Roitman, J. (2005), *Fiscal Disobedience. An Anthropology of Economic Regulation in Central Africa*, Princeton, Princeton University Press.

Rondeaux, C. and D. Sterman, (2019), *Twenty-First Century Proxy Warfare. Confronting Strategic Innovation in a Multipolar World Since the 2011 NATO Intervention*, Washington: New America.

Schmidt, E. (2013), *Foreign Intervention in Africa: From the Cold War to the War on Terror (New Approaches to African History)*, Cambridge: Cambridge University Press.

Singer, P. W. (2001–2002), "Corporate Warriors: The Rise of the Privatized Military Industry and its Ramifications for International Security", *International Security*, 26 (3): 186–220.

Titeca, K. and T. Costeur (2015), "An LRA for Everyone: How Different Actors Frame The Lord's Resistance Army", *African Affairs*, 114 (454): 92–114.

Tubiana, J. (2008), *The Chad-Sudan Proxy War and the "Darfurization" of Chad: Myths and Reality*, Geneva: Small Arms Survey.

Walter, B. F. (2015), "Why Bad Governance Leads to Repeat Civil War", *Journal of Conflict Resolution*, 59 (7): 1242–72.

Doui Wawaye, A.J. (2017), *La République centrafricaine à la croisée des chemins du droit : entre droit coutumier, droit de sécurité, force du droit positif et droit de la force*. Paris: Harmattan.

Welz, M. (2014), "Briefing: Crisis in The Central African Republic and the International Response", *African Affairs*, 113 (453): 601–10.

Williams, P. D. (2016), *War and Conflict in Africa*, 2nd edn, Cambridge: Polity.

Yanis, T. (2016), *Centrafrique: un destin vole. Histoire d'une domination française*, Paris: Editions Agone.

9

Libya: Fragmentation of the Country amid a Proxy War[1]

Mehmet Alper Sozer and Emirhan Darcan

Introduction

Since the fall of dictator Muammar al-Gaddafi more than ten years ago, Libya has not been at peace. Similarly, Iraq has never been a stable state, nor has it ever witnessed days without bombings as in the "old good days" under Saddam's dictatorship. Would having a ruling dictator be better than having so many somewhat equal powers that are unable to dominate others to maintain stability in the country? What happens amid all these shambles for the sake of reaching a democracy, endless conflicts in an attempt to consolidate power, and "all voices will be heard illusion" in underdeveloped oil-rich countries is just a cursed destiny? We do not know the answer to these arduous questions. We rather try to depict the turmoil in Libya ignited with the Arab uprising through a thorough look at proxy warfare stemming from conflicting interests of several countries.

Framing this chapter with an obscure phenomenon of "proxy war" would be definitely pretentious given the strong efforts of conceptualization in the literature (Mumford 2021: 40–6). Proxy war refers to the employment of intermediaries in the forms of mercenaries, private contractors, and indigenous armed groups in furthering the goal of an external force, namely a patron state (Kozera et al. 2020: 79), or may refer to something, as Fox (2019: 44) puts simply, repackaging the concept in an idea known as by, with, and through and security force assistance. Proxy warfare is not a new phenomenon; its use, however, was augmented after Second World War and seemingly became a new rule of modern warfare rather than an exception. Proxy wars are and have been attractive because they protect governments against unwelcome questions and internal investigations, they can avoid not only detailed inquiries about the cost and the number of casualties at home but also possible legal challenges of any possible violation of international law (Krieg and Rickli 2019: 66). The developed states, which have been shying away from military operations abroad, favor proxy wars due less to a strategic calculation than to fear of damaging effects on governments. Immigration waves, exponentially increasing costs of war, and martyrs' coffins sent to the homeland create huge displacement for the people which, in turn, not only erode the legitimacy of war but also generate negative consequences on the ballots.

The goal of proxy wars, unlike "traditional" military invasions, is not necessarily a victory. An outside power may also support local proxies in order to maintain a precarious status quo or with the aim of overthrowing an unwelcome government, in other words, simply to "feeding the chaos" (Groh, 2019: 9). This is what happens in Libya, another failing state affected by the devastating upshot of the Arab uprising. Several external forces in varying scales pursue opposing goals and seek to advance their geopolitics, geostrategic, and economic interests at the expense of Libya's constancy, which, in turn, amplifies the use of proxies (Laessing 2020: 121). Libya's proxy war, in contrast to Syria's, is mainly sponsored by the Libyan own money and fueled by local power brokers (Fetouri 2019). The increasing meddling of multiple states only worsens the situation. What is more dangerous in Libya is that the tension among the conflicting countries has gradually increased and has highly internationalized the conflict, approaching sometimes the edge of a conventional war that has the potential to strew over the region. This chapter is an effort to understand what has been happening in this very hotspot. It provides important aspects of proxy-based model warfare in Libya from a historical, political, and thematic perspective. In doing so, we start with a snapshot of Libya's history and continue to illustrate armed conflicts and the military intervention of external powers with specific emphasis on the use of proxies in the post-Gaddafi era. Finally, we conclude with recent political developments along with a damage report of this devastating proxy war.

Gaddafi's Libya

Gaddafi came to the power with the promise of constructing "Islamic Socialism" along with an even distribution of wealth blended with socialist democracy, Libya, however, has never witnessed a multi-party democratic process, nor did the people of Libya enjoy any better liberty and prosperous life. He played by the book of any dictator; he simply created an awkward ideology of his kind based on the Zawara Statement, which was reflected in the daily life of Libyans through the *Green Book*, a roadmap in understanding "terrorist activities" opposing to the Gaddafi regime (Chivvis 2013; Darcan 2015: 283–4). With this statement, the bureaucratic cadres in Libya were liquidated (Hagger 2009: 101–2) and the transition to the Shari'a law, which was considered a revolution in the legal system, took place (Vogler 2005: 121; Chivvis 2013).

Gaddafi pursued the goal of a pan-Arab union under Libyan leadership in foreign policy, but this did not materialize. After the failure of his pan-Arab goals, Gaddafi shifted gears and changed his target group from Arab countries to African countries with predominantly Muslim populations. He did not hesitate to extend his generous hands to terrorist organizations operating in Somalia and Niger, which was not pleasant for the western world. The 1986 attack on the "La Belle" discotheque in Berlin, which was frequented mainly by American soldiers, was the last straw, and as a result, the US severed all economic ties with Libya. Later on, things got worse as the UN Security Council imposed an air and trade embargo, and the US Air Force carried out attacks on the Libyan capital, Tripoli. One year later, in 1993, Libya officially renounced all its terrorist activities (Schwartz 2007: 553–80). Following up, as an expression of goodwill, Libya complied with the request of the UN Security Council and surrendered two terrorist suspects to the International Criminal Court (Zoubir 2009: 401–15). In response to attempts of political normalization, in October 2007, Libya was elected to a two-year term as a non-permanent member of the UN Security Council (Solomon and Swart 2005: 469–92). Nobody might have predicted that this short-term honeymoon was not anything more than "calm before the storm." The devastating effect of the Arab uprising made everything upside-down in Libya, and Gaddafi disappeared into the dark corridors of history.

Libya as a Proxy Battleground

Right after changing the political game in Tunisia, the turbulent wave of the Arab uprising did not take long to hit Libya. The forty-two-year-old tyranny of Gaddafi was toppled by a coalition of mixed groups, later became rivalry with each other, and by a NATO military intervention mainly orchestrated by the US and France. Framing what was happening in Libya at that time was quite a struggle. Melcangi and Mezran (2022: 15), devoted their article to understanding the character of the conflict in which they conclude the fragmented order that currently exists in Libya cannot be characterized as a pure proxy war because

142   *Proxy Wars from a Global Perspective*

Libyan players retain a greater degree of autonomy. To some it was a civil war, to others it was a proxy war in which various clans and tribal leaders fought each other, constantly changing their stakes according to power-shifts in the field, attempting to further their gains at all means (Fulvio 2020; Harchaoui and Lazib 2019). A non-state system with split sovereignty emerged during the post-Gaddafi transitional era as a result of rebels seizing control of key towns and areas, disputing the regime's claim to legitimacy, and appointing their own local military council heads (Lacher 2020: 9). The National Transition Council's (NTC) failed attempt to re-institutionalize the nation made it evident that the central government remained submissive to a number of local governments and militias, which operated with a localized, patronage-based system of government and had exclusive use of coercive military force. The Libyan Shield Force and the Supreme Security Committee (SSC) were the first attempts by the NTC to bring together independent militia groups under a single command with the intention of imposing control over them. The SSC became Libya's police force under the Ministry of the Interior, while the Libyan Shield was placed under the Ministry of Defense and became Libya's army. But despite the good intentions behind them, none of these initiatives could be successfully achieved (Melcangi and Mezran 2022: 8).

Libya, right from the beginning of the post-Gaddafi era has been a battleground for great powers, neighboring countries, adventurist Gulf States, and ex-colonial powers. Proxy wars in Libya worked in a reciprocal way. An array of armed groups in Libya swiftly attempted to gain influence over others and filled up spaces in the vacuum of any institutional government body. All of these groups and Libyan power brokers called for foreign aid, military support, and arms from external actors which were readily available and in search of proxies to reshape oil-rich Libya, aligning with their own interests. Qatar, the most assertive intervening power at the beginning, intersected with groups that were ideologically close to the Muslim Brotherhood, specifically supporting religious activist and scholar Ali Mohammed al-Salabi, whereas, the United Arab Emirates supported rival groups more prone to anti-Islamic tendencies (Wehrey 2020: 28). However, these two Gulf States did not operate without the scrutiny of greater powers. France, Saudi Arabia, Russia, and Egypt (after the Morsi era) aligned with the Emirates, on the other hand, Turkey and Sudan worked in line with Qatar.

Over time, disentangling the armed groups became a little bit easier. Following the June 2014 election, the nation was divided into two primary opposing powers, each claiming to represent Libya. The first crucial faction was the Libyan Dawn coalition rested on the authority of the General National Congress (GNC) in Tripoli backed by Qatar and its allies, an organization dominated by western cities' militias, while the other ran its operations from the eastern city of al-Bayda supported by Haftar's Libyan National Army[2] (LNA, one of the main movements largely known from Operation Dignity, supported by the Emirates and its allies) (Mezran 2018: 14). While this dual division made the lines in the Libya proxy war clear, it led to the emergence of two competing security administrations, central banks, and oil production companies in Libya (Melcangi and Mezran 2022: 9).

Ansar al-Sharia, a radical Salafist group, and the Islamic Youth Shura Council, an extremist Islamist group that had links to al-Qaida and later pledged allegiance to Islamic State, also played critical roles on the Libyan battleground (Reeve 2014).

Between the years 2011–2014, the Libyan conflict was not influenced by the direct military intervention of external actors, as it is today, even though officers from special operation forces of many countries were evident on the ground. The rival armed groups were trained, fueled with arsenal, fed with intelligence by external forces, and utilized as proxies in compliance with each country's own agenda. In 2014, with a new offensive initiated by Khalifa Haftar, a second civil war broke out (Fulvio 2020). Starting in 2014, Libya witnessed escalating tension between two groups, LNA and Government of National Accord (GNA), and their external allies. The Emirates' engaged with its air force and it was the first direct foreign military intervention in Libya since the NATO-led coalition's airstrikes in 2011. Since then, the tension in Libya has been constantly escalating and eventually has reached a point where regular forces of certain countries could clash.

Toward Possible Conventional Warfare

The Libyan conflict has been serving as an area for drone competitions along with mercenaries outsourced from a variety of conflict zones in and out of Libya. The Emirates attempted to control the air zone and establish air dominance through the use of their own piloted aircraft, Chinese-made armed drones, and French-made Mirages. As its opponent, Turkey struck back with its national-made TB2's. Many civilians lost their lives because of the haphazard use of drones on the battlefield (UNSC 2019). The Emirates, in particular, caused significant civilian casualties (Wehrey 2020: 10).

On the ground, conflicting external forces preferred using, by and large, infantries consisting of local militias, African mercenaries, and radical Islamist groups. Readily available warriors from African countries having fresh hands-on fighting experience in neighboring southern Libya served as a fighter market for both sides (Debos 2016: 131). However, fighting forces were not limited to outsourced mercenaries; countries not only deployed their own Special Forces personnel as trainers and advisors but also hired private military companies (PMCs) as contractors. Russia, through its Wagner group, is in the foreground as being very vivid in different parts of the world striving to restore the power of the old-great days of the Former Soviet Republic. Turning to hysteria, Putin's ambitions to be Alexander the Great, which he can no longer hide, is using Wagner as a subordinate force in Sudan, Libya, Syria, the Central African Republic (CAR), and Ukraine at the hands of a former restaurant owner, Prigozhin (Østensen and Bukkvoll 2022: 130–51). In Libya, Russia did not want to cede control to the West or lose ground in games of proxies. When Haftar and the Russian defense hierarchy met in Moscow, Prigozhin was also there (Reynolds 2019: 8). Despite predictions that Wagner won't play the same disproportionate role as it did in CAR, it conducted successful operations on the ground, its snipers had a devastating impact on the Sarraj-led GNA, and it later expanded its influence over the command level in the Khalifa Haftar-led LAAF.

At the end of March 2021, UN experts reported "serious human rights violations" committed by Russian Wagner mercenaries in the Central African Republic. The human rights violations included mass shootings, torture, enforced disappearances, indiscriminate attacks on civilian facilities, and attacks on humanitarian workers, eventually, based on these allegations in December 2021, the European Union imposed sanctions on "Wagner" (Masuhr and Friedrich 2020: 2), which obviously did not stop the group's and Putin's further rush into Ukraine.

In the same way, Turkey, with its military contractor, SADAT, founded in 2012 by retired Brigadier General Adnan Tanriverdi, a former general who was dismissed from the Army in 1996 for Islamist ties, operated on the battlefield. The company bills itself as a corporation that "provides consulting in the international defense sector and military training." According to several statements and media reports, despite the company's strong denial, Ankara allegedly contracted SADAT for some paramilitary services such as militia recruitment, training, logistics, and transportation of mercenaries to Libya from Syria (Cubukcu 2018; Eissenstat 2017). It has also long been reported that SADAT has trained fighters and provided military equipment for the opposition in Libya with the support of the Turkish government (Ersozoglu 2020). Based on an agreement signed with the United States in 2015, several militia groups were stationed in Turkey as part of a training and equipment program for Syrian opposition members. The use of these militias in Turkey's foreign operations reached a new level when Erdogan acknowledged the presence of Syrian mercenaries alongside the Turkish army in its operations in Libya which align with the assertation of Tanriverdi who has pushed for so long for Turkish deployment of PMCs in line with the private mercenary force for foreign operations like Blackwater or Wagner did (Wither 2020: 22–3).

Governments of these patron states officially denied their relationship with the aforementioned private military companies. However, according to Sukhankin (2018), Russian writers and military theorists, in the first place, consider PMCs to be on par with regular army units in the battle arena and to play an increasingly essential role in a conflict zone. Aside from battling proxies of patron-states, and terrorist organizations, ISIS as being the most influential along with the Maghreb branch of Al-Qaeda engaged in the Libyan war, either with their own manpower or with the proxies ISIS recruited from among Arabs, Berbers, and the Tuaregs, or from local terrorist groups that declared their affiliation with them (Manyuan 2020: 81).

From the battlefield, the proxy war spread into social and conventional media as well. Each side launched Twitter campaigns against the other. They used bot accounts and hired Twitter trolls to pump fake news into social media aligned with their interests, and also broadcasted through TV stations in order to gain influence and superiority in the propaganda realm that escalated tensions and fueling up the conflict (Wehrey 2020: 18).

To increase its influence, Turkey has centralized several revolutionary groups under an Islamist-nationalistic worldview and paired them with its own military (Yuksel 2019: 138). After signing an agreement on the maritime border with GNA in November 2019, Turkey has expanded its military presence in the field and deployed its own military force supported by Syrian militias. Ankara has basically attempted to consolidate its proxy architecture in Libya by integrating Syrian mercenaries into GNA-aligned battalions. While GNA-aligned militias act as proxies for Turkey, Syrian militias act as mercenaries (Yuksel 2019: 145). Turkey's last maneuver changed the equilibrium in favor of GNA, and as a result, two international conferences were held; one in Moscow, between Turkey and Russia in the aftermath of Turkish gains on the battlefield, and another in Berlin to secure concerns of the EU and the broader international community. Turkey's military deployment in Libya along with the Turkish search for hydrocarbon resources in the Mediterranean and the Aegean Sea, and rival ideological stances, provoked Egyptian repercussions.

The Egyptians are pursuing a gas project that could potentially be linked to facilities in Israel, Cyprus, and Greece to supply Europe. However, this goal is in direct conflict with the Turkish goal of creating a maritime zone with Libya to be used exclusively by these two powers and to secure sole control over Libya's energy resources. Moreover, Sisi threatened to send its own military in response to Turkey's operation. If that had happened, an enduring proxy war would have rapidly turned into a conventional battle between the two countries.

The Ceasefire and Recent Developments in Libya

On October 23, 2020, five officers from each of the Libyan warring parties signed an agreement in Geneva on a "complete and sustainable ceasefire." As members of a Joint Military Commission, they had been working for some time on measures for the disengagement of forces outside the central Libyan town of Syrte, the southern air base of al-Jufra, and on other local fronts, as well as for a withdrawal of foreign mercenary units from the immediate vicinity of the front. The result so far has been an unofficial cease-fire that has been held since July 2020. With the mediation of the United Nations Support Mission in Libya (UNSMIL) "the complete and sustainable ceasefire agreement in Libya between the GNA and the LNA" was negotiated. Significant terms of this agreement included: (1) the withdrawal of foreign mercenary units within three months, (2) the withdrawal of both sides from the front lines, (3) the establishment of a joint police force to take over the security of the cleared areas, and (4) the listing of all militias and fighting parties in a joint register to serve as a basis for their integration into the armies or their demobilization. The agreement also emphasizes the de-escalation in the media by implying "the media escalation and hate speech currently being disseminated via audio-visual propaganda channels and websites are to be stopped, and the judicial and relevant authorities are required to take the necessary measures to ensure serious and deterrent prosecution of these channels and their websites (Lacher 2020). Additionally, the military commission agreed to neutralize the powerful Petroleum Facilities Guard in the west and east of the country, which until now have been close to the Benghazi-based LNA, and to instruct its commanders to work with representatives of the National Oil Corporation in Tripoli on a proposal to restructure and organize the Facilities Guard. This allowed the immediate resumption of oil production and the shipment of oil to ports in eastern Libya (Capasso 2020: 545–67).

International experts fear "devastating developments" due to fights between Tuareg and Tubu, which have close ties with Chad, Niger, and Mali. Both of the two said groups are struggling for control of an area not only important for the water and oil supply, but also for long-established smuggling and trade routes that increase the risk that neighboring countries and other states will also be drawn into the militia war. Dramatically, fights between these tribes are not free from the influences of two Libyan governments, nor are they independent from the interference of foreign states such as Egypt, the Emirates, and Qatar (England, 2020).

UNSMIL facilitated a Switzerland-hosted intra-Libyan talk with the contribution of the Libyan Political Dialogue Forum (LPDF) that identified efforts to end the country's division as the most important task of the presidential council. The acting Special Adviser to the United Nations Secretary-General on Libya, Stephanie Williams, had promised an "open and transparent selection process." The sessions, during which candidates introduced themselves and answered questions from the public, were broadcast on the internet. As a result of this transparent election, a new prime minister and a three-member of the presidential council were elected in Geneva in order to finalize the legal framework for reaching national elections on December 24, 2021 (Lacher 2021).

Conclusion

Two days before the election date on December 24, 2021, the head of the electoral authority called off the vote. After a ceasefire since October 2020, the conflict in Libya seems to be reigniting. A rekindled truce cannot be won by either side. Libya is deeply divided in the face of different lines of conflict. The government of Fathi Bashagha can count on Turkey's support, while Abdulhamid Dbeiba receives help from Egypt, France, and Russia (Aljazeera 2022). Putin has meanwhile withdrawn some of the mercenaries of the private group Wagner stationed in the country, possibly to use them in the war in Ukraine, but this does not change the balance of power in Libya in the long term. Moscow is playing along again while Europe and the US are focusing primarily on Ukraine in the new East-West conflict with Russia, Putin is also expanding his country's position in the Middle East and creating new dependencies. World public opinion hardly notices this military and economic expansion.

The hybrid war strategy has several advantages for Russia. They do not have to fear reprisals from other countries, provided they cannot be proven to be actively involved in the war. Moreover, Russia can present itself as an officially "uninvolved party in the war" as a mediator without having to give up its military involvement. In addition, Moscow can secure control over the Libyan refugee corridor alongside parts of the energy business. This gives Russia a very strong migration power influence *vis-à-vis* Europe, which is already extremely burdened by the Syrian war and more recently by the Ukrainian war. A ceasefire has been in place in Libya for roughly two years. But after the Russian attack on Ukraine, the proxy war between Turkey and its Western partners on the one side and Russia on the other threatens to flare up again.

The proxy war in Libya has never mitigated conflicts nor done any good for the Libyan people; in contrast, it gradually escalated the tension and created a long-lasting battle zone like in Syria, Somalia, and Yemen. The multiplicity of meddling powers on the ground made it very hard, if not impossible, to generate unity and accord within the country. The region constantly experienced unintended consequences such as an uncontrolled flow of weapons, which poured into the hands of radical terrorist groups, a warning sign for possible future bloodshed and instability in the Sahara and beyond. Moreover, the enduring proxy war created a serious refugee problem. People of countries in conflict flew neither to Russia nor to the Gulf States. They preferred to reach Europe where they believe they can find a better life. Italy, in particular, stood as a gateway to the migrant flow from Africa, supporting proxy militias in controlling refugee crossings in the Mediterranean (Fulvio 2020). The recent election victory of the Italian first female prime minister, by and large, leans on her uncompromising stance against immigrants pouring from North Africa (Rizzo 2022).

The actual division of inheritance in Libya has yet to take place; however, it seems hard to prevent this partition. Nevertheless, the political solution is still a long way off. This means that a lasting ceasefire between the warring parties is unlikely for the time being. Although the ceasefire agreement and impending elections symbolize optimism, it is not enough to change the estimation that the ceasefire was only an interlude in Libya's war of succession and that the war could continue after a while. However, the remarkable role the Democratic regimes should have in Libya is to support any form of elected and legitimate governance and rule of law in Libya.

Libya 149

Notes

1 This chapter is an extended and revised version of the Libya part of the article published in the journal *Security and Defense* in 2020 (Kozera, C. A., P. Bernat, C. Gürer, B. Popławski and M. A. Sozer (2020), "Game of Proxies—Towards a new model of warfare: Experiences from the CAR, Libya, Mali, Syria, and Ukraine", *Security and Defense Quarterly*, 31 (4): 77–97).

2 The "Libyan National Army (LNA)" and "Libyan Arab Armed Forces (LAAF)" are two major armed forces among many others operating under a coalition led by Khalifa Haftar.

Bibliography

Capasso, M. (2020), "The War and the Economy: The Gradual Destruction of Libya", *Review of African Political Economy*, 47 (166): 545–67. https://doi.org/10.1080/03056 244.2020.1801405.

Chivvis, C. S. (2013), *Toppling Qaddafi: Libya and the Limits of Liberal Intervention*. New York: Cambridge University Press.

Cubukcu, S. (2018), "The Rise of Paramilitary Groups in Turkey", *Small Wars Journal*, 3 March. Available online: https://smallwarsjournal.com/jrnl/art/rise-paramilitary-groups-turkey (accessed 19 October 2020).

Darcan, E. (2015), "El Kaidenin Libya Versiyonu: Libya İslami Mücadele Örgütü", in B. Sevinç and I. Çiftçi (eds), *Terör ve Şiddet Sarmalında Orta Doğu & Afrika*, Ankara: Karinca Yayinlari.

Debos, M. (2016), *Living by the Gun in Chad: Combatants, Impunity and State*. London: Zed Books.

Eissenstat, H. (2017), "Uneasy Rests the Crown: Erdoğan and 'Revolutionary Security', in Turkey", *POMED Snapshot, Project on Middle East Democracy*. Available online: http://pomed.org/pomed-publications/pomed-snapshot-uneasy-rests-the-crown-erdogan-and-revolutionary-security-in-turkey/ (accessed 2 October 2020).

England, A. (2020), "Libya: How Regional Rivalries Fuel the Civil War", *Financial Times*, 24 February. Available online: https://www.ft.com/content/c113d340-51b1-11ea-90ad-25e377c0ee1f (accessed 2 October 2020).

Ersozoglu, E. (2020), "SADAT: Turkey's Shadow Army in Africa", *Grey Dynamics*, 2 July. Available online: https://greydynamics.com/sadat-turkeys-paramilitary-wings-take-flight-in-africa/ (accessed 19 October 2022).

Fetouri, M. (2019), "Who's fighting their proxy wars in Libya?", *Middle East Monitor*, 9 May. Available online: https://www.middleeastmonitor.com/20190509-whos-fighting-their-proxy-wars-in-libya/ (accessed 2 October 2020).

Fox, A. C. (2019), "Conflict and the Need for a Theory of Proxy Warfare", *Journal of Strategic Security*, 12 (1): 44–71. https://doi.org/10.5038/1944-0472.12.1.1701.

Fulvio, B. (2020), "Libya: Multiple Conflict, Proxy Wars", *Lindro*, 27 July. Available at: http://www.lindro.it/libya-multiple-conflict (accessed: 15 September 2020).

Groh, T. L. (2019), *Proxy War: the Least Bad Option*, Stanford: Stanford University Press.

Harchaoui, J. and M. E. Lazib (2019), *Proxy War Dynamics in Libya*, Blacksburg: Virginia Tech Publishing. https://doi.org/10.21061/proxy-wars-harchaoui-lazib.

Kozera, C. A., P. Bernat, C. Gürer, B. Popławski and M. A. Sozer (2020), "Game of Proxies–Towards a new model of warfare: Experiences from the CAR, Libya, Mali, Syria, and Ukraine", Security and Defense Quarterly, 31 (4): 77–97.

Krieg, A. and J. M. Rickli (2019), *Surrogate Warfare: The Transformation of war in the Twenty-First Century*, Washington DC: Georgetown University Press.

Lacher, W. (2020), *Libya's Fragmentation: Structure and Process in Violent Conflict*, London: Bloomsbury Publishing.

Lacher, W. (2021), *Grenzen der Einigung in Libyen: die Bildung der Einheitsregierung verbirgt alte und neue Gräben*, (SWP-Aktuell, 34/2021), Berlin: Stiftung Wissenschaft und Politik-SWP-Deutsches Institut für Internationale Politik und Sicherheit.

Laessing, U. (2020), *Understanding Libya Since Gaddafi*, New York: Oxford University Press.

Manyuan, D. (2020), "The Cross-Regional Impact and Direction of Proxy War in Libya", *China International Studies*, 84: 65–83.

Masuhr, N. and J. Friedrich (2020), "Söldner im Dienst Autoritärer Staaten", *CSS Analysen zur Sicherheitspolitik*, 274: 1–4.

Melcangi, A. and K. Mezran (2022), "Truly a Proxy War? Militias, Institutions and External Actors in Libya between Limited Statehood and Rentier State", *The International Spectator*, 57 (4): 1–18. https://doi.org/10.1080/03932729.2022.2061225.

Mumford, A. (2013a), "Proxy Warfare and the Future of Conflict", *The RUSI Journal*, 158 (2): 40–6.

Mumford, A. (2013b), *Proxy Wars*, Cambridge: Polity.

Mumford, A. (2021), "Disarmament, Demobilisation and Reintegration (DDR) after Proxy Wars: Reconceptualising the Consequences of External Support", *Third World Quarterly*, 42 (12): 1–18. https://doi.org/10.1080/01436597.2021.1981762.

Østensen, Å. G. and T. Bukkvoll (2022), "Private Military Companies–Russian Great Power Politics on the Cheap?", *Small Wars & Insurgencies*, 33 (1–2): 130–51. https://doi.org/10.1080/09592318.2021.1984709.

Otman, W. and E. Karlberg (2007), *The Libyan Economy: Economic Diversification and International Repositioning*, Berlin: Springer.

Reeve, R. (2014), "Libya's Proxy Battlefield", *Oxford Research Group Briefing*, January. Available online: https://www.files.ethz.ch/isn/187322/ORGJan15LibyaProxyBattlefield.pdf (accessed 15 September 2020).

Reynolds, N. (2019), *Putin's Not-so-Secret Mercenaries: Patronage, Geopolitics, and the Wagner Group*, Washington, DC: Carnegie Endowment for International Peace.

Rizzo, A. (2022), "Giorgia Meloni: She's Called for a Naval Blockade of Africa to Stop Migrants", *Sky News*, 24 September. Available online: https://news.sky.com/story/who-is-giorgia-meloni-far-right-leader-set-to-become-italys-first-female-pm-12703271 (accessed 15 October 2022).

Schwartz, J. B. (2007), "Dealing with a 'Rogue State': The Libya Precedent", *The American Journal of International Law*, 101 (3): 553–580. https://doi.org/10.1017/S0002930000029791.

Solomon, H., and G. Swart (2005), "Libya's Foreign Policy in Flux", *African Affairs*, 104 (416): 469–92. https://doi.org/10.1093/afraf/adi006.

Sukhankin, S. (2018) "Continuing War by Other Means": The Case of Wagner, Russia's Premier Private Military Company in the Middle East', *Jamestown Foundation*. Available online: https://jamestown.org/program/continuing-war-by-other-means-the-case-of-wagner-russias-premier-private-military-company-in-the-middle-east/ (accessed 15 September 2022).

Wehrey, F. (2020), "This War is Out of Our Hands": The Internationalization of Libya's Post-2011 Conflicts From Proxies to Boots on the Ground', *New America*, 14 September. Available online: http://newamerica.org/international-security/reports/this-war-is-out-of-our-hands/ (accessed 15 September 2020).

Wither, J. K. (2020), "Outsourcing warfare: Proxy Forces in Contemporary Armed Conflicts", *Security and Defence Quarterly*, 31 (4): 17–34. https://doi.org/10.35467/sdq/127928.

Yüksel, E. (2020), "Turkey's Approach to Proxy War in the Middle East and North Africa", *Security and Defence Quarterly*, 31 (4): 137–152. https://doi.org/10.35467/sdq/130916.

Zoubir, Y. H. (2009). "Libya and Europe: Economic Realism at the Rescue of the Qaddafi Authoritarian Regime", *Journal of Contemporary European Studies*, 17 (3): 401–15. https://doi.org/10.1080/14782800903339354.

10

The Spheres of Influence: Multiple Proxy Wars in Syria

Engin Yüksel

Introduction

The Syrian Uprising is frequently introduced as an example of how a civil war turns into multiple proxy wars waged by regional and global actors (Philips and Valbjørn 2018: 415). Subsequently, proxy warfare has become the primary mode of intervention on the Syrian battlefield after various forms of relationships between indigenous and external actors have come into existence (Mumford 2013: 40). Broadly speaking, contemporary proxy wars are driven by the empowerment and control of militia groups by foreign actors who are involved in a regional contest for dominance. The historical record of the Syrian Civil War seems to validate this statement. Foreign states have partaken in regional power competition by warring indirectly through local proxies, who are primarily mobilized based on shared identity such as ideology, religion, sect and tribe (Philips and Valbjørn 2018: 419–20). During the last decade, fierce battles between the Syrian opposition and the Assad regime's Syrian Arabian Army (SAA) have been indirectly and directly influenced by Turkey, the US, Qatar and Saudi Arabia on the one hand and Iran and Russia on the other hand. In addition to that, Turkey and the US have taken part in the violent competition between the Syrian Kurds led by the Democratic Union Party (PYD) and moderate and extremist Islamist groups of the Syrian Armed Opposition. However, what is less clear is the nature and character of the proxy relationships between foreign states and indigenous actors in Syria. The mechanisms that underpin the essential features of relationships between external actors and their local proxies on the Syrian battlefield are not fully understood. This indicates a need to understand the comparative examination of Turkish, Iranian and the USA's approaches to unleashing proxy wars in Syria. By this means, the findings of this chapter will make an essential contribution to the evolution of contemporary proxy warfare.

This chapter sets out to investigate in what ways various external actors have designed distinctive approaches to waging a proxy war on the Syrian battlefield. In this regard, this chapter gives an account of how Turkey, Iran, and the US have set up different arrangements with Syria's warring factions from 2011 onward to attain their broader political objectives. To that end, this chapter is designed to compare the essential features of these relationships. For the purpose of this research, this chapter will make use of Philips and Valbjørn's (2018: 419–20) identity-focused proxy war justification and Rauta's (2021: 11–12) definitional proxy war structure while investigating Turkish, Iranian and the USA's approaches to carrying out proxy war.

According to Philips and Valbjørn (2018: 419–420), identity has been an essential feature of building a relationship between an indigenous and external actor. In the case of Syria, shared identity plays a significant role for local and regional actors to establish various connections. Therefore, this chapter uses the argument that identity politics has transformed a local Syrian war into a theater of multiple proxy wars incorporating different actors with various identities. In addition to that, Rauta's theoretical observations are adopted to allow a more profound understanding of the essential features of proxy wars. Rauta's definitional proxy war structure is organized around three features. These are (1) a material-constitutive feature elaborating the provision of any particular form of assistance by an external actor, (2) a processual feature explaining the modalities through which the material-constitutive feature is provided, and (3) a relational feature specifying the character of association between a proxy and an external actor (Rauta 2021: 12–3).

Material-constitutive feature centers on providing different forms of external support to a local actor. This feature is considered an inalienable determinant of proxy wars, and it can range from direct or indirect support. While direct support refers to an external actor's own military forces, indirect support is characterized by various donated assistance strategies such as providing supplies of weapons, financial assistance, or sanctioned use of a neighboring state's territory (Rauta 2021: 16). Much of the literature categorizes proxy wars under indirect military interventions. For instance, Groh (2019: 29) defines proxy war as "directing the use of force by a politically motivated local actor to indirectly influence political affairs of a target state." Nevertheless, states' contemporary war strategies in Syria have demonstrated that direct military interventions could also be used to empower and enable proxy forces.

When it comes to the provision of material support, the direct/indirect dichotomy acquires a new dimension. In this regard, the processual feature examines the proxy relationship as an interactive process of provision and acceptance (Rauta 2021: 16). This feature is utilized to understand if an external actor assists a local warring faction through various chains of government institutions or entirely via external intermediaries. The processual feature has resulted in multiple linkages between local proxies and external factors such as delegation, sponsorship or empowerment (Rauta 2021).

Finally, the relational feature is applied to specify whether a relationship between a foreign state and an indigenous actor falls into the category of proxy, auxiliary or alliance (Rauta 2021: 15). Proxy relationships "are commonly seen as arrangements in which state sponsors work through non-state proxies typically rebel or insurgent groups" (Moghadam and Wyss 2018). On the other hand, auxiliaries are military forces that support the regular armed forces of a state militarily, as opposed to proxies (Rauta 2021: 15). Apart from these, alliances are formal agreements between official representatives of independent states that consists of a promise to aid one another in times of conflict (Leeds 2002: 238).

Therefore, this chapter is designed to compare how Turkey, Iran, and the US have put distinctive proxy war strategies into practice in Syria based on the theoretical framework discussed above. Therefore, a case-study approach is adopted to help understand the essential features of these countries' approaches to carrying out proxy wars. The findings of each case will be used to compare the data based on the pre-selected criteria: the drivers of intervention; the material-constitutive, processual and relational features of proxy war. The findings of this chapter should make an important contribution to the field of proxy war as it discovers the extent to which contemporary proxy war has evolved on the Syrian battlefield by different actors in distinctive forms.

Turkey's Approach to Proxy War in Syria

The antecedents of Turkey's involvement in the Syrian Civil War date back to 2011 when the Assad regime paid no attention to Ankara's proposal to integrate Muslim Brotherhood into the Syrian political structure. Turkey's ruling party, the Justice and Development Party (AKP), has been the staunch backer of Syria's political Islamists (primarily Sunni Arabs) and Turkmens since the beginning of the Syrian Civil War (Veen and Yüksel 2018: 22). Therefore, Ankara aimed to capitalize on existing Islamist and nationalist (Turkish) networks driven by shared identity while attempting to change the course of the Syrian Civil War. Subsequently, Turkey has sought to overthrow the Assad regime through the use of Syrian armed opposition, which encapsulates the secular revolutionary, nationalist Islamist and Salafi-jihadist groups (Yüksel 2019: 19). While the secular revolutionary groups, led by Free Syrian Army (FSA), do not have a religious agenda, the nationalist Islamists aims to build a Syrian Islamist state on the basis of sharia law. Apart from those, Salafi-jihadist groups boil down to the Islamic State of Iraq and Syria (ISIS) and Hay'at Tahrir Al-Sham (HTS), the Syrian branch of the transnational Al-Qaeda network (Yüksel 2019: 19). Between 2011 and 2016, Turkey provided indirect support to the secular revolutionary and nationalist Islamist rebel groups under Ankara's donated assistance strategies towards the Syrian opposition (Yüksel 2020: 141). To that end, these categories of groups enjoyed significant material support such as training, salaries and equipment not only from Turkey but also from the US and the Gulf states (Blanchard and Belasco 2015: 4–5).

After mid-2016, Turkey has relied on direct military interventions to implement its Syrian strategy due to two reasons. Firstly, the secular revolutionary and nationalist Islamist groups could not attain anticipated battlefield performance, especially after Salafi jihadist groups gained more ground in Syria. Secondly, Ankara has perceived the rise of the Kurdish PYD and its tendency to form democratic autonomy in northern Syria as existential threats (Acun and Keskin 2017: 8). By mid-2014, the PYD established three semi-autonomous cantons north of Syria (Afrin, Jazeera and Kobane) following its fight against ISIS. This development shifted Ankara's Syria strategy due to the PYD's organic links with the PKK (Kurdistan Workers' Party), a recognized terrorist organization by Turkey, the USA and the EU. Subsequently, Turkey prioritized undoing the gains of the PYD over toppling the Assad regime after mid-2016. This policy shift has been operationalized through Turkey's direct military involvement and its use of the Syrian Armed Opposition as a proxy element. Consequently, the Turkish military carried out three direct military interventions during Operation Euphrates Shield (2016/2017) against the ISIS and PYD between Al-Bab and Jarabulus, Operation Olive Branch (2018) against the PYD in Afrin, Operation Peace Spring (2019) against the PYD between Tal Abyad and Ras Al-Ayn. Likewise, expanding Syrian regime attacks backed by the Russian military's air support necessitated Turkey to employ the same strategy in Idlib during the fourth military intervention, Operation Spring Shield, in February 2020 (Veen 2021: 1). Selected groups of armed Syrian opposition participated in these operations as Turkish proxies.

Turkey's post-2016 proxy war strategy is predicated on two essential elements. Firstly, it has aimed to have a grip on the groups through "control-through-centralization" policy (Yüksel 2019: 15). This policy has tended to turn the fragmented armed Syrian opposition into a centralized organization with clear command and control structures (Yüksel 2019: 16). While the secular revolutionary and Islamist nationalist groups came to terms with Turkey's merge offer, Salafi jihadist groups with a transnational jihad agenda showed resistance. The transformation between 2017 and 2019 has created the Syrian National Army (SNA), which comprises about 90,000 irregular fighters under seven irregular corps (Özkizilcik 2020: 4). The primary purpose of this unification was to make armed Syrian groups more effective, united and compatible with Turkish military conventional operations. Under Turkey's new proxy war strategy, presumably Turkish National Intelligence (MIT), in coordination with the Turkish military, has relatively easily directed the acts of various armed groups by earning the loyalties of brigade and corps commanders. For instance, apart from Operation Spring Shield in 2020, in none of the operations did the SNA clashed against the Assad regime's Syrian Arabian Army, even though undermining the Syrian regime has long been the primary purpose of the Syrian revolution. Instead, most operations aimed to deliver a heavy blow against PYD's attempts to form democratic autonomy along Turkey's southern borders with Syria (Netjes and Veen 2021: 1). Therefore, a centralized grip over the armed groups has incentivized Turkey to use the Syrian armed opposition as an instrument of influence to change the course of the Syrian Civil War in accordance with Ankara's own agenda.

Secondly, Turkey's acts also incorporate direct military intervention mechanisms. Proxy wars are generally accepted as an instrument of indirect influence (Rauta 2021: 10). In Syria, Turkey has combined its proxy warfare strategy with direct military means and methods. First of all, this strategy was designed to make up for the poor battlefield performance of the Syrian armed opposition in realizing Turkish political objectives. The PYD's progressing autonomy attempt in mid-2015 cordoning Turkey's southern borders under Rojava idea (eastern Kurdistan) and the armed Syrian groups' inability to cope with it has created a perception of existential threat among Turkey's Islamic and nationalist elite (Çandar 2020: 261). Subsequently, Turkey put its military weight into the Syrian Civil War. In some cases, Turkish army units carried out offensive maneuvers in open fields along the main highways, while Syrian armed groups dealt with the adversarial elements in urban centers (Yüksel 2019). In this regard, direct military interventions enhanced the efficacy of Turkey's proxy war strategy in Syria. According to Yüksel (2020: 147), "one of the most distinctive features of Turkish proxy war strategy in Syria is the extent to which it has been able to combine its proxies with its own military units during the military incursions in Syria between 2016 and 2020."

In respect of the provision of support, Turkey's has provided Syrian armed groups payroll, training, equipment and weapons through state institutions instead of intermediaries. In that regard, Turkish institutions such as the Turkish Military and presumably Turkish National Intelligence Agency have engaged with the armed Syrian opposed groups directly without a need for external intermediaries or the Syrian opposition's political body: National Coalition of Syrian Revolution and Opposition Forces. Even though the SNA is technically positioned under the Ministry of Defense of the Syrian National Council, Turkey has contacted straightforwardly with armed groups and has had a tighter grip on them. Until now, the SNA has functioned as the core irregular component of the Turkish military's effective control in northern Syria's imagined safe zones, 30 km stretching outside the Turkish border. Under nearly complete Turkish control via training, equipment and payroll, the SNA has become a full Turkish proxy in northern Syria.

Iran's Approach to Proxy War in Syria

Arab Spring has offered avenues of opportunities for Iran as the totalitarian regimes of the region have been challenged by protest movements and the expansion of insurgencies. Nevertheless, the Syrian revolution's principal objective to undermine Syria's Assad regime has been considered a threat to Iran's national security (Ostovar 2019: 180). Some high-level Iranian officials have gone further to introduce Syria as "a strategic province for Iran", more vital than Iran's own southern Khuzestan Province in case of a simultaneous enemy attack (Ostovar 2019: 176). This is mainly because Iran's Axis of Resistance, "which is the most vital pivot of Iran's unconventional alliance and patronage network [with Lebanese Hezbollah]", stretches from Tehran to Beirut through Syria in Israel's immediate neighborhood (Behravesh 2020: 9). Tehran's priority of maintaining this strategic connection stimulated Iran's political elite to defend the Assad regime at all costs.

Sectarian and geopolitical drivers offer a compelling explanation for the importance attached by Tehran to Damascus. Firstly, the sectarian dynamics of the Syrian Civil War has set Sunni Rebels against Alawite Assad regime. Even though theological and cultural differences exist, the Alawite sect is derived from Shi'a Islam, which has led to an affinity between Damascus and Tehran (Ostovar 2018). As a result of this, Iran has allied with Assad regime since the 1980s. In this regard, Philips and Valbjørn's (2018: 419–20) shared-identity justification of proxy wars applies to Iran's acts in Syria. Iran has long capitalized on the existing Shia-Sunni sectarian divide, as the advocator of the former, within the region to foster ties with Tehran-affiliated governments and sub-state Shia actors (Crepy, 2019). Secondly, converging political interests have stimulated cooperation between two countries. The Assad regime has partnered with Tehran in backing Hezbollah, and it has shared Iran's anti-Israel agenda (Ostovar 2019: 186). Due to the aforementioned reasons, Tehran has provided its support to the Assad regime in various ways since the early stages of the Syrian Civil War.

Iran has relied on primarily irregular methods during its involvement in the Syrian Uprising. Thus, Tehran's approach to waging a proxy war in Syria could be examined under three categories; (1) donated assistance to the Assad regime, (2) the deployment of Iran's primary paramilitary organization, Islamic Revolutionary Guards Corps-Quds Force (IRGC-QF), to Syria, and (3) the use of non-Syrian intermediaries on the Syrian battlefield as a proxy force.

IRGC-QF began providing military assistance to Assad regime immediately after protest movements commenced in mid-March 2011 (Ostovar 2019: 176). Thus, weapons, equipment and military personnel were transferred from Tehran to Damascus via air. High-ranking IRGC-QF members served as advisors for the Syrian Arabian Army (SAA). In addition to that, IRGC-QF trained Assad's National Defense Forces (NDF), acted as an umbrella paramilitary organization with 90,000 personnel from pro-Assad Alawites, Shias and Christians, in Tehran (Philips and Valbjørnb 2018: 420). To that end, IRGC-QF relied on the NDF as the local proxy force. Therefore, Iran predominantly empowered Assad's military and paramilitary forces, as local proxies, in order to shape the course of the Syrian Civil War.

However, Iran's involvement in Syrian Civil War increased as different factions of the Syrian revolution, united under the FSA, received considerable assistance from Turkey, the US and Gulf Countries between 2011 and 2013. As a result, IRGC-QF began taking active roles on the Syrian battlefield covertly, for instance, by fighting near or at the frontlines (Denghan 2013). Especially in 2013, IRGC-QF's foothold saw an increase in the number of low-ranking and non-commissioned officers and specialists from Iran's regular Army (Bucala 2017: 8). Therefore, Iran added another layer to its Syrian war proxy war strategy by directly intervening when the battlefield situation necessitated.

The multi-faceted Syrian War has required Iran to put another strategy in place in addition to the existing two strategies: using Assad's forces as a local proxy and relying on (covertly) direct intervention mechanisms. Under the third strategy, Iran has intended to use intermediary forces, predominantly non-Syrian Shia paramilitary organizations in the region, in support of the Assad regime. These forces include about 8,000 Lebanon's Hezbollah fighters, Shiite militias from Iraq such as Asaib Ahl al-Haq and Kataib Hezbollah, between 10,000 and 15,000 Afghan paramilitaries under the Fatemiyoun Brigade, roughly 2,000 Pakistan fighters under the Zaynabiyoun Brigade and Shia militias from Bahrain (Jones 2019; Ostovar 2019; Knights and Lewitt 2018). These regional Shia militias were organized, trained and funded by Iran's IRGC-QF in the context of Iran's substantial assistance to the Assad regime. Therefore, Shia militias operated as Iran's intermediary proxies on the Syrian battlefield. These militias helped the Assad regime entrench its rule in Damascus while Iran secured its axis of resistance from Tehran to Beirut.

The USA's Approach to Proxy War in Syria

At the outset of the Syrian Uprising, the USA initially advocated for Syrian political transition. When this policy failed, the USA began being indirectly involved in the Syrian Civil War to isolate extremist groups and empower the moderate Syrian Opposition (Williams 2016: 276). To that end, the CIA and Turkish National Intelligence Agency (MIT) facilitated the flow of lethal and non-lethal assistance to the FSA in 2012 under the donated assistance strategy (Philips and Valbjørnb 2018). The purpose of this strategy was to empower the Syrian opposition in overthrowing the Assad regime. However, the USA was increasingly concerned about the possible handover of USA weapons from moderate to extremist groups in Syria (Williams 2016: 271). As a result, the Obama Administration began providing training to the vetted, namely secular-leaning groups, of the Syrian armed opposition under the train and equip program in 2014 (Blanchard and Belasco 2015).

The rise of ISIS changed the USA's geopolitical calculations. Since then, defeating ISIS and maximizing leverage against the Assad regime and Russia for peace talks have become the USA's main priority (Hof 2019). In the beginning, the USA-trained armed groups were asked to fight ISIS. However, this strategy proved ineffective, and the US plan to train the vetted groups of the Syrian armed opposition (in Saudi Arabia) was canceled in 2015 (Williams 2016). Resultingly,

The Spheres of Influence 161

the US formed a broad international coalition to overcome ISIS when the group conquered as much as one-third of Syria and posed a threat to international security in September 2014 (The USA Department of State 2021). After Syria's Kurdish People's Protection Units (YPG) and their connected political party, the Democratic Union Party (PYD), won fierce battles against ISIS in northeast Syria (i.e. battle for Kobane), the US built a tactical partnership with Syria's PYD-led Kurdish groups since 2015 (Netjes and Veen 2021). The partnership has continued to play an active part in the USA's Syria policy even though Washington's objectives has gradually leaned towards countering the Syrian regime and Iran.

The USA's war against ISIS in Syria (as well as in Iraq) relies predominantly on carrying out air operations and using proxy warfare methods. Former President Barrack Obama made the details of this public in September 2014. During a speech, Obama stated that "[w]e will use our air power. We will train and equip our partners. We will advise them, and we will assist them" (Williams 2016: 296). The test case of confronting ISIS by proxy forces was the battle for Kobane (northeast Syria), where the YPG defended the city against the ISIS attacks. In this operation, the US military's waves of precision-guided airstrikes and airborne weapon deliveries earned the YPG a victory after a four-month fight. Subsequently, the US introduced the PYD as a reliable and effective proxy partner in its war against ISIS. After Kobane, Pentagon Press secretary, summarized the results of USA's new proxy war strategy, stating, "I think the airstrikes helped a lot. It helped when we had a reliable partner on the ground in there who could help us fine-tune those strikes" (Hürriyet Daily 2015).

After Kobane, the USA's military assistance continued as the YPG conducted a series of offensives on the ISIS-controlled territories of northeast Syria, i.e., Tal Abyad and Manbij (Williams 2016: 300). The US training, weapons and air support paid off as the YPG operations gained further momentum, liberating about 40 percent of the territories previously held by ISIS in 2016. About several hundred USA Special Forces took part in these operations as an ancillary component (Williams 2016: 312). Nevertheless, the role of USA military forces would be characterized by capacity building which aimed to advise and support the YPG in their fight against ISIS (Seligman 2021). Signifying a major shift in US operations between 2003 and 2011 against Al-Qaeda in Iraq, the US military did not involve kinetic operations in Syria, such as conducting raids or making patrols.

Turkey was growing increasingly uneasy about the PYD's organic links with the PKK, an outlawed terrorist organization in Turkey, and the group's increasing momentum to build democratic autonomy along Turkey's southern borders (Acun and Keskin 2017). To mitigate Turkey's concern, the US facilitated a rebranding of the rebel coalition as Syrian Democratic Forces (SDF), in which several Arab tribal brigades enlisted their support to the PYD in late 2015. This partnership allowed the YPG to expand its operations beyond Kurdish majority and minority areas (Netjes and Veen 2021). As a result, the USA-backed SDF attained to liberate the capital of ISIS, Raqqa, in October 2017. Since then, the USA troops have operated in northern Syria in support of SDF to help prevent ISIS from reconstituting, hamper the Iranian axis of resistance route from Tehran to Beirut and counter-balance Russian and Syrian forces' further territorial gains in northeast Syria (Netjes and Veen 2021: 70–3).

Philips and Valbjørn's (2018) identity theory is inadequate for explaining the USA's involvement in the Syrian Civil War. Until the emergence of ISIS, the USA assisted the Syrian opposition to overthrow an autocratic regime with a record of human rights violations. Therefore, an indirect intervention to promote democracy offers a more compelling driver. Since late 2014, the USA has introduced Syria's SDF as the efficient fighting force against ISIS under the USA-led Operation Inherent Resolve. Like the previous period, this effort is associated with the USA's ambition to counter terrorist groups that posed a danger to Western democracies after 9/11. Therefore, the USA's relationship with the local Syrian actors is predominantly driven by ideology in the form of promoting democracy and countering global terrorism.

The Synthesis of Multiple Proxy Wars in Syria

Table 1 illustrates some of the main features of Turkish, Iranian and the USA's proxy war practices in Syria between 2011 and 2021. Close inspection of the table shows that it investigates the characteristics of proxy wars by using drivers of states, and material-constitutive, processual and relational features.

To begin with, Turkey's proxy warfare in Syria is mainly driven by a shared identity that privileged Syria's Sunni Arabs and Turkmen over other entities such as Alawites and PYD-led Kurds. In addition to that, the Turkish Syrian strategy has relied on performing a mixture of direct and indirect military interventions that varies from providing military assistance to the SNA to carrying out conventional military operations through Turkish military units in northern Syria. Under this strategy, Turkish institutions have straightforwardly engaged with the SNA. Given the level of control that Ankara has ensured on Syria's armed groups, the SNA is described as a Turkish proxy in Syria.

The Spheres of Influence 163

As to Iran, its intervention is in part stimulated by shared identity driven by Shiism. Like Turkey, Iran's proxy war encapsulates an assortment of direct and indirect warfare mechanisms ranging from militarily backing, deploying its own military force to the Syrian battlefield and using regional Shia armed groups. Therefore, Iran has tended to influence the Syrian War through its own institutions and external Shia intermediaries. Apart from these, the relational feature of Iran's proxy war would be characterized by a mixture of auxiliary and proxy arrangements. On the one hand, IRGC-QF's military assistance to the Syrian Arabian Army can be categorized as an auxiliary relationship because it is a covert association between the military forces of two states. On the other hand, regional (non-Syrian) Shia paramilitary groups in Syria have functioned as Iranian proxies.

Table 1 The Synthesis of Turkish, Iranian, and the US Approaches to Waging Proxy Wars in Syria

Actor/ Features	Driver	Material-constitutive	Processual	Relational
Turkey	Shared identity driven by political Islam and Turkish nationalism	A mixture of indirect (btw. 2011–2016) and direct (2016–present)	Turkish institutions' direct assistance to armed Syrian groups	The SNA functioning as a Turkish proxy
Iran	Identity driven by Shiism	A mixture of direct and indirect proxy war strategies	Iranian IRGC-QF and via Shia intermediaries	Auxiliary relation btw. The IRGC-QF and SAA; Proxy relationship with external Shia armed groups
The USA	Ideology driven by democracy and combatting extremism.	A mixture of indirect (2011–2014, to FSA and 2014 to present to PYD/SDF) and direct (2014–present, air and special operations)	The US institutions support for FSA (2011–2014) and PYD/SDF (2014–present)	FSA and SDF functioned as the USA proxies

Source: author

Finally, the USA military intervention in Syria is driven by an ideology (as opposed to identity) that has sought to promote democratic revolutions and eliminate extremism that posed a threat against Western democracies. Like Turkey and Iran, the USA has performed an array of direct and indirect military interventions in Syria that varies from assisting local rebel groups to carrying out airstrikes. In terms of processional features, the USA institutions engaged straightforwardly with local proxies without a need for local intermediaries. Finally, both the FSA and SDF have operated as the US proxies on the Syrian battlefield.

Conclusion

This chapter sets out to investigate the different ways in which Turkey, Iran and the US have performed various proxy war strategies in Syria. This study has found that regional actors, namely Turkey and Iran, have capitalized on the existing (shared) identity networks in building proxy relationships, whereas the USA has pragmatically established linkages to promote democracy and eliminate extremism threat against international security. The research has also demonstrated that the three countries have incorporated their military units, as the decisive or ancillary component, with local proxy forces during their operations. Therefore, these investigations have confirmed that direct military interventions are used to enable, empower and supplement proxy forces. One of the more significant findings to emerge from this study is that, unlike Turkey and the USA, Iran has employed peculiar relational and processual methods of waging proxy war, such as utilizing non-Syrian Shia groups as intermediaries or building an auxiliary relationship with the Syrian Arabian Army. The findings from this study make several contributions to the current literature. First, these findings have extended our knowledge of contemporary proxy wars by showing how three key regional and global actors of the Syrian Civil War have designed atypical approaches. Secondly, this new understanding should help improve predictions of the impact of the Syrian War on the evolution of global proxy warfare.

Bibliography

Acun C. and B. Keskin (2017), "PKK'nın Suriye Örgütlenmesi PYD-YPG", *SETA*. Available online: https://setav.org/assets/uploads/2016/12/20160222181213_pkknin-kuzey-suriye-orgutlenmesi-pyd-ypg-pdf.pdf (accessed 12 October 2021).

The Spheres of Influence 165

Behravesh, M. (2020), "Iran's Unconventional Alliance Network in the Middle East and Beyond", *The Middle East Institute*. Available online: https://www.mei.edu/ publications/irans-unconventional-alliance-network-middle-east-and-beyond (accessed 21 September 2021).

Blanchard, C. and A. Belasco (2015), "Train and Equip Program for Syria: Authorities, Funding, and issues for Congress", *Congressional Research Service*. Available online: https://fas.org/sgp/crs/natsec/R43727.pdf (accessed 18 September 2021).

Bucala, P. (2017), "Iran's New Way of War in Syria", *The Institute for the Study of War*, Available online: https://www.understandingwar.org/sites/default/files/Iran%20 New%20Way%20of%20War%20in%20Syria_FEB%202017.pdf (accessed 12 October 2021).

Çandar, C. (2020), *Turkey's Mission Impossible: War and Peace with the Kurds*, London: Lexington Books.

Crepy, P. (2019), "Proxy Warfare's Impact on Sectarianization: The Case of Saudi-Iranian Rivalry", *Flux International Relations Review*, 9 (1): 23–35.

Denghan, S. K. (2013), "Elite Iranian General Assassinated Near Syria-Lebanon Border," *The Guardian*, 14 February. Available online: https://www.theguardian.com/ world/2013/feb/14/elite-iranian-general-assassinated-syria-lebanon (accessed 12 September 2021).

Groh, T. L. (2019), *The Proxy War: The Least Bad Option*, Stanford: Stanford University Press.

Hof, F. C. (2019), "The United States in Syria: Why It Still Matters?", *Atlantic Council*. Available online: https://www.atlanticcouncil.org/in-depth-research-reports/ issue-brief/the-united-states-in-syria-why-it-still-matters/ (accessed 20 September 2021).

Hürriyet Daily (2015), *Too Soon to Say "Mission Accomplished" in Kobane: US Official*, 28 January. Available online: https://www.hurriyetdailynews.com/too-soon-to-say-mission-accomplished-in-kobane-us-official-77549 (accessed 25 September 2022).

Jones, S. G. (2019), "War by Proxy: Iran's Growing Footprint in the Middle East," *Center for Strategic International Studies*. Available online: https://www.csis.org/war-by-proxy (accessed 12 October 2021).

Knights M. and M. Levitt (2018), "The Evolution of Shia Insurgency in Bahrain", *CTC Sentinel*. Available online: https://ctc.usma.edu/ evolution-shia-insurgency-bahrain/ (accessed 1 October 2021).

Leeds, B., J. Ritter, S. Mitchell and A. Long (2002), "Alliance Treaty Obligations and Provisions, 1815–1944", *International Interactions*, 28 (3): 237–60. https://doi. org/10.1080/03050620213653.

Moghadam, A. and M. Wyss (2018), "Five Myths about sponsor-proxy relationships", *Lawfare*, 16 December. Available online: https://www.lawfareblog.com/five-myths-about-sponsor-proxy-relationships (accessed 16 December 2021).

Mumford, A. (2013), "Proxy warfare and the future of conflict", *RUSI Journal*, 158 (2): 40–46. https://doi.org/10.1080/03071847.2013.787733.

Netjes, R. and V. E. Van (2021), "Henchman, Rebel, Democrat, Terrorist", *Clingendael*, 19 April. Available online: https://www.clingendael.org/publication/ypgpyd-during-syrian-conflict (accessed: 12 October 2021).

Ostovar, A. (2018), "Iran, its Clients, and the Future of the Middle East: The Limits of Religion", *International Affairs*, 94 (6): 1237–55.

Ostovar, A. (2019), "The Grand Strategy of Militant Clients: Iran's Way of War", *Security Studies*, 28 (1): 159–88. https://doi.org/10.1080/09636412.2018.1508862.

Özkizilcik, Ö. (2019), "Uniting the Syrian Opposition: The Components of the National Army and the Implications of the Unifications", *SETA*. Available online: https://setav.org/en/assets/uploads/2019/10/A54En.pdf (accessed 12 September 2021).

Philips, C. and M. Valbjørnb, (2018), "What is in a Name?": The Role of (Different) Identities in the Multiple Proxy Wars in Syria', *Small Wars & Insurgencies*, 29 (3): 414–33. https://doi.org/10.1080/09592318.2018.1455328.

Rauta, V. (2021), "Proxy War": A Reconceptualization', *Civil Wars*, 23 (1): 1–24. https://doi.org/10.1080/13698249.2021.1860578.

Seligman, L. (2021), "Troops to Stay Put in Syria Even as Biden Seeks to End America's 'Forever Wars", *Politico*, 11 November. Available online: https://www.politico.com/news/2021/07/27/troops-to-stay-in-syria-biden-500848 (accessed 12 October 2021).

The US Department of State (2021), "The Global Coalition to Defeat ISIS". Available online: https://www.state.gov/about-us-the-global-coalition-to-defeat-isis/ (accessed 12 October 2021).

Van, V. E. (2021), "Turkey's Interventions in Its near Abroad: The Case of Idlib", *Clingendael*, 6 September. Available online: https://www.clingendael.org/publication/turkeys-interventions-its-near-abroad-case-idlib (accessed 12 October 2021).

Van, V. E. and E. Yüksel (2018), "Too Big for Its Boots: Turkish Foreign Policy Towards the Middle East from 2002 to 2018", *Clingendael*, July. Available online: https://www.clingendael.org/pub/2018/too-big-for-its-boots/ (accessed 18 September 2020).

Williams, B. G. (2016), *Countering Jihad: America's Military Experience in Afghanistan, Iraq, and Syria*, Philadelphia: University of Pennsylvania Press.

Yüksel, E. (2019), "Strategies of Turkish Proxy Warfare in Northern Syria", *Clingendael*, November. Available online: https://www.clingendael.org/pub/2019/strategies-of-turkish-proxy-warfare-in-northern-syria/ (accessed 18 September 2021).

Yüksel, E. (2020), "Turkey's Approach to Proxy War in the Middle East and North Africa", *Security & Defence Quarterly*, 31 (4): 137–55. https://doi.org/10.35467/sdq/130916.

11

Iran's Hybrid Proxy Warfare through Palestinian Terrorism against Israel

Ori Wertman and Christian Kaunert

Introduction

Palestinian terrorist organizations have been conducting a hybrid terror campaign against the State of Israel, which includes executing suicide attacks against civilians, firing rockets and missiles at Israeli population centers, and other notorious activities. Similar to the Lebanese Shiite terrorist organization Hezbollah (Kaunert and Wertman 2020), Hamas, Palestinian Islamic Jihad (PIJ) and other Palestinian Islamic terror organizations have received financial and logistical support from Iran and have served as Iranian proxies. Thus, Hamas and PIJ are integrated as part of the Iranian strategy of indirect war through its proxies against Israel, the West, and other regimes in the Middle East (Orion 2018). Since the violent takeover by Hamas of the Gaza Strip in the summer of 2007, during which the Palestinian Authority (PA) lost its control over the territory, Israel has dealt with a hybrid terrorist organization that controls land inhabited by more than two million Palestinians. Thus, taking advantage of the fact that it is hiding behind a civilian population that serves as a buffer between Israel and Hamas, which in turn continues to conduct hybrid terrorism against Israel, the latter had to face an even more significant challenge in the form of a terrorist entity on its southern border. This chapter reviews how Hamas and PIJ, serving as Iranian proxies have conducted a hybrid terror campaign against Israel, and how the latter confronted this security threat.

The Evolution of Hamas and Palestinian Islamic Jihad

Hamas and PIJ are Palestinian terror organizations leading the fight against the Jewish State. Originating from the Muslim Brotherhood movement, both groups receive direct assistance from the Islamic Revolutionary Guards Corps (IRGC) and are in fact part of the circle of proxy organizations in the service of Iran, which for its part is working to deter Israel from realizing offensive intentions against its nuclear facilities through strong support for terrorist organizations, especially to improve their missile launch capabilities (Mansharof 2020; Orion 2018). Compared to PIJ, which does not enjoy broad support among Palestinian society, Hamas is the leading Islamic movement among the Palestinians, constituting an alternative to the national-secular Fatah movement that leads the Palestine Liberation Organization (PLO), which signed the Oslo Accords with Israel and is heading the PA. In practice, both Hamas and PIJ advocate the complete elimination of Israel and the liberation of Palestine from the sea to the river (Chehab 2007: 202–3; Eldar 2012: 155–60).

Historically, until 1967 when the Gaza Strip was under Egyptian rule, members of the local Muslim Brotherhood were persecuted by the Nasser regime. But after the Six Day War and the Israeli occupation of the Gaza Strip, the Muslim Brotherhood enjoyed relative peace under Israeli rule (Chehab 2007: 4–5). In fact, until the early 1980s, the Israeli authorities did not perceive the Muslim Brotherhood as a threat, and Israel's main security challenge on the Palestinian side was the PLO led by Yasser Arafat, which carried out notorious terror attacks, including the murder of eleven athletes at the 1972 Munich Olympics (Morris 2003: 343–60). Thus, the Muslim Brotherhood, led by a disabled cleric named Ahmad Yassin, had freedom of action on the part of Israel to operate in the Gaza Strip, concentrating on social activities for the Gaza community including providing education and medical services (Tamimi 2007: 36; Chehab 2007: 20; Baconi 2018: 16–7; Eldar 2012: 22–3). In the early 1980s, there was a split amongst the Palestinian Muslim Brotherhood branch. Fathi Shaqaqi, a member of the movement who supported the Islamic revolution in Iran and argued that the Muslim Brotherhood should start an armed struggle for the liberation of Palestine, withdrew from it and founded PIJ (Baconi 2018: 18; Tamimi 2007: 43). Contrary to Shaqaqi's militant line, Yassin argued that prior to the armed struggle, Palestinian society must embrace the values of Islam (Bartal 2012: 96). But clandestinely, Yassin ordered his men to organize militarily and purchase weapons, an operation that was thwarted by the Israeli authorities and led to the incarceration of the movement's members until their release as part of a prisoner exchange in 1985 (Bergman 2018: 412–5; Tamimi 2007: 45; Chehab 2007: 21). The imprisonment did not lower the motivation of Yassin and his men to fight Israel, and in June 1987 they established a military wing (Eldar 2012: 88).

During the mid-1980s, it was PIJ that led the armed struggle against Israel, executing several shooting attacks against Israel Defense Forces (IDF) soldiers (Tamimi 2007: 50; Ganor 2021: 90). But the outbreak of the First Palestinian Intifada in December 1987, an uprising that erupted spontaneously without any prior planning by the PLO or the Palestinian leadership in the territories, devoured the cards for the Muslim Brotherhood in the Gaza Strip. Fearing that they would lose their status among the Palestinian public in favor of Fatah and PIJ, the Muslim Brotherhood decided to focus on the armed struggle, and on December 9, 1987 they founded the "Islamic Resistance Movement," whose acronym in Arabic is Hamas. Thus, all Palestinian terror organizations, both the nationalist PLO and the Islamic organizations Hamas and PIJ, used the circumstances of the intifada to portray themselves as leading the Palestinian people, and in fact competed against each other over who was leading the armed struggle against Israel (Tamimi 2007: 52–4; Chehab 2007: 23–5; Baconi 2018: 1–3; Eldar 2012: 28–30). In August 1988, Hamas published the organization's charter, which was anti-Semitic towards the Jews and portrayed them as a source of the world's problems. Also, the Hamas Charter clearly refused to recognize Israel and saw Palestine as Islamic land, and that the way to liberation is only through armed struggle (Baconi 2018: 21–3).

During the first intifada, Hamas began carrying out terror attacks against Israeli targets through the organization's military wing, Izz ad-Din al-Qassam Bridges. One of its notorious actions was the abduction and murder of two Israeli soldiers in 1989, which led to the imprisonment of Hamas leader Sheikh Ahmad Yassin and the transfer of the movement's center of gravity outside the territories (Tamimi 2007: 57–61; Bergman 2018: 416–7; Baconi 2018: 26; Eldar 2012: 30–1). PIJ also continued the armed struggle against Israel, such as the terrorist attack executed by the organization in February 1990 near Cairo in which nine Israeli tourists were murdered, an activity that had received Iranian support. Perceiving PIJ as the leading organization in the Palestinian struggle against Israel, Tehran allowed the organization to establish a base in Damascus and provided it with economic support and weapons (Bergman 2018: 430), which effectively turn the latter into an Iranian proxy.

Although the first intifada started to diminish in 1991, mainly due to the beginning of the peace process between Israel and the Palestinians at the Madrid Conference in October 1991, Hamas continued to carry out terror attacks against Israeli targets. Hamas' heyday came in December 1992, during which six Israeli soldiers were killed in shooting attacks, and a Border Police soldier was abducted and murdered. In response, the Israeli government led by Yitzhak Rabin decided

170 *Proxy Wars from a Global Perspective*

to deport 415 Hamas and PIJ members to Lebanon (Tamimi 2007: 64–6; Bergman 2018: 417–9). The Israelis were confident that the deportation would be an appropriate reaction of harming Palestinian terrorist organizations. Yet in practice, the deportation led to the unification of the internal and foreign leadership of Hamas, which was based in Jordan and led by Mousa Abu-Marzook, and to global media exposure (Tamimi 2007: 68–9). Most importantly, the deportation enabled the liaison between the Hamas deportees and Hezbollah and IRGC, who came to Lebanon with the aim of assisting the Palestinian terror organization. Thus, IRGC and Hezbollah taught Hamas deportees methods of warfare and the preparation of explosives, knowledge that would be used later to carry out terrorist attacks in Israel. Eventually, in April 1993, Hamas carried out its first suicide bombing, when a suicide bomber blew himself up in a car bomb in the Jordan Valley (Bergman 2018: 416–21).

Sabotaging the Oslo Peace Process using Suicide Terrorism

The terror attacks of Hamas and PIJ escalated after the signing of the Declaration of Principles (DOP) in September 1993, in which Israel and the PLO began a peace process to end the Israeli-Palestinian conflict. Hamas and PIJ vehemently opposed the Oslo Accords and saw them as a betrayal of the Palestinian people, claiming that Palestine is Islamic Waqf land and that no one has the right to give it up (Chehab 2007: 190; Tamimi 2007: 105–6; Gunning 2007: 199; Mishal and Sela 2006: 83; Bartal 2012: 96–7). But in addition to the ideological opposition to any compromise with Israel, Hamas saw the agreements signed by Arafat and the PLO as a strategic threat to its existence, which would distance Hamas from setting the agenda of the future Palestinian state (Mishal and Sela 2006: 107; Eldar 2012: 70). The terror policy of both organizations received clear support and backing from the ayatollahs' regime in Tehran, who in turn transferred their financial support from the PLO to Hamas and PIJ (Azizi 2020: 165). The preferred method by the two organizations was executing suicide terror attacks, such as those conducted on October 19, 1994, on a bus in Tel Aviv in which twenty three Israelis were murdered, and on January 22, 1995, at the Beit Lid junction in which twenty one Israelis were killed (Bergman 2018: 422–3; Morris 2003: 583). Israel responded directly against the Palestinian terror organizations by arresting hundreds of their activists. Nevertheless, despite the continuation of the Palestinian terrorism, The Israeli government decided not to halt to negotiation with the PLO (Inbar 2004: 206).

Iran's Hybrid Proxy Warfare through Palestinian Terrorism against Israel   171

For Hamas, the suicide terror attack, a method that was learned from Iran and Hezbollah, were a weapon aimed at resetting the balance of power with Israel. Perceived by them as the only means of pressuring Israel to recognize the rights of the Palestinians (Tamimi 2007: 161–5), this notorious method also received religious legitimacy. Both the Mufti of Jerusalem and the PA, Sheikh Ikrima Sabri, and many other clerics in the Muslim and Arab world having expressed support for the suicide attacks in Palestine, arguing that it is a noble act of sacrifice for the sake of God (Tamimi 2007: 181–4).

Despite the Israeli expectation that handing over control to Arafat and the PLO would lead to a decline in Palestinian terrorism, and that the PA would try to thwart terrorist attacks as required by the Oslo Accords, Arafat and his men chose not to seriously confront Hamas and PIJ (Ganor 2021: 129–32; Bergman 2018: 425; Chehab 2007: 115; Tamimi 2007: 83), and the PA also helped Hamas members escape from Israeli security forces (Chehab 2007: 127). Despite the PA's unwillingness to fight terrorism, negotiations between Israel and the PLO have continued. Eventually, both sides signed the interim agreement on September 28, 1995, in which the PA was given control of the concentrations of the Palestinian population in the West Bank and Gaza Strip, an area equivalent to twenty six percent of the West Bank (Interim Agreement 1995).

Simultaneously with the implementation of the Interim Agreement, the Israeli security forces continued to fight the Palestinian terrorist organizations. On October 26, 1995, PIJ leader Fathi Shaqaqi was assassinated in Malta by the Mossad (Bergman 2018: 432–6). But on January 5, 1996, Israel recorded another significant achievement in the war on terror, when it succeeded in eliminating the head of Hamas' military wing in the West Bank Yahya Ayyash, who was responsible for the deaths of fifty-six Israelis in suicide bombings in 1994–1995 (Bergman 2018: 436–44; Chehab 2007: 59–60). But in retaliation for Ayyash's assassination and with the aim of thwarting the continuation of the Oslo Peace Process and harming Arafat and the PA, Hamas executed two suicide terror attacks on February 25 in Jerusalem, in which twenty-three Israelis were murdered, and on March 3 in Jerusalem, in which nineteen were murdered. The next day, March 4, PIJ also carried out a suicide attack in Tel Aviv in which fifteen Israelis were murdered (Bergman 2018: 445–6; Chehab 2007: 62–4; Hroub 2006: 54; Eldar 2012: 81–2).

Hamas and PIJ's terror attacks continued in 1997: on March 12 in Tel Aviv killing three Israelis; on July 30 in Jerusalem where fifteen Israelis were murdered, and on September 4, in Jerusalem murdering four Israelis. (Naveh 1999: 72–9). In Israel, there were those who believed that Arafat had given the green light to the

172 *Proxy Wars from a Global Perspective*

terror organizations to carry out terror attacks to signal to the new right-wing Israeli government headed by Benjamin Netanyahu, that it must move forward in the peace process. Indeed, in contrast to what was agreed in the agreements with Israel, Arafat released Hamas members from prison, and refrained from disarming the Palestinian terror organizations (Eldar 2012: 73–84). In response to the Hamas attacks, on September 25, Israel tried to eliminate the deputy chairman of Hamas political bureau, Khaled Mashal, who was based in Amman, the capital of Jordan. But the operation failed, during which two Mossad fighters were captured by the Jordanian security forces. Aiming to release the Mossad fighters and to appease the Jordanian King Hussein, who was furious that Mossad operated in his kingdom without his knowledge, Netanyahu accepted to release Hamas leader Sheikh Yassin from Israeli prison (Yatom 2009: 13–31; Bergman 2018: 448–66; Eldar 2012: 19). Despite Mashal's failed assassination attempt, Israel continued to act against Palestinian terrorism and recorded considerable successes: in March 1998, Israel eliminated Mohiyedine Sharif, Hamas' master bombmaker, by planting an explosive device in his car (Bergman 2018: 448–66); and in September 1998, Israeli security forces succeeded in eliminating the head of Hamas' military wing in the West Bank, Adel Awadallah, an action that led to the arrest of all members of Hamas' military wing in the West Bank (Ayalon 2020: 156–64; Bergman 2018: 448–66). In parallel, further progress was made in the peace process, when on October 1998, Israel and the PLO reached an agreement, in which Israel transferred thirteen percent of the West Bank to the PA (Israel Ministry of Foreign Affairs 1998), an agreement that was perceived by Hamas and PIJ as a betrayal (Tamimi 2007: 120).

After Ehud Barak's victory in the Israeli elections in May 1999, progress was made in the peace process, and it seemed that both sides were on the verge of historic peace agreements. However, following the failure of the Camp David Summit in July 2000, during which Arafat refused Barak's proposal whereby a Palestinian state would be established on approximately ninety percent of the territory (Ben-Ami 2004: 187; Karsh 2004: 187; Harel and Issacharoff 2004: 68–70), and the outbreak of the Second intifada at the end of September 2000 (Harel and Issacharoff 2004: 18–9; Ben-Ami 2004: 292; Bregman 2005: 127), Palestinian terrorism returned to strike in Israeli cities. In fact, in early October, Arafat met with the heads of all Palestinian terror organizations and gave them the green light to carry out terror attacks, and again ordered the release of hundreds of Hamas prisoners from PA prisons (Tamimi 2007: 199–200; Eldar 2012: 86–7). Thus, with the help of funding from Hamas' headquarters abroad, which began operating from Syria after its men were deported from Jordan in August 1999

Iran's Hybrid Proxy Warfare through Palestinian Terrorism against Israel 173

(Chehab 2007: 132–3; Tamimi 2007: 121–5), Hamas has returned to carrying out suicide terror attacks in Israel, the first of these was in early March 2001 in the city of Netanya, where three Israelis were murdered (Eldar 2012: 87–91).

The Second Intifada: The Culmination of Palestinian Terrorism

Terror attacks significantly increase during the second Palestinian intifada, when Fatah, Arafat's organization, also joined Hamas and PIJ (Tamimi 2007: 199–200), executing a total of 146 suicide terror attacks, in which 518 Israelis were murdered (Ganor 2021: 204). In addition to the suicide attacks, Hamas began from April 2001 to launch rockets from the Gaza Strip at southern towns in Israel located a few kilometers from the border (Harel and Issacharoff 2004: 122–3; Drucker and Shelah 2005: 56). In response to Palestinian terrorism, one of the counter-terrorism measures used by Israel during the second intifada was the targeted killing, which enabled Israel to target Palestinian terrorists groups without harming civilian population (Bergman 2018: 494–5; Harel and Issacharoff 2004: 98). Using this method, twenty-four terrorists were eliminated in 2000, eighty-four in 2001, 101 in 2002, and one hundred and thirty-five in 2003 (Bergman 2018: 501–4). In addition, Israel was successful in locating arms smuggling to the PA. The most notable case was in January 2002 with the capture of the ship "Karine A" in which fifty tons of weapons purchased from Iran through Hezbollah were discovered (Harel and Issacharoff 2004: 180–1; Drucker and Shelah 2005: 169–70).

After Palestinian terrorism reached its peak in March 2002, in which 133 Israelis were murdered, the Israeli government headed by Ariel Sharon has decided to launch a large-scale military operation ("Defensive Shield") with the aim of dismantling the Palestinian terrorist infrastructure in the West Bank (Ganor 2021: 214–6; Bergman 2018: 493). Although Israel managed to severely harm Palestinian terrorist organizations during the operation, Palestinian terrorism did not cease: in May 2002, Hamas carried out a terrorist attack on a club in Rishon LeZion and killed fifteen Israelis, and in June 2002, PIJ carried out a suicide bombing at the Megiddo junction and killed seventeen Israelis. In response, Israel continued to use targeted counterterrorism weapons, when in July 2002 it eliminated the head of Hamas' military wing, Salah Shehadeh. This phenomenon in which the terror organizations continued to carry out suicide bombings and in response Israel continued to directly attack the heads of the terrorist organizations through targeted killing also continued in the years 2003–2004: in August 2003, Hamas carried out a terror attack on a bus in Jerusalem in which twenty three Israelis were murdered, and in October 2003 PIJ executed a suicide attack on a restaurant in Haifa in which twenty one Israelis were killed. In response, using targeted killing method, Israel succeeded to eliminate Hamas leader Sheikh Yassin in March 2004, and his successor Abdel Aziz al-Rantisi in April 2004. In fact, throughout the second intifada (October 2000–May 2004), Israel eliminated 237 terrorists through the method of targeted killing (Ganor 2021: 217–23; Bergman 2018: 553–6; Eldar 2012: 50–62).

Another prominent measure to fight Palestinian terrorism was the Israeli decision from mid-2002 to build a separation fence between it and the PA (Ganor 2021: 217–8). In fact, the existence of the separation fence substantially reduced the number of terrorist attacks. While from the beginning of the second intifada in September 2000 until the construction of the separation fence, 73 suicide bombings were carried out in which 293 Israelis were killed, since its establishment (albeit partially) in August 2003 until August 2004, five suicide bombings have been carried out from the West Bank in which 28 Israelis were killed (Ganor 2021: 226–7).

Eventually, following Arafat's death in November 2004 and the election of Abu Mazen as PA chairman in January 2005, there was a significant decline in the scale of the violence. All in all, Palestinian suicide terrorism posed a significant security challenge to Israel during the second intifada and caused many casualties on the Israeli side: four suicide bombings were executed and fourty four Israelis were killed in 2000; thirty five attacks with 207 Israelis dead in 2001; fifty nine attacks with 451 Israelis dead in 2002; twenty six attacks with 208 Israelis dead in 2003; and twelve attacks with 117 Israelis dead in 2004 (Ynet 2009). In addition, rocket fire by Palestinian terrorist organizations also intensified during the second intifada period: fourty two in 2002, 105 in 2003, and 159 in 2004 (Ganor 2021: 221). Eventually, despite the efforts of Palestinian terror organizations, Israel managed to neutralize suicide terrorism using a method of targeted killing, an instrument that led Hamas leaders to offer Israel a ceasefire agreement through the intermediary Egypt that essentially stipulated cessation of Hamas' terrorist attacks in exchange for an Israeli cessation of targeted assassinations. In addition, after Abbas came to power in 2005, the PA began to take the Palestinian terrorist organizations seriously while conducting security cooperation with Israel (Bergman 2018: 556–63; Eldar 2012: 62–3). However, the second intifada illustrated to Israel the Iranian support for Palestinian terror organizations, with Iranian fingerprints on weapons, explosives and methods of warfare clearly visible. In practice, Palestinian terrorist organizations began to resemble the Lebanese Hezbollah organization, the central proxy organization under Iranian auspices (Katz and Hendel 2011: 45).

Post-Yassin Era: Strengthening Relations Between Iran and Hamas

Following Yassin's assassination, there was a significant rapprochement between Hamas and Iran. In fact, Sheikh Yassin opposed close ties with Iran because he wanted to maintain organizational independence. In addition, the religious aspect also had weight in Yassin's decision to keep his distance from the Shiite Iranian leadership, with Hamas being a Sunni organization (Eldar 2012: 342; Bergman 2018: 565). Thus, while PIJ was an Iranian proxy organization in the broadest sense of the word, until Yassin's assassination the connection between Hamas and Iran was loose. Yassin preferred to maintain close ties with the Sunni states, especially Egypt and Saudi Arabia, as the latter poured large sums of money into Hamas charities without demanding anything in return. On the other hand, the Iranians perceived Hamas as a branch of the Muslim Brotherhood whose main struggle is with Arafat and the PA and not with Israel, but still transferred several tens of millions of dollars a year to Hamas. In practice, until the outbreak of the second intifada, Iran did not believe that Hamas had a great chance of succeeding in the frontal struggle against Fatah, and instead preferred trying to directly influence Arafat and even transferred weapons to him, as the case of the Karine A illustrated (Eldar 2012: 190–2).

There was controversy in Hamas over ties with Iran: While Hamas leaders in the Gaza Strip feared strengthening ties with Iran, Hamas leaders abroad in Damascus led by Khaled Mashal found in Tehran the key to building the organization's power. Another aspect of the connection with Iran was the fact that Hamas, which feared Israel's targeted assassination method and therefore reached an agreement with it to stop the attacks in exchange for stopping the assassinations, had to find a suitable alternative to suicide terror attacks. The answer was to fire rockets at Israel, as Hezbollah in Lebanon did from southern Lebanon (Eldar 2012: 193–5). Thus, Hamas in the post-Yassin era under Mashal has established close ties with Iran. Hamas' contact person with the Iranians was Izz el-Deen al-Sheikh Khalil, through whom Tehran began sending missile parts to the Gaza Strip in an effort to increase the range of the rockets (Bergman 2018:

582–3). Although Sheikh Khalil was assassinated by Israel in September 2004 from his car bombing in Damascus (Eldar 2012: 100–1; Bergman 2018: 583; Chehab 2007: 147–8), Iranian support for Hamas continued. At the same time, PIJ also received assistance from Iran, when with the help of Hezbollah, dismantled rockets were transferred from Iran and Syria into the Gaza Strip and assembled by PIJ members (Bergman 2018: 570–1).

In the summer of 2005, Israel decided to unilaterally disengage from the Gaza Strip, an action that was interpreted by Hamas as a victory through resistance and as the first step on the road to the liberation of all of Palestine (Baconi 2018: 89). The disengagement practically helped Hamas to criticize Fatah and present PA Chairman Abu Mazen as a weak leader who does not influence Israel, and was an important element that aided Hamas' victory in the January 2006 Palestinian parliamentary elections (Baconi 2018: 94–7; Tamimi 2007: 219–21). In the summer of 2007, Hamas completed its takeover of the Gaza Strip by carrying out a violent coup against the PA (Eldar 2012: 244–61; Baconi 2018, 131–2), an action that led Israel to impose a siege on the Gaza Strip, with the support and encouragement of PA officials including Abbas himself, who claimed that the siege would cause Hamas to fold and relinquish its rule (Eldar 2012: 266–8). In practice, the disengagement and Hamas takeover of the Gaza Strip have had a major impact on the armament of Palestinian terror organizations in the Gaza Strip, as the rate of their acquisition of weapons and the firing of rockets increased afterwards (Siboni 2014: 27). Thus, with the help of Hezbollah and the IRGC, Hamas significantly expanded its military arm, which in effect became an army of ten thousand fighters (as of the end of 2008), which included snipers, anti-tank units, combat intelligence, tunnel diggers, infantry, naval commando and artillery. Furthermore, Hamas continued to develop its military industries to manufacture rockets and munitions while relying almost entirely on Iranian knowledge and smuggling network (Katz and Hendel 2011: 176–8). Following Sheikh Khalil's assassination, the man in charge of Hamas' relations with Iran was Mahmoud al-Mabhouh, who ensured the flow of weapons from Iran to Sudan, from there to Egypt, and then smuggled through Sinai desert to Gaza through underground tunnels located on the border between Gaza and Egypt (Bergman 2018: 610–9; Katz and Hendel 2011: 138–41). In addition, with Iran's support, Hamas set up munitions' depots in the Gaza Strip in a similar format set up by Hezbollah in Lebanon, and Hamas operatives were trained in Iran and Lebanon, acquiring knowledge in military guerrilla warfare, tank warfare, communications, intelligence and sabotage methods (Katz and Hendel 2011: 180–2).

2008–2021: Four Violent Rounds Between Israel and Palestinians Proxies

After realizing that the rocket threat posed by Palestinian terror organizations with Iranian funding had become unbearable, Israel decided to launch a large-scale operation against Hamas and PIJ in in Gaza Strip. During Operation Cast Lead, which began at the end of December 2008 and lasted until mid-January 2009, 558 rockets were fired at southern Israel by Palestinian terrorist organizations, an average of twenty three rockets per day (Elran 2012). The strategy of the Palestinian terror organizations was to fire from population centers, in direct violation of international law, in order to both deter Israel from firing back for fear of harming Palestinian civilians, and to provoke international criticism against Israel if the latter does respond and fire back at the source of the shooting (Katz and Hendel 2011: 58–9). During the operation, the IDF destroyed dozens of targets, including rocket launchers, ammunition depots, and underground passages to the launch sites. In practice, fifty percent of Hamas' launch capabilities built with the help of the Iranians were destroyed, and dozens of underground tunnels were eliminated by the Israeli Air Force. Yet at the end of the operation, Hamas declared victory, claiming that Israel had failed to disarm the organization and stop firing rockets at it (Eldar 2012: 296–322; Baconi 2018: 154–9; Katz and Hendel 2011: 192–204).

Even after Operation Cast Lead, the Iranians continued their policy of arming the Palestinian terror organizations in the Gaza Strip, endeavors that were frequently thwarted by Israel. For example, in January–February 2009, Israel destroyed convoys of trucks carrying the weapons in Sudan that delivered weapons to Egypt and from there through underground tunnels to Gaza, including dismantled Fajr three rockets with a shooting range of forty kilometers (Katz and Hendel 2011: 247–8). Another smuggling route was through the sea, which Israel also knew how to deal with, as the capture of the ship Francop in November 2009 on which 500 tons of weapons were found well illustrated (Katz and Hendel 2011: 221–33). Mabhouh's assassination in January 2010 (Katz and Hendel 2011: 138–41) also did not prevent Iran from continuing its efforts to arm Palestinian terror organizations, as weapons transfers from Iran to the Gaza Strip continued. These included medium-range and short-range rockets and advanced anti-tank and anti-aircraft missiles, which Israel defined it as a tie-breaking weapon. Therefore, the Israeli efforts to prevent the transfer of advanced weapons from Iran to the Gaza Strip continued: In October 2012, when F15 aircraft of the Israeli Air Force attacked in Khartoum, Sudan, which served as a transit station for the shipment of weapons from Iran to Gaza Strip (Bergman 2018: 625).

In order to overcome the rocket fire, Israel began to deploy at the end of 2010 the Iron Dome, an interception system specially designed to handle short-range rockets. Apart from the interception capability of the Iron Dome system, which prevents serious harm to civilians and property, it has allowed the Israeli leadership freedom of maneuver. Thus, while before the Iron Dome era, Israel was forced to launch an operation in Gaza in order to undermine the rocket capability of Palestinian terrorist organizations, thanks to the Iron Dome, Israel can contain rockets firing from the Gaza Strip up to a certain limit by reducing pressure on the Israeli government to respond (Katz and Hendel 2011: 79–87).

Although the Syrian civil war started in 2011 led to a rupture in Hamas-Iran relations and a significant reduction in Iranian funding of the Palestinian terrorist organization (twenty three million US dollars monthly), with the latter expressing support for the Assad regime while Hamas supported its downfall, Iran continued to support PIJ economically and militarily (Eldar 2012: 336–7; Baconi 2018: 186; Levin 2021). In November 2012, another violent round was held between Israel and Hamas, Operation Pillar of Cloud. The fighting lasted a week, during which more than 1,400 rockets were fired at Israel, a daily average of 175, when rockets were also fired at Tel Aviv and Jerusalem for the first time. Yet the Iron Dome system, whose interception rate was eighty four percent, managed to significantly reduce the number of casualties and damage on the Israeli side (Elran 2012: 29). Operation Pillar of Cloud, which began with the assassination of Hamas army chief Ahmed Jabari, ended in an Egyptian-mediated ceasefire (Baconi 2018: 193–5). Another round of fighting between Israel and the Palestinian terror organizations took place in the summer of 2014, Operation Protective Edge, when in response to the abduction and murdering of three Jewish teenagers by Hamas terrorists and the continuation of massive rocket fire at a city, Israel launched a large-scale operation against Hamas and Palestinian terrorist organizations in the Gaza Strip. During fifty days of fighting, 4,300 rockets were fired at Israel, which, thanks to the Iron Dome system, failed to cause significant damage to the Israeli home front. Like in the last round in 2012, the fighting finally ended with the help of Egyptian mediation (Baconi 2018: 212–21).

Not only Hamas had a crisis in relations with the Iranian patron against the background of Tehran's policy in the region. In mid-2015, PIJ also had a crisis in relations with Iran, after the former refused to support Tehran's involvement in Yemen and their support for the Houthi movement in the country. But a year later, the crisis was resolved, and Iran returned to support PIJ allocating seventy million US dollars annually. Eventually, Hamas-Iran relations returned to normal in 2017, as Tehran again began funding the Palestinian terror organization and enhancing its rockets arsenal (Levin 2021). The outcome was illustrated in May 2021, when another round of fighting ensued between Israel and Hamas, after seven years of relative calm, after Hamas launched a rockets attack on Israel. During Operation Guardian of the Walls, which lasted eleven days, Hamas and PIJ fired 4,400 rockets at Israel, ninety percesnt of them were intercepted by the Iron Dome (Terrorism-Info, 2021). In fact, Iranian sponsorship played a major role in enabling Hamas to start this round, maintaining frequent barrages of up to twenty seven rockets per minute against targets in Tel Aviv, with the aim of overwhelming Iron Dome (Levi 2021). One of the types of rockets used in this round is the Badr 3, an Iranian rocket which carries a warhead weighing between 300 kg and 400 kg with a range of at least thirteen kilometers (Hinz 2021). In addition to the assistance with weapons, the Iranians have also funded the families of Palestinian terrorists. For example, in January 2020, the Al-Ansar Charity Association, affiliated with PIJ, distributed Iranian funds to "martyr" families, who were killed from the beginning of the second intifada until Protective Edge. It is estimated that this is an amount of close to two million US dollars paid to 4,800 families, with each family receiving an amount ranging from three to six hundred US dollars (Terrorism-Info 2020).

Summary and Conclusions

This chapter presented how Iran supported the Palestinian terrorist organizations, which for Tehran serve as proxy organizations for the day of command in the fight against Israel. As early as the 1990s, Palestinian terrorist organizations Hamas and PIJ have received assistance from IRGC. Thanks to Iranian funding and knowledge, Hamas and PIJ have been able to carry out suicide bombings against Israel during the Oslo process, terror attacks that have hampered the progress of the peace process, and during the second intifada as part of the Palestinian terrorist attack on the Jewish state. After Israel managed to neutralize Palestinian suicide terrorism at the end of the second intifada, the Iranian aid has been a key component in improving the military capability of Hamas and PIJ, especially in upgrading their rocket array which became their main weapon against Israel. Thus, while in Operation Cast Lead at the end of 2008, the rockets of Palestinian terrorist organizations managed to threaten only cities and towns located in southern Israel, in May 2021 during Operation Guardian of the Walls, the rockets of Hamas and PIJ reached as far as Jerusalem and Tel Aviv and the rest of central Israel. Thus, we can conclude that, not only have Palestinian terrorist organizations been conducting a hybrid terror campaign against the State of Israel, including suicide attacks against civilians, firing rockets and missiles, etc, similarly to the Lebanese Shiite terror organization Hezbollah (Kaunert and Wertman 2020), they have also received financial and logistical support from Iran; thus, serving as Iranian proxies. In conclusion, Hamas and PIJ are integral to the Iranian strategy of indirect war through its proxies against Israel, the West, and other regimes in the Middle East.

Bibliography

Ayalon, A. (2020), *Friendly Fire: How Israel Became Its Own Worst Enemy*, London: Scribe.

Azizi, A. (2020), *The Shadow Commander: Soleimani, the US and Iran's Global Ambitions*, London: Oneworld.

Baconi, T. (2018), *Hamas Contained: The Rise and Pacification of Palestinian Resistance*, Stanford: Stanford University Press.

Bergman, R. (2018), *Rise and Kill First: The Secret History of Israel's Targeted Assassinations*, New York: Random House.

Bregman, A. (2005), *Elusive Peace: How the Holy Land Defeated America*, London: Penguin Books.

Chehab, A. (2007), *Inside Hamas: The Untold Story of Militants, Martyrs and Spies*, London: I.B. Tauris.

Eldar, S. (2012), *Getting to Know Hamas*, Israel: Keter [Hebrew].

Elran, M. (2012), "The Civilian Front: Learning from Success", in S. Brom (ed.), *In the Aftermath of Operation Pillar of Defense: The Gaza Strip, November 2012*, 33–8, Institute for National Security Studies (INSS).

Ganor, B. (2021), *Israel's Counter Terrorism Strategy: Origins to the Present*, New York: Columbia University Press.

Harel, A. and A. Issacharoff (2004), *The Seventh War*, Israel: Yedioth Ahronoth [Hebrew].

Hinz, F. (2021), "Iran Transfers Rockets to Palestinian Groups Terrorism", *Wilson Center*, 19 May. Available online: https://www.wilsoncenter.org/article/irans-rockets-palestinian-groups (accessed 1 October 2021).

Inbar, E. (2004), *Rabin and Israel's National Security*, Israel: Ministry of Defense [Hebrew].

Interim Agreement (1995), "Israeli Palestinian Interim Agreement on the West Bank and the Gaza Strip", 28 September. Available online: https://web.archive.org/

web/20021115180646/http://knesset.gov.il/process/docs/heskemb_eng.htm (accessed 1 October 2021).

Israel Ministry of Foreign Affairs (1998), "The Wye River Memorandum", *Israel Ministry of Foreign Affairs*, 23 October. Available online: https://mfa.gov.il/MFA/ForeignPolicy/Peace/Guide/Pages/The%20Wye%20River%20Memorandum.aspx (accessed 1 October 2021).

Karsh, E. (2004), *Arafat's War: The Man and His Battle for Israeli Conquest*, Israel: Ma'ariv [Hebrew].

Katz, Y. and Y. Hendel (2011), *Israel vs. Iran*, Israel: Kinneret, Zmora-Bitan, Dvir [Hebrew].

Kaunert, C. and O. Wertman (2020), "The Securitization of Hybrid Warfare through Practices within the Iran-Israel Conflict: Israel's Practices to Securitize Hezbollah's Proxy War", *Security and Defence Quarterly*, 31 (4): 99–114. https://doi.org/10.35467/sdq/130866.

Levi, I. (2021), "How Iran fuels Hamas Terrorism", *Washington Institute for Near East Policy*, 1 June. Available online: https://www.washingtoninstitute.org/policy-analysis/how-iran-fuels-hamas-terrorism (accessed 1 October 2021).

Levin, D. (2021), "Iran, Hamas & Palestinian Islamic Jihad", *Wilson Center*, 21 May. Available online: https://www.wilsoncenter.org/article/iran-hamas-and-palestinian-islamic-jihad (accessed 1 October 2021).

Mansharof, Y. (2020), "The Relationship between Iran and Islamic Jihad", *The Jerusalem Institute for Strategy and Security*, 27 February. Available online: https://jiss.org.il/en/mansharof-the-relationship-between-iran-and-palestinian-islamic-jihad/ (accessed 1 October 2021).

Morris, B. (2003), *Righteous Victims: A History of the Zionist-Arab Conflict 1881-2001*, Israel: Am Oved [Hebrew].

Naveh, D. (1999), *Government Secrets*, Israel: Yedioth Ahronoth [Hebrew].

Orion, A. (2018), "The Response to the Iranian Proxy War: Jerusalem's Power vs. the Quds Force", *Strategic Assessment*, 21 (2): 29–40.

Siboni, G. (2014), "Operations Cast Lead, Pillar of Defense, and Protective Edge: A Comparative Review", in A. Kurz and S. Brom (eds), *In the Lessons of Operation Protective Edge*, 27–34, Institute for National Security Studies (INSS).

Tamimi, A. (2007), *Hamas: Unwritten Chapters*, London: Hurst & Company.

Terrorism-Info (2020), "Iranian Support for Palestinian Terrorism: Distribution of Iranian Funds to Shaheeds' Families in the Gaza Strip by PIJ-affiliated Al-Ansar Charity Association", *The Meir Amit Intelligence and Terrorism Information Center*, 13 February. Available online: https://www.terrorism-info.org.il/en/iranian-support-palestinian-terrorism-distribution-iranian-funds-shaheeds-families-gaza-strip-pij-affiliated-al-ansar-charity-association/ (accessed 1 October 2021).

Terrorism-Info (2021), "Escalation from the Gaza Strip: Operation Guardian of the Walls Summary", *The Meir Amit Intelligence and Terrorism Information Center*, 24 May. Available online: https://www.terrorism-info.org.il/en/escalation-from-the-gaza-strip-operation-guardian-of-the-walls-summary/ (accessed 1 October 2021).

Yatom, D. (2009), *The Confidant: From Sayeret Matkal to the Mossad*, Israel: Miskal [Hebrew].

Ynet (2009), "A Decade of Terrorism: Wars are Happening in the Home Front", 25 December. Available online: https://www.ynet.co.il/articles/0,7340,L-3820279,00.html (accessed 1 October 2021) [Hebrew].

12

The Conflict in Yemen through the Prism of Proxy War

James K. Wither

Introduction

The United Nations (UN) has described Yemen as the "world's worst humanitarian crisis" (UNFPA 2020: 10). Over 230,000 people have died as a result of the war since 2014 and nearly four million have been displaced. Fighting has destroyed much critical infrastructure, impacting supplies of food, water and energy. As a result, eighty percent of the population is dependent on humanitarian assistance. All sides in the conflict have been guilty of significant human rights' abuses.

The current civil war started in 2014 when northern Houthi rebels, officially known as Ansar Allah, supporting former president Ali Abdullah Saleh seized the capital Sanaa and forced President Abd Rabbu Mansour al Hadi into exile. But Yemen is no stranger to violent conflict. The fighting has been described as the latest outburst of a "sixty-year civil war" caused by poor governance, corruption and systematic institutional failure since the establishment of modern Yemen in the 1960s (Feierstein 2019). Saudi Arabia, along with the United Arab Emirates (UAE) and other countries, entered the war against the Houthis in support of Hadi's internationally recognized government in 2015. This internationalized the conflict and created a perception that the Yemen civil war was essentially a proxy conflict between Saudi Arabia and its rival Iran, which backed the Houthis. But a UNSCR report in 2020 recognized the complexity of the war, stating that: "The country's many conflicts are interconnected and can no longer be separated by clear divisions between external and internal actors and events" (UNSCR 2020).

All types of military forces have been involved in the war. Saudi Arabia led an intense air campaign that inflicted heavy casualties on Yemen's civilians. The UAE took the leading role in the ground force campaign against the Houthis and their allies in support of pro-Hadi forces, along with smaller air and land force contingents from Jordan, Sudan, Egypt, Morocco and other Gulf States. The US and major allies initially backed the Saudi coalition and provided weapons, intelligence and military contractors in support. In a separate counterterrorism campaign since the early 2000s, the US has conducted hundreds of air strikes against Salafi terrorist group, Al Qaeda in the Arabian Peninsula (AQAP). Iran supports the Houthis with weapons, military advisers and finance but has not been directly involved in the fighting. There is also a sectarian dimension to the conflict, as the Houthis are predominantly Zaydi Shia and their adversaries mainly Sunnis. According to a recent study, there are tens of thousands of religiously motivated fighters involved in the civil war (Salisbury 2021: 6). The Houthis, for example, have conscripted and indoctrinated thousands of child soldiers. There are many other non-state actors that are parties to the conflict that sometimes support the government or the rebels, but often have objectives that are not directly related to the core struggle for power. These include Salafi and Islamist groups such as AQAP, al Islah, Islamic State (IS) and Dar al Hadith. There is also a UAE supported southern separatist movement, the Southern Transitional Council (STC), which has clashed with Hadi government forces. The war defies simple labelling or explanations. On the ground, personal relationships, geography, familial and business ties have often determined the shifting allegiance of local politicians and militias rather than ideology or geopolitical issues (Baron and al Hamdani, 2019a, p. 30). Yemeni parties to the conflict have also proved adept at exploiting foreign sponsors for money and arms to pursue their local agendas, turning the normal proxy, principal—agent relationship on its head (al Muslimi 2019).

UN sponsored negotiations between the Saudi-backed government and Houthi rebels, as well as recent diplomatic dialogue between Saudi Arabia and Iran, have not yet translated into a genuine peace process for Yemen. The Houthis are unlikely to negotiate seriously as long as they clearly have the military advantage. Saudi Arabia, on the other hand, is very keen to end the war as it has been a disastrous failure. It has highlighted Saudi military weaknesses and vulnerability, soured relations with the United States and increased the relative regional power of its rival Iran.

This chapter does not attempt to provide a comprehensive survey of the war in Yemen. Instead it analyzes the current civil war through the lens of contemporary proxy warfare. Firstly, it examines the difficulties involved in defining the term proxy in the current conflict environment, highlighting the problems of classifying the complicated relationships between states and non-state actors involved in the Yemen war. As the civil war in Yemen is often described as an Iranian/Saudi proxy war, the article examines and critiques this perspective on the conflict, with a particular focus on Yemen's role in Iran's overall strategic and security policies. The chapter also addresses the UAE proxy war in Yemen as a regional case study that illustrates how minor powers can exploit local proxies to advance their strategic objectives. Finally, the chapter concludes with observations regarding the place of Yemen's civil war in the lexicon of contemporary proxy warfare.

Yemen and the Character of Contemporary Proxy Warfare

Earlier chapters have provided a detailed examination of the growing academic literature on proxy warfare. It is not the intention to reprise that material here. However, preliminary discussion of some of the relevant recent literature provides insights into the complex Yemen case study. Proxy warfare was defined by Geraint Hughes as an armed conflict "... in which belligerents use third parties as either a supplementary means of waging war, or as a substitute for the direct employment of their own armies" (Hughes 2012: 2). Proxy wars were a common feature of the Cold War, but were less common in the decades following the end of that conflict. Now, renewed strategic competition between the major powers has brought proxy warfare back center stage in contemporary armed conflict as states with an interest in foreign, internal wars seek to influence strategic outcomes in their favor without incurring the political and financial costs and risks of direct military involvement. As the Yemen case illustrates, contemporary proxy warfare is more complicated than during the Cold War. It is no longer a feature of bilateral superpower competition, but rather involves multiple states and sometimes coalitions of both regional and global powers. State and even non-state sponsors of proxy forces have multiplied in contemporary wars, with formal and informal partnerships between states, corporations, mercenaries, militias, insurgents and criminal gangs. Ready access to sophisticated armaments has also made non-state military actors much more capable and lethal than hitherto.

Hughes' definition captures the essential character of proxy warfare. Nevertheless, the diverse forms of contemporary armed conflict, the variety of combatants, the differing objectives of states and non-state actors and the complexity of relationships between them have prompted much debate over the classification of proxy forces. The most challenging element of this discussion is to characterize the relationship between state principals and their agents. Words such as surrogate, ally, partner and other terms are often used alongside proxy to describe the status of combatants and their relationship with outside powers (Sterman 2019; Rauta et al. 2019: 416–20; Krieg and Rickli 2018: 115). Analysts Hoffman and Orner, for example, have referred to degrees of "proxiness" to try to define principal-client relationships (2021). This lack of clarity was already illustrated by a written statement to the US Senate Foreign Relations Committee in 2013, which described an Iranian non-state threat network that comprised "an alliance of surrogates, proxies, and partners such as Hizballah, HAMAS, and Iraqi Shi'a militants, among others" without distinguishing between these categories (Sherman 2013: 5).

Scholars use the term agency theory to describe the normal relationship between a sponsor and a sponsored party (Lupia 2001). The "principal" is the sponsor who delegates authority, the "agent" is the sponsored individual or organization to which authority is delegated. Agency theory implies a hierarchical relationship and in law a proxy is an agency over which the principal has effective control (Proxy 2008). In the martial, proxy force context, however, both principal and agent agree to enter a relationship and may have different objectives for working together. The military proxy relationship is dynamic. Relative power, objectives and interests can change over time (Zorri et al. 2020: 3). Iran's relationship with its non-state proxies, including the Houthis, reflects these tendencies and does not meet strict agency theory criteria. RUSI Fellow, Jack Watling, argues that states do not usually seek effective control, but rather the minimum degree of influence to ensure a proxy acts in the sponsoring state's interests (2019: 6). Looser control allows a principal to maintain a degree of plausible deniability regarding its direct involvement in a conflict and is less likely to undermine an agent's local legitimacy through too close an identification with a foreign power. As discussed below, the UAE's relationship with its proxy militias in Yemen post 2019 illustrates these considerations.

Heinkelmann-Wild and Mehrl identify two types of support relationships according to the degree of control that a state principal has over its non-state agent in a conflict environment. What they call "delegation" refers to hands-on control, while "orchestration" suggests a looser relationship (2021). Their research concluded that orchestration was more likely when a rebel group shared ethnic ties with the state principal, whereas delegation was the preferred approach when the principal had salient interests at stake in a conflict (2021: 21). Arguably, in the case of the Houthis, the relationship fits the orchestration model because, unlike Iraq, Syria and Lebanon, Yemen has not been an area of vital interest for

Iran (Juneau 2016: 659). However, given the intrinsic strength and autonomy of the Houthis, Combating Terrorism Center (CTC) researcher, Nakissa Jahanbani, excludes them from a recent comprehensive study of Iranian proxy force operations (Jahanbani 2020), classifying them as a "non-state partner" rather than a proxy. The rise of "state-like," non-state actors has added further complexity to the proxy debate. Lebanese Hezbollah (LH) is commonly referred to as the principal Iranian proxy force, but has raised and trained its own proxy militias, notably in Syria (Jahanbani 2020). LH has also operated on its own initiative to provide advice and training to the Houthis (Esfandiary and Tabatabai 2016: 165). Analyst, Vladimir Rauta, has even argued that LH has the status of an Iranian ally, having "long outgrown its proxy status" (2020: 45). Such discussion of the status of the Houthis and LH illustrates once again the terminological confusion and ambiguity inherent in any discussion of proxy forces.

Daniel Byman (2018) makes a useful distinction between ally and proxy relationships. He defines an alliance as a situation where a state makes a significant, direct and open military contribution in support of a foreign government. He describes a proxy relationship as one where the external state's involvement in a conflict remains indirect, with assistance normally limited to weapons, finance and military advisers. Applying Byman's criteria, the Saudi coalition has an alliance with Yemen's government, while the Houthis' relationship with Iran meets proxy criteria. However, Rondeaux and Sterman acknowledge that a "thin gray line" can separate an ally from a client state (2019a: 21). Their argument is that the status of ally means that both states share a common threat perception and retain their independence. In practice, one state is often materially dependent on a more powerful partner, which can create a client, proxy relationship. Yemen is a failed state and President Hadi's government is dependent on Saudi Arabia for survival. In 2020, a UN report noted that the Riyadh Agreement of 2019 had removed the sovereign ability of the Yemeni government to make military decisions independently from Saudi supervision, an action which moves Yemen closer to Saudi client status (UNSCR 2020).

Saudi Arabia's War in Yemen

The strategic rivalry between the principal Sunni and Shia powers, Saudi Arabia and Iran, is a major Middle East regional faultline and dates back to Iran's Islamic revolution in 1979. As noted above, the civil war in Yemen is often described as an Iranian/Saudi proxy war (Rondeaux and Sterman 2019: 50; Zorri et al. 2020:

71; Deutsche Welle 2019; Fahim 2018), although to view the war in Yemen primarily as a proxy conflict rather than a civil war ignores the critical longstanding domestic divisions and grievances that lie behind the fighting. Saudi Arabia has a long history of involvement in Yemen, primarily to secure its vulnerable southern border and ensure that instability in Yemen does not undermine its vital interests. Some years before Iran's involvement, Saudi Arabia had already provided military support to campaigns by the Yemeni government against the Houthis (Feierstein 2019: 20–2; Counter Extremism Project 2021a). Still, the perception that the Houthis were an Iranian proxy was a major factor in prompting direct military intervention in 2015. Saudi Arabia used the proxy war narrative as a means of obtaining international political and material support for its coalition (al Jubeir 2016; Baron and Hamdani 2019b: 18). However, Saudi Arabia may have felt compelled to intervene militarily in order to prevent a Houthi takeover in Yemen, regardless of Iran's involvement, especially given the Houthis' raids and territorial claims on its southern border (Knights 2018: 16).

Hadi's government remains weak and reliant on Saudi Arabia. The Yemeni army and the plethora of non-state militias that support the Hadi government depend on the Saudis for finance and equipment. Despite these considerations, the term proxy war is employed too freely as regards Saudi Arabia's role in Yemen. As the internationally recognized head of state, President Hadi formally requested military intervention from Gulf Cooperation Council (GCC) members in March 2015 citing the self-defense under Article 51 of the UN Charter. The Saudi coalition's intervention was granted a Chapter VII mandate by UN Security Council Resolution 2216 (UNSCR 2015). Although, there has been some discussion as to whether Hadi retained the governmental authority to legally request assistance from other states (Weizmann, 2015, Rondeaux and Sterman 2019: 26–6), the Saudi coalition's direct and legally sanctioned military intervention does not meet the usual criteria for a proxy war. Nevertheless, from a geopolitical perspective, it is easy to understand why the international community tends to view the Yemen war from an Iranian/Saudi proxy perspective given the two states' perennial rivalry.

Iran's Proxy Strategy and the Resistance Axis

Iran's support for the Houthis reflects the state's broader regional security objectives and strategy. Iran provides the best contemporary example of a state

The Conflict in Yemen through the Prism of Proxy War 189

that has a national security strategy based on regional non-state partnerships. Since the 1980s, Iran has maintained close ties with a range of militant groups in the Middle East, cultivating relationships for long term strategic benefit (Katz 2019). Initially its agenda focused on the export of the Iranian Islamic revolution, but this rapidly evolved into more pragmatic deterrent objectives against Iran's enemies. Iran has created what is often referred to as a "resistance axis" against Israel, the US and American backed governments in the Middle East (Mohseni and Kalout 2017). US officials refer to this axis as "Iran's Threat Network" (ITN), which a RAND study described as "Tehran's most potent deterrent at its disposal against the United States" and a "primary means of power projection and preferred instrument of influence in the Middle East" (Tabatabai et al. 2019: 1). Iran's network includes cornerstone partner LH, Iraq's Kaita'ib Hezbollah, Ansar Allah and the Afghan Fatemiyoun and Pakistani Zaynabiyoun Brigades. Iran has also shown flexibility in working with non-ideologically aligned groups, such as Hamas, and even Salafi-jihadists when it serves mutual interests. The increase in radical Sunni fundamentalism has even enabled Iran to pose as a moderate alternative for Arab minorities and nationalist regimes threatened by extremism. Mohseni and Kalout have referred to this as a relationship based on "sectarian identity without sectarian ideology" (2017). Opposition to the status quo, rather than ideology, has been a common factor in Iran's relationships with regional non-state partners.

Iran has weak conventional military forces in comparison to its enemies. Therefore, the resistance axis strategy aims to deter opponents by demonstrating Iran's capability to employ irregular military forces against them. In classic proxy warfare terms, Iran seeks to achieve its strategic objectives while avoiding a direct conventional military confrontation that could lead to an inter-state war (Levitt 2020). Iran has been described as "the quintessential gray zone actor whose entire modus operandi is influenced by this particular way of war" (Eisenstadt 2021: 78). Iran uses its elite Quds Force of the Islamic Revolutionary Guard Corps (IRGC) to recruit, train and advise proxy militias and provide intelligence and logistic support for their operations. LH also operates independently to support proxy forces for the common cause in the role of Iran's primary "strategic deterrent" (Watling 2019: 8). As noted above, Iran's relationship with individual partners varies. There are differences in terms of their strategic importance, the degree of command and control exercised by Iran and the extent to which a partner is dependent on political, financial, organizational or military support. Michael Eisenstadt's reference to a Shi'ite "foreign legion" to support Iran's power projection capabilities may exaggerate the state's ability to mobilize and direct all of the individual components of its resistance axis (2021: 81). The term "Shi'ite foreign legion" may apply to LH and the Hazara Shi'ite Fatemiyoun Brigade, but not to Hamas and, arguably not yet to the Houthi Ansar Allah.

The Iran/Houthi Partnership

The Houthi movement dates back to the 1980s when its founder, Hussein Badr al-Din al-Houthi, sought to protect Shia Zaydism from the encroachment of Saudi-backed Salafism in northern Yemen. The Houthi movement was also influenced by Iran's Islamic revolution, although there are significant religious differences between Yemeni Zaydi (Fiver) and Iranian Twelver Vilayet-e Faqih Shism and the extent of the ideological links between Iran and the Yemeni Shias remains a matter of dispute (Zorri et al. 2020: 93–4; al Dawsari 2021). Increased demands for regional autonomy led to a series of wars between the Houthis and the Yemeni government after 2004. Over time, a combination of tactical lessons learned in combat and the mobilization of aggrieved Zayidi tribes turned the Houthis into a highly effective military force that was able to capture the capital, Sanaa, and overthrow the government by 2015.

Unlike Saudi Arabia, Iran has not historically played a role in Yemen's internal affairs. Despite former president Saleh's claims, there was little evidence of Iranian military support for the Houthis during the wars between 2004 and 2010 (Juneau 2016: 655; Feierstein 2019: 21). The Houthi military successes, however, presented an opportunity for the IRGC to influence the regional balance of power. Analysts have discussed the extent to which the Houthis' continued military success is the result of Iranian military, financial and political assistance (Knights 2018: 20–1; Tabatabai et al. 2019: 14). Initially, the Houthis were able to capitalize on widespread discontent with the Yemeni government to grow their support from local militias. Their alliance with former president Saleh between 2014 and 2017 also increased their strength as units defecting from the Hadi government's army provided the Houthis with heavy weaponry, including missile systems. Iranian support was not required for the Houthis to defeat their divided and disorganized opponents. But, there is no question that the Houthis welcomed assistance from the IRGC and LH, in the form of military training and technical assistance, especially after 2014 (Knights 2018: 17–22; Juneau 2016: 657; Tabatabi et al. 2019: 14). Over time Iran managed to increase the delivery of armaments, including advanced technology to Houthi fighters. This equipment was combined with locally acquired or produced material to manufacture relatively sophisticated weapons with IRCG and LH assistance (Juneau 2021: 4–9; Watling 2019: 25–6). The Houthis have deployed anti-ship cruise missiles and "drone boats" in the Red sea and used long range drones and missiles to attack infrastructure targets in Saudi territory (UNSCR 2021: 3–284).

The Houthis have been described as a "natural partner" for Iran and LH to cultivate (Zorri et al. 2020: 86). From the start of the relationship, the Houthis shared strategic interests with Iran and LH. All three opposed Saudi Arabia, Israel and US power and influence in the region. Support for the Houthis offered Iran a low-cost opportunity to undermine Saudi Arabia's power, influence and reputation without direct involvement in the Yemen war. From the perspective of Iran, the Yemen civil war can be categorized as a proxy war, although it would be simplistic and inaccurate to classify its relationship with the Houthis in conventional principal—agent terms. In the context of Yemen, the relationship can be described as symbiotic. As Thomas Juneau states "Iran has bandwagoned on Houthi successes as much as it has caused them" (Juneau 2021: 11). The Houthis benefit from Iranian support, but are not dependent on it to the extent that small proxies usually are on an external principal. Iran has indeed acknowledged that it has no veto power over Houthi decision making (International Crisis Group 2021).

Inevitably, the Houthis' relationship with Iran became closer after 2014 as they faced the internationally backed Saudi military coalition with no other source of external support (Malley and Pomper 2021; Zorri 2020: 89). The hardliners that currently dominate the Houthi movement have also become more ideological aligned with Iran and both the Houthis and Iran openly acknowledge the importance of their partnership (UNSCR 2021: 13–284; Juneau 2021: 5–6). Some analysts have claimed that religious differences alone will prevent a long-term Iran/Houthi partnership (Zorri et al. 2020: 89–90; Watling 2019: 24). But Houthi military and spiritual leader, Abdul-Malik al-Houthi, has already declared that Ansar Allah is a member of Iran's resistance axis (Counter Extremism Project 2021b). There are claims that the Houthis could become a "southern Hezbollah" serving as part of Iran's resistance axis on the southern flank of Saudi Arabia and Israel (Juneau 2021d: 16–8; Knights 2018d: 21). Like LH, the Houthi movement is now a regional power in its own right. As noted by the UNSCR's recent report on Yemen "The Houthis ability to project power beyond Yemen remains a threat to regional stability and a challenge for future peace negotiations" (UNSCR 2021: 3–24).

"Little Sparta"—the UAE's proxy war in Yemen

The UAE has become a significant regional power under the influence of Crown Prince Muhammed bin Zayed. With the international focus on Saudi/Iran rivalry, the UAE's activities in Yemen have tended to be overlooked. However, the UAE case study offers an example of a national proxy war within a broader, multifaceted armed conflict. In classic proxy warfare terms, the UAE has sought to shape the outcome of the war in Yemen to its strategic advantage through the use of local militias, mercenaries and deft diplomacy. The UAE joined the coalition to support its principal ally Saudi Arabia, fight the Iranian-backed Houthis and combat AQAP and the Islamist group, al Islah. The UAE also embarked on an ambitious, national agenda in South Yemen. The UAE mobilized, trained and equipped southern tribal militias, in particular the Aden based Security Belt forces. These militias worked with UAE Special Forces to fight common enemies, principally the Houthis and AQAP (Heras 2018; UNSCR 2020). Working closely with the US, the UAE also established elite paramilitary units, notably the Shabwani and Hadrami Elite Forces, to seize areas occupied by AQAP (Heras 2018; Augustin 2019). By 2019, the UAE provided advisers, training, logistics and finance for an estimated 90,000 fighters (Jalal 2020). Most of The UAE's armed and trained South Yemen security forces are aligned with the Southern Transitional Council (STC) formed in 2017 to provide overarching leadership for the various tribal units (Augustin 2019). The STC fights the Houthis, but also campaigns for southern independence (Rauta et al. 2019: 423). Secession would in essence restore the pre-1990 status of two Yemeni states. Potentially, it would also provide the UAE with an important base to expand its political and economic power in the Red Sea and the Horn of Africa. Officially, the Emirates still recognizes the authority of the Hadi government, but the extent to which it supports the preservation of a unified Yemen has been questioned (Al-Qassab 2018; Guardian 2019; Harb, 2017).

The UAE withdrew its forces from Yemen during 2019 as part of a claimed switch from a "military-first to a peace-first process" (Yaakoubi 2019). However, its proxies ensured continuing influence on the ground and Emirati forces still control the strategic island of Soqotra, as well as air bases and sea ports on the mainland (Khalel 2021). A number of factors influenced the UAE's decision to withdraw (Bakir and Cafiero 2019; Juneau 2020: 195–202). The costs of an intractable and stalemated war were exceeding the benefits for the UAE. Continued direct involvement in the fighting was endangering the UAE's relations with both Saudi Arabia and the US. Withdrawal enabled the UAE to distance itself from the political and military quagmire on the ground. Therefore, international criticism, not least in the US, has focused on Saudi Arabia's brutal bombing campaign rather than human rights abuses committed by the UAE's proxies. The UAE was also aware that its role in the US's controversial counter terrorist campaign, heavy-handed military operations and its growing influence on regional politics had angered the population in southern Yemen and provoked widespread protests (Heras 2018; Juneau 2020: 201).

Although still a member of the coalition, the UAE's support for the secessionist STC soured relations with Saudi Arabia and nominal ally, the Hadi government. The latter's heavy reliance on the Islamist al Islah militias was a major source of friction with the UAE (Juneau 2020: 191). Matters came to a head in summer 2019, when UAE-aligned STC forces clashed with Yemeni government troops (UNSCR 2020). Therefore, it was not surprising that the UAE backed a unity agreement, brokered by Saudi Arabia, between the STC and the Yemeni government in December 2019. Both parties "agreed to form a unity government" (The Riyadh Agreement 2019). The agreement acknowledged the power and reach of the STC without curbing its secessionist ambitions. It also allowed the UAE to retain its political influence in southern Yemen (Jalal 2020). However, recent diplomatic outreach to Turkey and Qatar and rapprochement with Saudi Arabia suggest that economic pressures and military overreach in Libya and Yemen have forced the UAE to rethink its aggressively ambitious foreign policy (Economist 2021). Despite the UAE's role in combating the Houthis, pragmatic security considerations have also influenced recent attempts to improve diplomatic relations with Iran (Juneau 2020: 199).

Former US Defense Secretary, General Mattis, referred to the UAE as "little Sparta," not least because its armed forces proved highly effective in operations against the Houthis (Economist 2017). With a population of just 10 million, only 1 million of which are citizens, the state lacks the manpower for effective military power projection. The Crown Prince imposed military conscription on UAE citizens in 2014, but his ambitious strategic agenda, especially in Libya and Yemen, would not have been possible without large scale "outsourcing." Consequently, the UAE has relied on hundreds of mercenaries, mainly recruited from a range of Latin American and African countries (Al-Qassab 2018; Wood 2018; Fenton-Harvey 2020). It is also reported to have hired former US navy SEALS from the private military company (PMC), Spear Operations Group, to assassinate leaders of al Islah (Roston 2018). The UAE has spent lavish sums on US arms and defense services, employing former American officers to train and advise its armed forces. It has also embedded experienced foreigners in command positions in the armed forces (Roston 2018; Wood 2018).

Mercenaries and more formal PMCs, such as Russia's Wagner Group, have become a major feature of contemporary proxy warfare, providing a versatile, comparatively cheap and often deniable means of supporting strategic objectives. The UAE has led regional powers in this respect and it remains to be seen if its attempts to further develop sovereign military capabilities over time will enable it to reduce its dependence on mercenaries. Mercenaries are not normally as effective or reliable as state armed forces and pose political, economic and reputational risks to states that employ them (Wither 2020: 10–1).

Conclusions

The war in Yemen cannot be described simply as a proxy war between Saudi Arabia and Iran. Nor is it just a binary conflict between the Houthis and the Saudi backed government. Rather, it is a multiparty power struggle and the tendency to view the Yemen civil war in binary terms obscures the complex, local origins of the conflict and differing military and political objectives of domestic combatants. The involvement of outside powers, particularly Iran, makes the war harder to end. The focus on external powers also tends to put too much weight on their ability to influence events on the ground in what remains essentially an internal conflict, the outcome of which can only be determined by the Yemenis themselves. Not that this is a conflict that is ripe for resolution, even if the Houthi movement decisively defeats the divided and irresolute pro-Hadi forces. Yemen is likely to remain in practice a failed state, prone to continued armed conflict that will periodically draw in regional powers and provide potential safe havens for international terrorist groups. The focus on the war between the Houthis and pro-Hadi government forces may even be providing temporary unity among disparate groups on both sides and helping to suppress even worse chaotic violence.

The Yemen conflict may be better described as a "modern" war rather than a proxy war. For example, it has many parallels with Libya, a failed state with an internationally recognized but powerless government; a plethora of non-state armed groups, some of which act as proxies for external powers; the presence of mercenaries and PMCs, and little prospect of a lasting peace. The Yemen conflict also illustrates the inadequacy of the principal-agent theory's application to contemporary proxy forces. Scholars struggle to characterize relations between

The Conflict in Yemen through the Prism of Proxy War

principals and agents, when so called proxies become powerful enough to be principals in their own right or act more as allies and partners than traditional agents. In Yemen, as elsewhere, many local proxies have proved adept at exploiting their sponsors to pursue their own agendas.

Iran and its Houthi partner are the current beneficiaries in the Yemen war, if such a term is appropriate in view of the humanitarian catastrophe that the war represents. Iran has once again demonstrated its ability to exploit internal armed conflicts in the region to enhance its power and influence. The war has also humiliated its principal regional rival, Saudi Arabia. The failure of the Saudi coalition to defeat the Houthis is one more example of the problems involved in using foreign, conventional military forces to combat complex insurgencies. Even the UAE, which has managed its role in Yemen much more adeptly than the Saudis, found direct military involvement to be problematic. All these developments, along with the more dramatic failures of the US and its allies in Iraq and Afghanistan, will likely encourage powers to rely even more on indirect involvement through proxies in future wars. As Yemen illustrates, there is a growing pool of experienced foreign fighters created by recent wars in the Middle East, Afghanistan and elsewhere. Unfortunately, there are plenty of potential mercenaries for hire as proxy forces for ambitious states, Salafi–jihadist terrorist groups and even transnational organized crime syndicates. This development poses a significant, growing challenge to international security and stability.

Bibliography

AFP (2019), "Saudi—UAE 'Rift' Weakens Fight Against Common Yemen Foe", *The Guardian*. 13 August. Available online: https://guardian.ng/news/saudi-uae-rift-weakens-fight-against-common-yemen-foe/ (accessed 28 December 2022).

Al Dawsari, N. (2021), "The Houthis and the Limits of Diplomacy in Yemen", *The Middle East Institute*, 6 May. Available online: https://mei.edu/publications/houthis-and-limits-diplomacy-yemen (accessed 28 December 2022).

Al Jubeir, A. B. A. (2016), "Can Iran Change?", *New York Times,* 19 January. Available online:

Al Muslimi, F. (2019), "The Tea Merchant's War", *The World Today*, October/November, 28–30.

Al Qassab, A. (2018), "Strategic Considerations of the UAE's Role in Yemen", *Arab Center Washington DC*, 9 March. Available online: https://arabcenterdc.org/resource/strategic-considerations-of-the-uaes-role-in-yemen/ (accessed 28 December 2022).

Augustin, A. (2019), "Security in South Yemen", *Middle East Institute*. 31 July. Available online: https://www.mei.edu/publications/security-south-yemen (accessed 28 December 2022).

Bakir, A. and G. Cafiero (2019), "The UAE's Yemen Withdrawal Leaves Saudi Arabia Exposed", *Middle Easy Eye*, 22 July. Available online: https://www.middleeasteye.net/opinion/how-will-riyadh-cope-uaes-yemen-withdrawal (accessed 28 December 2022).

Baron, A. and R. al Hamdani (2019), "The Proxy War Prism and Yemen", *New America*, 9 December. Available online: https://d1y8sb8igg2f8e.cloudfront.net/documents/The_Proxy_War_Prism_on_Yemen_KjH1dNB.pdf (accessed 28 December 2022).

Byman, D. L. (2018), "Why Engage in Proxy War? A State's Perspective", *Brookings*, 21 May. Available online: https://www.brookings.edu/blog/order-from-chaos/2018/05/21/why-engage-in-proxy-war-a-states-perspective/ (accessed 28 December 2022).

Counter Extremism Project (2021a), "Houthis", *Counter Extremism Project*. Available online: https://www.counterextremism.com/threat/houthis (accessed 28 December 2022).

Counter Extremism Project (2021b), "Abdul-Malik al Houthi, June 3, 2021", *Counter Extremism Project*. Available online: https://www.counterextremism.com/content/abdul-malik-al-houthi-june-3-2021-0 (accessed 28 December 2022).

Deutsche Welle (2019), "Saudi and UAE Leaders Meet to Heal Yemen Rift", *Deutsche Welle*, 12 August. Available online: https://www.dw.com/en/saudi-and-uae-leaders-meet-to-heal-yemen-rift/a-49998790 (accessed 28 December 2022).

Economist (2017), "The Gulf's 'Little Sparta': The Ambitious United Arab Emirates", *The Economist*, 6 April.

Economist (2021), "Middle Eastern Foes are Giving Diplomacy a Shot", *The Economist*, 18 September.

Eisenstadt, M. (2021), "Iran's Gray Zone Strategy: Cornerstone of its Asymmetrical Way of War", *PRISM*, 9 (2): 77–97. Available online: https://ndupress.ndu.edu/Journals/PRISM/PRISM-9-2/ (accessed 28 December 2022).

Esfandiary, D. and A. Tabatabai (2016), "Yemen: an Opportunity for Iran–Saudi Dialogue?", *The Washington Quarterly*, 39 (2): 155–74. https://doi.org/10.1080/0163660X.2016.1204415.

Fahim, K. (2018), "U.N. Probe Details Fallout of Proxy War in Yemen Between Saudi Coalition and Iran", *The Washington Post*, 11 January. Available online: https://www.washingtonpost.com/world/un-probe-details-fallout-of-proxy-war-in-yemen-between-saudi-coalition-and-iran-/2018/01/11/3e3f9302-f644-11e7-9af7-a50bc3300042_story.html (accessed 28 December 2022).

Feierstein, G. M. (2019), "Yemen: The 60-Year War", *Middle East Institute*, February. Available online: https://www.mei.edu/sites/default/files/2019-02/Yemen%20The%2060%20Year%20War.pdf (accessed 28 December 2022).

Fenton-Harvey, J. (2020), "How the UAE Mercenaries Serve Its Foreign Policy Ambitions", *Al Sharq Strategic Research*, 16 March. Available online: https://research.

sharqforum.org/2020/03/16/how-uae-mercenaries-serve-its-foreign-policy-ambitions/# (accessed 28 December 2022).

Harb, I. K. (2017), "Troubling Ambiguities in the UAE's Role in Yemen", *Arab Center, Washington DC,* 8 September. Available online: https://arabcenterdc.org/resource/troubling-ambiguities-in-the-uaes-role-in-yemen/ (accessed 28 December 2022).

Heinkelmann-Wild, T. and M. Mehrl (2021), "Indirect Governance at War: Delegation and Orchestration in Rebel Support", *Journal of Conflict Resolution*, 66 (1): 115–43. https://doi.org/10.1177/00220027211027311.

Heras, N. A. (2018), "Security Belt": The UAE's Tribal Counterterrorism Strategy in Yemen', *Jamestown Foundation: Terrorism Monitor*, 16 (12), 14 June. Available online: https://jamestown.org/program/security-belt-the-uaes-tribal-counterterrorism-strategy-in-yemen/ (accessed 28 December 2022).

Hoffman. F. G. and A. Orner (2021), "Dueling Dyads: Conceptualizing Proxy Wars in Strategic Competition", *Foreign Policy Research Institute*, 30 August. Available online: https://www.fpri.org/article/2021/08/dueling-dyads-conceptualizing-proxy-wars-in-strategic-competition/ (accessed 28 December 2022). https://www.nytimes.com/2016/01/19/opinion/saudi-arabia-can-iran-change.html (accessed 28 December 2022).

Hughes, G. (2012), *My Enemy's Enemy: Proxy Warfare in International Politics*, Eastbourne: Sussex Academic Press.

International Crisis Group (2021) "After al-Bayda, the Beginning of the Endgame for Northern Yemen?" *Briefing*, 84, 14 October. Available online: https://www.crisisgroup.org/middle-east-north-africa/gulf-and-arabian-peninsula/yemen/b84-after-al-bayda-beginning-endgame-northern-yemen (accessed 28 December 2022).

Jahanbani, N. (2020), "Reviewing Iran's Proxies by Region: A Look Toward the Middle East, South Asia, and Africa", *CTC Sentinel*, 13 (5): 39–49. Available online: https://ctc.usma.edu/reviewing-irans-proxies-by-region-a-look-toward-the-middle-east-south-asia-and-africa/ (accessed 28 December 2022).

Jalal, I. (2020), "The UAE May Have Withdrawn From Yemen, But Its Influence Remains Strong", *Middle East Institute*, 25 February. Available online: https://www.mei.edu/publications/uae-may-have-withdrawn-yemen-its-influence-remains-strong (accessed 28 December 2022).

Juneau, T. (2016), "Iran's Policy towards the Houthis in Yemen: A Limited Return on a Modest Investment", *International Affairs*, 92 (3): 647–63.

Juneau, T. (2020), "The UAE and the War in Yemen: From Surge to Recalibration", *Survival*, 62 (4): 183–208.

Juneau, T. (2021), "How War in Yemen Transformed the Iran-Houthi Partnership", *Studies in Conflict and Terrorism*. https://doi.org/10.1080/1057610X.2021.1954353.

Katz, B. (2019), "What the US Can Learn From Iranian Warfare", *The Atlantic*, 19 October. Available online: https://www.theatlantic.com/politics/archive/2019/10/what-us-can-learn-iranian-warfare/600082/ (accessed 28 December 2022).

Khalel, S. (2021), "UAE Deeply Involved in Yemen despite Claims of Withdrawal, Experts Say", *Middle East Eye*, 22 February. Available online: https://www.middleeasteye.net/news/uae-yemen-conflict-deeply-involved-experts-say (accessed 28 December 2022).

Knights, M. (2018), "The Houthi War Machine: From Guerilla War to State Capture", *CTC Sentinel*, 11 (8): 15–23. Available online: https://ctc.usma.edu/houthi-war-machine-guerrilla-war-state-capture/ (accessed 28 December 2022).

Krieg, A. and J. M. Rickli (2018), "Surrogate Warfare: The Art of War in the 21st Century?", *Defence Studies*, 18 (2): 113–30. https://doi.org/10.1080/14702436.2018.1429218.

Levitt, M. (2020). "Fighters Without Borders'—Forecasting New Trends in Iran Threat Network Foreign Operations Tradecraft', *CTC Sentinel*, 13 (2): 1–8. Available online: https://ctc.usma.edu/fighters-without-borders-forecasting-new-trends-iran-threat-network-foreign-operations-tradecraft/ (accessed 28 December 2022).

Lupia, A. (2001). "Delegation of Power: Agency Theory", *International Encyclopedia of the Social and Behavioral Sciences,* 3375–7. Oxford: Elsevier Science Limited.

Malley, R. and S. Pomper (2021), "Accomplice to Carnage: How America Enables War in Yemen" *Foreign Affairs*, March/April. Available online: https://www.foreignaffairs.com/articles/united-states/2021-02-09/how-america-enables-war-yemen (accessed 28 December 2022).

Mohseni, P. and H. Kalout (2017), "Iran's Axis of Resistance Rises", *Foreign Affairs*, 24 January. Available online: https://www.foreignaffairs.com/iran/irans-axis-resistance-rises (accessed 28 December 2022).

Proxy (2008), "Proxy", *West Encyclopedia of American Law*, 2 edn. Available online: https://legal-dictionary.thefreedictionary.com/proxy (accessed 28 December 2022).

Rauta, V. (2020), "Proxy Warfare and the Future of Conflict: Take Two", *The RUSI Journal*, 165 (2):38–47. https://doi.org/10.1080/03071847.2020.1736437.

Rauta, V., M. Ayton, A. Chinchilla, A. Krieg, C. Rickard and J-M. Rickli (2019), "A Symposium—Debating 'Surrogate Warfare' and the Transformation of War", *Defence Studies*, 19: 410–430. 10.1080/14702436.2019.1680290.

Reuters (2019), "Special Report: 'Time to Take out the Swords'—Inside Iran's Plot to Attack Saudi Arabia", *Reuters*, 25 November. Available online: https://www.reuters.com/article/us-saudi-aramco-attacks-iran-special-rep-idUSKBN1XZ16H (accessed 28 December 2022).

Rondeaux, C. and D. Sterman (2019), "Twenty-First Century Proxy Warfare", *New America*, 21 February. Available online: https://www.newamerica.org/international-security/reports/twenty-first-century-proxy-warfare-confronting-strategic-innovation-multipolar-world/ (accessed 28 December 2022).

Roston, A. (2018), "A Middle East Monarchy Hired Ex-Soldiers to Kill Its Political Enemies", *BuzzFeed News*, 16 October. Available online: https://www.buzzfeednews.com/article/aramroston/mercenaries-assassination-us-yemen-uae-spear-golan-dahlan (accessed 28 December 2022).

The Conflict in Yemen through the Prism of Proxy War

Salisbury, P. (2021), "Misunderstanding Yemen, *International Crisis Group*, 20 September. Available online: https://www.crisisgroup.org/middle-east-north-africa/gulf-and-arabian-peninsula/yemen/misunderstanding-yemen (accessed 28 December 2022).

Sherman, W. (2013), "US Policy Towards Iran", *Senate Foreign Relations Hearing*, 15 May. Available online: https://www.foreign.senate.gov/imo/media/doc/Sherman_Testimony.pdf (accessed 28 December 2022).

Sterman, D. (2019), "How Do We Move Beyond 'Proxy' Paralysis", *New American Weekly*, 7 March. Available online: https://www.newamerica.org/weekly/redfine-proxy-warfare-strategy-identity/ (accessed 28 December 2022).

Tabatabai, A. M, J. Martini and B. Wasser (2019), "The Iran Threat Network (ITN): Four Models of Iran's Nonstate Client Partnerships", *RAND*, September. Available online: https://www.rand.org/pubs/research_reports/RR4231.html (accessed 28 December 2022).

The Riyadh Agreement (2019), "The Riyadh Agreement". Available online: https://saudiembassy.net/sites/default/files/Riyadh%20Agreement%20Fact%20sheet.pdf (accessed 28 December 2022).

UNFPA [United Nations Population Fund] (2020), "Humanitarian Action: 2020 Overview", available online: https://www.unfpa.org/sites/default/files/pub-pdf/HAO_2020_publication_Lo_Res_10_Feb.pdf (accessed 30 December 2022)

UNSCR [United Nations Security Council] (2015), "Resolution 2216, S/RES/2216(2015)", 14 April. https://www.undocs.org/S/RES/2216%20(2015) (accessed 28 December 2022).

UNSCR [United Nations Security Council] (2020), "Final Report of the Panel of Experts on Yemen", 27 January. Available online: https://undocs.org/en/S/2020/326 (accessed 28 December 2022).

UNSCR [United Nations Security Council] (2021), "Final Report of the Panel of Experts on Yemen", 25 January. Available online: https://undocs.org/S/2021/79 (accessed 28 December 2022).

Watling, J. (2019), "Iran's Objectives and Capabilities: Deterrence and Subversion", *RUSI Occasional Paper*, February. Available online: https://rusi.org/explore-our-research/publications/occasional-papers/irans-objectives-and-capabilities-deterrence-and-subversion (accessed 28 December 2022).

Weizmann, N. (2015), International Law on the Saudi-led Military Operations in Yemen. *Just Security*. 27 March. Available online: https://www.justsecurity.org/21524/international-law-saudi-operation-storm-resolve-yemen/ (accessed 28 December 2022).

Wither, J. K. (2020), "Outsourcing Warfare: Proxy Forces in Contemporary Armed Conflicts", *Security and Defence Quarterly*, 31 (4): 17–34. https://doi.org/10.35467/sdq/127928.

Wood, J. (2018), "Outsourcing Warfare: How Foreigners and Mercenaries Power UAE's Military", *Middle East Eye*, 13 July. Available online: https://www.middleeasteye.net/

news/outsourcing-war-how-foreigners-and-mercenaries-power-uaes-military (accessed 28 December 2022).

Yaakoubi, A. Z. (2019), "UAE Troop Drawdown in Yemen was Agreed with Saudi Arabia: Official, *Reuters*, 8 July. Available online: https://www.reuters.com/article/us-yemen-security-emirates-idUSKCN1U31WZ (accessed 28 December 2022).

Zorri, D. M., Sadri, H. A., & Ellis, D. C. (2020), Iranian Proxy Groups in Iraq, Syria, and Yemen: A Principal-agent Comparative Analysis. MacDill, FL: Joint Special Operations University Press.

13

When Proxies Win: The Impact of the Taliban's Changing Fortune on Pakistan's Leverage

Tova Norlen and Vinay Kaura

Introduction

In an increasingly volatile global environment, where strategic competition between states is played out on multiple domains through irregular and hybrid means, the proxy concept is gaining renewed prominence among scholars and security practitioners to describe how large states can use an intermediary to achieve their objectives beyond their own territory without putting "boots on the ground" (Fox 2019; Mumford 2013; Bar-Siman-Tov 1984). But does the understanding of proxy relationships account for the current paradigm shift in global security? Given the growing tendency of scholars and practitioners to describe both old and new power relationships between states and non-state actors through the "proxy" conceptual lens, there is both a need as well as an interest to better understand how changing power dynamics over the course of time impact proxy-patron relationships in contemporary conflicts (Fox 2021: 1).

Ever since the Afghan Taliban captured power in Afghanistan by eliminating all resistance in the wake of the departing American forces, the relationship between Kabul's new rulers and Pakistan has again generated widespread interest from a proxy perspective. It has been conventional wisdom that the Afghan Taliban is a Pakistani puppet, which traces its origins in religious seminaries in the Pashtun-dominated region of Pakistan during the Afghan jihad under the Soviet occupation. There is no doubt that the Afghan Taliban enjoyed an all-embracing relationship with both religious and political institutions in Pakistan, but the popular view of the Afghan Taliban being an extension of Pakistani state oversimplifies the political dynamics in Afghanistan as well as underestimates the local conditions that sustained the Taliban insurgency for almost two decades. It also overlooks the enormous efforts that Pakistan has invested for several decades to both manage and exert control over their Afghan Taliban proxy.

Given these dynamics, the Pakistan-Taliban relationship exemplifies the complexity of proxy relationships in the new global security landscape. Proxy relationships are hierarchical and depend on two elements in particular: the *coherence* of interests and policy objectives between principal and proxy/agent, as well as on the principal's ability to *control* and/or *manage* the agent (Groh 2019). When a principal's leverage changes, it affects the principal's ability to control the agent, and when a proxy's goals are achieved, the coherence of interests is threatened. If a principal is unable to regain control and re-align divergent interests and objectives, the proxy may become vulnerable to exploitation by outside actors seeking influence. The Taliban-Pakistan relationship is a recent example where both *coherence* and *control* have shifted in the proxy relationship as a result of the Taliban's return to power in August, 2021. Thus, while the exit of Western-led forces from Afghanistan led to an expectation that Pakistan had almost unhindered leverage over the new Afghan authorities, an understanding of proxy relationships predicts a much messier, and more contentious scenario, as a result of the agent (Taliban) having gained leverage to counteract the principal (Pakistan).

The purpose of this chapter is to describe how the changed dynamics between the Taliban and Pakistan, and the divergent goals between the two actors, have impacted Pakistan's ability to control the Taliban to do its bidding. We explore the history of the Pakistan-Taliban relationship, the changing dynamics during the Doha peace process, as well as more recent developments since the return of the Taliban to Kabul, in order to explain how Pakistan is being forced to re-examine its policy objectives and interests in the principal-agent relationship and revise its strategy to focus on stability and counterterrorism, rather than primarily on the Indian threat. We find that the Afghan Taliban's new position as a "state actor" and the increasingly divergent goals between Pakistan and the Afghan Taliban have greatly diminished Pakistan's ability to exert control over their proxy, arguably giving rise to an inverted proxy-patron relationship, in which the proxy partially dictates its patron's policies (Qazi 2022; Fox 2019: 14).

Conceptual Discussion

Traditionally used to describe a relationship where a dominant actor (or principal) leverages an intermediary (or proxy) against an adversary in order to achieve the dominant actor's objectives, the term *proxy* is now often used to describe any type of influence operation where states use external actors (whether states, groups, or individuals) to impact an outcome to their advantage (Fox 2021: 4). For the purpose of this chapter we limit a proxy relationship to that between a principal and an agent, where the principal is a state and the agent is either a smaller and/or weaker state, or a non-state actor.

States engage proxies when they want to keep their own troops and resources out of harm's way as well as in situations when they want to maintain plausible deniability and avoid direct blame for intervening in a regional conflict (Byman 2018; Mumford 2013). With the current trend of diminishing interventions by western states in some of the world's most vulnerable regions, including Afghanistan, Iraq, and the Sahel, states are more likely to use over the horizon capabilities or local proxies to pursue their objectives (Berman and Lake 2019). However, proxy relationships are both costly and risky as principals often need to use both enticements and punishments to ensure that the agent continues to fight and die for their interests (Fox 2019; Fox 2021).

As far as Pakistan is concerned, the Afghan Taliban has always been treated as a proxy through whom indirect management of Afghan political affairs could be ensured. But this was not a plan originally conceived in Rawalpindi, the military headquarters of the all-powerful Pakistan army. The Taliban had emerged as a socio-political reaction to the chaos following the Soviet withdrawal from Afghanistan in 1989 and the fall of the Najibullah government. Multiple Mujaheddin groups, who had fought against the Soviets, turned against each other as the US support ceased and Western countries lost interest in Afghanistan. The country disintegrated into multiple regions controlled by warlords. As foreign funding dried out, many regions experienced chaos, lack of governance and corruption.

As a result of disillusionment among local Mujaheddin, a new group, known as the Taliban, was formed under the leadership of Mullah Omar. The Taliban was initially a local Pashtun movement with a narrow agenda of restoring security and enforcing Sharia laws in Afghanistan. According to Ahmed Rashid in *Taliban*, its sudden rise and expansion in "Robin Hood fashion" was aided by their firm stand against Kandahari warlords (Rashid 2010). As the Taliban's popularity grew and their ranks swelled, Pakistan's power elite was quick to realize the strategic potential of the organization. It gradually gained considerable influence over the Taliban through the provision of weapons and money (Rashid 2010; Griffin 2000).

In some cases, the principal-agent relationship could be greatly strengthened by ethnic or ideological ties. When these exist, they strengthen the capacity of the principal to manage the agent. In the Pakistani-Taliban relationship ideological ties have been central, and although Pakistan's ultimate objective in Afghanistan was a government friendly to Islamabad and hostile to New Delhi, supporting the Taliban's nationalist ambitions and nurturing the ethnically driven proxy relationship was the most effective way to ensure this goal. However, the recent Taliban pre-occupation with politics has diminished the importance of such ties in favor of political objectives. Pakistan's divergent policies towards the Taliban in Afghanistan and the groups on their own side of the border (*Tahrik-e-Taliban*) also greatly undermine its ability to take advantage of ethnic kinship ties.

When proxies achieve their objectives, they seldom continue to do the bidding of their principal. In addition, as the power relationship shifts, proxies often develop relationships with a range of external sponsors for their own ends. This was true of the Afghan government and their relationship to their US patrons, and is also true of the Taliban today. The Afghan Taliban has always pursued a dual strategy with respect to Pakistan's priorities; despite sheltering transnational terrorist groups like Osama bin Laden's Al Qaeda and fighting against Western forces, the Taliban's political and ideological objectives remained focused on the Afghan nationalist agenda. The August 2021 return to power was therefore a trigger for a relationship change between the Taliban and its main sponsor. As Taliban's political objectives have changed, Pakistan has struggled to "align" their interests with that of its proxy in order to maintain the ability to exert leverage. The changing power dynamics between the Taliban and Pakistan has led to both opportunities and risks, as the Taliban reaches out to other regional or global actors, such as India, Iran, and China, to help them pursue their governing priorities (Commuri 2022; Abbasian 2022; Akbarzadeh and Ibrahimi 2019).

The Historic Relationship

It was due to Pakistan's significant support that enabled the Taliban to take control of Afghanistan and eventually emerge as the de facto regime during 1996 to 2001. The phase witnessed Pakistan exercising extensive political control in Afghanistan through strategic convergence between the ISI and the Taliban, widely regarded as proxy force of Pakistan's military and its civilian government. But the Taliban was never as pliant as Pakistan might have wished and in fact,

When Proxies Win 205

consistent with proxy theory, as the group expanded it demonstrated considerable autonomy, directly challenging Pakistan's strategic objectives (Coll 2005).

The Taliban's autonomy became even more evident after they took control of the state in 1996. Much to Pakistan's frustration, the Taliban refused to recognize the Durand Line[1] as the legitimate international border. Pakistan also failed to persuade the Taliban to reverse its decision of destroying historic Bamiyan Buddha statues. Most importantly, Pakistan failed to persuade Mullah Omar to hand over Osama bin Laden to the US after the 9/11 terrorist attacks. Understanding the possible consequences, Pakistan's military dictator, Pervez Musharraf, asked Lt. Gen. Mahmood Ahmed, the chief of the Pakistani intelligence, to knock some sense into the Taliban leadership. However, the ISI efforts were neither convincing, nor successful (Abbas 2014).

Faced with President Bush's ultimatum to cooperate in the "War on Terror," Pakistan allowed the use of Pakistani territory for the US military intervention. Without Pakistani patronage, the Taliban regime collapsed quickly, losing estimated 8,000–12,000 fighters (about twenty percent of their fighting force) and 7,000 taken prisoner (Committee on Foreign Relations 2009). While Musharraf's demands that the anti-Taliban Northern Alliance must not occupy Kabul went unheeded,[2] his personal intercessions with President Bush to covertly rescue Pakistani military and intelligence officers deployed in Afghanistan were successful. It is believed that the operation also brought some prominent Taliban figures to safety (Abbas 2014: 74). Many Taliban commanders and fighters took refuge in Pakistan's tribal belt where they enjoyed close networks among refugees, religious madrassas, and most importantly, the Pakistan's intelligence community.[3] Since Pakistan officially supported the US war efforts, it could only support the Afghan Taliban through covert channels. However, Pakistan's government looked the other way when the Afghan Taliban began to take advantage of their safe haven in Pakistan to rebuild their resistance. Some CIA analysts felt that elements of Pakistani intelligence helped bin Laden elude American capture inside Afghanistan (Hersh 2002).

It was Pakistan's willingness to offer safe haven that allowed the weakened Afghan Taliban not only to survive but make a comeback as an insurgency movement. As the Haqqani branch strengthened, Pakistani support intensified and by early 2003, the Taliban were promised refuge in North Waziristan, South Waziristan, Quetta, Bajaur and Peshawar. Taliban's leaders and commanders chose to re-group in Quetta. Their initial inability to return to Afghan soil due to being the target of the Kabul government remarkably reinforced Pakistan's leverage over them and the poor performance and greed of local Afghan warlords undermined the legitimacy of the western-backed regime in Kabul, strengthening the Taliban's cause.

India's growing influence in Kabul and the unlikely chance of reconciliation between the Afghan regime and the Taliban strengthened Pakistan's resolve to support its proxy (Giustozzi 2019: 30). In addition to offering safe haven on its territory, the Taliban was also provided military training and logistical help (Perlez, 2021). The Taliban insurgency gained momentum as small teams were infiltrated into Afghanistan during 2003–05 to mobilize local support (Bacon 2018). At this stage, the money and weapons the Taliban obtained from Pakistan's security establishment were critical. However, the sanctuary in Pakistan was equally crucial as it not only offered protection but also allowed Taliban leaders to travel to the Gulf countries to make political connections and raise funds (Perlez 2021; Azami 2021).[4]

While it is too simple to claim that Taliban fought the insurgency at Pakistan's behest, Pakistan's patronage and support was decisive in the Taliban's ability to sustain the insurgency. Pakistan's and the Taliban's interests converged as Pakistan became more convinced that preventing Indian influence and ensuring a Pakistan-friendly regime in Kabul required the removal of the western-led government. Thus, Pakistan's active support for the insurgency grew as the new Kabul government became more India-friendly.

By late 2005, the Taliban's activities and support in rural areas along Pakistan's border grew significantly, and violence increased (Johnson 2013). As several doubts about Washington's commitment to Afghanistan were raised, the ISI support for the insurgency also increased and the government looked for ways to provide support to the Taliban without being caught red-handed (Coll 2018).[5] However, an emboldened Taliban with more autonomy over operations and decision-making made it difficult for Pakistan to keep the relationship a smooth affair. A growing internal threat from various jihadist groups, many of them being ideologically aligned with the Taliban, tested the competence of Pakistan's security establishment including its intelligence agencies. In particular, Pakistan's initial counter-insurgency operations in 2007 against the Pakistani branch of the Taliban suffered from "cognitive dissonance" as it treated the Pakistani branch as adversaries and the Afghan branch as allies (Zaidi 2010).

But Pakistan's overt and covert support to the Afghan Taliban did not go unnoticed. Since early 2006, the US government had voiced its public displeasure that Pakistan was aiding the insurgency (Kleiner 2014).[6] The Taliban's growing influence in Afghanistan and tactical improvement in war-fighting abilities against the Afghan security forces suggested that they were receiving substantial help. In some cases, Pakistan's paramilitary force even provided cover for the Taliban to infiltrate across the Afghanistan-Pakistan border. In response, the Taliban sometimes obliged Pakistan, as in its targeting of the Indian Embassy in Kabul. Evidence shows that the perpetrators had links to the Quetta Shura and the ISI-supported Haqqani Network (Chaudhuri 2010). Thus, through sanctuary as well as support to the Afghan Taliban, but also arrest of those who stepped out of line, the ISI was able to exert considerable influence on Taliban strategy (Waldman 2010).

When the Obama administration set a deadline for exit in 2014, Pakistan used the opportunity to control the Taliban's growing penchant for autonomy. As Pakistan sought to convey the message that the Taliban's secret negotiations with Americans without Pakistan would not be tolerated, tensions rose significantly. Pakistan arrested several Taliban senior leaders who may not have been compliant with Pakistan's wishes, including Mullah Baradar. Many, like Mullah Obaidullah Akhund, died in Pakistan's custody (Reuters, 2008). Obaidullah's death in March 2010 in Pakistani custody was quite bizarre as his high-profile arrest in early 2007 had coincided with the visit of the US Vice President Dick Cheney, after which he was released in a prisoner swap but re-arrested a few months later (King 2012).[7] Such incidents only underlined an extremely complicated nature of the Afghan Taliban's proxy relationship with Pakistan. As the Taliban grew in strength by getting embedded in the social and political life of Afghanistan, it became more difficult for Pakistan to maintain its control.

In an effort to retain its control over the political outcome in Afghanistan and ensure a continued proxy relationship with the Taliban, Pakistan adopted coercive measures to bring the Taliban to the negotiating table. However, the Taliban resisted Pakistan's efforts to insert itself as the deal maker with the US and insisted on participating in the negotiations in Qatar. This severely undermined Pakistan's ability to directly influence negotiations.

The death of Mullah Akhtar Mansour in a US drone strike in Balochistan in 2016 was more evidence of Pakistan's pressure. Mansour, who had replaced Mullah Omar as supreme leader, had managed to consolidate his position in the organization and chart an independent path but failed to unite the two groups of the Taliban that had split after Mullah Omar's death. As relationship with Pakistan's security establishment worsened, Mansour tried to establish closer ties with Tehran to reduce his dependence on Islamabad, even moving his own family to Iran (ANI 2016). The fact that Mansour was killed while traveling back to Pakistan from Iran was a sign of displeasure from Pakistan, and is in fact a common occurrence when a principal assesses that the proxy was gaining too much influence (Fox 2020: 6). The new Taliban chief Mullah Haibatullah Akhundzada was a religious leader rather than a military commander. This made unification easier but it was also something that Pakistan could exploit. Akhundzada's deputy, Sirajuddin Haqqani, with strong ties to the Pakistani ISI, would run the political and military affairs of the Taliban. Officially Pakistan objected to all US airstrikes on its territory, though State Department cables leaked by WikiLeaks claimed that Islamabad secretly gave its consent (Walsh 2010). The killing happened shortly after Pakistan, Afghanistan, the US and China held talks in Islamabad about how to draw the Taliban into peace negotiations.

Doha Peace Talks

The Doha peace talks were an attempt by the Trump administration to fulfill its 2016 campaign promise to draw down American forces by 2020. However, the decision had bipartisan consensus in domestic foreign policy circles as many Democratic candidates also expressed their support to bring an end to the Afghan war. Sensing this broad consensus, the US began to prepare for direct negotiation with the Taliban.

In an effort to persuade Pakistan to rein in the Taliban and the Haqqani network on the Afghan border and crack down on Taliban sanctuaries on its territory, Trump suspended a $1.3 billion US military aid package to Pakistan in January 2018 (Mohammed and Landay 2018; Economic Times 2018). However, punishments were unable to change Islamabad's Afghan policy. Given Pakistan's value in bringing the Taliban to the negotiation table, and the Trump administration's unwillingness to alienate a nuclear-armed country with 200 million people, the administration reversed their approach and entered into direct talks with the Taliban to end America's longest war (Yousafzai 2022: 83).

The appointment of former US Ambassador to Afghanistan, Zalmay Khalilzad, as *Special Representative for Afghanistan Reconciliation* in September 2018, further demonstrated that the US Afghanistan policy that was full of contradictions. The Taliban consistently refused to negotiate with the Afghan government or consider a cease fire, arguing that doing so would remove their bargaining power with the government (London 2020). The Taliban's reluctance was thus a function of their growing power and influence on the battlefield, which allowed a gradual hardening of their positions. On the other hand, Pakistan's disinterest in the peace could be attributed to Trump's open criticism of Pakistan's Afghan policy. However, the role that the US decision to negotiate directly with the Taliban had in emboldening the organization should not be underestimated (Behuria 2019).

The opening talks in Doha in October 2018 led to no real breakthrough but the parties agreed to meet again in December 2018, that time with Pakistani and Saudi participation (Sediqi 2018). The Taliban team refused to meet with the Afghan government delegation that was present despite Saudi pressure (Kermani and Yousafzai 2019). Following negotiations in January and March 2019, Khalilzad announced that an agreement "in draft" had been reached in which: "Taliban have committed, to our satisfaction, to do what is necessary that would prevent Afghanistan from ever becoming a platform for international terrorist groups or individuals," in return for which American troops would withdraw from the country (Mashal 2019). Despite the fact that the March dialogue brought no final agreement, the Taliban were now convinced that they were close to achieving their objective, and stepped up their violence against Afghan security forces while still refusing to dialogue with the government.

The US seemed happy to exclude the Ashraf Ghani government from the talks, since many in the Trump administration felt that he was a spoiler (Stewart et al. 2019). This led the Afghanistan National Security Advisor, Hamdullah Mohib, to accuse Khalilzad of undercutting the Afghan government to propel his own political ambitions, of legitimizing the Taliban, and downgrading the legitimacy of the Afghan government (Hansler and Atwood 2019). Similarly, at the end of the sixth round of talks in May 2019, an Indian observer suggested that the Afghan peace process was faltering and that Khalilzad sent the wrong signal, in effect emboldened the Taliban and giving the group undue legitimacy while undermining the elected government in Kabul. He also claimed that Khalilzad's negotiating strategy was one "of desperation, which the Taliban leaders have read as victory" (Sirohi 2019). The growing marginalization of the Ghani government and their frustration was music to Pakistan's ears and it only increased Islamabad's confidence about its proxy's imminent success.

Despite President Ashraf Ghani's pleas that Afghanistan's future "cannot be decided outside [Afghanistan], whether in the capital cities of our friends, nemeses or neighbours" the eighth round of talks was concluded in August 2019 without any agreement (Gul 2009). However, there were multiple reports detailing the outlines of an emerging deal. Khalilzad confirmed in an interview on September 2 that "we have reached an agreement in principle" in which the US agreed to withdraw around 5,000 of its 14,000 troops from five bases within 135 days if the Taliban reduced violence in two key Afghan provinces, and a final withdrawal set for the end of 2020. However, when a Taliban terror attack killed an American soldier on September 7, Trump cancelled his planned meeting with Taliban leaders and Afghan President Ghani at Camp David, and tweeted that the Afghan peace process was "dead" (Baker et al. 2019). With the terror attack the Taliban clearly indicated that they were not interested in sharing power with the legitimate Afghan government; they were interested in overthrowing it. This converged with Pakistan's main objective—to bring an end to the India-friendly regime in Kabul.

As talks with Khalilzad in Doha continued in 2021, Afghanistan saw higher levels of violence than the country had experienced in decades from the Taliban. It became clear that the Taliban's ultimate aim was not to secure peace, but to finalize a deal that facilitated American withdrawal and cleared the way for its ascent to power in Kabul. The false narrative that the Taliban were amenable to join the Afghan government was legitimized by those in Pakistan advocating for a peace deal at all costs. It paired nicely with the Trump administration's intent to withdraw from Afghanistan at any cost. The US "recognition" of the Afghan Taliban as a negotiation partner in the Dohan peace Talks legitimized the group, and in February 2020, as the world watched in stunned amazement, the US signed a peace deal with the Afghan Taliban that gave them much of what they had been fighting for. As one analyst noted, the US effectively abandoned the Afghan government's military while putting "the future of counterterrorism in the region in the hands of the Taliban and their Pakistani patrons" (Riedel 2020). The Taliban infrastructure in Pakistan where numerous terrorists have enjoyed sanctuary was never mentioned.

Pakistan's Interests

It is difficult to overstate how much Pakistan's India policy drives its relations with its neighbors, especially Afghanistan. Supporting radical Jihadi groups, like the Afghan Taliban and the Haqqani network in their fight against Afghan and American security forces, has been crucial in Pakistan's asymmetric strategy against India. Pakistan joined the Bush administration's "global war on terror" in 2001 reluctantly, providing tactical help to US-led international troops fighting Al Qaeda. Not surprisingly, that commitment was never translated into action. Instead, Pakistan's security establishment demonstrated that it would go to any extent to frustrate friendly relations between India and Afghanistan, and the Taliban proved to be a useful instrument for that purpose.

But the relationship has been far from smooth. All of Islamabad's early diplomatic efforts, including the 2015 Pakistan-brokered talks and those involving the four-nation group, proved unsuccessful due to deep mistrust between the Taliban and Pakistan.[8] By delivering political legitimacy to the Afghan Taliban, Pakistan's security establishment hoped to gain a much bigger political role in Afghan affairs. However, Pakistan's desire for full control of its proxy generated deep mistrust at a time when the Taliban was expanding its influence and control, making them less pliable to Pakistani demands. Changing power dynamics and diverging goals thus made it more difficult for Pakistan to manage its proxy. However, despite pressure from the Trump administration to deny safe haven to terrorist groups, Pakistan continued to bet on an early US withdrawal from Afghanistan. The Trump decision to withdraw US troops fully from Afghanistan vindicated that strategy.

While Pakistan made efforts to portray the Afghan Taliban as an autonomous entity free from Pakistani influence, Pakistan's multi-dimensional patronage to the Taliban was never lost and remained crucial for the Afghan insurgency (Threlkeld and Easterly 2021).[9] Islamabad also held the key to getting the Taliban to the table. To placate the Americans, Pakistan's security services released Taliban co-founder, Mullah Abdul Ghani Baradar, in October 2018. Khalilzad remarked that Baradar had been released at his request, in order to bring a more open, "pro-peace" voice to the table. Khalizad also thanked Pakistan for facilitating the travel of the Taliban delegates to Doha, giving credit to Prime Minister Imran Khan's claims that he was the main facilitator of the talks (The Hindu 2019b).

Understandably, India was averse to the idea of bringing Islamabad back into the Afghan endgame without adequate safeguards. In response to Pakistan's statement that "India has no role in Afghanistan," India's MEA issued a strongly asserted statement that "it is not for Pakistan to decide as to what role another country has in regional or global affairs. Pakistan also cannot decide on behalf of the independent and sovereign country Afghanistan and dictate them as to how to conduct their foreign policy" (Spokesperson, Government of India 2019). This presented the Taliban with a dilemma, since Pakistan continues to insist that the Kabul regime owes Islamabad good relations but that close ties to New Delhi must be prevented at all costs. Pakistan's India focus was confirmed by a 2019 Congressional Research Service (CRS) report claiming that "Pakistan's security establishment, fearful of strategic encirclement by India, apparently continues to view the Afghan Taliban as a relatively friendly and reliably anti-India element in Afghanistan" (Thomas 2019: 46; The Hindu 2019a). Pakistan's policy to give sanctuary to a number of other Jihadi groups active in (and against) India, including Lashkar-e-Tayyiba (LeT) and Jaish-e-Mohammad (JeM), further highlights this (The Hindu 2019b). In 2018, the US State Department criticized Pakistan for its dual policy of supporting reconciliation while its security services allowed the Afghan Taliban and the Haqqani network to operate from its territory (US Department of State 2019).

Changing Dynamics After Taliban's Takeover

The Taliban have always claimed that they are a nationalistic force with a legitimate claim to Afghanistan but the power of Pakistan and its security establishment over its Taliban proxy became obvious with the selection of the interim Afghan government led by Mullah Hasan Akhund from the powerful Haqqani network, which had close ties to the ISI. The presence of Lt. General Faiz Hameed, chief of ISI, to assist the Taliban in their shift from insurgency to governance, was a sign of Islamabad's influence and signaled the success of Pakistan's long-term objectives to install the Taliban as a Pakistan-friendly regime in Kabul (Roy 2021; Asthana 2021).

The Taliban cabinet was also filled with members who ruled Afghanistan from 1996 to 2001, when the group was led by Mullah Omar, almost all of them close with the ISI. The choice of Sirajuddin Haqqani as interior minister left no one in doubt of ISI's influence. Sirajuddin's father, Jajaluluddin Haqqani, was once a favorite protégé of American and Pakistani intelligence agencies during the Afghan jihad, but later a close ally to Bin-Laden (Zaidi 2009).

The powerful roles given to members of the Haqqani network effectively marginalized the Taliban leadership team that handled the Doha political process. In particular, the head of the delegation, Mullah Abdul Ghani Baradar, was edged out, and given only a token position as deputy prime minister. Except for Abdul Salam Hanafi, an Uzbek, who was appointed the second deputy prime minister, the government was Pashtun and all-male, reflecting the fundamentalist . and conservative Pashtun ideology (Yousaf and Jabarkhail 2022).

With the Taliban in absolute control of Kabul, Pakistan's primary goal will remain geostrategic, focused on ensuring that its proxy, the Afghan Taliban, maintain their anti-India stance (Ganguli 2022). Thanks to Pakistani patronage and local and regional alliance-building, the Haqqani network has avoided the consequences of harboring Al Qaeda and other terrorist groups. Thus, Pakistan expects Sirajuddin to ensure that opposition to Islamabad's interference in

Afghanistan's internal affairs is suppressed. Al Qaeda's long association with the Haqqani network has been mutually beneficial, contributing to the development of Al Qaeda's capacity to wage global jihad and reinforcing the Haqqani network's standing among various jihadist groups. The killing of Ayman al-Zawahiri in the center of Kabul is testament to the fact that those relations between the groups remain strong.

The Haqqani network is at the nexus of religious extremism, state sponsorship of terrorism, and global jihad unleashed by the Taliban, Pakistan, and al-Qaeda. All of these actors have a vested interest in ensuring that the Haqqani network remains a key decision-maker in the Islamic Emirate of Afghanistan. However, these networks also point to a growing complexity of groups with competing agendas and ties, leaving the environment vulnerable to sponsorship from external actors. Pakistan will face increasing challenges and growing costs in its efforts to exert influence on an emboldened proxy whose interests have shifted significantly from that of its principal.

Inverting Patron-Proxy

The significant role Pakistan played in the early stages after the August 2021 Taliban takeover raised concern that Afghan interests, identity, and institutions under the Taliban regime would be dictated by Pakistan. However, there is plenty of evidence that Pakistan's grip is slipping as the Afghan Taliban become preoccupied with regime survival rather than their proxy's political objectives. The new circumstances have opened up opportunities for hardliners within the Taliban to pursue their ideological objectives, and/or pursue Pashtun nationalism. Thus, what counts as Pakistan's great achievement could also prove its disaster (Riedel 2021). The Taliban victory had an inspirational effect on those who seek the imposition of Sharia law in Pakistan. There are therefore ample reasons to worry about a security blowback from a Taliban regime across the Durand Line.

Decades of Islamization in Pakistan since the time of General Zia ul-Haq has turned many in Pakistan into religious conservatives. According to Hassan Abbas, Pakistan's practice, since the time of the Soviet jihad, of never completely "decommissioning" its Islamic warriors, is now coming back to haunt them in the form of rising sectarianism and misguided religious fervor (Abbas 2014: 39). Additionally, the contradictory policy of distinguishing between the "good" and the "bad" Taliban ensured that radical Islam remained a grossly under-examined phenomenon. Ironically, the ideological connection that has helped Pakistan control its proxy forces in Afghanistan has simultaneously inspired radicalization in Pakistan. Thus, as the Taliban regime imposes their specific brand of Islamic rule in Afghanistan, it may thus further radicalize Pakistani society, creating a significant challenge for the country.

The Taliban were groomed to be an asset for Pakistan's security establishment in its anti-India policies, but it remains doubtful if the strategic advantages will extend much further. The Taliban gains little from keeping India at bay, especially as the country can provide much-needed financing and serve as a mediator between the Taliban and international organizations and western states. Given Afghan Taliban's request to complete India-funded projects, New Delhi reopened its embassy in Kabul in June 2022, almost a year after it was shut down in the wake of the Taliban takeover of Afghanistan (Subramanian 2022). In an astonishing interview, which must have raised alarm bells in Islamabad, the Afghan Defense Minister Mullah Yaqoob, has expressed his wish to have close and cordial relations with India, mentioning both humanitarian aid and infrastructure support, as well as the past training of Afghan military officers in Indian defense colleges (Gupta 2022).

The Afghan Taliban are clearly signaling that they may be less amenable to getting instructions from their prime patron, and that they at least want to maintain the charade of autonomy in front of global and regional audiences. While Pakistan is the major beneficiary of a Taliban-led regime in Kabul, the Taliban were brought to the negotiating table also by regional powers including Russia, China, and Qatar. Moscow and Beijing believed that the Taliban could mollify some of their common concerns about "their own" terrorist groups operating in Afghanistan. The Taliban leaders also understand the importance of American support that will enable their regime to engage with the international community to ensure needed political, financial, and diplomatic support (Domingo 2021).

Another reason why the Taliban are careful not to be seen as a mere puppet of Pakistan is the latter's unpopularity in Afghanistan. The Tehrik-i-Taliban Pakistan (TTP),[10] which has carried out terror attacks against the Pakistani state, trained at the same religious seminaries that produced the Afghan Taliban. The TTP is a direct outcome of the dangerous policy of propping up jihadist proxies, and it is now testing the limits of Pakistan's toleration towards the Afghan Taliban (Iqbal 2022), leading to significant tensions.

Greatly emboldened by the Afghan Taliban ascent to power, the TTP have declared the Afghan Taliban as their role model and launched an escalating terror campaign inside Pakistan from its base in North Waziristan (Sayed 2021;

Qazi 2022). Hundreds of TTP fighters were released from prisons in Kabul when the Afghan Taliban came to power and they now enjoy operational freedom in the country. Pakistan's security forces are facing direct attacks from the TTP in tribal areas, including in Peshawar and the Swat Valley, leading the government to complain about terrorist safe havens in Afghanistan. Reversely, when Pakistani jets bombed the Afghan provinces of Khost and Kunar in April 2022 in retaliation to the bombing of a Pakistani military convoy in North Waziristan, the Taliban regime was furious with the Defense Minister, Mullah Yaqoob, warning Pakistan that Afghanistan would not tolerate such attacks in the future (Reuters 2022). A tentative peace agreement between the TTP and Pakistan was reached in November 2021 as a result of Afghan Taliban mediation, although the Afghan spokesman denies any involvement (Smith 2021).

Indeed, the alliance between the Afghan and Pakistani Taliban seems stronger than ever and there are signs of integration across the border (AFP 2022). In his address to the United Nations General Assembly in September 2022, Pakistan's Prime Minister, Shehbaz Sharif, noted that Pakistan shared global concerns about "the threat posed by the major terrorist groups operating from Afghanistan, especially Islamic State, ISIL-K and TTP, as well as Al Qaeda, ETIM, and IMU" (Yousaf 2022). Clearly, Pakistani policymakers need to be realistic about the Taliban's commitment on preventing the use of Afghan territory for terrorism.

In view of the changed political scenario in Afghanistan, Pakistan will need to re-orient its priorities if they want to maintain control over their proxy. Because of the shifting power balance and the Taliban's achievement of their primary objective, Pakistan faces a choice to adopt the goals of their proxy in order to get continued support, or "punish" the proxy into compliance by withholding needed assistance. Obviously, the second option is risky, as there would be several external powers, including India, that are ready to step in to exploit the vacuum.

Conclusion

This chapter has shown that the Pakistan-Taliban relationship is a marriage of necessity. For Pakistan, the Taliban are not easy to manage, which leads to periodic frustrations. For the Taliban, Pakistan tries to use coercive measures to control it. Though the Taliban have returned to power in Kabul, Pakistan can still apply substantial pressure on the Taliban in order to discourage it from taking actions detrimental to Pakistan's core security interests. Since August 2021, there has been little reason to expect that the Afghan Taliban will easily temper its ideological aspirations and sever its ties with terrorist groups such as al-Qaeda and the TTP.

However, the pragmatic and changing dynamics of the Taliban's geopolitical worldview signal that Pakistan will not be the sole beneficiary of a Taliban-controlled Kabul. Though Pakistan still holds substantial sway over the group, the Taliban's increasing independence, evident in its attempts to find equilibrium as a state actor, will only deepen the tension between the patron and the proxy, leading to possible problems in the near future. The tide is slowly turning against Pakistan's military control over Kabul and, with the security cover from the West out of sight, the Pakistan government finds itself isolated, caught in the complexities of domestic political maneuverings. A political unstable Pakistani may be in the best interest for the Afghan Taliban as it would keep the former's attention away from the latter.

With India remaining the core concern that drives Pakistan's Afghanistan policy, the loss of control over the proxy relationship, as well as the looming possibility of a deepening Afghan-Indian friendship, has driven one Pakistani analyst Raza Khan Qazi to push for the impossible: Open a dialogue with arch-rival India. If not, he warns, "the security threat to the region emanating from Afghanistan could in time prove existential" (Qazi 2021).

Notes

1 Afghanistan's and Pakistan's dispute over the Durand Line is rooted in the Pashtunistan issue. By rejecting the 1893 treaty with the British Raj that created the Durand Line, all Afghan regimes including the Taliban claim all the territories inhabited by Pashtuns. Pashtunistan is thus a territory that stretches across Afghanistan and Khyber Pakhtunkhwa of Pakistan, where most Pashtuns live.

2 In the mid-1990s, while Pakistan supported the Taliban, India, Russia and Iran threw their support behind the anti-Taliban Northern Alliance led by Ahmad Shah Massoud.

3 Comprising various intelligence agencies that work internally and externally to manage and collect intelligence to protect Pakistan's national security. The best known is the Inter-Services Intelligence (ISI).

4 The Taliban links with Individual donors from the Gulf is long standing. In 2008, a classified US intelligence report estimated that the Taliban received $106m from foreign sources, in particular from the Gulf states.

5 Steve Coll's book, *Directorate S*, about the most secretive wing of ISI responsible for relations with the Taliban, documents ISI's consistent strategy to promote the

Afghan Taliban in Afghanistan's politics and shows America's miscalculation about Pakistan's long-term vision about Afghanistan & India.

6   In June 2006, the US ambassador in Islamabad asked Pakistani Prime Minister "to address the increasing Taliban influence in Balochistan and FATA."

7   Obaidullah was very close to Mullah Omar and had served defense minister during the Taliban's brief reign in 1990s.

8   The 4-nation group included Pakistan, Afghanistan, the US and China,

9   The Taliban relied on Pakistan almost completely for military logistics, medical care and sanctuary.

10 Pakistan's crack-down on safe havens in Pakistan resulted in violent backlash, prompting Pakistani jihadists to band together formally with al-Qaeda and the Afghan Taliban, establishing the TTP in 2007.

Bibliography

Abbas, H. (2014), *The Taliban Revival: Violence and Extremism on the Pakistan-Afghanistan Frontier*, Wales: Yale University Press.

Abbasian, P. (2022), "My Enemy's Enemy: Iran's Approach to the Re-emergence of the Taliban", *Journal of Asian Security and International Affairs*, 9 (3): 493–512. https://doi.org/10.1177/23477970221130144.

AFP (2022), "Afghanistan Death Toll in 'Pakistan Strikes' Rises to at Least 47: Officials", *The Defense Post*, 17 April. Available online: https://www.thedefensepost.com/2022/04/17/pakistan-strikes-afghanistan/ (accessed 29 December 2022).

Akbarzadeh, S. and N. Ibrahimi (2019), "The Taliban: A New Proxy for Iran in Afghanistan?", *Third World Quarterly*, 41 (5): 764–82. https://doi.org/10.1080/01436597.2019.1702460.

ANI (2016), "Pakistan Benefited Most From Mullah Akhtar Mansour's Death", *The Indian Express*, 17 June. Available online: https://indianexpress.com/article/world/world-news/pakistan-benefited-most-from-mullah-akhtar-mansours-death-reports-taliban-terrorism-2859278/ (accessed 29 December 2022).

Asthana, N. C. (2021), "Pakistan's Support to the Taliban is One of the Greatest Feats of Covert Intelligence", *The Wire*, 5 September. Available online: https://thewire.in/south-asia/pakistans-support-to-the-taliban-is-one-of-the-greatest-feats-of-covert-intelligence (accessed 29 December 2022).

Azami, D. (2021), "Afghanistan: How do the Taliban make Money?", *BBC*, 28 August. Available online: https://www.bbc.com/news/world-46554097 (accessed 29 December 2022).

Bacon, T. (2018), "Slipping the Leash? Pakistan's Relationship with the Afghan Taliban", *Survival* Global Politics and Strategy, 60 (5): 159–80. https://doi.org/10.1080/00396338.2018.1518379.

Baker, P., M. Mashal and M. Crowley (2019), "How Trump's Plan to Secretly Meet with the Taliban Came Together, and Fell Apart", *New York Times*, 8 September.

Bar-Siman-Tov, Y. (1984), "The Strategy of War by Proxy", *Cooperation and Conflict*, 19 (4): 263–73.

Behuria, A., Y. Ul Hassan and S. Saroha (2019), "US-Taliban Talks for Afghan Peace: Complexities Galore", *Strategic Analysis*, 43 (2): 126–37. https://doi.org/10.1080/0970 0161.2019.1595483.

Berman, E. and D. Lake, eds (2019), *Proxy Wars: Suppressing Violence Through Local Agents*, Ithaca: Cornell University Press.

Byman, B. (2018), "Why Engage in Proxy War? A State's Perspective", *Brookings*, 21 May.

Chaudhuri, R. (2010), "The Proxy Calculus: Kabul, not Kashmir, Holds the Key to the Indo-Pakistani Relationship", *The RUSI Journal*, 155 (6): 52–9. https://doi.org/10.108 0/03071847.2010.542674.

Coll, S. (2005), *Ghost Wars: The Secret History of the CIA, Afghanistan, and Bin Laden, from the Soviet Invasion to September 10, 2001*, London: Penguin Books.

Coll, S. (2018), *Directorate S: The C.I.A. and America's Secret Wars in Afghanistan and Pakistan*. New York: Penguin Books.

Committee on Foreign Relations, United States Senate (2009), "Tora Bora Revisited: How We Failed To Get Bin Laden And Why It Matters Today", 30 November. Available online: https://www.govinfo.gov/content/pkg/CPRT-111SPRT53709/html/CPRT-111SPRT53709.htm (accessed 29 December 2022).

Commuri, G. (2022), "Mulling the Contours of India's Taliban Policy: Past, Present and Future Prospects", *Journal of Asian Security and International Affairs*, 9 (3): 475–92. https://doi.org/10.1177/2347797022112990.

Domingo, M. (2021), "Post-Afghanistan Destinies: America and the Middle East at a Crossroads", *Israel Journal of Foreign Affairs*, 15 (3): 425–39. https://doi.org/10.1080/2 3739770.2021.2017674.

Economic Times (2018), "US suspends $2 billion military aid to Pakistan over terror inaction", *Economic Times*, 6 January. Available online: https://economictimes. indiatimes.com/news/defence/us-suspends-2-billion-military-aid-to-pakistan-over-terror-inaction/articleshow/62386728.cms?from=mdr (accessed 29 December 2022).

Fox, A. (2019), "In Pursuit of a General Theory of Proxy Warfare", *Land Warfare Paper 123*, The Institute of Land Warfare, The Association of the United States Army.

Fox, A. (2021), "Strategic Relationships, Risk, and Proxy War", *Journal of Strategic Security*, 14 (2): 1–24.

Ganguly, S. (2022), "Kabul and a Strategic Triangle" *The Washington Quarterly*, 45 (2): 59–71. https://doi.org/10.1080/0163660X.2022.2090758.

Giustozzi, A. (2019), *The Taliban at War 2001–2018*, London: C. Hurst & Co.

Government of India (2019), "Official Spokesperson's Response to Media Query," 18 January.

Griffin, M. (2000), *Reaping the Whirlwind: The Taliban Movement in Afghanistan*, Pluto Press.

Groh, T. L. (2019), *Proxy War: The Least Bad Option*, Stanford: Stanford University Press.

Gul, A., (2019), "Taliban, US End Latest Round of Talks Without Announcing Outcome", *VOA*, 12 August. Available online: https://www.voanews.com/a/south-central-asia_taliban-us-end-latest-round-talks-without-announcing-outcome/6173668.html (accessed 29 December 2022).

Gupta, M. (2022), "Great Expectations of India, Gave Crucial Help in Past: Afghan Defence Minister to News18", Interview, *CNN-News18*, 2. June. Available online: https://www.news18.com/news/world/great-expectations-of-india-gave-crucial-help-in-past-afghan-defence-minister-to-news18-global-exclusive-5292811.html (accessed 29 December 2022).

Hansler, J. and K. Atwood (2019), "Senior Afghan Official Accuses US Envoy of 'Delegitimizing' Afghan Government", *CNN*, 14 March. Available online: https://edition.cnn.com/2019/03/14/politics/mohib-khalilzad-afghanistan-row/index.html (accessed 29 December 2022).

Hersh, S. (2002), "The Getaway: Questions Surround a Secret Pakistani Airlift", *New Yorker*, 20 January. Available online: https://www.newyorker.com/magazine/2002/01/28/the-getaway-2 (accessed 29 December 2022).

Iqbal, A. (2022), "Bilawal Wants Taliban Rulers to Use Their Influence on TTP for Peace", *The Dawn*, 29 September. Available online: https://www.dawn.com/news/1712522/bilawal-wants-taliban-rulers-to-use-their-influence-on-ttp-for-peace (accessed 29 December 2022).

Johnson, T. H. (2013), "Taliban Adaptations and Innovations", *Small Wars & Insurgencies*, 24 (1): 3–27. https://doi.org/10.1080/09592318.2013.740228.

Kermani, K. and S. Yousafzai (2019), "Taliban Talks: Pakistan Arrest 'Sends Militants Message", *BBC News*, 15 January. Available online: https://www.bbc.co.uk/news/world-asia-46865955 (accessed 29 December 2022).

King, L. (2012), "Top Taliban Official Died in Pakistani Prison, Movement Says", *Los Angeles Times*, 13 February. Available online: https://www.latimes.com/archives/blogs/world-now/story/2012-02-13/top-taliban-official-died-in-pakistani-prison-movement-says (accessed 29 December 2022).

Kleiner, J. (2014), "How Many Lives Do the Taliban Have?", *Diplomacy & Statecraft*, 25 (4): 708–31. https://doi.org/10.1080/09592296.2014.967133.

London, D. (2020), "Why the Taliban Will Never Agree to a Real Peace Deal", *The New York Times*, 27 February. Available online: https://www.nytimes.com/2020/02/27/opinion/afghanistan-war-taliban.html (accessed 29 December 2022).

Mashal, M. (2019), "US and Taliban Agree in Principle to Peace Framework, Envoy Says", *New York Times*, 28 January. Available online: https://www.nytimes.com/2019/01/28/world/asia/taliban-peace-deal-afghanistan.html (accessed 29 December 2022).

Mohammed, A. and J. Landay (2018), "US Suspends at Least $900 Million in Security Aid to Pakistan", *Reuters*, 4. January. Available online: https://www.reuters.com/article/us-usa-pakistan-aid-idUSKBN1ET2DX (accessed 29 December 2022).

Perlez, J. (2021), "The Real Winner of the Afghan War? It's Not Who You Think", *The New York Times*, 26 August. Available online: https://www.nytimes.com/2021/08/26/world/asia/afghanistan-pakistan-taliban.html (accessed 29 December 2022).

Qazi, R. K., (2022), "As Pakistan's Afghanistan Policy Fails, the Afghan Taliban Moves Against Islamabad", *South Asia Source*, Atlantic Council, 6 September. Available online: https://www.atlanticcouncil.org/blogs/southasiasource/as-pakistans-afghanistan-policy-fails-the-afghan-taliban-move-against-islamabad/ (accessed 29 December 2022).

Rashid, A. (2010), *Taliban: The Power of Militant Islam in Afghanistan and Beyond*, London: I.B. Tauris.

Reuters (2008), "Arrest Of Senior Taliban Chief In Pakistan Raises Western Hopes", *Reuters*, 23 July. Available online: https://www.rferl.org/a/Taliban_Arrest_In_Pakistan_Raises_Western_Hopes/1185555.html (accessed 29 December 2022).

Reuters (2022), "Afghanistan Will not Tolerate 'Invasions', Defense Minister Says", *Reuters*, 24 April. Available online: https://www.reuters.com/world/asia-pacific/afghan-defence-minister-says-will-not-tolerate-invasions-2022-04-24/ (accessed 29 December 2022).

Riedel, B. (2020), "The Mess in Afghanistan", *Brookings Institution*, 4 March. Available online: https://www.brookings.edu/blog/order-from-chaos/2020/03/04/the-mess-in-afghanistan/ (accessed 29 December 2022).

Riedel, B. (2021), "Order from Chaos: Pakistan's problematic victory in Afghanistan", *Brookings*, 24 August. Available online: https://www.brookings.edu/blog/order-from-chaos/2021/08/24/pakistans-problematic-victory-in-afghanistan/ (accessed 29 December 2022).

Roy, S. (2021), "As Taliban Factions Bicker, ISI Chief in Kabul to Find Berths for Haqqanis" *Indian Express*, 5 September. Available online: https://indianexpress.com/article/world/pakistan-powerful-intel-chief-arrives-in-kabul-7488925/ (accessed 29 December 2022).

Sayed, A. (2021), "The Evolution and Future of Tehrik-e-Taliban Pakistan", *Carnegie Endowment for International Peace*, December. Available online: https://carnegieendowment.org/2021/12/21/evolution-and-future-of-tehrik-e-taliban-pakistan-pub-86051 (accessed 29 December 2022).

Sediqi, A. Q. (2018), "Afghan Taliban Say Will Continue Talks with US Peace Envoy", *Reuters*, 13 October. Available online: https://www.reuters.com/article/us-usa-afghanistan-idUSKCN1MN0EU (accessed 29 December 2022).

Sirohi, S. (2019), "Is the Afghan Peace Process Going Anywhere?", *Observer Research Foundation*, 25 May. Available online: https://www.orfonline.org/expert-speak/is-the-afghan-peace-process-going-anywhere/ (accessed 29 December 2022).

Smith, J. (2021), "The Haqqani Network: The New Kingmakers in Kabul," *War on the Rocks*, 12 November. Available online: https://warontherocks.com/2021/11/the-haqqani-network-afghanistans-new-power-players/ (accessed 29 December 2022).

Stewart, P., J. Landay and H. Shalizi (2019), "In US Pursuit of Peace Talks, Perilous Rift Opens with Afghan Leader", *Reuters*, 27 March. Available online: https://www.reuters.com/article/us-usa-afghanistan-idUSKCN1R809V (accessed 29 December 2022).

Subramanian, N. (2022), "Taliban: Asked India to Complete its Development Projects in Afghanistan", *Indian Express*, 16 August. Available online: https://indianexpress.com/article/world/asked-india-to-complete-its-projects-in-afghanistan-taliban-8090476/ (accessed 29 December 2022).

The Hindu (2019a) "Pakistan views Afghan Taliban as Reliable Anti-India Element in Afghanistan: US Congressional Report", *The Hindu*, 6 November. Available online: https://www.thehindu.com/news/international/pakistan-views-afghan-taliban-as-reliable-anti-india-element-in-afghanistan-us-congressional-report/article29901277.ece (accessed 29 December 2022).

The Hindu (2019b), "Mullah Baradar released by Pakistan at the behest of US: Khalilzad", *The Hindu*, 9 February. Available online: https://www.thehindu.com/news/international/mullah-baradar-released-by-pakistan-at-the-behest-of-us-khalilzad/article26222102.ece (accessed 29 December 2022).

Thomas, C. (2021), "US Military Withdrawal and Taliban Takeover in Afghanistan: Frequently Asked Questions", *Congressional Research Service*, Report R46879, 17 September. Available online: https://crsreports.congress.gov/product/pdf/R/R46879 (accessed 29 December 2022).

Threlkeld, E. and G. Easterly (2021), "Afghanistan-Pakistan Ties and Future Stability in Afghanistan," *United States Institute of Peace*, 175.

United States Department of State (2019), "Country Reports on Terrorism 2018", *United States Department of State Bureau of Counterterrorism*, October.

Waldman, M. (2010), "The Sun in the Sky: The Relationship Between Pakistan's ISI and Afghan Insurgents", *Crisis State Research. Centre*, Discussion Paper 18, June. Available online: https://www.files.ethz.ch/isn/117472/dp%2018.pdf (accessed 29 December 2022).

Walsh, D. (2010), "WikiLeaks Cables: US Special Forces Working Inside Pakistan", *The Guardian*, 30 November. Available online: https://www.theguardian.com/world/2010/nov/30/wikileaks-cables-us-forces-embedded-pakistan (accessed 29 December 2022).

Yousaf, F. and M. Jabarkhail (2022), "Afghanistan's Future Under the Taliban Regime: Engagement or Isolation?", *Journal of Policing, Intelligence and Counter Terrorism*, 17 (1): 117–34. https://doi.org/10.1080/18335330.2021.1982139.

Yousaf, K. (2022), "Shehbaz's UNGA Speech Sparks Row with Kabul", *The Express Tribune*, 25 September. Available online: https://tribune.com.pk/story/2378510/shehbazs-unga-speech-sparks-row-with-kabul (accessed 29 December 2022).

Yousafzai, Z. (2022), *The Troubled Triangle: US-Pakistan Relations under the Taliban's Shadow*, Oxon: Routledge.

Zaidi, S. M. A. (2009), "The Taliban Organisation in Pakistan", *The RUSI Journal*, 154 (5): 40–7. https://doi.org/10.1080/03071840903411954.

Zaidi, S. M. A. (2010), "Pakistan's Anti-Taliban Counter-Insurgency", *The RUSI Journal*, 155 (1): 10–9. https://doi.org/10.1080/03071841003683377.

Part Three

Proxy Wars: The Emergence of a New Paradigm

14

Transnational Organized Crime Groups as State Proxies

Ümit Namli and Cüneyt Gürer

Introduction

This chapter departs from the traditional understanding of proxy forces and local armed groups as proxies and introduces transnational organized crime (TOC) groups as State proxies. The overall argument of the chapter's discussion relies on the strategic competition concept that has become a crucial global paradigm in international relations. Previous proxy discussions in the literature pay significant attention to the interaction between states and non-state armed groups within a principle-agent framework in which the State is considered as the "principle" defining the terms of the relationship and the proxy as the "agent" following the principle guidance and interests in the conflict (Mumford 2013: 40–6; Berman and Lake 2019: 1–27). Studies looking at the structure of the principle-agent relationship consider the conflict as a constant factor of a given situation and disconnects external competition among states when analyzing the relationship between a proxy and a State. In a recent study, Ivanov (2020: 38) argues that it is necessary to go beyond proxy discussions, such as what proxy is and how states engage on the traditional battlefield. Instead, the discussion should be expanded further by connecting the proxy use to the global political context, which includes the power competition among states. He places the geopolitical environment at the center of his analysis of proxy structures. He argues that the entire geostrategic environment must also be included in the discussion to understand the dynamics of proxy use by states fully. (Ivanov 2020: 37–51).

Starting with a similar assumption, this chapter considers the strategic competition among states as the primary independent variable of the geostrategic environment that defines the outcome of state-state interactions and state and non-state engagements. This approach allows us to consider other forms of non-state actors serving as states' proxies; therefore, in this chapter, we will examine the role of transnational organized crime groups as state proxies in the context of the contemporary strategic competition among states. This chapter will use the model introduced by Gürer (2021) that looks at TOC-State interaction differently, where the traditional interaction highlights the TOC groups trying to infiltrate State institutions to keep their operation away from State intervention. However, in the "Strategic Competition Model of TOC" (Gürer 2021; Gürer and Lauer 2022), competing States at the global level use TOC groups for their strategic gain; therefore, they become an instrument of the competition.

Competition among states is not a new phenomenon; however, the contemporary competition among global actors became part of their national security strategies and was voiced openly as a priority. The National Security Strategy of the United States (2022) prioritizes the rivalry between the US and China as a security challenge. It highlights Russian aggression as a threat to the international rule-based order. China and Russia are not shy to express their intention to challenge the US-led international order. Both countries published a joint statement on February 4, 2022, stating that both sides "call for the establishment of a new kind of relationship between world powers," and mentioning that both China and Russia are superior to political and military alliances of the Cold War era (Official Internet Resources of the President of Russia 2022). Their joint statement gives a clear message about the cooperation between China and Russia against Western global dominance. They indicate that their collaboration has no limits and there are no "forbidden areas" of cooperation. When the Presidents of the two countries met on September 15, 2022, in Samarkand, they repeated their willingness to cooperate, despite Chinese concerns over the developments of the unprovoked Russian war in Ukraine, which eventually led China to modify their foreign policy (Wei 2022). According to Christensen (2022) China and Russia have different attitudes toward strategic competition. While China benefits from the current international system and does not directly attack it or export the Chinese model, Russia attempts to overthrow the present system because it sees itself as a victim of the current international order, which prevents the development of its economy and society.

Power struggles between these nations are also seen as conflicts between political regimes, namely between democracies and non-democratic states (Bunde 2021). With their authoritarian regime practices, China and Russia both pose a threat to the rule-based system of international law. To understand the relationship between the State and TOC organizations, political regime differences in the strategic struggle have significant explanatory power. In this context, authoritarian regimes use TOC groups as a tool to reach their foreign policy objectives, and TOC groups become part of the "gray zone" tactics in contemporary irregular warfare. In fact, the traces of this long-standing approach of Russia were made even more evident by the findings of Grinda, the prosecutor of the 2010 operation against the Russian mafia in Spain. In his assessments, Grinda first noted that the Russian mafia's control of strategic sectors such as oil and metals had increased its influence on the global economy. In his second observation, he noted that the murder of Alexander Litvinenko in London, who was conducting intelligence work on organized crime, should be seen as an obstruction of efforts to uncover these links. Moreover, he remarked that there are still unanswered questions in the investigation of the links between Russian politicians and mafia groups (Harding 2010). The sanctions on the oligarchs after the war in Ukraine show that, over time, not only organized criminal groups but any group or person backed by Russia have developed into powerful global actors. Within this context, this study will examine how TOC groups are used as a proxy by mostly non-democratic regimes and explore the interaction under a competition framework among States.

Strategic Competition and TOC Groups as Proxies

In the competitive environment, States use both hard and soft security options to balance each other (Gürer 2021). It is not a new phenomenon for states to use non-state criminal actors as a proxy and to operate in illicit markets to protect their national interests at the international level (Ullman 1983; Popovic 2017; Biberman 2016; Wither 2020). Similarly, political parties frequently use them to intimidate rivals at the national level. This narrative dates back several centuries, making it quite ancient. For example, one of the earliest examples of criminals being used as proxies is State-sponsored piracy that happened in the sixteenth and seventeenth centuries (Chamblis 1989; Roth 2014: 8). Pirates were used by states to smuggle gold, precious metals, and other goods to other countries and continents which were under the dominance of Spanish and Portuguese colonization (Chamblis 1989). In further years they have been used not only to smuggle valuable commodities but also to support state operations in different countries financially, especially by intelligence agencies (Chamblis 1989: McCoy 1972), and to smuggle weapons in order to carry out an illegal operation in other countries or to support insurgent groups against the hostile governments and states (Chamblis 1989).

However, in the course of history, not only TOC groups but also other types of unconventional methods, such as media, trades, energy sources, propaganda, etc., were used by the states (Lutsevych 2016: Wither 2020). Especially during the cold war, western and old eastern bloc countries used those methods to avoid armed confrontation to undermine each other (Lutsevych 2016), and proxy wars became the era's norm (Hoffman and Orner 2021). After the cold war, proxy use involved local armed groups collaborating with States or pursuing State agendas in a conflict (Lutsevych 2016; Wither 2020). Despite the differences between the Cold War and the contemporary competitive environment, proxy use is the common method of challenging sides. As Hoffman and Orner (2021) argue, great powers competed for each other supporting proxies throughout history, and "there is no reason to think that US competition with China and Russia will be any different than earlier periods of history." Nevertheless, a recent Foreign Affairs Article by Thomas J. Christensen (2022) argues that US-China strategic competition differs from the cold war era: ideological component and interconnected global economic structure. These countries are not leading opposing alliance systems that are created local conflicts. A lack of ideology and a high degree of interdependence decreases the chance of a large-scale military conflict. Still, they increase the importance of non-State players in the struggle since they can act independently of States while upholding States' interests.

In a recent analysis, Gürer and Lauer (2022) demonstrated case studies that the contemporary strategic environment is redefining the interaction between States and criminal actors at the international level. Based on the model created by Gürer (2021), he argued that "non-democratic practices and the spread of democratic backsliding give rise to opportunities for authoritarian countries not only to cooperate with criminal actors but also to control these non-state actors and to use them for their own benefits." They develop a model suggesting a new understanding of TOC groups as instruments of the undemocratic countries in the competition among States. Non-democratic regime structure allows State institutions to engage with the criminal underworld to use their resources, skills, and influence for the benefit of the State. The lack of transparency in the internal system, not having a clear line between legal and illegal State practices, the desire to control every element in the social structure, being able to bend the laws, and the desire to control these groups rather than completely destroying them makes these groups likely candidates of cooperation at the international level. In his book *Weaponization of Everything* Mark Galeotti, furthermore, argues that authoritarian States are not only stretching the limits of international law, institutions, and the system itself (2022: 149), but they are also benefiting from the vague distinction between legal and illegal by interpreting them based on their interests (Galeotti 2022: 87).

Analyzing the State-TOC Proxy Relationship

This section explores further how States and transnational organized crime groups connect to each other and how they operate in the principle-agent relationship where States use TOC groups as a proxy at the international level. Before analyzing the relationship further, this section first looks at the difference between the traditional way of understanding the TOC-State interaction.

In the traditional understanding, organized crime (O.C.) groups are founded at the national level with hierarchical structures with a crime boss at the top of the organization (Kleemans 2014: 34). This image of organized crime has been reiterated by the Hollywood impact and complements the image of organized crime as a system of hierarchies connected to various ethnicities in a given society. Although this structure exists, it doesn't reflect the entire reality of organized crime structures as organized crime groups become more transnational. They tend to act in network structures as enterprise models rather than organized hierarchies (Dijk and Spapens 2014: 215). Considering that their primary objective is to make money, organized crime groups have also had to change their organizational structure. Thus, they are able to communicate with any organization in the world and carry out their operation faster and more effectively (Albenese 2007). The new network structure also allows them to benefit from each other's capabilities and become flexible to adjust to the changing dynamics of illicit markets.

On the other hand, in the traditional Model, Gürer (2021) argues that the interaction between O.C. and State is mainly in a direction that O.C. groups target state institutions to keep their illicit businesses running by protecting them from law enforcement intervention. O.C. groups use various tools to infiltrate state structures using corruption, establishing close ties with political figures, and supporting candidates they prefer during the elections. In this model, States try to protect themselves from external O.C. actors, and the primary assumption in this traditional model conveys that States consider O.C. groups as a threat to public order and public safety. An alternative way of looking at the connection between States and TOC, presented by Gürer (2021) considers strategic competition as an important contextual reality establishing a new way of interaction between the State and O.C. groups. Calling the new model, the "Strategic Competition Model of CTOC", the author argues that the competitive positions of both political regimes and states determine their level of engagement with TOC groups. According to this model, authoritarian governments compete strategically against democracies, and because of the nature of their regime type, they frequently use O.C. groups to their advantage. This model also makes countering transnational organized crime (CTOC) more than a law enforcement issue and carries the threat posed by TOC groups to global political discussions.

Comparing Advantages and Disadvantages of Proxy Use

Using non-state actors provides numerous advantages for the sponsoring State, including avoiding direct confrontation with rivalries and conflicts due to the indirect relation between the sponsor country and proxy (Risse et al. 2018). States also recruit proxies to reduce the cost of war and political pressure on the sponsoring country (Popovic 2017: Wither 2020), to increase the effectiveness of the operation since local groups have more local, ethnic, and cultural knowledge in the combat locations (Biberman 2016; Wither 2020), to keep distance from the conflicting areas, to divert the revenge attacks from sponsoring states, and to increase deniability of certain attacks (Wither 2020). Despite the advantages, there are also certain disadvantages of using proxies. For example, the effectiveness and success rate of the proxies may be lower than regular forces, and the number of casualties might be higher (Biberman 2016; Wither 2020). Of course, all these defeats also harm the reputation of the sponsoring country even though most times don't publicly declare that they support their proxies (Wither 2020). Secondly, since the proxies are not regular forces, they are not entirely under control (Biberman 2016; Popovic 2017; Wither 2020) and use power that might exceed legal boundaries, including massacres and war crimes (Biberman 2016; Wither 2020). Within this context, they are not entirely reliable since they also have their own agenda, which might result in conflict with allies in the meantime (Popovic 2017). Thus, unsuccessful efforts or failures of proxies seriously harm the reputation of the supporting or sponsoring countries (Wither 2020). Thirdly, while strong countries that have robust institutions and powerful governments can manage such scandals or live with them, weak countries that are dependent on their proxies have proxy backfires, such as insurgence, which damages state power (Popovic 2017; Wither 2020).

It's important to emphasize several differences between TOC organizations and regular armed groups utilized as a proxy. The first difference between the two is related to their motivations. While traditional proxies such as insurgents, terrorists, and militias are mostly ideologically, politically, and/or religiously motivated (Beare and Naylor 1999; Mullins and Wither 2016; Shelley and Picarelli 2002; Stanislawski 2005), TOC groups are economically motivated groups (Mullins and Wither 2016; Shelley and Picarelli 2002; Stanislawski 2005). Secondly, while the main objective of the armed groups and insurgencies used as traditional proxies is to surpass or overthrow the adversary state/regime/government, the main purpose of TOC groups is to infiltrate the existing system and capture key actors and institutions to increase their economic gains rather than taking down the government or regimes. Therefore, there are operational and motivational differences between the two types of proxies even though the majority of the advantages and disadvantages of using proxies listed in the literature are compatible with using proxies within the military concept, which may not accurately reflect all aspects of using TOC groups as a proxy from a criminological perspective. However, most of the listed advantages and disadvantages of using proxies in the literature are compatible with using proxies within the military concept, not necessarily reflecting the advantages or disadvantages of using criminals as a proxy.

Entangled Relationship: TOC Groups and Politics

Undoubtedly, TOC groups are one of the biggest threats to democracies, economies, societies, sustainable development, and peace in the regions (Demirbüken et al. 2009; Ekici 2014; Finklea 2010; Global Initiative Against Transnational Organized Crime 2018; Mani 2018; Sari 2015; Shelley 1995; Zoutendijk 2010; Stanislawski 2005). Especially considering their entangled relations with corrupted politicians and bureaucrats, the threat they pose against society is getting even more significant, specifically the post-conflict environment provides opportunities for criminals to engage in activities allowing them to work with people with State affiliations. In the meantime, if the post-conflict environment could not be managed effectively, political and criminal actors could converge, and some of the actors that engaged in criminal activities during the conflict or war could shift to politics without disconnecting their criminal ties. In this type of interaction, these individuals become the face of the criminal world in the country's post-conflict structure. When the connection between criminal groups and politics is established, O.C. groups hire individuals who previously worked for the country's security services.

Galeotti (2018) claims in his article that some former military staff who served in the Russian army and were skilled with weapons, as well as athletically gifted individuals such as wrestlers, fighters, etc., were invited and joined organized crime groups due to their ideologies or financial considerations, and some of them served time in prison before dying. In the meantime, those organized crime groups evolved into transnational crime groups involving drug, weapon, human trafficking, money laundering, and cybercrimes. Disputes between organized crime organizations stopped after the Berlin Wall fell at the beginning of the 1990s, commencing after perestroika, and Russian organized crime groups gathered after Putin took office; these conflicts also had a connection to the kleptocracy government (Galeotti 2018). In the new regime established after the conflict or war, those criminal groups operating not against the regime and government but operating within and by the side of the government. As the circumstances changed, certain businesspeople, politicians, and government officials started to employ those criminal organizations as their proxies.

However, in this scenario, legitimate business owners seek protection from corrupt law enforcement officials or organized crime organizations in order to execute their operations and safeguard their companies from competing organized criminal organizations. The financial gain was so big that police found more than 120 million dollars in Col. Dmitry Zakharchenko's residence during one of the corruption operations targeting high-level anti-corruption officers (Galeotti 2018). Especially in antidemocratic countries, leaders designate candidates who are dependable from the perspective of the regime to ensure that regular forces like the army and law enforcement are kept under control. These individuals are chosen among those with ties to the government on a political, familial, ethnic, or religious level (Ash 2016). Eventually, they are used as a parallel military force (revolutionary guards in Libya and Iran) to protect themselves against threats to their reign (Carey and Mitchell 2017) and observe the military (Ash 2016). Political leaders also use corruption to support their election campaigns (Gürer 2021).

TOC Activities and Proxy Practices

Many traditional TOC activities serve very well to the objectives of undemocratic state objectives to increase their influence in other states. Karlsen (2019: 1–14) analyzes forty official reports of eleven Western countries covering the period of

2014–2018 to examine the Russian political influence in these countries. He finds out that, among others, Russia uses an extensive network of alliances and front organizations to operate in these countries and establish long-term political influence. Russian organized crime networks play an important role in establishing a Russian influence in Europe. They have been used for various purposes, such as a source of "black cash," to create political influence, and to carry out targeted assassinations (Galeotti 2017: 6). For example, in the ongoing Russian invasion of Ukraine, it is not certain what role organized crime groups played in both the initiation of the events and in the process of the invasion. Furthermore, it hasn't been researched or investigated yet how much organized crime groups influenced local politicians in those regions and how much these politicians played critical roles in the referendum for separation from Ukraine, which is one of the grounds Russia uses as a political argument. However, prior investigations and research have revealed that Russian-organized criminal gangs are racially concentrated and functional, particularly in the Luhansk, Donbas, and Donetsk areas, where the invasion began, which needs to be probed (Home Office 2016; Galeotti 2014).

Similarly, China also has a long history of working with organized crime groups in the country. Although China launched a significant and widely publicized anti-corruption campaign after Xi Jinping came into office as the General Secretary of the Chinese Community Party in 2012, the Chinese government does not isolate criminal elements from its overall strategy of increasing its influence in global politics (Aukia 2021). According to Cole (2021: 57), the Chinese Communist Party presented an offer to all criminal groups in the nation in 1949 following the Chinese conflict, asking them to cooperate with the State or face destruction. Those groups accepting the offer were asked to develop a relationship with the party-state structure and, whenever asked and obliged to assist in intimidating civil society and the opponents of the party (Cole 2021: 57). Later, China incorporated the O.C. structure into its global aspirations and delegated coordination of non-State actors outside of China to the United Front Work Department, an official organization charged with gathering intelligence and influencing people and institutions both inside and outside of China, under the authority of the 2017 Chinese National Intelligence Law. The law imposes a legal obligation for Chinese individuals and organizations to report back to the authorities and work in coordination with them. The law increased the concerns about China's use of private companies operating abroad and individuals living in other countries are required by law to act as State proxies, and the law gave a legal base for the United Front to recruit individuals from the non-State actors (Aukia 2021: 21).

234   *Proxy Wars from a Global Perspective*

This part of the chapter highlighted some of the key issue areas that China and Russia operate by using TOC groups as their proxies. The following points will be emphasized to demonstrate how the State uses TOC organizations and some of their strategies to achieve its global objectives in the context of strategic competition: Corruption, smuggling of weapons, cash flows, money laundering, infiltration into local politics, and destabilizing effects.

Infiltration into Domestic Politics

There are many reasons why antidemocratic regimes infiltrate a State's domestic politics; however, in the strategic competition environment, one of the most important reasons is to help populist leaders to be elected or to keep authoritarians in power. Undemocratic regimes prefer to work with similar regimes to gain flexibility in their interaction at the international level. The collaboration of tyrants on a global scale is seen as a novel approach for them to learn from one another and adapt to the changing needs of the international system. In order to accomplish this, authoritarians do not hesitate to intervene in the internal politics of States to manipulate the re-election of their preferred leader to remain in power. For this reason, they prefer to keep other authoritarians (including populist leaders) in power once they are elected in their countries. Especially during the election, they become a useful tool for their sponsors (Carey and Mitchell 2017). In the event of any slip-a-side crisis, TOC organizations form alliances with the governing political regimes, either with pro-government institutions and troops or against regular forces (Carey and Mitchell 2017). So, they are basically insurance for autocratic regimes since they don't accept democratic results.

On the other hand, especially in underdeveloped democratic countries, organized crime groups, corrupted politicians, and bureaucrats use shell companies as proxies to launder money that comes from illegal activities, including drug trafficking, corruption, weapons trafficking, and financial crimes. Corrupted politicians and bureaucrats use the money to empower their political status in the country or against other political rivals to keep their position in the country. Similarly, bureaucrats use that money to keep their position in their organizations or to use it as leverage to promote the bureaucracy. Organized crime groups are using the system to make money, which is the major reason for their existence, to gain political power and to strengthen themselves against their rivals (OCCRP 2011).

The symbiotic relationship between organized crime groups and corrupted politicians and bureaucrats eventually leads to oppressive and authoritarian regimes (Farah 2012; OCCRP 2011; Sung 2004), which are structured strictly in the hierarchy from top down. While corrupted politicians are financially supported by TOC groups, corrupted prominent figures provide protection for their long arms and endure their rule (Farah 2012; Skaperdas 2001). On the other hand, TOC groups also involve in the election process. They buy votes, intimidate electorates and opponents, and influence or manipulate votes to make money or keep immunity under the supported regimes (Sung 2004).

Destabilizing Effect

Authoritarian governments use O.C. groups to increase their influence in disputed areas, frozen conflict regions, and post-conflict environments either to keep the conflict protracted or to justify their involvement later. This happens to be a very active Russian strategy in a different conflict that Russia involved. The operations of Russia in Donbas are one of the most obvious examples of how it exploited criminal organizations to expand its influence and afterward to justify its presence. Galeotti and Arutunyan (2022) conducted extensive research on the criminal activities and illicit markets facilitated by groups affiliated with Russian security agencies and how these connections shaped the social influence campaigns and established a political structure in favor of Russia over time. Russian involvement in the region using various methods destabilized the region, and later it was used as a justification by Russia for further involvement. Another example of Russia using organized crime as a proxy in regional conflicts is Abkhazia and South Ossetia. Earlier reports on the activities of Russian OC groups in the Caucasus indicate that the growing smuggling and criminal networks decreased the stability of the region as well as provided a strong ground for criminals (Curtis 2002; Kukhianidze 2004) which later turned to Russia and became Russian proxies during the Russian invasion of these two regions in the 2008 War with Georgia.

Cash Flows and Money Laundering Activities

TOC groups manage a significant amount of cash which is the lifeblood of criminal activities, and they are considered a great resource for illegal activities when they align themselves with authoritarian State interests (Gregson and

Crang 2017; Leuprecht et al. 2015), specifically in underdeveloped countries, which have unstable democracy and have been suffering from conflicts (Galeotti 2018; Vorrath 2015; Stanislawski 2005). TOC groups, additionally, pose a threat to commercial and financial institutions. Businesses, which are entangled with money laundering, commingle legitimate revenues with criminal proceeds; thus, they access greater sources to endow their businesses, which creates a significant advantage for the businesses involved in money laundering compared to legitimate businesses and companies in the free market.

However, this doesn't only have negative effects on businesses, again since dirty money entangled businesses don't intend to make a profit from the legitimate business but conceal the origin of the money; these businesses produce low-quality products and services, which empty the businesses. Moreover, these cash flows coming from unknown sources, especially in underdeveloped countries, harm the economic policies of the governments. Thus, corrupted politicians, bureaucrats, and members of organized criminal organizations in developing nations live in lavish homes and drive the newest models of cars. At the same time, their citizens suffer from financial difficulties, poverty, inadequate housing, unpaid credit debts, etc. (OCCRP 2011). Meanwhile, tolerating money laundering operations attracts more organized crime groups and, eventually, terrorist organizations that are funded by organized crime and money laundering to the nations. Moreover, money laundering also has an increasing factor in corruption in both public and private institutions.

Corruption

TOC groups use corrupted politicians and bureaucrats to cover their illegal activities and to provide protection from prosecution (Skaperdas 2001); vice versa, those corrupted politicians and bureaucrats use them to support and endure their rule and existence (Farah 2012; Galeotti 2018; Gürer 2021; Carey and Mitchell 2017), and to funnel public funds for their private usage (OCCRP 2011). Corruption begins with politicians and high-level bureaucrats and then spreads across society and through all levels of bureaucracy, which eventually leads to the destruction of the social and economic environment (Terziev and Petkov 2018). In the meantime, corruption erodes trust between citizens and the government at the national level and ruins the reputation of the government and regimes at the international level, which causes the escape of foreign investment from the country (Terziev and Petkov 2018). To remain off track, both parties use offshore accounts through phantom or shell companies and third parties/other tools (OCCRP 2011). Thus, this degenerated relationship prevents the equal distribution of public resources to citizens, which gives unlawful and unethical opportunities for those who involve in corruption to both public servants and beneficiaries (Warren 2004) (Terziev and Petkov 2018).

Weapon Smuggling

One of the great sources of intelligence services is arms smuggling. So far, intelligence agencies have used TOC groups to sell weapons to different countries that have a conflict with each other, even their rivalries, to profit from the business (Chamblis 1989). Additionally, in order to support paramilitary groups which, operate against the sponsoring states, TOC groups were used to give weapons to those (Chamblis 1989). In the meantime, some countries allowed TOC groups to smuggle drugs, even helped in some occasions to the TOC group in their operation, and illegal substances to the paramilitary groups so that they could financially support their activities against targeted countries (Chamblis 1989). Organized crime groups also avoid any kind of legal action against them by using their powerful allegiances. Therefore, this symbiotic relationship between the parties endangers national and international securities. Not only corrupted bureaucrats and politicians but also those who hide behind patriotic ideologies using organized crime groups and criminals to fight with others in their asymmetric wars (Galeotti 2018). For example, in the case of Chinese organized crime member Wan Kuok Koi, who is also involved in drug trafficking, illegal gambling, human trafficking, etc., extended his operation under the cover of legal businesses backed by the Chinese government with Beijing's Belt and Road Initiative Project (Gürer 2021).

Conclusions

Due to their mentioned characteristics, TOC groups are a useful tool to be used as a proxy (Risse et al. 2018). Yet, there are differences between traditional proxies and organized crime groups as a proxy. For example, while traditional proxies such as insurgents, terrorists, and militias are mostly ideologically, politically, and religiously motivated (Beare and Naylor 1999; Mullins and Wither 2016; Shelley and Picarelli 2002; Stanislawski 2005), TOC groups are economically motivated groups (Mullins and Wither 2016; Shelley and Picarelli 2002; Stanislawski 2005). Within this context, while the main purpose of traditional proxies is to surpass or take down the adversary state/regime/government, the primary purpose of organized crime groups is to infiltrate the existing system and capture it to increase economic gains rather than overthrowing the government and regimes. Therefore, even though most of the listed advantages and disadvantages of using proxies in the literature are compatible with using proxies within the military concept, they do not necessarily reflect all aspects of using TOC groups as a proxy from the social science perspective. Moreover, the role of TOC groups' tremendous damage to society and the economy in great power competition has yet to be comprehensively examined (Gürer 2021). Even though democracy is not the only factor in preventing the spread of organized crime in countries, it is definitely a significant contributor to understanding the threat posed by TOC groups and the size/greatness of the problem (Sung 2004).

Bibliography

Albanese, J. S. (2007), *Organized Crime in Our Times*, 5th edn, Newark, NJ: Lexis/Nexis.

Ash, K. (2016), "Threats to Leaders' Political Survival and Pro-Government Militia Formation", *International Interactions*, 42 (5): 703–728.

Aukia, J. (2021), "China as a Hybrid Influencer: Non-State Actors as State Proxies", *Hybrid CoE Research Report* 1. Available online: https://www.hybridcoe.fi/publications/hybrid-coe-research-report-1-china-as-a-hybrid-influencernon-state-actors-as-state-proxies/ (accessed 20 September 2022).

Beare, M. E. and Naylor, R. T. (1999), "Major Issues Relating to Organized Crime: Within the Context of Economic Relationships". *Paper Prepared for the Law Commission of Canada*, 61. Available online: https://www.ojp.gov/ncjrs/virtual-library/abstracts/major-issues-relating-organized-crime-within-context-economic (accessed 30 December 2022).

Berman, E. and D. A. Lake, eds (2019), *Proxy Wars: Suppressing Violence Through Local Agents*, Ithaca: Cornell University Press.

Biberman, Y. (2016), "Self-Defense Militias, Death Squads, and State Outsourcing of Violence in India and Turkey", *Journal of Strategic Studies* 41 (5): 751–81. https://doi.org/10.1080/01402390.2016.1202822

Bunde, T. (2021), "Beyond Westlessness: A Readout From the Munich Security Conference", *Munich Security Brief*. Available online: https://securityconference.org/en/publications/munich-security-brief/msc-special-edition-2021/ (accessed 30 December 2022).

Carey, S. C. and N. J. Mitchell (2017), "Progovernment Militias", *Annual Review of Political Science*, 20: 127–47. https://doi.org/10.1146/ANNUREV-POLISCI-051915-045433.

Chambliss, W. J. (1989), "State-Organized Crime: The American Society of Criminology, 1988 Presidential Address." *Criminology*, 27 (2): 183–208. https://doi.org/10.1111/j.1745-9125.1989.tb01028.x.

Christensen, T. J. (2022), "There Will Not be a new Cold War", *Foreign Affairs*. 24. Available online: https://www.foreignaffairs.com/articles/united-states/2021-03-24/there-will-not-be-new-cold-war (accessed 25 April 2021).

Cole, J. M. (2021), "On the Role of Organized Crime and Related Substate Actors in Chinese Political Warfare Against Taiwan. Ministry of Justice Investigation Bureau, Prospect and Exploration." *Outlook and Exploration Monthly,* 19 (6): 55–88. Available online: https://www.mjib.gov.tw/FileUploads/eBooks/6f2646ebb06a4ddba2449c950a42533d/Section_file/8a0b255919bc48e1bc3d2a38825cd3c8.pdf (accessed 15 July 2022).

Curtis, G. E. (2002), *Involvement of Russian Organized Crime Syndicates, Criminal Elements in the Russian Military, and Regional Terrorist Groups in Narcotics Trafficking in Central Asia, the Caucasus, and Chechnya,* Washington DC: Library of Congress Federal Research Division.

Demirbüken, H., H Mili, J. Townsend, U. Rahmonberdiev, O. Kurbanov, R. Johansen, S. Kunnen, K. Kuttnig and T. Le Pichon (2009), "Addiction, Crime, and Insurgency: The Transnational Threat of Afghan Opium", *United Nations Office on Drugs and Crime*. Available online: https://www.unodc.org/documents/data-and-analysis/Afghanistan/Afghan_Opium_Trade_2009_web.pdf (accessed 30 December 2022).

Dijk, Van J. and T. Spapens (2014), "Transnational Organized Crime Networks", in P. Reichel and J. Albanese eds , *Handbook of Transnational Crime and Justice*, 213–26, Thousand Oaks: Sage.

Ekici, B. (2014), "International Drug Trafficking and National Security of Turkey", *Journal of Politics and Law*, 7 (2): 113–26. https://doi.org/10.5539/jpl.v7n2p113.

Farah, D. (2012). *Transnational Organized Crime, Terrorism, and Criminalized States in Latin America: An Emerging Tier-one National Security Priority*, US Army War College, Strategic Studies Institute.

Finklea, K. M. (2010), *Organized Crime in the United States: Trends and Issues for Congress*, Washington D.C.: Congressional Research Service.

Galeotti, M. (2014). "Ukraine's Mob War", *Foreign Policy*, 1 May. Available online: https://foreignpolicy.com/2014/05/01/ukraines-mob-war/ (accessed 08 August 2022).

Galeotti, M. (2017), "Crimintern: How the Kremlin Uses Russia's Criminal Networks in Europe", *ECFR*, 2 (3): 1–12. Available online: https://ecfr.eu/publication/crimintern_how_the_kremlin_uses_russias_criminal_networks_in_europe/ (accessed 14 January 2021).

Galeotti, M. (2018), "Gangster's Paradise: How Organized Crime Took Over Russia", *The Guardian*, 23 March. Available online: https://www.theguardian.com/news/2018/mar/23/how-organised-crime-took-over-russia-vory-super-mafia (accessed 30 December 2022).

Galeotti, M. (2022), *The Weaponization of Everything: A Field Guide to the New Way of War*, New Haven: Yale University Press.

Galeotti, M. and A. Arutunyan, A. (2022), "Rebellion as Racket: Crime and the Donbas conflict, 2014–2022", *Global Initiative Against Transnational Organized Crime*. Available online: https://globalinitiative.net/wp-content/uploads/2022/07/GITOC-Donbas-Rebellion-as-racket.pdf (accessed 21 November 2021).

Global Initiative Against Transnational Organized Crime (2018), "Organized Crime and its Role in Contemporary Conflict: An Analysis of U.N. Security Council Resolutions", *Global Initiative Against Transnational Organized Crime*, September. Available online: https://globalinitiative.net/wp-content/uploads/2018/09/TGIATOC-UNSC-Policy-Note-1962-web.pdf (accessed 13 March 2021).

Gregson, N., and M. Crang (2017), "Illicit Economies: Customary Illegality, Moral Economies and Circulation", *Transactions of the Institute of British Geographers*, 42 (2): 206–19. https://doi.org/10.1111/TRAN.12158/FORMAT/PDF/OEBPS/PAGES/2.PAGE.XHTML.

Gürer, C. (2021), "Strategic Competition: International Order and Transnational Organized Crime", *George C Marshall European Center for Security Studies: Security Insights,* 69. Available online: https://www.marshallcenter.org/en/publications/security-insights/strategic-competition-international-order-and-transnational-organized-crime-0 (accessed 03 April 2022).

Gürer, C. and L. Lauer (2022), "Political Regime Changes and Transnational Organized Crime", *Clock Tower Security Series*. Available online: https://www.marshallcenter.org/en/publications/clock-tower-security-series/political-regime-changes-and-transnational-organized-crime (accessed 22 September 2022).

Harding, L (2010), "WikiLeaks Cables: Russian Government Using Mafia for its Dirty Work", *The Guardian*, 1 December. Available online: https://www.theguardian.com/world/2010/dec/01/wikileaks-cable-spain-russian-mafia (accessed 30 December 2022).

Hoffman, F. and A. Orner (2021), "The Return of Great-Power Proxy Wars", *War on the Rocks*, 2 September. Available online: https://warontherocks.com/2021/09/the-return-of-great-power-proxy-wars/ (accessed 21 November 2022).

Home Office (2016), "Country Information and Guidance Ukraine: Fear of Organised Criminal Gangs", *United Kingdom Home Office*. Available online: https://www.refworld.org/docid/5853df354.html (accessed 30 December 2022). https://doi.org/10.1080/03050629.2016.1138108.

Ivanov, Z. (2020), "Changing the Character of Proxy Warfare and its Consequences for Geopolitical Relationships", *Security and Defence Quarterly*, 31 (4): 37–51. https://doi.org/10.35467/sdq/130902.

Karlsen, G. H. (2019), "Divide and Rule: Ten Lessons About Russian Political Influence Activities in Europe", *Palgrave Communications*, 5 (1): 1–14. https://doi.org/10.1057/s41599-019-0227-8.

Kleemans, E. R. (2014), "Theoretical Perspectives on Organized Crime", in L. Paoli (ed.), *The Oxford Handbook of Organized Crime*, 32–52. https://doi.org/10.1093/oxfordhb/9780199730445.013.005.

Kukhianidze, A. (2004), "Organized Crime and Smuggling Through Abkhazia and South Ossetia", *Publication Series: European Institute for Crime Prevention and Control*, 87–101.

Leuprecht, C., O. Walther, D. B. Skillicorn and H. Ryde-Collins (2015), "Terrorism and Political Violence Hezbollah's Global Tentacles: A Relational Approach to Convergence With Transnational Organized Crime", *Political Violence*, 29 (5): 902–21. https://doi.org/10.1080/09546553.2015.1089863.

Lutsevych, O. (2016), "Agents of the Russian World: Proxy Groups in the Contested Neighbourhood", Policy Commons, 14 April. Available online: https://policycommons.net/artifacts/613721/agents-of-the-russian-world/1593810/ (accessed 25 November 2022).

Mani, K. S. (2018), "Organised Crime—A Growing Threat to National and International Security", *International Journal of Legal Developments and Allied Issues*, 4 (6): 134–91. Available online: https://thelawbrigade.com/wp-content/uploads/2019/05/Dr.-S.-Krishnan-Mani.pdf (accessed 25 November 2022).

McCoy, A. W. (1972), *The Politics of Heroin in Southeast Asia*, New York: Harper Colophon Books.

Mullins, S. and J. K. Wither (2016), "Terrorism and Organized Crime", *Connections: The Quarterly Journal*, 15 (3): 65–82. https://doi.org/10.11610/connections.15.3.06.

Mumford, A. (2013), *Proxy Warfare*, Cambridge: Polity.

National Security Strategy of the US (2022), *The White House*. Available online: https://www.whitehouse.gov/wp-content/uploads/2022/10/Biden-Harris-Administrations-National-Security-Strategy-10.2022.pdf (accessed 23 December 2022).

OCCRP (2011), "The Proxy Platform", *Organized Crime and Corruption Reporting Project*. Available online: https://www.reportingproject.net/proxy/en/the-proxy-platform (accessed 30 December 2022).

Official Internet Resources of the President of Russia (2022), "Joint Statement of Russian Federation and the PRC on the International Relations Entering a New Era and the Global Sustainable Development", *President of Russia*, 4 February. Available online: http://en.kremlin.ru/supplement/5770 (accessed 20 February 2022).

Popovic, M. (2017), "Fragile Proxies: Explaining Rebel Defection Against Their State Sponsors", *Terrorism and Political Violence*, 29 (5): 922–42. https://doi.org/10.1080/09546553.2015.1092437.

Risse, T., T. A. Borzel and A. Draude, eds (2018), *The Oxford Handbook of Governance and Limited Statehood*, Oxford: Oxford University Press. https://doi.org/10.1093/oxfordhb/9780198797203.001.0001.

Roth, M. P. (2014), *Handbook of Transnational Crime and Justice*, 2nd edn, Thousand Oaks, CA: Sage Publications.

Sari, I. (2015), "The Nexus Between Terrorism and Organized Crime: Growing Threat?", *Journal of Judgements by the Court of Jurisdiction Disputes*, 1 (6): 463–503. Available online: https://dergipark.org.tr/tr/download/article-file/155620 (accessed 31 December 2022).

Shelley, L. (1995), "Transnational Organized Crime: An Imminent Threat to the Nation-State?", *Journal of International Affairs*, 48: 463–89.

Shelley, L. I. and J. T. Picarelli (2002), "Methods Not Motives: Implications of the Convergence of International Organized Crime and Terrorism", *Police Practice and Research*, 3 (4): 305–18. https://doi.org/10.1080/1561426022000032079.

Skaperdas, S. (2001), "The Political Economy of Organized Crime: Providing Protection When the State Does not", *Economics of Governance*, 2 (3): 173–202.

Stanislawski, B. H. (2005), "Transnational Organized Crime, Terrorism, and WMD", *International Studies Review*, 7 (1): 158–160. https://doi.org/10.1111/j.1521-9488.2005.479_10.x.

Sung, H.-E. (2004), "Democracy and Organized Crime Activities: Evidence from 59 Countries", *Security Journal*, 17 (4): 21–34. https://doi.org/10.1057/palgrave.sj.8340181.

Terziev, V. and M. Petkov (2018), "Corruption and National Security", *Evrazijskij Sojuz Uchenyh*, 33 (1): 90–6.

Ullman, R. H. (1983), "Redefining Security", *International Security*, 8 (1): 129–53.

Vorrath, J. (2015), *Organized Crime and Development: Challenges and Policy Options in West Africa's Fragile States* (No. RP 9/2015), SWP Research Paper. Available online: https://www.swp-berlin.org/publications/products/research_papers/2015RP09_vrr.pdf (accessed 31 December 2022).

Warren, M. E. (2004), "What Does Corruption Mean in a Democracy?", *American Journal of Political Science*, 48 (2): 328–43. https://doi.org/10.1111/j.0092-5853.2004.00073.x.

Wei, L. (2022), "China Declared Its Russia Friendship Had 'No Limits.' It's Having Second Thoughts", *The Wall Street Journal*, 3 March. Available online: https://www.wsj.com/articles/china-russia-xi-putin-ukraine-war-11646279098?st=2cdpf21bx0vubyd&reflink=desktopwebshare_twitter (accessed 31 December 2022).

Wither, J. K. (2020), "Outsourcing Warfare: Proxy Forces in Contemporary Armed Conflicts", *Security and Defence Quarterly*, 31 (4): 17–34. https://doi.org/10.35467/sdq/127928.

Zoutendijk, A. J. (2010), "Organised Crime Threat Assessments: A critical Review", *Crime, Law and Social Change*, 54 (1): 63–86. https://doi.org/10.1007/s10611-010-9244-7.

15

The Salience of the New Proxy War Paradigm

Graeme P. Herd

Introduction

After the Second World War, the former dominant way of direct inter-state war came to an end, to be replaced by indirect, irregular or war by proxy. The Cold War paradigm was defined by political-ideological competition, military confrontation, and economic opposition between the first and second Worlds (the US and its allies versus the USSR and its allies) and as a struggle for influence in the non-aligned "Third World," now understood as the "Global South". The major proxy war flashpoints in the Cold War were located outside the European theater and included the Korean War, the Vietnamese War, the Cuban Missile Crisis, and the Afghan-Soviet War. China was also an actor in this respect: "From the late 1950s through the 1970s, China pursued a militant anti-imperialist (and anti-Soviet) foreign policy and sponsored a variety of rebel factions engaged in "wars of national liberation." Beijing sent tens of thousands of troops to North Vietnam; backed leftist political groups in Laos, South Korea, Thailand, and Oman; and armed rebels in approximately twenty African countries, including Algeria, Zimbabwe, Guinea-Bissau, Congo, Angola, and South Africa" (Tierney 2021). Superpowers avoided direct interventions leading to inter-state conventional clashes which risked "nuclear Armageddon" by recruiting, training, arming and leading third party military surrogates or proxy forces to further their influence and reduce that of the adversary. Ideologically-driven insurgencies were the proxy wars of choice. As President Dwight D. Eisenhower noted in 1955, proxy wars represent "the cheapest insurance in the world" (Winter-Levy 2022).

The following assumptions, conditions and characteristics appear common features of "proxy war" in the modern era. Two or more parties should have conflicting political-ideological, military or economic interests, for proxy of third-party forces to be employed. In addition to indigenous irregular armed forces that use violence (separatists, insurgents, paramilitaries, vigilantes, and militias), proxies could include Private Military Corporations (PMCs), transnational terrorist groups, transnational organized crime gangs and cartels and, very latterly, "cyber warriors" or hackers for hire. The relationship between external actor and proxy would be sustained through the provision of direct assistance, including lethal material aid, by the external actor to its proxy. The assistance from external sponsor to proxy would be conditional and represent some sort of alignment between the aims of both parties against a common target. (Rauta 2021) Proxy relationships are inherently hierarchical. Two assumptions: "the *coherence* of interests and policy objectives between principal and proxy/agent, as well as on the principal's ability to *control* and/or *manage* the agent" (Kaura and Norlen 2022). That the sponsor chooses undeclared indirect proxy rather than declared direct military attack suggests that the sponsor seeks a number of possible benefits, including reducing costs and limiting the risk of escalation to inter-state conflict, obscuring casualties and avoiding domestic and international legal challenges and political exposure, and, if the external proxy sponsor remains unrecognized as a party to the conflict, it reserves the option to act as mediator in the conflict itself (combining fireman and arsonist roles). State-sponsors of proxies could use their own territory as a safe-haven, a base of operations and a training and recruitment facility. Proxy force conflicts were more manageable than inter-state war. Many proxies offered additional benefits, with the sponsor able to make use both of their greater knowledge of local physical and human terrain, as well as their specific tactical and operational capabilities which the external sponsor otherwise lacks.

The End of the Cold War—In Search of a Paradigm?

After the collapse of the bipolar world order, proxy wars (and so proxies) continued to operate, with new ones emerging but within a different international order paradigm. In this new order the ideological constraints of the Cold War became much less relevant. The stable balance of power system gave way to uncertainty, ambiguity and unpredictability. Old alliances withered and a seemingly enduring set of patron-client relations were weakened. Resource wars and illicit political economies run by non-state and state sponsored actors increased. The assumptions of Keohane and Nye (2012) was that multilateral interstate negotiations between multiple actors would lead to complex interdependence—that is, reciprocal mutual cooperative gains, entanglements, and the emergence of decentralized networks that generate new opportunities for cooperative diplomacy. Power would become "power with," rather than "power over" (Slaughter 2017). This understanding translated into the notion of market-democratic universalism in the 1990s, with Fukuyama's "End of History" thesis. Within this paradigm of ever-expanding peace, proxy wars would be redundant. However, as economic interdependence increased and nuclear weapons proliferated, not least to South Asia (India and Pakistan), major inter-state war became less likely. Global order became more uncertain, unpredictable and ambiguous.

By the early 2000s, in an increasingly multipolar and polycentric world, we could envisage a Global Concert of Great Powers. This would be the equivalent of the nineteenth century European Concert of Nations. In this world order paradigm, a "Yalta-2" or "Helsinki III" conference of the UN Security Council permanent members (P-5) and India and Japan, who collectively represent 70 percent of global GDP, would exercise an influential leadership role on the world stage (Haass and Kupchan 2021). Through transactional strategic dialogue and informal negotiation, this Global Concert would direct and manage the global strategic agenda (for example, over WMD proliferation, climate change, terrorism, regional crises, and terrorism), while still able to take unilateral action in its sphere of privileged interest. In this context, proxies would not have a global role—mitigation and management of such conflict would be the prerogative of resourced UN mandated multilateral peace operations. Proxies would operate regionally, within the geographically defined sphere of influence, on behalf of the center. Their role would be to police elites, enforce the doctrine of limited sovereignty and discipline societies states within the sphere. Clearly this is not the case, as our case studies demonstrate.

Rather than a Global Concert, are we reaching a "Cold War 2.0" inflection point, as relations between the United States, its friends and allies on the one hand, and Russia and China on the other, rapidly deteriorate? If this is the case, we can expect that "proxy war" will also take on a "2.0" hue. However, national interest likely places limits on the inevitability of a slide into "Cold War 2.0." First, unlike the late 1940s, the world is globalized and increasingly multi-polar. In this context, Cold War style "containment" is not possible. Second, in the current strategic context of great power competition "short of war," the US prioritizes countering China over Russia. From a US perspective, countering China is enabled by the support of coalition partners, not least Japan, South Korea and Germany. Thus, transatlantic unity is at a premium. This suggests targeted

"Containment 2.0," in that the political West seeks to contain (or constrain) Russian aggressive and malign strategic behavior within "stable and predictable" lines. Moreover, a Russian alliance with China would expose Moscow's asymmetric dependencies on Beijing and render Russia a junior partner within a Sino-centric technology-trade bloc (*Pax Sinica*), with little or no strategic autonomy.

By the twenty first century, key global economic networks have converged toward "hub and spoke" systems, with important consequences for power relations. Adversaries, understanding the structure of the internet, food or energy supply network, can directly or using proxies exploit network chokepoints to weaponize interdependence (Farrell and Newman 2019). Analysts point to fifty "black spots" globally (Brown and Hermann 2020), where we witness the entangled threat of crime, corruption, and terrorism. At a national level transnational organized crime groups try and infiltrate state structures to protect themselves from and so avoid state law enforcement intervention (Gürer 2021) but internationally and in the context of strategic competition, states utilize TOC proxies to further their respective interests—power and profit. (Gürer and Lauer 2022; Namli and Gürer 2023) Civil wars evolve into multiple proxy wars waged by regional and global actors. Regional crises and fragile states are driven by economic and demographic inequalities, the rise of ethnic and sectarian violence, climate change, the growth of technology, and the failure of current institutions to respond (Shelley 2014). Given the proliferation of nuclear weapons and rise of global economic interdependence, as in the Cold War, states avoid direct inter-state war and advance strategic competition through various proxies, including military capable ones. In this digital age of space-enabled warfare, for example Elon Musk, the owner of Space-X, shapes Ukraine's ability to wage war as Ukraine is dependent on Musk's satellite Starlink for military communications and command and control. Market principles apply: demand signals (sponsors in need of proxies) generate supply (proxies). Increased financing, expanded recruitment opportunities based on a glut of foreign fighters and more advanced communication technologies enabled the emergence of more lethally capable (e.g., drones, cyber weapons, and anti-ship missiles) PMCs, such as Blackwater (US), Wagner (Russia) and SADAT (Turkey), and other proxies.

These trends, drivers and dynamics highlight the difficulties of a group of states exerting leadership and management of the global strategic agenda. The UN Security Council is increasingly paralyzed using Permanent Five veto power. This world order can be termed G-Zero i.e., a Group with no members leads or to put it another way, leadership of the global strategic agenda is absent (Bremmer 2016). A G-Zero world order favors states that thrive in ambiguity, unpredictability, contestation, where transactionalism is the order of the day. States with well-developed alliance systems are disadvantaged, while states without (not least, Russia, China, and DPRK) are freer to maneuver. Russia in decline can participate in great-power asymmetric competition by embracing asymmetric strategies and the use of proxies, irregular warfare and hybrid tools to close the gap. States that have a spoiler role ability and a higher tolerance for risk-taking thrive and flourish. A G-Zero world order best secures and protects a Russia in power decline relative to China. Russia cannot achieve G3 status, and can hardly accept unipolarity or even bipolarity if it cannot be one of the poles. Russia's order-producing and managerial role in its shared neighborhood is increasingly compromised by third parties, not least the EU, Turkey and China. This G-Zero world order is the default and most likely outcome of current confrontation, systemic rivalry and strategic competition.

The New Proxy Paradigm in a G-Zero World Order

Given this G-Zero paradigm constitutes the operating environment within the current international order, how does it impact on the salience of proxy warfare, in particular: "who fights, for whom and at whose request, against whom, why, how, where, and for how long"? (Rauta 2021). Building on the work of Heinkelmann-Wild and Mehrl (2021), Farasoo (2021), and Newton (2022), we can highlight four distinct defining features of the structure of proxy use in the contemporary era: first, the multiplicity of sponsors; second, the fluidity and complexity of proxy sponsor motivations; third, sponsor delegation or orchestration relations with proxies are governed by increasingly complex costs/benefits trade-offs; and, fourth, proxy-sponsor relations trend towards convergence. Let us examine each in turn, highlighting the features empirically evidenced by the case study chapters in this book, and referencing other examples not included in this book but which appear to validate the new paradigm.

- First, the types of Principal or Beneficiary external sponsors of proxies have widened to include the full range of states and non-state actors. As well as China, Russia and the US as external sponsors, new regional players, as well as smaller and weaker nations, are now exploiting the role of proxies in conflicts to advance their own strategic agendas. Small states not just the battlegrounds for proxy wars, but can be sponsors of proxies themselves. In the Syrian or Libyan theaters of proxy operations (relatively) small states like Qatar, United Arab Emirates or Israel evidently support opposing parties to these conflicts. Rwanda in the DRC would be another example or Lithuania in Ukraine. (Isoda 2022) In the case of Ukraine, the target state of Russian direct full-scale warfare, itself employs proxies in its own defense. Actors the sponsor proxies are not simply state actors, but can consist of non-state illicit power structures, such as transnational terrorist or criminal groups and private military companies (PMC's).

- Coalitions of major, regional and local states as well as non-state proxy actors can form dynamic alliances of surrogates, proxies, states and state-like non-state partners. The case of Yemen demonstrates that coalitions of major, regional and local states as well as non-state proxy actors can create dynamic alliances of surrogates, proxies, states and state-like non-state partners (Wither 2023). Libya is another case in point. Qatar supports pro-Muslim Brotherhood internal actors and is aligned with Turkey and Sudan and is more dominant by land. The UAE supports anti-Islamisist actors, alongside France, Saudi Arabia, Russia and Egypt and is stronger in the air war (Sozer and Darcan 2023). Iran's approach to proxy war in Syria is regional, locating the Syrian conflict in an "Axis of Resistance" to Israel and the West which stretches from Tehran to Beirut, with Shia militias in Syria linked to Hamas and Palestinian Islamic Jihad (PIJ), Houthi forces in Lebanon and its Fatemiyoun Brigade in Afghanistan (Wertman and Kaunert 2023).

- Second, the strategic and policy motivations that shape the support relationship between principal/sponsor and third-party proxy surrogate have become more complex and fluid. External actor motivation is especially hard to classify (Farasoo 2021). Sponsors can enter a conflict with different aims—to win, as a holding or freezing effort, to meddle or to feed the conflict. (Groh 2019) Each require or necessitate different levels of support and types of relations between external sponsor and proxy. External sponsor aims can change over time, just as the loyalties of proxies can be very fluid. We witness a blurring of internal and external actors and activities and such complex interconnectedness poses challenges to identify causes, explain the cause and assess the consequences of such conflicts. This ever-widening range of potential proxy groups and types were, and continue to be, motivated by creed/belief, need and greed. Ideological belief is a critical component of any network in that it sustains motivation, mindset, decision-making processes and command-and-control relationships,

The Salience of the New Proxy War Paradigm

supports organizational dynamics, recruitment and appeal. Ideologies are patterned thinking, clusters of ideas, beliefs, opinions, values and attitudes. Ideologies are structured as follows 1) What is the problem? *Problem diagnosis* provides explanation for cause of problems, issues, and grievances. 2) Who is to blame? *Responsibility attribution* points to scapegoats or actual causes of problems (individuals, groups, state policies). 3) What is the solution? *Prognostic framing* suggests viable solutions to the problems and calls individuals and groups to action to offer a future alternative governance paradigm although any professed vision of society may cloak a desire for profit, that is, to control of rent distribution and the illicit economy. Proxies communicate a narrative to sponsors, supporters and adversaries that highlight problems, apportion blame to their adversaries and identify themselves as the only necessary solution. In this sense the proxy is a needed service provider able to meet public demand. Proxy groups can fight each other for power, authority and supremacy, to establish their prestige, status, and honor.

- Mali and France both utilize local tribal militias and other armed groups in northern Mali to secure their interests but adopt different approaches as their motivations are not aligned: "Whilst the central government in Bamako was interested in retaining status quo and the precarious (dis)order in the conflict-ridden north of the country (and later the center), frequently resorting to the *divide et impera* strategy, the French intervening forces were focused on careful cooperation with "vetted" local actors. For Bamako, it allowed to supplement their lack of resources and will to resolve local animosities, while for Paris it limited their operational cost, risk of loss of life and allowed to gain access to intimate human and physical terrain knowledge" (Kozera 2023). In the case of Ukraine, for example, proxy war is understood and fought very differently by Russia and the West. In 2014, Russia sought to use hybrid and proxy warfare to exploit the "fog of war" and thereby create uncertainty and dampen western response (Bernat et al. 2023). In 2022 Russia understands Ukraine to be a proxy of the West and that it fights in Ukraine an existential war against the West. The West understands Russia to fight Ukraine using proxies and Western military and other support to Ukraine upholds Ukraine's right to self-defense against a nuclear armed aggressor. Yemen can be understood in geo-political rivalry terms as Iranian/Saudi Arabia proxy war. Saudi Arabia supports President Haddi's predominantly Sunni government forces with the help of the UAE, US, Jordan, Sudan, Egypt and Morocco while Iran supports predominantly

Zavdi Shia Houthis in a low-cost effort to undercut Saudi Arabian power, influence and reputation (Wither, 2023). Iran adopts a national security strategy based on a "resistance axis" (characterized by the US as "Iran's Threat Network"), a network of anti-status quo regional non-state partnerships as a means of power projection. In the Central African Republic (CAR), a post-colonial majority Christian farming-based political elite fights a minority Muslim pastoralist periphery, with the corrupt center using militias and PMCs to uphold their power. Opposing proxies are supported by France, Libya, Russia, DRC, Chad, and Sudan, but for different reasons—Chad and Sudan, for example, seek to secure their borders and influence border oil field exploitation (Popławski 2023). In Syria, Turkey, Iran and the US have all designed distinctive proxy war strategies to obtain their differing political objectives. "Turkey and Iran, have capitalized on the existing (shared) identity networks in building proxy relationships, whereas the USA has pragmatically established linkages to promote democracy and eliminate extremism threat against international security" (Yüksel 2023).

- Third, sponsor-proxy relations are governed by increasingly complex costs/benefits trade-offs which are embedded in the mode of control itself. First, delegation, where a sponsor can exert "hands-on" hierarchical control over a rebel group and effectively monitor agent compliance activities and sanction bad behavior and so avoid escalation, but may undercut proxy's local legitimacy and the ability of the sponsor to claim plausible deniability. Second, orchestration occurs when a sponsor takes a "hands-off" approach, steering rebels by inducements (material, financial, or informational support) rather than enforcing compliance. This boosts the proxy's local legitimacy and the sponsors' plausible deniability but the loss of control relative to delegation generates strategic risks. Orchestration represents a sponsor preference when inducements in-built—through aligned goals based on shared interest and identity and/or market principles (supply dependency of proxy on sponsor) and/ or the sponsor is a great power better able "to afford efficiency losses due to rebels' partially non-compliant behavior." (Heinkelmann-Wild and Mehrl 2021). Our Ukraine case study demonstrates that Russia adopted a versatile, flexible and differentiated approach to Crimea and Donbas in 2014, using regular Russian-supported militias as proxies, alongside Russian special forces. (Bernat et al. 2023) Ukraine itself creates a Foreign Legion in part to highlight international support for its struggle and so the saliency of the struggle itself in the international arena. Plausible deniability is not an objective (Sinai 2023).

The Salience of the New Proxy War Paradigm

251

- Fourth, the nature of the relationship between sponsors and proxies has been addressed, but what of the relationship between proxies and sponsors? Rondeaux and Sterman (2019: 18) argue proxy warfare is "sponsorship of conventional or irregular forces that lie outside the constitutional order of states." However, a convergence between proxy and sponsor is notable current dynamic. Convergence includes increased collusion, communication, cooperation, collaboration, connections, coordination, linkages, interactions and nexus—all appear as descriptors in the literature—for mutual gain. This can translate into activity convergence, when militaries under the direct control of a state sponsor and non-state proxies under indirect control adopt the practices, procedures, and tactics of each other. This goes beyond goal alignment based on shared identity, shared or compatible interests/goals and/or ideology and beliefs.

- Proxies can also be directly integrated into the state apparatus law enforcement and conventional military forces, as is the case in Russia where the LNR and DNR 1st and 2nd Corps, are integrated into the regular military (Galeotti et al. 2022). In Ukraine the Foreign Legion consists of noncitizens who become uniformed members of Ukraine's military, integrated into its chain of command. Such close relationships can then result in organizational convergence between different proxies and the proxies themselves and sponsors official structures. Libya represents these tendencies. A fragmented order is enabled by a non-institutionalized state. Several competing autonomous internal clan or tribal-based actors that fight and ally with each other and each group actively solicit external sponsorship and assistance. Libya is as much a civil war as proxy war. In Libya non-state transnational terrorist groups such as ISIS create its own proxy affiliates, recruiting amongst Arabs, Berbers and Tuaregs and the Tabu tribe has close ties with Chad, Niger and Mali. (Kozera 2023) In a case study not addressed in the book, a little-known militant group, the Kashmiri Freedom Fighters (KFF) operating in Jammu and Kashmir is believed to be a proxy of the Lashlar-e Taiba (LeT) which was responsible for the Mumbai terrorist attacks in November 2008 and is itself a proxy of Pakistan (Macander 2021). In addition, the Pakistan (sponsor)-Taliban (proxy) relationship provides an example of *coherence* and *control* shifting, after the proxy was elevated to state actor in August 2021, and the interests and policy goals of the two diverged. This resulted in an "inverted proxy-patron relationship, in which the proxy partially dictates its patron's policies." Convergence—proxy become state, state becomes proxy (Kaura and Norlen 2022).

- When it comes to states as external sponsors, regime type of the sponsor provides direction that shapes the behavior of the proxy—Wagner PMC atrocities in CAR, Libya, Syria, and Mali being a case in point. (Kozera 2023) The state sponsor can adopt the threat perception, assessment, agenda and motivation of the proxy itself. We can call this "threat convergence". CAR provides evidence of this monetization of Russian foreign policy. Russia through Wagner PMC pursues profit derived from access to natural resources, not least oil, diamonds, gold, iron, uranium, timber, cotton and coffee (Popławski, 2023). The mineral-rich Great Lakes conflict, a case study not addressed in this book, has been described as "La guerre sans fin" and "Africa's World War", with the DRC (the Democratic Forces for the Liberation of Rwanda, or FDLR, is a DRC proxy), Rwanda (M23 is a proxy group supported by the Rwandan Defense Force), and Uganda fighting proxy wars over the production and export of precious natural resources. In this sense the market place for proxy activity—unresolved conflicts in resource rich regional crisis contexts—may become a priority for the erstwhile sponsoring state. Market convergence between sponsor and proxy is a logical outcome.

Conclusions

On the diverse empirical studies offered in this book the four distinct defining features of the structure of proxy use in the contemporary era are validated. The chapters collectively highlight a multiplicity of external sponsors; the fluidity and complexity of proxy and sponsor motivations; an increasing range of complex costs/benefits trade-offs that govern relations between both parties and a trend towards convergence. Given the diversity of examples offered by this book, we can further conclude that case studies and actors not addressed here will likely still validate this paradigm. China as a core contemporary external sponsor of proxy groups, for example, builds on a rich Cold War history of proxy use: the "United Wa State Army in neighboring Myanmar is an effective Chinese proxy. The Wa rebels speak Chinese and use Chinese currency, and Beijing reportedly supplies the group with financial support and heavy weaponry, including missiles and armored vehicles" (Tierney, 2021). But today China's use of proxies has broadened to include PMCs guarding the Belt and Road Initiative, shadow "police stations" abroad to monitor its own diaspora and embraces cyber actors and algorithmic authoritarian surveillance.

The Salience of the New Proxy War Paradigm   253

Given a G-Zero world order will be heavily shaped by the nature of Sino-Russian strategic alignment—what are the trends and significance for proxy war? We see multifaceted, broad security and other policy coordination between China and Russia, facilitated by respective State Council-Security Council and Xi-Putin dialogue. China and Russia have not formed a treaty-based alliance with mutual defense commitments for defensive or offensive military collaboration against shared threat, but retain their strategic autonomy, flexibility, and policy independence. They do though share great power pragmatic alignment based on common interest of strategic counterweight vs. US hegemony/liberal international order. However, both states have different development trajectories and so there is no "deep-rooted and long-lasting convergence" between the two. Rather, China determines the level/tempo of bilateral engagement and as Russia becomes less integrated in the global economy, PRC cooperation becomes more challenging for China—there is no replacement for the Western market. Russia aligns its positions with India, Japan, and SE Asia to counterbalance China's geopolitical influence and become "third pole" and leader of a new Non-Aligned Movement.

Both seek different global orders—Beijing wants a revisionist, stable sphere of influence system in which China exercises global leadership via control of Asia, but Moscow wants revolutionary G-Zero world order of uncertainty and crisis, where no global leadership exists. As a result, proxy wars fought to prevent escalation are also "one of the most likely ways whereby the United States will come to blows with its great-power adversaries" (Hoffmann and Orner 2021).

Bibliography

Bernat, P., V. Semenenko, P. Openko and D. Michalski (2023), "Russian Proxy Use in the Hybrid War against Ukraine before the 2022 Invasion", in P. Bernat, C. Gürer and C. A. Kozera (eds), *Proxy Wars From a Global Perspective: Non-State Actors and Armed Conflicts*, 61–76, London: Bloomsbury.

Bremmer, I. (2016), "After the G-Zero: Overcoming Fragmentation", Eurasia Group. Available online: https://www.eurasiagroup.net/siteFiles/Issues/After_The_G_Zero_.pdf (accessed 30 December 2022).

Brown S. S. and M. G. Hermann (2020), *Transnational Crime and Black Spots: Rethinking Sovereignty and the Global Economy*, London: Palgrave.

Farasoo, A. (2021), "Rethinking Proxy War Theory in IR: A Critical Analysis of Principal-Agent Theory", *International Studies Review*, 23 (4): 1835–58. https://doi.org/10.1093/isr/viab050.

Farrell, H. and A. L. Newman (2019), "Weaponized Interdependence: How Global Economic Networks Shape State Coercion", *International Security*, 44 (1): 42–79. https://doi.org/10.1162/isec_a_00351.

Galeotti, M., P. Baev and G. P. Herd (2022), "Militaries, Mercenaries, Militias, Morale, and the Ukraine War", *In Moscow's Shadow*, 16 November. Available online: https://inmoscowsshadows.wordpress.com/author/markgaleotti/ (accessed 30 December 2022).

Groh, T. L. (2019), *Proxy War: The Least Bad Option*, Stanford: Stanford University Press.

Gürer, C. (2021), "Strategic Competition: International Order and Transnational Organized Crime", *George C Marshall European Center for Security Studies*, Security Insights, No. 69. Available online: https://www.marshallcenter.org/en/publications/security-insights/strategic-competition-international-order-and-transnational-organized-crime-0 (accessed 30 December 2022).

Gürer, C. and L. Lauer (2022), "Political Regime Changes and Transnational Organized Crime", *Clock Tower Security Series*. Available online: https://www.marshallcenter.org/en/publications/clock-tower-security-series/political-regime-changes-and-transnational-organized-crime (accessed 30 December 2022).

Haass, R. N. and C. A. Kupchan (2021), "A Concert of Powers for a Global Era", *Project Syndicate*, 25 March. Available online: https://www.project-syndicate.org/commentary/concert-of-powers-for-global-era-by-richard-haass-and-charles-a-kupchan-2021-03 (accessed 30 December 2022).

Heinkelmann-Wild, T. and M. Mehrl (2021), "Indirect Governance at War: Delegation and Orchestration in Rebel Support", *Journal of Conflict Resolution*, 66 (1): 1–29. https://doi.org/10.1177/00220027211027311.

Hoffmann, F. and A. Orner (2021), "The Return of Great-Power Proxy Wars", War on the Rocks 2 September. Available online: https://warontherocks.com/2021/09/the-return-of-great-power-proxy-wars/ (accessed 30 December 2022).

Isoda, V. (2022), "Can Small States Wage Proxy Wars? A Closer Look at Lithuania's Military Aid to Ukraine", *Cooperation and Conflict*, 9 (2). https://doi.org/10.1177/00108367221116532.

Keohane, R. O. and J. S. Nye Jr. (2012), *Power and Interdependence*, 4th edn, New York: Longman.

Kozera, C. A. (2023), "Auxiliary and Proxy Forces in Mali (2012–2022): New Rendition of *Divide et Impera* and Cautious French Saviourism", in P. Bernat, C. Gürer and C. A. Kozera (eds), *Proxy Wars From a Global Perspective: Non-State Actors and Armed Conflicts*, 107–22, London: Bloomsbury.

Macander, M. (2021), "Examining Extremism: Lashkar-e-Taiba", *Center for Strategic and International Studies*, 28 October. Available online: https://www.csis.org/blogs/examining-extremism/examining-extremism-lashkar-e-taiba (accessed 30 December 2022).

Namli, Ü. and C. Gürer (2023), "Transnational Organized Crime Groups as State Proxies", in P. Bernat, C. Gürer and C. A. Kozera (eds), *Proxy Wars From a Global Perspective: Non-State Actors and Armed Conflicts*, 225–42, London: Bloomsbury.

Newton, R. D. (2023), "Proxy Warfare's New and complex Paradigm?", in P. Bernat, C. Gürer and C. A. Kozera (eds), *Proxy Wars From a Global Perspective: Non-State Actors and Armed Conflicts*, 23–39, London: Bloomsbury.

Norlen T. and V. Kaura (2023), "When Proxies Win: The Impact of the Taliban's Changing Fortune on Pakistan's Leverage", in P. Bernat, C. Gürer and C. A. Kozera (eds), *Proxy Wars From a Global Perspective: Non-State Actors and Armed Conflicts*, 201–21, London: Bloomsbury.

Popławski, B. (2023), "The Bifurcation of Violence. The Proxy Forces in the Central African Republic", in P. Bernat, C. Gürer and C. A. Kozera (eds), *Proxy Wars From a Global Perspective: Non-State Actors and Armed Conflicts*, 123–37, London: Bloomsbury.

Rauta, V. (2021), "Proxy War"—A Reconceptualisation', *Civil Wars*, 23 (1): 1–24. https://doi.org/10.1080/13698249.2021.1860578.

Rondeaux, C. and D. Sterman (2019), "Twenty-First Century Proxy Warfare: Confronting Strategic Innovation in a Multipolar World Since the 2011 NATO Intervention", *New America*. Available online: https://d1y8sb8igg2f8e.cloudfront.net/documents/Twenty-First_Century_Proxy_Warfare_Final.pdf (accessed 10 November 2022).

Sinai, T. (2023), "Ukraine's Use of Proxies in Conventional and Unconventional Warfare Against Russia", in P. Bernat, C. Gürer and C. A. Kozera (eds), *Proxy Wars From a Global Perspective: Non-State Actors and Armed Conflicts*, 77–93, London: Bloomsbury.

Shelley, L. I. (2014), *Dirty Entanglements: Corruption, Crime, and Terrorism*, New York, NY: Cambridge University Press.

Slaughter, A. (2017), *The Chessboard and the Web: Strategies of Connection in a Networked World,* New Haven, Conn.: Yale University Press.

Sozer, M. A. and E. Darcan (2023), "Libya: Fragmentation of the Country amid a Proxy War", in P. Bernat, C. Gürer and C. A. Kozera (eds), *Proxy Wars From a Global Perspective: Non-State Actors and Armed Conflicts*, 139–51, London: Bloomsbury.

Tierney, D. (2021), "The Future of Sino-US Proxy War", *Texas National Security Review*, 4 (2). http://dx.doi.org/10.26153/tsw/13198.

Wertman, O. and C. Kaunert (2023), "Iran's Hybrid Proxy Warfare through Palestinian Terrorism against Israel", in P. Bernat, C. Gürer and C. A. Kozera (eds), *Proxy Wars From a Global Perspective: Non-State Actors and Armed Conflicts*, 167–82, London: Bloomsbury.

Winter-Levy, S. (2022), "A Proxy War in Ukraine Is the Worst Possible Outcome—Except For All the Others", *War on the Rocks*, 28 March. Available online: https://warontherocks.com/2022/03/a-proxy-war-in-ukraine-is-the-worst-possible-outcome-except-for-all-the-others/ (accessed 30 December 2022).

Wither, J. (2023), "The Conflict in Yemen through the Prism of Proxy War", in P. Bernat, C. Gürer and C. A. Kozera (eds), *Proxy Wars From a Global Perspective: Non-State Actors and Armed Conflicts*, 183–200, London: Bloomsbury.

Yüksel, E. (2023), "The Spheres of Influence: Multiple Proxy Wars in Syria", in P. Bernat, C. Gürer and C. A. Kozera (eds), *Proxy Wars From a Global Perspective: Non-State Actors and Armed Conflicts*, 153–66, London: Bloomsbury.

Afterword

Writing in 2020 the article 'Game of Proxies—Towards a new model of warfare: Experiences from the CAR, Libya, Mali, Syria, and Ukraine' for the *Security and Defence Quarterly* journal, we argued that states would not seek to confront their counterparts on the conventional battlefield yet rather resort to subversive methods, hybrid tools, and outsourcing of warfare to various kinds of proxies. We might have been mistaken in this prediction regarding Russia and its post-Soviet inclination towards the "solve it with pure force and hardware" approach. On the other hand, the Russian conventional conflict of 2022 against Ukraine, arguably, falls into an exception and one which stems from miss-assessments and leads to failures. An exception that only confirms the assumption that proxy warfare will be yet more popular in the future battlespace.

As of the time of writing this text, the global response to this conflict remains firm, resolved, and united while Putin's Russia is isolated, deprived, and—all points to that direction—declining. This ex-KGB-agent-turned-dictator's last attempt at restoring the "glory" and power of Soviet Russia seems to fail. The "panzer" power of modern Russian and (increasingly) Soviet tanks and artillery has not crushed Ukrainian resistance supported by the Western allies. It rather forced Moscow to employ yet more mercenaries and affiliated forces as Russia's proxies. The approach that the Kremlin has not refrained from in other parts of the world, notably in the Central African Republic, Mali, Mozambique, Sudan, and Venezuela. Wherever Russia could not project its force otherwise, it tried to undermine the international system "on the budget" by using hybrid and subversive means, including proxies, rather than direct confrontation it could not have won.

The Russian conventional war in Ukraine of 2022 neither did encourage other states to exploit the situation (we can ignore here Azeri's minor border clashes with Armenia). Simultaneously, with the assertive and united response, the West and primarily the US only cemented its reputation as a reliable ally. China has not invaded Taiwan and does not seem to be willing to do so militarily, rather focusing on paying lip service to this cause at big party gatherings. Furthermore, if one pays attention to the Chinese political and cultural analysts, and we do not mean the Sun-Tzu clichés, their conclusions are not pointing towards an imminent China-started Third World War yet rather a continuous, long-term, and economically-oriented takeover of the global system with any military action seen rather as a remote, minor, and crowning endeavor. Any deviation from that path could only be undertaken by a Putin-alike Chinese dictator in a frantic attempt at achieving some earthen glory and reliving some imaginary past—and in Chinese politics, that certainly would be yet a bigger exception than in Russian.

Furthermore, from the realist perspective, the war in Ukraine can be considered a perfect opportunity and a proxy war per se. A war that the US is waging against its second global contender—Russia, and it costs the US pennies to do so. Within this conceptual framework, the US can obtain a strategic gain of defeating a global contender with no direct involvement by just arming an ally, a proxy in this context, that does all the dirty job of fighting, dying, and at the same time, weakening the enemy. After almost a year of successful struggle, it has cost the US defense budget several percent of its total spending planned for 2022 and no US soldier casualties. It is a very low price to pay for totally neutralizing the Russian conventional threat. For the US, it is a strategic bargain.

Putin's dream of re-imperializing Russia has rather pushed her into pariah status. An outcast that can count only on erratic support of—besides Iranian Ayatollahs—coup-makers in Sub-Saharan Africa, South American post-communist relics, or the Kremlin-bred second-league dictators in the post-Soviet pseudo-republics. For others, Russia's struggle in Ukraine rather serves as an example that the conventional war strategically does not pay off anymore. If this trend holds, as all suggest in the Russian-Ukrainian conflict, it will more likely push contenders of the liberal system yet more towards hybrid methods and subversive tools, of which proxy warfare is one of the most efficient.

Even with Russia's demise, the global competition between the two key powers of the US and China will not slow down but, we predict, intensify, specifically in the gray zone. Meanwhile, the Western world has been awoken by the Russia-Ukraine war and arms itself in accordance with the ancient sentence: *si vis pacem—para bellum.* We could only add: and brace for more proxy warfare in the future.

The Authors
Paweł Bernat, Cüneyt Gürer, Cyprian Aleksander Kozera

Index

Abbasid Empire 95
Abéché 126
Abkhazia 235
Abu Ali, *see under* al-Hakim, Abdullah
Abu Dhabi 102
Abu-Marzook, Mousa 170
Addis Ababa 29
Aden 192
Adrar des Ifoghas 115–16
Afaghis 109
Afghan Taliban 7, 201–7, 210–17
Afghanistan (*also* Afghan, Afghans) 4, 7,
    14, 15, 24, 26–8, 31, 33, 36, 53, 95,
    97, 103, 115, 160, 195, 201–17, 243,
    248
Africa (*also* African) 5, 6, 24, 29, 32, 34, 36,
    78, 95–9, 102–3, 108–11, 123–4,
    126–7, 129–34, 141, 144, 148, 192–3,
    243, 250, 252, 257–8
African Union Mission in Somalia
    (AMISOM) 32, 34–5
Afrin 156
ag Gamou, El Hadj 110–12
ag Ghali, Iyad 110–11
ag Najim, Mohamed 111
Air Force (*also* Airborne forces) 25, 29, 35,
    66, 141, 143, 177
Akhund, Obaidullah, Mullah 207, 212
Akhundzada, Haibatullah, Mullah 208
al-Assad, Bashar, President 51, 101–2, 153,
    155–60, 178
al-Assad, Hafez, President 101
al-Ayn, Ras 156
al-Bab 156
al-Din al-Houthi, Hussein Badr 190
al-Gaddafi, Muammar Muhammad Abu
    Minyar, President 6, 97, 111, 139–41
al-Ghaliboun 102
al-Hadi, Abd Rabbu Mansour, President
    183
al-Hakim, Abdullah 103
al-Harith ibn Jabalah 13

al-Houthi, Abdul-Malik 191
al-Islah 184, 192–3
al-Itihaad-al-Islamiya 31
al-Khatim, Mahamat 129
al-Qaeda 31–2, 34–6, 111, 116, 143, 145,
    156, 161, 213, 216–17
al-Qaida, *see under* al-Qaeda
al-Quds, *see under* Jerusalem
al-Razzami, Abdullah Eida 103
al-Sadr 100
al-Salabi 142
al-Sarraj, Fayez 144
al-Shabaab 31, 32, 34–6
al-Zawahiri, Ayman 32, 213
Algeria (*also* Algerian) 111, 115–16, 243
Algiers 110
Alliance for Revival and Rebuilding 126
Amal 100–1
amenokal 109
America, *see under* United States of
    America
AMISOM, *see under* African Union
    Mission in Somalia
Anefis battle 112
Angola (*also* Angolan) 95, 124, 243
Ansar Allah, *see under* Houthi
Anti-Balaka 127–31, 133
anti-Taliban Northern Alliance, *see under*
    Northern Alliance
Anushirvan, *see under* Khosrow I
Anya Naya rebellion 98
Arab-Fulani 108, 113, 125, 128
Arab Movement of Azawad 116
Arabia (*also* Arab) 6, 13, 16, 27, 28, 97–9,
    103, 108, 110–14, 116, 139–42, 153,
    158, 160, 162, 171, 175, 183–4,
    187–9, 190–5, 24–9
Arab Spring 6, 158
Arafat, Yasser 168, 170–2, 175
ARC, *see under* Autonomous Republic
    of Crimea
Arestovych, Oleksiy 86

Arethas. *see under* al-Harith ibn Jabalah
Asa'ib Ahl al-Haq 102
Asia (*also* Asian) 7, 24, 26, 98–9, 102,
  217–18, 245, 253
ATO, *see under* Ukraine, Anti-Terrorist
  Operation
Australia 83
Austria 14
Autonomous Republic of Crimea 66–7
Avakov, Arsen 81
Azov Battalion 82

Bagram Air Base 28
Bahrain 160, 165
Bakhmut 87
Balkan 68
Bamako 108, 110–13, 115, 117–19, 249
Bambara ethnic group 113
Bamingui-Bangoran 125
Banda tribe 125, 128
Bangui 125–9, 132–3
Banu Lakhm 13
Barkhane Operation 117, 119
Barré, Mohammed Siad, General 29–31
Bashagha, Fathi, Prime Minister 147
Bay of Pigs 96, 105
Beijing 214, 243, 246, 237, 252–3
Beirut 99–101, 158, 160, 162, 248
Belarus (*also* Belarussian) 79, 85–6
Belgium 89, 123
Berbera 30
Berbers 145, 251
Berengo, military base 132
Berlin 141, 145, 232
Bezler, Igor 69
Biden, Joe, President 36, 38, 166
bin Laden, Osama 31, 204–5, 212
Birao 129
Black Sea 66–7
Blackwater, private military contractor 95,
  145, 246
Boko Haram 52–3
Borno, Nigeria 52
Bozizé, François, President 125, 127–9, 134
British 14, 24, 27, 95, 216
  see also United Kingdom
Buckley, William Francis 101
Budapest Memorandum 61, 80
Burundi 34

Bush, George W., President 32, 205, 210
Byzantine Empire 13–14

Cairo 169
Camp David 172, 210
CAR, *see under* Central African Republic
Caribbean 96
Carter, Jimmy, President 27–8
Carthage 13
Castro, Fidel 96
Caucasus 68, 82, 235
Central African Patriotic Movement
  129–30
Central African Republic 124–34, 144, 250,
  252, 257
Central Intelligence Agency 24, 31, 34, 101,
  160, 205
Chad (*also* Chadian) 115, 124–7, 129,
  133–4, 147, 250–1
Chaly, Oleksiy 67
Che Guevera 96
Chechen 79, 82, 84
Cheney, Dick, Vice President 207
China (*also* Chinese) 4, 24, 29, 34, 36, 96,
  133, 143, 204, 208, 214, 217, 226,
  228, 233–4, 237, 243, 245–7, 25–3,
  257–8
CIA, *see under* Central Intelligence
  Agency
Civilian Joint Task Force 52
CJTF, *see under* Civilian Joint Task Force
Clinton, Bill, President 30
Coalition of Patriots for Change 130
Cold War 3–5, 11–19, 23–4, 26, 28–9, 33,
  36, 72, 65, 96–8, 102–4, 123, 185,
  226, 228, 243–6, 252
Congo 123–5, 243
Convention 126
Council of Europe 63
CPC, *see under* Coalition of Patriots for
  Change
Crimea (*also* Crimean) 4, 61, 62, 66–70,
  72–3, 79, 81, 85, 250
Cuba (*also* Cuban) 27, 29, 96, 105, 243
Cuban Missile Crisis 96, 243

Damascus 158–60, 169, 175–6
Danab Brigade 35
Dan Na Ambassagou 113, 118

Index

Dar al-Hadith 32, 184
Darassa, Ali 129–30
Darfur 98, 126
Dbeiba, Abdulhamid 147
Déby, Idriss, President 126
Democratic Front of the Central African
People 126
Democratic People's Republic of Korea, *see*
under North Korea
Democratic Republic of Congo, *see under*
Congo
Democratic Union Party 153, 156, 161–3
Dhaffane, Mohamed-Moussa 126
Dinka tribe 98
Djibouti 34
Djotodia, Michel Am-Nondokro,
President 126–7
Dogon ethnic group 113
Doha Peace Process 202, 208–12
Donbas 70, 81–5, 233, 235, 250
Donetsk 4, 68–70, 72, 233
Donetsk People's Republic 68
Dozo tribe 113
DPRK, *see under* North Korea
Durand Line 205, 213, 216
Dzhemal, Orkhan 132
Dzhokhar Dudayev Battalion 82

ECCAS, *see under* Economic Community
of Central African States
Economic Community of Central African
States 127
Edjezekanne, Salvador 126
Egypt (*also* Egyptian) 14, 27–8, 142, 146–7,
174–8, 184, 248, 249
el-Khalil (*also* Il-Khalil) 116–18
El Salvador, *see under* Salvador
el-Sisi, Abdel Fattah Saeed Hussein Khalil,
President 146
Erdogan, Recep Tayyip, President 145
Eritrean Liberation Movement 98
Ethiopia (*also* Ethiopian) 29–32, 34, 98
EU, *see under* European Union
Euromaidan 64, 81
Europe (*also* European) 13, 24–5, 34, 36,
62–3, 70, 80, 86, 88–9, 104, 110, 115,
119, 144, 146–8, 233, 243, 245
see also European Union
European Concert of Nations 245

European Union 34, 64, 70–1, 144–5, 156,
247

Fadlallah, Muhammad Hussein, Grand
Ayatollah 100
Farabundo Martí National Liberation
Front 27
Fatemiyoun Brigade 101–2, 160, 189–90,
248
FDPC, *see under* Democratic Front of the
Central African People
Federal Security Service 66
Filipino, *see under* Philippines
Finland (also Finnish) 14, 87–8
Foreign Legion, Ukraine 87, 250–1
FPRC, *see under* Popular Front for the
Rebirth of Central African Republic
France (*also* French) 5–6, 14, 16, 24, 77, 89,
107, 109, 111, 113–20, 123, 125–7,
129, 131, 134, 141–2, 147, 248–50
Freedom of Russia Legion 86
French Foreign Legion 89 12930
Front for the Return of the Constitutional
Order 128
FSB, *see under* Federal Security Service

Gaddafi, *see under* al-Gaddafi, Muammar
Muhammad Abu Minyar
Gadhafi, *see under* al-Gaddafi, Muammar
Muhammad Abu Minyar
Ganda Izo 112
Ganda Koy 110, 112
Gao 117
GATIA, *see under* Imghad Tuareg
Gaza Strip 167–9, 171, 173, 175–8
Gbaya tribe 125, 127–8
General National Congress 142
Georgia (*also* Georgian) 79, 82, 84–7, 235
Georgian Legion, *see under* Georgian
National Legion
Georgian National Legion 82, 84–5, 86
Germany (*also* German) 1, 8, 14, 77, 83,
245
Ghani, Ashraf 209–12
Ghassanid tribe 13
Girkin, Igor 69
Global Concert of Great Powers 245
GNA, *see under* Government of National
Accord

Gorbachev, Mikhail, President 28
Goula 130
Government of National Accord 97, 143–6
Green Book 141
GRU, *see under* Main Directorate of the
    General Staff of the Armed Forces
    of the Russian Federation
Gurkha Brigade 89

Haftar, Khalifa 143–4
Hamas 6–7, 167–80, 178–9, 186, 189–90,
    248
Haqqani Network 207, 208, 210, 212–13
Harakat al-Nujaba 102
Hashd al-Shaabi 102
Haut-Mbomou 130
Havana 27
Hay'at, Tahrir Al-Sham 156
Hezbollah (*also* Hizballah) 7, 99–103,
    158–60, 167, 170–1, 173, 175–6, 180,
    186–7, 189, 191, 241
Horn of Africa 29, 98, 192
Houthi 7, 99, 102–3, 178, 183–4, 186–95,
    248, 250
Hussein, King of Jordan 172

IDF, *see under* Israel Defense Forces
Idnan clan 109, 111, 116
Ikkwan, *see under* Muslim Brotherhood
Imezzekarren clan 109
Imghad clan 109, 111–12
Imghad Tuareg 108, 112, 117–18
India (*also* Indian) 34, 95, 202, 204, 206–7,
    209–12, 214–17, 245, 253
International Legion, Ukraine 79–80, 86
Investigations Management Center 132
Iran (*also* Iranian) 6–7, 16, 27–8, 45,
    98–104, 153–5, 158–64, 167–9, 171,
    173–80, 183–95, 204, 207, 216, 232,
    248–50, 258
Iranian Revolutionary Guard Corps, *see*
    under Islamic Revolutionary Guard
    Corps
Iraq (*also* Iraqi) 13, 24, 26, 36, 98, 100, 102,
    139, 156, 160–1, 186, 189, 195, 203
IRGC, *see under* Islamic Revolutionary
    Guard Corps
IRGC-QF, *see under* Islamic Revolutionary
    Guards Corps-Quds Force

Iriyaken clan 109
ISIS, *see under* Islamic State
Islamabad 204, 207–9, 211–12, 214, 217
Islamic Courts Union 31
Islamic Movement of Azawad 117
Islamic Revolutionary Guard Corps
    99–103, 168, 170, 176, 179, 189, 190
Islamic Revolutionary Guards Corps-
    Quds Force 102, 159–60, 163
Islamic State 31, 45, 51, 53, 84, 143, 145,
    156, 160–2, 184, 215, 251
Islamic Youth Shura Council 143
Israel (*also* Israeli) 6, 7, 18, 56, 83, 98–101,
    103, 146, 158, 167–80, 189, 191, 248
Israel Defense Forces 167, 177
Ivorian Civil Wars 124
Iwellemmedan 114–15
Izz ad-Din al-Qassam Brigades 169

Janjaweed 126
Japan (*also* Japanese) 24, 245, 253
Jarabulus 156
Jerusalem 100, 171, 174, 178, 180
Jordan (*also* Jordanian) 13, 170, 172, 184,
    249
Justinian 13

Kabul 202, 205–7, 209–16
Kalinouski Battalion 86
Kampala 131
Kashmir 251
Kashmiri Freedom Fighters 251
Kata'ib Aimmah al-Baqiyah 102
Keïta, Ibrahim Boubacar 111–12
Kel Adagh 109, 114–16
Kel Afella 109
Kel Ahaggar 114
Kenya (*also* Kenyan) 32, 34
Kerch strait 67
Khalilzad, Zalmay 208–11
Khan, Mohammad Daoud 27
Kharkiv 68–9
Khartoum 126, 131, 133, 177
Kherson 70
Khodorkovsky, Mikhail 132
Khomeini, Ruhollah, Imam 100
Khosrow I, Emperor 13
Kidal 111, 116, 118
Kony, Joseph 130

Index

Korea (*also* Korean) 14–15, 243, 245
Korean War 14–15, 243
Kramatorsk 69
Kremlin 62, 82, 131–2, 257–8
Kunta Arabs 114
Kurdistan (*also* Kurdish, Kurds) 45, 53, 153, 156–7, 161–2
Kyiv 64, 81–3, 85, 87, 89
Kyivan Rus 84

Laddé Baba 127
Lakhmids 13
Laos 243
Lashkar-e-Tayyiba 212
Lebanese Hezbollah 99, 102–3, 158, 175, 187, 189–91
Lebanon (*also* Lebanese) 7, 53, 98–103, 158, 160, 167, 170, 175, 176, 180, 186–7, 248
LH, *see under* Lebanese Hezbollah
Liberian Civil Wars 124
Libya (*also* Libyan) 6, 52, 78, 97, 110–11, 124–5, 132, 139–49, 193, 194, 232, 248, 250–2, 257
Libyan National Army 97, 143, 146, 149
Libyan Shield Force 142
Lithuania 248
Litvinenko, Alexander 227
LNA, *see under* Libyan National Army
Lord's Resistance Army 130
Luhansk 4, 68–70, 72, 233
Luxembourg 89
Lysychansk 87

MAA, *see under* Arab Movement of Azawad
Macina Liberation Front (*Katiba Macina*) 112
Madagascar 132
Madrid 169
Maghreb 111, 116, 145
Magsaysay, Ramon 26
Main Directorate of the General Staff of the Armed Forces of the Russian Federation 132
Makkah 103
Mali (*also* Malian) 5, 53, 97, 107–19, 132, 147, 249, 251–2, 257
Mamertines 13

Mandjia ethnic group 125, 128
Mansour, Akhtar, Mullah 207
Maoist 97
Mariupol 70
Maronite 99
Massi, Charles 126
Massoud, Ahmad Shah 97, 216
Matafans 14
Mbum ethnic group 125, 128
Menaka Battle 112
Messene 13
Mexico 14
Middle East 5–7, 24, 36, 45, 95–9, 104, 147, 167, 180, 187, 189, 195
Minsk Agreements 69, 71, 73
Minsk Protocol 71
Miskine, Abdoulaye 126
MNLA, *see under* National Movement for the Liberation of Azawad
Mogadishu 30–2, 34
Mokom, Maxime 128
Mopti 112
Morocco (*also* Moroccan) 114, 184, 249
Moscow 15, 23–4, 33, 67, 80, 86, 119, 132, 144, 145, 147, 148, 214, 246, 253, 257
Mossad 171–2
Movement for Oneness and Jihad in West Africa 111
Movement for the Salvation of Azawad 117
Mozambique 95, 132, 257
MPC, *see under* Central African Patriotic Movement
Mujaheddin (*also* Mujahideen, Mujahidin) 28, 52, 203
Multinational Force of the Central African Economic and Monetary Community 134
Mumbai 251
Munich 168, 238
Musk, Elon 246
Muslim Brotherhood 100–1, 142, 155, 167–9, 175

National Movement for the Liberation of the Central African Republic 129
National Movement for the Liberation of Azawad 111, 115–17
National Transition Council 142

NATO, *see under* North Atlantic Treaty
Organization
Ndjamena 126–7, 131
Nepal 97
Netanyahu, Benjamin 172
Ngaissona, Patrice-Edouard 128
Ngbanki ethnic group 125
Niger 108, 141, 147, 251
Nigeria (also Nigerian) 30, 52, 124
Nixon, Richard, President 23, 36, 38
North Atlantic Treaty Organization 80, 87,
141, 143
Northern Alliance 97, 205, 216
North Korea 247
Norway 89
Noureddine, Adam 126
Novorossiya 69
NPT, *see under* Treaty on Non-
Proliferation of Nuclear Weapons
NTC, *see under* National Transition
Council
Nyala 126

Ogaden 29, 30
Oman 243
Omar, Mullah 203, 205, 207, 212, 217
Orange Revolution 63
Organization for Security and Co-
operation in Europe 63, 70–1
OSCE, *see under* Organization for Security
and Co-operation in Europe
Oslo Accords 168, 170, 171, 179
Oslo Peace Process, *see under* Oslo
Accords

Pakistan (*also* Pakistani) 7, 27, 28, 99, 160,
189, 201–8, 205–17, 245, 251
Palestine (*also* Palestinian) 6, 99–100,
167–80, 176, 248
Palestine Liberation Organization 99, 100,
168–72
Palestinian Authority 167
Palestinian Islamic Jihad 6–7, 167–80,
248
Paris 115–18, 249
Patriotic Convention for Saving the
Country 126
People's Army for the Restoration of
Democracy 126

People's Defense Units 53
Persia 13
Peru 97
Peuhl, *see under* Arab-Fulani
Philippines (*also* Filipino, Philippine) 4,
24, 26, 36
PIJ, *see under* Palestinian Islamic Jihad
PLO, *see under* Palestine Liberation
Organization
PMC, *see under* Private Military
Corporations
Pontifical Swiss Guard 89
Popular Front for the Rebirth of Central
African Republic 129–30
Poroshenko, Petro 64
Portugal (*also* Portuguese) 14, 227
Prigozhin, Yevgeny 132, 144
Private Military Corporations 124, 132–3,
144–5, 193–4, 244, 246, 248, 250,
252
Prussia 14
Putin, Vladimir, President 64, 66–7, 70, 73,
85, 90, 119, 132, 144, 147, 232, 257,
258
PYD, *see under* Democratic Union Party

Qaddafi, *see under* al-Gaddafi, Muammar
Muhammad Abu Minyar
Qatar 142–3, 147, 153, 193, 207, 214, 248
Qatif 99
Quwat al-Ridha 102

Rabin, Yitzhak 169
Radchenko, Kirill 132
Reagan, Ronald, President 27–8
Red Cross 52
Red Sea 103, 191–2
Return, Reclamation, Rehabilitation
129–30
Rhodesia 95
Rhodesian Bush War 123
Riyadh 102, 187, 193
Rome (*also* Roman) 13, 95
Rostorguev, Aleksandr 132
Runga ethnic group 130
Russia (*also* Russian) 1, 4–6, 14, 16, 18,
23–4, 27–9, 34, 36, 61–73, 77, 79–88,
90, 95, 97, 103–4, 119, 131–4, 142,
144–5, 147, 148, 153, 156, 160, 162,

194, 214, 216, 226–8, 232–5, 245–53, 257–8
Rwanda (*also* Rwandan) 98, 131, 248, 252

Sabri, Ikrima 171
SADAT 144, 246
Saddam, Hussein, President 139
Sahel (*also* Sahelian) 5, 113, 115, 117, 131, 203
Saleh, Ali Abdullah 183, 190
Salvador (*also* Salvadoran) 4, 27, 36
Samarkand 226
Samba-Panza, Catherine 127
Samoan Civil War 14
Sanaa 183, 190
Sandinistas 96
Sara ethnic group 125
Sasanian Empire, *see under* Persia
Sassanians 13
Saudi 7, 13, 16, 27–8, 98, 99, 102–4, 142, 153, 160, 175, 183–5, 187–8, 190–5, 209, 248–50
Saudi Arabia (*also* Saudi Arabian) 13, 16, 27–8, 98–9, 103–4, 142, 153, 160, 175, 183–4, 187, 188, 190–5, 248–50
Second Intifada 172–5, 179
Second World War 14, 17, 24, 62, 77, 123, 139, 243
Security Service of Ukraine 66
Séléka 125–30, 133
Sendero Luminoso (the Shining Path) 97
Serval Operation 111, 115–17
Sevastopol 66–7
Sewa Sécurité Services 132
Shaamba Arabs 114
Shaqaqi, Fathi 168, 171
Sheikh Mansur Battalion 82, 84
Shia (*also* Shiite) 6–7, 159–60, 163–4, 167, 175, 180, 184, 187, 190, 248, 250
Shiism 163
Sidiki Abbas 129
Sierra Leone Civil War 124
Simferopol 67
SNA, *see under* Somali National Army
SOF, *see under* Special Operations Forces
Somali National Army 34–5, 157–8, 162–3
Somalia (*also* Somali) 4, 29–36, 141, 148
Songhai tribe 108
Soqotra 192

South Africa (*also* South African) 123, 243
South America 24, 258
South Korea 243, 245
South Ossetia 235
South Sudan 130–1
Southern Transitional Council 184, 192–3
Soviet Union (*also* Soviet) 4, 14, 15, 23–31, 33, 62, 66, 80, 96–8, 103, 110, 119, 123–4, 127, 144, 201, 203, 213, 243, 257
Space-X 246
Spain (also Spanish) 14, 24, 27, 227
Spanish Civil War 14
Spear Operations Group 193
Special Operations Forces 24–5, 35–6
Spetsnaz 132
Starlink 246
STC, *see under* Southern Transitional Council
Sub-Saharan Africa 5, 97, 108, 124, 258
Sudan (*also* Sudanese) 98, 114, 120, 125–6, 129–33, 142, 144, 176–7, 184, 248–50, 257
Sunni 98–9, 155, 158, 162, 175, 184, 187, 189, 249
Supreme Security Committee 142
Syria (*also* Syrian) 6, 13, 44–5, 51–3, 78, 84, 98–9, 101–2, 140, 144, 148, 153–64, 172, 176, 178, 186–7, 248, 250, 252, 257
Syrian National Army 157
Sysenko, Volodymyr 69

Takuba Task Force 119
Taliban 7, 53, 201–17, 251
Tamanrasset Accord 110
Tanriverdi, Adnan, General 144–5
Tatar 67
Tehran 98, 101–2, 158–60, 162, 169–70, 175, 178–9, 189, 207, 248
Thailand 243
3R, *see under* Return, Reclamation, Rehabilitation
Timbuktu 113–14, 118
Tora-Bora 115
Touadéra, Faustin-Archange 130, 131–3
Touré, Amadou Toumani 110–11
Transitional Federal Government 31
Traoré, Moussa 108

Index

Treaty on Non-Proliferation of Nuclear Weapons 62, 80
Trump, Donald, President 36, 208–11
Tuareg 108–18, 145, 147, 251
Tumgoev, Timur 84
Tunisia 141
Turchynov, Olexander 64, 67
Turkey (also Turkisch) 6, 16, 44–5, 53, 97, 142–8, 153–64, 193, 246–8, 250
Turkish National Intelligence 157–8, 160

UAE, *see under* United Arab Emirates
UFDR, *see under* Union of Democratic Forces for Unity
Uganda (*also* Ugandan) 32, 34, 98, 130–1, 252
UK, *see under* United Kingdom
Ukraine (*also* Ukrainian) 4–5, 61–73, 77–90, 95, 103, 104, 144, 147–8, 226–7, 233, 246, 248–51, 257–8
Ukraine, Anti-Terrorist Operation 69–70, 74
Ukrainian Volunteer Corps 82, 84
ul-Haq, Zia, General 213
Ummayad Empire 95
UN, *see under* United Nations
UN Security Council, *see under* United Nations Security Council
Unified Task Force 30
Union of Democratic Forces for Unity 126, 134
Union for Peace in the Central African Republic 129–30
United Arab Emirates 28, 97, 104, 142, 183–6, 192–5, 248–9
United Kingdom 14, 32, 61, 80, 83, 86, 89
United Nations 23, 30, 32, 52, 67, 70, 112, 113, 131, 141, 144, 146–7, 183–4, 187–8, 215, 245–6
United Nations Operation in Somalia 30
United Nations Security Council 32, 67, 141, 188, 245–6
United States of America (*also* American) 4, 6, 8, 14, 16, 23–33, 35–7, 45, 51–3, 61, 65, 70–1, 80, 83, 86, 89, 96, 98,

100–1, 103–4, 123, 141, 145, 147, 153–6, 159–64, 184, 186, 189, 191–3, 195, 203–12, 216–17, 226, 228, 245–6, 249–50, 253, 257
UNOSOM, *see under* United Nations Operation in Somalia
UPC, *see under* Union for Peace in the Central African Republic
US, *see under* United States of America
USA, *see under* United States of America
USSR, *see under* Soviet Union
Utkin, Dimitri 132

Vakaga 125
Vietnam (*also* Vietnamese) 14, 15, 23, 27, 37, 243

Wagner Group 1, 95, 119, 131–3, 144–5, 147, 194, 246, 252
Washington 15, 33, 36, 97, 161, 206
Wehrmacht 77, 89
West Bank 171–4
Williams, Stephanie 147

Xi Jinping 233, 253

Yanukovych, Viktor 63–4
Yaqoob, Mullah 214–15
Yassin, Ahmad 168–9, 172, 174–5
Yemen (*also* Yemeni) 7, 29, 99, 102–3, 148, 178, 183–8, 190–5, 248–9
YPG, *see under* People's Defense Units
Yushchenko, Viktor 63

Zaghawa ethnic group 126
Zakharov, Valery 132
Zande-Nzakara ethnic group 125
Zaporizhzhia 70
Zaydi 102, 184, 190
Zayed 192
Zayidi tribe 190
Zaynabiyoun Brigade 160, 189
Zelenskyy, Volodymyr, President 77, 86
Zia 213
Zimbabwe 243

Printed in the USA
CPSIA information can be obtained
at www.ICGtesting.com
LVHW021521160624
783249LV00004B/370